Ferguson

America's Breaking Point

By Tim Suereth

Tim Suereth

Cover design: Bryce Chapnick

Copyright © 2015 Elwood Press

Publisher: Andrew Miller

ISBN: **0692300937**
ISBN-13: **978-0-692-30093-0**

DEDICATION

This book is dedicated to the Citizens of the United States of America

CONTENTS

CONTENTS

CONTENTS

Tim Suereth

ACKNOWLEDGMENTS

United States Constitution

CHAPTER 1

INTRODUCTION

On August 9th, 2014, 18-year-old Michael Brown and his 22-year-old friend Dorian Johnson set into motion a day that would lead to the death of Brown, a discussion around the world over the proper use of police force, and the beginning of a renewed civil rights movement in America.

Race-based tensions in the United States have been smoldering for many years. The civil rights movement, which began in the 1950's, largely died with the death of Dr. Martin Luther King Jr. in the 1960's. Although some progress has been made in civil and racial rights since King's passing, the movement has stalled.

The seeds of inter-racial conflict, sewn a century and more ago, germinated with the police shooting of Michael Brown, in the small St. Louis suburb of Ferguson, Missouri. The Ferguson protests galvanized support among minorities, as well as many Caucasians, to form a new movement for civil rights, to finally ensure liberty, justice and freedom for all Americans, as promised by the founders of the United States.

America was founded; and has flourished, substantially on the economic principles of slavery. Before oil-powered reciprocating engines became available, the energy to grow, process and manufacture the products that the United States produced, for both internal consumption and international export, was provided in large measure by slave labor.

Slavery didn't begin in America. It had been around since the dawn of mankind. The Eastern European Slovaks were enslaved in such high numbers that the term slave descends from the slang name for Slovaks, who were known as "Slavs." "Slavs" were "Slaves." Eventually the name became more synonymous with African Americans than with Eastern Europeans, especially in North America, which is why slavery, in the minds of most Americans, is associated with African Americans and almost never thought to include white Eastern Europeans.

When slavery finally ended in America, not much changed for African Americans. They were mainly stuck in the South, trying to forge a working relationship with their ex-owners as sharecroppers, or trying to eke out an existence though whatever means possible. It probably seemed nearly impossible for African Americans to sustain themselves in the South after the Civil War, especially after the passage of restrictive "Jim Crow" and "Pig" laws. These laws were enacted to enable de facto slavery to be maintained in the South, or at least prevent former slaves from experiencing real freedom or upward economic mobility.

This period of "Reconstruction," after the Civil War, gave rise to "the Negro Problem." White ex-slave owners and black ex-slaves were unwilling, or unable, to find a way to co-exist peacefully. The unhappy result was a mass rioting across much of the country (but primarily in the South) and the widespread practice of lynching, which is the killing of a person by mob action, without the benefit of judicial sanction. Entire communities of African Americans were driven from their homes, beaten and killed by mobs of white men, women and children who were determined to drive away any Negros aspiring to reside in their communities.

It was a time in the nation's history when lynchings were so common that Federal Legislation had to be passed to curtail them.

Mark Twain was so moved by a lynching near his hometown in Hannibal Missouri that he wrote an essay about it, entitled "The United States of Lyncherdom." After he wrote it, Twain decided against publishing this scathing rebuke of racism in America, and also canceled a book he had planned on writing on the subject. He told his publisher to never publish the essay because he thought the world was not prepared for the truths it revealed. Twain stated at the time, "I shouldn't have even half a friend left down there in the South, after it issued from the press." The executor of Mark Twain's will, perhaps mistakenly, released "The United States of Lyncherdon," along with some of his other books and articles, 13 years after Twain's death. It was eventually published in Europe, but received very little press in the United States.

Lynchings were mainly a southern activity. Some lynchings did occur in the North, but most of them happened in the South. lynchings In the south were most often employed to punish or abuse individual Negros, but in the North, in the early 1900's, white mobs resorted to racial cleansing of entire black communities as a way to remove and exclude minorities from their white neighborhoods and their workforce.

The white-on-black violence and rioting that occurred in East St. Louis, Illinois, in 1917 was one of the most violent examples of barbarism that has ever occurred in the United States. The events which unfolded were so horrific that the United States Government classified the witness accounts of the black massacre as "Confidential Information," until 1986, due to the belief that Americans could not handle hearing the realities of what occurred in East St. Louis, in 1917. There were implications that the National Guard and police had participated in the "wholesale slaughter" of black citizens. One witness to the atrocities testified, "African American men had their fingers cut off by the mob and their heads split open with axes. Will Morgan saw the mob make the African Americans swim into the Cahokia River, then shoot them, one being killed instantly. The others managed to struggle back to shore, only to be stoned to death by children. He saw them beat men down with revolvers and clubs; white men knocked African American women down, and then the white women would finish by beating them to death or nearly so." Approximately 10,000 African Americans were driven from their homes in East St. Louis, never to return. All of their possessions were looted or burned during the massacre. It was not an isolated incident. Rioting by white mobs against black communities continued into the 1950's, when a black resistance movement took shape. Minorities began to arm themselves, with weapons and words, to confront their white oppressors in the streets and in the courts.

During the civil rights movement of the 1950's, African Americans began to rise-up, demand equal rights, and fight for their freedom. Some activists, such as Malcolm X, chose the violent approach of civil disobedience. Others, such as Dr. Martin Luther King Jr., chose a more radical, peaceful approach. Neither of them produced a quick change, or drastically improved lives in the inner city and surrounding suburban ghettos. King was close to achieving some success, but he was gunned down before he could make a larger contribution to the fight for civil rights. However, his life and his message were a beacon for the civil rights movement in the years following his death.

In the 1960's, African Americans began to fight back, violently, against the oppression they endured at the hands of an over-aggressive police force, and public officials who conspired to keep them contained and controlled. The 1960's race-riots raged on, through the end of the decade. Finally, the Federal Government took drastic action to break-up the slums into smaller, more manageable mini-ghettos, both within the inner cities and throughout the surrounding suburbs. After the desegregation of schools and housing allowed African Americans to move about more freely, Ferguson was inundated with minorities and quickly changed from being mainly white to having mainly black residents. In many communities around the country, including Ferguson, the white political power structure remained in place and prevented minorities from having a voice in their community's governance or any control of their own destiny.

Toward the end of the 1960's race riots, a Presidential Commission was established to find the root cause of the racial divide in America, and recommend solutions to prevent the mass violent racial rioting of the 1960's from ever recurring in America. The "National Advisory Commission on Civil Disorders" stated that governmental housing discrimination, discriminatory police practices, and attempts toward emasculation of the black man contributed to the mass rioting of the 1960's. The report concluded that the nation was "moving toward two societies, one black, one white – separate and unequal," and warned, "If we are heedless, none of us shall escape the consequences."

The report also warned of a black uprising. It stated, "A new mood has sprung up among Negroes, particularly among the young, in which self-esteem and enhanced racial pride are replacing apathy and submission to 'the system'. The police are not merely a 'spark' factor. To some Negroes police have come to symbolize white power, white racism and white repression. And the fact is that many police do reflect and express these white attitudes. The atmosphere of hostility and cynicism is reinforced by a widespread belief among Negroes in the existence of police brutality and in a 'double standard' of justice and protection—one for Negroes and one for Whites."

The National Advisory Commission on Civil Disorders, in 1968, concluded, "Segregation and poverty have created in the racial ghetto a destructive environment totally unknown to most white Americans. What white Americans have never fully understood—but what the Negro can never forget—is that white society is deeply implicated in the ghetto. White institutions created it, white institutions maintain it, and white society condones it. It is time now to turn with all the purpose at our command to the major unfinished business of this nation. It is time to adopt strategies for action that will produce quick and visible progress. It is time to make good the promises of American democracy to all citizens—urban and rural, white and black, Spanish, American Indian, and every minority group. To pursue our present course will involve the continuing polarization of the American community and, ultimately, the destruction of basic democratic values."

Reverend Martin Luther King said, at the time that the 426 page report was released, that it was "a physician's warning of approaching death, with a prescription for life." But before Martin Luther King could promote the conclusions of the Presidential report, he was shot in the face while on his hotel balcony and died, one month after the Commission report was released. He was killed soon after he called for an end to the Vietnam War and demanded that the United States government pay $50 billion in restitution for the racial policies and practices committed by the U.S. Government in the past. After King's death, the nation of black mourners were left leaderless, with no one to fill his shoes. The movement had stalled, with few interludes, until the riots in Ferguson, Missouri galvanized support within the black community once again, to band together to fight for their equal rights, in Ferguson, and in every other similar city across the country. This uprising, if not managed properly, could descend into another civil war in America--whites and blacks, fighting in urban combat. It's a fear that the U.S Government is also concerned with, and it is probably the primary reason local police departments are over-militarized, in preparation for a mass uprising in America, caused either by another economic collapse or through a race-riot that leads to an all-out war between the races; reminiscent of the days of the East St. Louis massacre.

America is at a breaking point. If the United States doesn't attend to the "unfinished business of our nation," we will all suffer the consequences, which could lead to larger and more violent riots throughout the United States and possibly another civil war over the inequalities in America, both race-based and economically driven. Ferguson should be an urgent wake-up call, to take swift action to promote peace, and protect the civil rights of all Americans—to forestall a race war in America, and to live up to the Democratic ideals that American politicians attempt to propagate around the world.

CHAPTER 2

FIGHTING FOR FREEDOM

The fight against oppression is core to America's history, and an innate instinct in every human being.

By rebelling against the King of England in 1776, the founders of the United States orchestrated the first acts of civil disobedience in America, to raise awareness of the injustices being perpetrated against the 13 original colonies. Incidents like the Boston Tea Party were intended to provoke change and end the ongoing oppression by the King, who ruled the U.S. until victory in the Revolutionary War allowed America to secede from Great Britain and form a new nation based on less government control and more freedoms for its citizens.

Rebellious rioting is as American as apple pie. The Declaration of Independence condones it, and actually calls for it--when governments become destructive.

The writers of the Declaration stated in 1776:

We hold these truths to be self-evident, that all men are created equal, that they are endowed by their Creator with certain unalienable Rights, that among these are Life, Liberty and the pursuit of Happiness. --That to secure these rights, Governments are instituted among Men, deriving their just powers from the consent of the governed, --That whenever any Form of Government becomes destructive of these ends, it is the Right of the People to alter or to abolish it, and to institute new Government, laying its foundation on such principles and organizing its powers in such form, as to them shall seem most likely to effect their Safety and Happiness. Prudence, indeed, will dictate that Governments long established should not be changed for light and transient causes; and accordingly all experience hath shewn, that mankind are more disposed to suffer, while evils are sufferable, than to right themselves by abolishing the forms to which they are accustomed. But when a long train of abuses and usurpations, pursuing invariably the same Object evinces a design to reduce them under absolute Despotism, it is their right, it is their duty, to throw off such Government, and to provide new Guards for their future security.

Although the Declaration of Independence proclaimed that all men were created equal, African Americans were not entitled to the same type of independence or equality that white Americans were entitled to, but that was due to how Africans became African American slaves and the ramifications of slavery in the United States and abroad.

The new nation of the United States was based largely on the economic principle of slavery and the profitable business of slave trading. The 13 original colonies of the United States originally accepted slavery within their borders. Although the Declaration of Independence proclaimed that all men were equal, the United States continued to condone the practice of slavery, even after the Civil War abolished it.

Slavery dates back to the beginning of recorded history. It was used throughout the world as a way for societies to enjoy cheap labor or to punish the enemies they conquered--and then to sell or trade them for profit. Africa has always been a large source of slaves for nations across the globe but the Slavs (Slovics) of Central and Eastern Europe (Russians, Ukrainians, Poles) have been so enslaved that the term slavery is derived from their long history of enslavement. Millions of Slavs, and also Africans, were captured and taken to Islamic states to become mercenaries, servants, construction workers and concubines between the 7th and 19th centuries A.D.

Contrary to practices in North and South America, most of the male slaves taken by Islamic countries were castrated, to deter sexual urges in their slaves, who often served in their masters' houses, which may explain why these countries do not have a large lineage of African or European slave descendants. Most male Slavs and African slaves perished without passing on any offspring, but the women were used as sex slaves and concubines, and to produce mixed-race babies, many of which were sold into slavery. Eventually, the African slaves and the European slave bloodlines became so intermixed with Middle Eastern inhabitants that their physical characteristics are not now distinguishable, whereas slavery in most other parts of the world has left an indelible imprint on the face each society it's touched.

The Slavs were the most desired slaves for Middle Eastern countries. The girls were pretty and the men were strong. They produced the highest value when sold or traded. When the supply of white European slaves could not be sustained any longer due to the insatiable appetite of the Islamic countries, the world turned to Africa for an almost unlimited supply of cheap servants, served-up by their own African countrymen and sold in boatloads destined for the Middle East as servants, and to the Americas as slave laborers.

Slavery appears to be as old as human history on earth. The Koran approves of it and actually institutionalized it throughout most of the Middle East. The Prophet Muhammad set out clear rules for the taking of slaves, and for their treatment in captivity. For more than a thousand years, countries in the Middle East bled the European and African nations of their men and women and subjugated them to lives of servitude.

Unlike the Atlantic slave trade which primarily provided slave labor for farming and industry to the new world of South and North America, the Eastern slave trade by the Islamic states employed their slaves mainly as personal servants, sex slaves and warriors. The women often became concubines for noble gentlemen of Islam, like the prophet Muhammad, who had many slaves and several concubines.

Slavery is still found in the Middle East today, but it is a taboo subject to talk about and is rarely, if ever, discussed. Even so, slavery is a reality in today's modern Middle East.

The business of selling slaves has been practiced by African merchants for thousands of years. Warring African tribes often sold their captives into slavery, either to other African nations or elsewhere around the world.

The Atlantic Slave trade was responsible for transporting millions of African hostages to South, Central, and North America, and to the Caribbean to tend to the tobacco, coffee, cocoa, cotton, sugar, and timber plantations, or work in the gold and silver mines which Europe had become dependent on.

The Portuguese were the first to exploit the slave trade in the Americas, beginning in Brazil, before expanding to North America and becoming the largest importer, by far, of African slaves into the Americas.

The most prolific slave trading nation, by number of slaves transported into the new world, was Portugal, followed by Britain, France, Spain, The Netherlands, and the United States. The Portuguese have a long history of slave trading, both inside and outside of their country. They started the Atlantic Slave trade business when Portuguese navigator Prince Henry sent an expedition of boats to Africa in 1441 to explore the coast and establish merchant relations with the continent. The expedition brought back boats filled with human cargo, totaling 235 African slaves in the year 1444. The Portuguese soon opened a Sugar plantation on the African island of Madeira, which was mainly manned by African slaves. The Portuguese, realizing how profitable businesses could be with slave labor, quickly formed relationships with African kings to buy as many of their war captives as they could conquer. African wars were deliberately begun solely for the purpose of acquiring new slaves to sell to the Portuguese, to be eventually shipped to the Caribbean, and North and South America to work in the mines and on the plantations.

Two mass waves of slave importation occurred in the Americas. The first began in South America in the early 1500's with Portugal being the main importer of human cargo to supply the Portuguese and Spanish businesses in South America with cheap labor. This continued until 1580 when Portugal and Spain became united, and temporarily prohibited professional slave trading. The English, Dutch and French stepped-up to fill the gap and continued the flow of slave laborers to the mines and plantations of South America, unabated. A second mass wave of slaves were imported into North America and The Caribbean beginning in the 1600's, driven by the labor needs of the rapidly growing colonies and the industrialization of North America.

Americas first settlement, in Jamestown Virginia, depended on slave labor to help tend the crops and do the manual labor that a new nation required. In 1619, Jamestown residents traded some of their last possessions to purchase twenty captured slaves from a Dutch merchant ship to establish the first slave colony in the new world. It was the first of many ships that would eventually bring ten to twenty million Africans to the Americas, to be sold into servitude as slave laborers.

By the 1700's gold was found in Brazil, cotton was growing in the new colonies of North America and sugar was being mass-produced in the Caribbean. The slave trade needed to continue. And it did, undisturbed, until resident slaves reached a breaking point--and began to fight for their freedom.

In the 1700's, 80% of the inhabitants of Caribbean islands were enslaved Africans. The large number of Africans on the islands overwhelmed the police forces and rioting broke out throughout the Caribbean continuously. A successful slave revolt that began in Santo Domingo in 1791 led to liberation of the islands slaves and the establishment of Haiti as the first independent black nation outside of Africa, in 1804. Numerous other slave revolts in the Caribbean were violently crushed by military force, leaving a tragic legacy along the entire Caribbean island chain. Many descendants of these slaves are now trying to eek out an existence selling trinkets to tourists or offering jet ski rides.

Even though the businesses of America and the rest of the world were becoming dependent on the easy money the slave trade enabled, there was a great deal of opposition to it internationally, especially in the northern United States.

In America, slave-owning sentiments were mainly based on northern or southern values and attitudes. Residents of the northern states had a general distain for slavery since they didn't depend on it, and thought it was a morally corrupt practice. The southern states, which depended on slave labor, whole-heartedly approved of it. This conundrum split the country in two and caused the deadliest war ever fought on America soil, to be fought against its own people, sometimes brother against brother, in an effort to preserve slavery by the southerners and eradicate it by the northerners. [1]

---

[1] http://abolition.e2bn.org/slavery_45.html

CHAPTER 3

DRED SCOTT DECISION

The final act which solidified the northern states resolution against slavery was the controversial U.S. Supreme Court Dred Scott Decision of 1857, which ruled that slaves or ex-slaves could never be free and were not entitled to protection under the United States Constitution, because they were considered to be "property" and not "people" deserving U.S. Constitutional protection. This decision provoked an outpouring of support for the abolitionist movement by people who thought the ruling went against the principles that America was founded upon.

The Dred Scott Ruling of 1857 became a rallying point for those who supported a national effort to eradicate slavery. The case was filed in 1857 by a St. Louis slave named Dred Scott who fought for his Constitutional right to be a free man, all the way through the United States court system. Although he lost his case for freedom in

St. Louis local courts, the Supreme Court decided to hear his argument, but they too conclude that no slave or ex-slave could ever be afforded any protection under the U.S. Constitution, even in free states where freed slaves had always been considered free. It was a reversal of fortunes for African Americans who saw all of their constitutional rights they thought they attained, quickly evaporate by a quorum of Supreme Court appointees who were determined to keep slavery alive in America.

The Majority Opinion of 7 of the 9 Supreme Court Justices stated:

The language of the Declaration of Independence is conclusive: 'We hold these truths to be self-evident: that all men are created equal.' It is too clear for dispute, that the enslaved African race were not intended to be included, and formed no part of the people who framed and adopted this declaration. They perfectly understood the meaning of the language they used, and how it would be understood by others; and they knew that it would not in any part of the civilized world be supposed to embrace the negro race, which, by common consent, had been excluded from civilized Governments and the family of nations, and doomed to slavery. The brief preamble to the Constitution declares that it is formed by the people of the United States; that is to say, by those who were members of the different political communities in the several States; and its great object is declared to be to secure the blessings of liberty to themselves and their posterity. It speaks in general terms of the people of the United States, and of citizens of the several States, when it is providing for the exercise of the powers granted or the privileges secured to the citizen. It does not define what description of persons are intended to be included under these terms, or who shall be regarded as a citizen and one of the people. There are two clauses in the Constitution which point directly and specifically to the negro race as a separate class of persons, and show clearly that they were not regarded as a portion of the people or citizens of the Government then formed. The right of property in a slave is distinctly and expressly affirmed in the Constitution. The right to traffic in it, like an ordinary article of merchandise and property, was guaranteed to the citizens of the United States, in every State that might desire it, for twenty years. And the Government in express terms is pledged to protect it in all future time, if the slave escapes from his owner. This is done in plain words—too plain to be misunderstood. And no word can be found in the Constitution which gives Congress a greater power over slave property, or which entitles property of that kind to less protection than property of any other description. The only power conferred is the power coupled with the duty of guarding and protecting the owner in his rights.

The dissenting Opinion of the 2 Supreme Court appointees who opposed the Dred Scott ruling, stated:

The question is whether any person of African descent, whose ancestors were sold as slaves in the United States, can be a citizen of the United States. If any such person can be a citizen, this plaintiff has the right to the judgment of the court that he is so, for no cause is shown by the plea why he is not so, except his descent and the slavery of his ancestors. To determine whether any free persons, descended from Africans held in slavery, were citizens of the United States at the time of the adoption of the Constitution of the United States, it is only necessary to know whether any such persons were citizens of either of the States under the Confederation at the time of the adoption of the Constitution. Of this there can be no doubt. At the time of the ratification of the Articles of Confederation, all free native-born inhabitants of the States of New Hampshire, Massachusetts, New York, New Jersey, and North Carolina, though descended from African slaves, were not only citizens of those States, but such of them as had the other necessary qualifications possessed the franchise of electors, on equal terms with other citizens. Did the Constitution of the United States deprive them or their descendants of citizenship? That Constitution was ordained and established by the people of the United States, through the action, in each State, or those persons who were qualified by its laws to act thereon in behalf of themselves and all other citizens of that State. In some of the States, as we have seen, colored persons were among those qualified by law to act on this subject. These colored persons were not only included in the body of "the people of the United States" by whom the Constitution was ordained and established, but, in at least five of the States, they had the power to act, and doubtless did act, by their suffrages, upon the question of its adoption. It would be strange if we were to find in that instrument anything which deprived of their citizenship any part of the people of the United States who were among those by whom it was established.

15

Politicians rose from complete obscurity to national prominence almost overnight through their protests, demonstrations and speeches in opposition of the Dred Scott ruling.

Escaped slave and civil rights activist Frederick Douglass gave the following speech about the unconstitutionality of the U.S Supreme Courts' Dred Scott decision. Douglas stated:

I have a quarrel with those who fling the Supreme Law of this land between the slave and freedom. The Constitution says "We, the people"—not we, the white people—not we, the citizens, or the legal voters—not we, the privileged class, and excluding all other classes but we, the people; not we, the horses and cattle, but we the people—the men and women, the human inhabitants of the United States, do ordain and establish this Constitution. I ask, then, any man to read the Constitution, and tell me where, if he can, in what particular that instrument affords the slightest sanction of slavery? Where will he find a guarantee for slavery? Will he find it in the declaration that no person shall be deprived of life, liberty, or property, without due process of law? Will he find it in the declaration that the Constitution was established to secure the blessing of liberty? Will he find it in the right of the people to be secure in their persons and papers, and houses, and effects? Will he find it in the clause prohibiting the enactment by any State of a bill of attainder? These all strike at the root of slavery, and any one of them, but faith-fully carried out, would put an end to slavery in every State in the American Union.

President Abraham Lincoln was one of America's most outspoken advocates for civil rights. His intense opposition to the Dred Scott decision and his activism for African Americans propelled him from an obscure mainly unknown politician from Illinois to the President of the United States.

Abraham Lincoln gave the following speech on the Dred Scott Decision in 1857:

Chief Justice Taney, in delivering the opinion of the majority of the Court, insists at great length that Negroes were no part of the people who made, or for whom was made, the Declaration of Independence, or the Constitution of the United States. The Chief Justice does not directly assert, but plainly assumes, as a fact, that the public estimate of the black man is more favorable now than it was in the days of the Revolution. This assumption is a mistake. In those days, our Declaration of Independence was held sacred by all, and thought to include all; but now, to aid in making the bondage of the Negro universal and eternal, it is assailed, and sneered at, and construed, and hawked at, and torn, till, if its framers could rise from their graves, they could not at all recognize it. I had thought the Declaration contemplated the progressive improvement in the condition of all men everywhere; but no, it merely "was adopted for the purpose of justifying the colonists in the eyes of the civilized world in withdrawing their allegiance from the British crown, and dissolving their connection with the mother country." Why, that object having been effected some eighty years ago, the Declaration is of no practical use now—mere rubbish—old wadding left to rot on the battle-field after the victory is won. And now I appeal to all—are you really willing that the Declaration shall be thus frittered away?—thus left no more at most, than an interesting memorial of the dead past? ...shorn of its vitality, and practical value; and left without the germ or even the suggestion of the individual rights of man in it?

The southern slave states did not support Lincoln and his abolitionist agenda. He was so hated that eleven southern states refused to place Lincoln on their ballot as a candidate for President. Even though Abraham Lincoln promised to allow slave-holding states to remain slave-holding states while he was campaigning for the Presidential election, once he was elected President, southern states began to succeed from the Union, knowing that Lincoln was setting the stage to end slavery, and doom the southern economy that depended on slave labor. His election to President in 1861 caused the southern states to secede from the Union in rapid succession, to create their own southern nation of confederate slave-owning states. Georgia, Louisiana, Alabama, Florida, Texas, Mississippi and South Carolina all seceded from the United States and formed the Confederate States of America. Jefferson Davis was named President of the new nation. Within a couple of months, North Carolina, Virginia, Arkansas, and Tennessee also joined the Confederacy. Something had to be done to preserve the Union, so Lincoln declared a civil war against the southern states--so they would be forced to stay in the Union. The Civil War was fought from 1861 until 1865, as a means of preserving the Union of the United States, and to prevent the country from being split apart through successive secessions of states leaving the Union to join the Confederacy.[2]

---

[2] http://www.historynet.com/dred-scott

CHAPTER 4

EMANCIPATION PROCLAMATION

In 1863 after several years of civil war, the nations first Republican Party President, Abraham Lincoln, issued an Emancipation Proclamation, declaring that all African Americans in the "rebellious" southern states "shall be then, thenceforward, and forever free."

It was mainly a political ploy to encourage southern blacks to flee from the south and enlist in the union army, to fight for their own freedom, and to give the northern states the manpower and the moral inspiration needed to win the war. The Emancipation Proclamation was a turning point. It gave the northern soldiers a new purpose - to fight on and fight harder for the freedom of slaves, and also to perform their patriotic duty to preserve the new nation.

With the added manpower and the new resolve, the Union Army won the war, the slaves were freed and the Union would survive.

Unfortunately, not much would change for African Americans in the south.

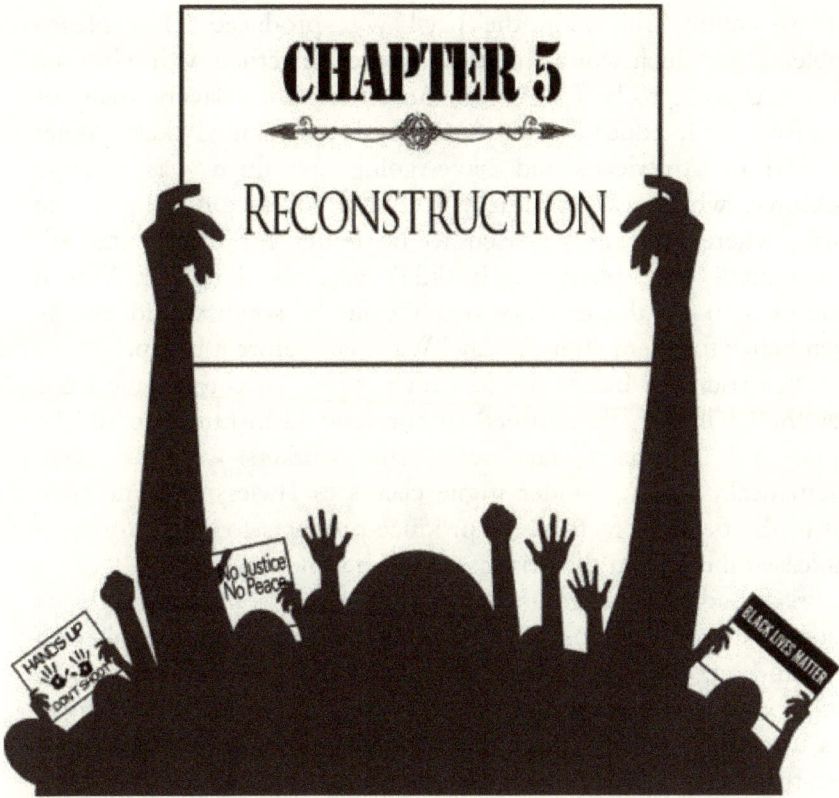

CHAPTER 5

RECONSTRUCTION

The Negro Problem:

After slavery ended, African Americans were trying to find a place for themselves in white America. They found it very difficult to find work to sustain themselves economically after slavery ended. Blacks were free but they were not independent. Many were kept in bondage or servitude, or prison, and many more turned to share cropping as a way to continue a partial working relationship with the plantation owners who once enslaved them, until other opportunities became available.

Those opportunities never came to fruition for the southern blacks. In fact, once the Civil War was won by the North, and slavery was abolished throughout the United States, the southern states enacted restrictive "Jim Crow" laws that kept slavery essentially alive and the races separate and unequal. This period of "reconstruction" following the Civil War produced "The Negro Problem," in which white Americans were concerned with what the future was going to be for African Americans after slavery, many of whom had little education, little resources and limited skills. What the African Americans did have going for them was a large workforce, which was eventually recruited for factory jobs in the North, where life was reported to be better for blacks and job opportunities were plentiful. It didn't take too long for African Americans to get the message that life in the south would not be much better for them after the Civil War than before it began.

Once southern businesses lost their supply of cheap slave labor after the Civil War, they turned to correctional institutes to fill the farms and southern factories with workers. Blacks were systematically arrested under vague claims of lawlessness, and then sent to the fields or factories to produce products for the businesses that leased them from the prisons, for $9 per month. [3]

Prison administrators made huge profits from renting black prisoners to corporations and the companies saved considerably on the man-hour rate paid to the prisons. Corporate America in the south found a new source of slave labor. Many of the "Jim Crow" laws turned law-abiding black citizens into common criminals, who were thrown in jail and then into the farms and factories to work essentially as slave laborers.

Southern blacks in Louisiana were rapidly loosing the rights they had attained through the Civil War. Louisiana had 130,000 black registered voters in 1896 but after only eight years of Jim Crow laws, the number of registered black voters had dwindled to only 1,342 due to rules that restricted black voting. The Southern states went back to their radical racial roots once national troops pulled out of the south after the Civil War ended, leaving blacks to fend for themselves, to fight a legal system that was intent on keeping them contained in segregated areas of a community, to do specific types of menial work and to continue to live life as second class citizens. [4]

Even though the Civil War seemed to free African Americans

---

[3] SLAVERY after Slavery (12 Years a slave documentary)

[4] http://www.crf-usa.org/black-history-month/a-brief-history-of-jim-crow

from slavery, the Jim Crow laws of the south produced a patchwork of outrageous laws that prevented white and black workers from being in the same room together, walking though the same doorways, drinking out of the same water fountains, using the same restrooms or living on the same streets. A poll tax was even established for the purpose of monetarily preventing minorities from voting. Unions prevented black workers from being hired and many industries also followed suit and refused to hire a "negro." Additionally, curfews were put in place to prevent blacks from roaming the streets at night. There was nowhere in the south that the blacks could go to realize the constitutional rights they hoped would protect them, so they fled for a better life, which they thought was going to be available to them in the north.

CHAPTER 6

LYNCHINGS

The term "lynching" comes from the Revolutionary war era to describe a way for neighbors to form their own system of justice and determine who were lawbreakers or individuals whom were bad for their community, and then enact their own justice, as the felt appropriate, through vigilantism. This usually entailed the loss of property, beatings, bondage, being tarred and feathered and hanging. Lynching, according to an article written for the *Southern Literary Messenger* magazine in 1836 by Edgar Allen Poe, was based on a written agreement between a Virginia landowner named William Lynch and his neighbors to dispel their own "justice" on those who were deemed to be unfit for their community. According to Edgar Allen Poe, this agreement was called "Lynch's Law." [5]

Since Edgar Allen Poe was such a good teaser, some historians

---

[5] www.yale.edu/ynhti/curriculum/units/1979/2/79.02.04.x.html

discount his writings on Lynching as just being propaganda for his magazine. Another view that is commonly considered is that the term Lynching comes from the accounts of Col. Charles Lynch, who held illegal trials of local lawbreakers on the front porch of his mansion. Once Col. Lynch proclaimed someone's guilt, the "Lynchings" began, which usually led to the accused being tied to a tree and beaten. Lynchings later escalated to hangings; mainly of black men, as a way to spark fear in the African American communities and to put "uppity niggers" in their place.

Lynch's Law or Lynching would eventually lead to Lynch mobs forming across the south to expel African Americans from white towns and to punish them for being black. It was also a recreational activity to break-up the boredom of everyday life in a small town. The name of Lynch continues to this day to reference the act of hanging an individual, usually a black man, without a trial or due process of law.

The hanging of blacks, and whites who were black sympathizers, had been happening since slaves were introduced to America, but the act now had a name and it was becoming more popular among white gangs who used it as a way to get rid of problem Negros, It was believed that freed slaved were trying to exercise too much freedom, and needed to be controlled after their release from bondage once the Civil War ended. After the war, lynchings became an epidemic in America. The National Guard was called in repeatedly to stop the lynchings, but instead of preventing them, the Guard typically joined-in with the white rioters. Lynching became an institutionalized tool used by whites to terrorize blacks and to maintain supremacy. Lynching is an American invention, and it was a family tradition in some of the southern states.

Lynching was so prevalent in the Untied States that Congress had to pass an anti-lynching bill to outlaw the practice and force law enforcement agencies to prosecute lynching cases within their community. There was even a penalty put in place to pay families of lynched victims $10,000 by each county that failed to prosecute a case of lynching. Section 5 of the Anti-Lynching Bill stated, "any county in which a person is put to death by a mob or riotous assemblage shall, if it is alleged and proven that the officers of the State charged with the duty of prosecuting criminally such offense under the laws of the State have failed, neglected, or refused to proceed with due diligence to apprehend and prosecute the participants in the mob or riotous assemblage, forfeit $10,000, for the use of the family."

The Anti-Lynching Bill provided penalties if two separate counties are involved in a Lynching. Section 6 states, "in the event that any person so put to death shall have been transported by such mob or riotous assemblage from one county to another county during the time intervening between his capture and putting to death, the county in which he is seized and the county in which he is put to death shall be jointly and severally liable to pay the forfeiture herein provided."

Law enforcement was so complicit in the lynchings and so corrupt that special provisions had to be addressed to hold police officers criminally liable if they participated in Lynching's or fail to halt them. It is estimated that at least one-half of the lynchings were carried out with the participation of police officers and in nine-tenths of the remaining cases, police officers condoned the mob activity.

The Anti-Lynching Bill states:

Any State or municipal officer, acting as such officer under authority of State law, having in his custody or control a prisoner, who shall conspire, combine, or confederate with any person to put such prisoner to death without authority of law as a punishment for some alleged public offense, or who shall conspire, combine, or confederate with any person to suffer such prisoner to be taken or obtained from his custody or control for the purpose of being put to death without authority of law as a punishment for an alleged public offense, shall be guilty of a felony, and those who so conspire, combine, or confederate with such officer shall likewise be guilty of a felony. On conviction the parties participating therin shall be punished by imprisonment for life or not less than five years.

Although laws were put in place to prevent Lynchings, they could not be contained. Nine-tenths of the lynching's came from the southern states. Mississippi, Georgia, Texas, Louisiana, and Alabama produced more than half of the total lynching victims, but the hanging of black men was commonplace throughout most of the south.

The main reasons for Lynchings were for assault and for rape, but just looking at a white women was enough cause for a back man to be hanged. According to research from the Tuskegee Institute, 41 percent of Lynchings were based on accusations of felonious assaults, 19.2 percent for rape, 6.1 percent for attempted rape, 4.9 percent for robbery, 1.8 percent for insult to white persons, and 22.7 percent for miscellaneous offenses, or no offense at all, other than racial prejudices. Other offenses were for arguing with a white man, attempting to register to vote, unpopularity, self-defense, testifying against a white man, asking a white woman in marriage, and peeping in a window. It is estimated that approximately one-third of the victims were falsely accused, through fraudulent accusations or mistaken identity.

Even when there were clear cases of unlawful killings, the Sheriffs, judges, jurors, prosecutors, and witnesses were all white and usually sympathized with the lynchers, and pardoned or exonerated most of them. Mark Twain, a famous writer from Missouri, wrote heatedly about Lynchings in and around Missouri--but he was too afraid to publish his works. He wrote *The United States of Lyncherdom* in 1901 to explain the horrid details of a lynching near his hometown, but he never published it. He told his publisher he could not publish *The United States of Lyncherdom* or his planned book on lynching because he thought the country was not ready for the truths it revealed. He stated, "I shouldn't have even half a friend left down there in the South after it issued from the press."

Mark Twain felt that cowardice and herd mentality caused most lynching's to occur. He proposed that if there was at least one noble person in each town who had the courage to stand-up and say no to the lynchings when they occurred, most lynchers would prefer to just go home, and not participate in the hangings at all.

His executor released his writings, including *The United States of Lyncherdom*, thirteen years after Twains death.

Mark Twain's purposefully unpublished article on race relations, the human condition and lynchings is written in its entirety, below:

For the world will not stop and think--it never does, it is not its way; its way is to generalize from a single sample. It will not say, 'Those Missourians have been busy eighty years in building an honorable good name for themselves; these hundred lynchers down in the corner of the state are not real Missourians, they are renegades.' No, that truth will not enter its mind; it will generalize from the one or two misleading samples and say, 'The Missourians are lynchers.' It has no reflection, no logic, no sense of proportion. With it, figures go for nothing; to it, figures reveal nothing, it cannot reason upon them rationally; it would say, for instance, that China is being swiftly and surely Christianized, since nine Chinese Christians are being made every day; and it would fail, with him, to notice that the fact that 33,000 pagans are born there every day, damages the argument. It would say, "There are a hundred lynchers there, therefore the Missourians are lynchers"; the considerable fact that there are two and a half million Missourians who are not lynchers would not affect their verdict.

Oh, Missouri!

The tragedy occurred near Pierce City, down in the southwestern corner of the state. On a Sunday afternoon a young white woman who had started alone from church was found murdered. For there are churches there; in my time religion was more general, more pervasive, in the South than it was in the North, and more virile and earnest, too, I think; I have some reason to believe that this is still the case. The young woman was found murdered. Although it was a region of churches and schools the people rose, lynched three negroes--two of them very aged ones--burned out five negro households, and drove thirty negro families into the woods.

I do not dwell upon the provocation which moved the people to these crimes, for that has nothing to do with the matter; the only question is, does the assassin take the law into his own hands? It is very simple, and very just. If the assassin be proved to have usurped the law's prerogative in righting his wrongs, that ends the matter; a thousand provocations are no defense. The Pierce City people had bitter provocation--indeed, as revealed by certain of the particulars, the bitterest of all provocations--but no matter, they took the law into their own hands, when by the terms of their statutes their victim would certainly hang if the law had been allowed to take its course, for there are but few negroes in that region and they are without authority and without influence in over-awing juries.

Why has lynching, with various barbaric accompaniments, become a favorite regulator in cases of "the usual crime" in several parts of the country? Is it because men think a lurid and terrible punishment a more forcible object lesson and a more effective deterrent than a sober and colorless hanging done privately in a jail would be? Surely sane men do not think that. Even the average child should know better. It should know that any strange and much-talked-of event is always followed by imitations, the world being so well supplied with excitable people who only need a little stirring up to make them lose what is left of their heads and do things which they would not have thought of ordinarily. It should know that if a man jumps off Brooklyn Bridge another will imitate him; that if a person venture down Niagara Whirlpool in a barrel another will imitate him; that if a Jack the Ripper make notoriety by slaughtering women in dark alleys he will be imitated; that if a man attempt a king's life and the newspapers carry the noise of it around the globe, regicides will crop up all around. The child should know that one much-talked-of outrage and murder committed by a negro will upset the disturbed intellects of several other negroes and produce a series of the very tragedies the community would so strenuously wish to prevent; that each of these crimes will produce another series, and year by year steadily increase the tale of these disasters instead of diminishing it; that, in a word, the lynchers are themselves the worst enemies of their women. The child should also know that by a law of our make, communities, as well as individuals, are imitators; and that a much-talked-of lynching will infallibly produce other lynchings here and there and yonder, and that in time these will breed a mania, a fashion; a fashion which will spread wide and wider, year by year, covering state after state, as with an advancing disease. Lynching has reached Colorado, it has reached California, it has reached Indiana--and now Missouri! I may live to see a negro burned in Union Square, New York, with fifty thousand people present, and not a sheriff visible, not a governor, not a constable, not a colonel, not a clergyman, not a law-and-order representative of any sort.

Increase in Lynching.--In 1900 there were eight more cases than in 1899, and probably this year there will be more than there were last year. The year is little more than half gone, and yet there are eighty-eight cases as compared with one hundred and fifteen for all of last year. The four Southern states, Alabama, Georgia, Louisiana and Mississippi are the worst offenders. Last year there were eight cases in Alabama, sixteen in Georgia, twenty in Louisiana, and twenty in Mississippi--over one-half the total. This year to date there have been nine in Alabama, twelve in Georgia, eleven in Louisiana, and thirteen in Mississippi--again more than one-half the total number in the whole United States.--Chicago Tribune.

It must be that the increase comes of the inborn human instinct to imitate--that and man's commonest weakness, his aversion to being unpleasantly conspicuous, pointed at, shunned, as being on the unpopular side. Its other name is Moral Cowardice, and is the commanding feature of the make-up of 9,999 men in the 10,000. I am not offering this as a discovery; privately the dullest of us knows it to be true. History will not allow us to forget or ignore this supreme trait of our character. It persistently and sardonically reminds us that from the beginning of the world no revolt against a public infamy or oppression has ever been begun but by the one daring man in the 10,000, the rest timidly waiting, and slowly and reluctantly joining, under the influence of that man and his fellows from the other ten thousands. The abolitionists remember. Privately the public feeling was with them early, but each man was afraid to speak out until he got some hint that his neighbor was privately feeling as he privately felt himself. Then the boom followed. It always does. It will occur in New York, some day; and even in Pennsylvania.

It has been supposed--and said--that the people at a lynching enjoy the spectacle and are glad of a chance to see it. It cannot be true; all experience is against it. The people in the South are made like the people in the North--the vast majority of whom are right-hearted and compassionate, and would be cruelly pained by such a spectacle--and would attend it, and let on to be pleased with it, if the public approval seemed to require it. We are made like that, and we cannot help it. The other animals are not so, but we cannot help that, either. They lack the Moral Sense; we have no way of trading ours off, for a nickel or some other thing above its value. The Moral Sense teaches us what is right, and how to avoid it--when unpopular.

It is thought, as I have said, that a lynching crowd enjoys a lynching. It certainly is not true; it is impossible of belief. It is freely asserted--you have seen it in print many times of late--that the lynching impulse has been misinterpreted; that it is act the outcome of a spirit of revenge, but of a "mere atrocious hunger to look upon human suffering." If that were so, the crowds that saw the Windsor Hotel burn down would have enjoyed the horrors that fell under their eyes. Did they? No one will think that of them, no one will make that charge. Many risked their lives to save the men and women who were in peril. Why did they do that? Because none would disapprove. There was no restraint; they could follow their natural impulse. Why does a crowd of the same kind of people in Texas, Colorado, Indiana, stand by, smitten to the heart and miserable, and by ostentatious outward signs pretend to enjoy a lynching? Why does it lift no hand or voice in protest? Only because it would be unpopular to do it, I think; each man is afraid of his neighbor's disapproval--a thing which, to the general run of the race, is more dreaded than wounds and death. When there is to be a lynching the people hitch up and come miles to see it, bringing their wives and children. Really to see it? No--they come only because they are afraid to stay at home, lest it be noticed and offensively commented upon. We may believe this, for we all know how we feel about such spectacles--also, how we would act under the like pressure. We are not any better nor any braver than anybody else, and we must not try to creep out of it.

A Savonarola can quell and scatter a mob of lynchers with a mere glance of his eye: so can a Merrill or a Beloat. For no mob has any sand in the presence of a man known to be splendidly brave. Besides, a lynching mob would like to be scattered, for of a certainty there are never ten men in it who would not prefer to be somewhere else--and would be, if they but had the courage to go. When I was a boy I saw a brave gentleman deride and insult a mob and drive it away; and afterward, in Nevada, I saw a noted desperado make two hundred men sit still, with the house burning under them, until he gave them permission to retire. A plucky man can rob a whole passenger train by himself; and the half of a brave man can hold up a stagecoach and strip its occupants.

Then perhaps the remedy for lynchings comes to this: station a brave man in each affected community to encourage, support, and bring to light the deep disapproval of lynching hidden in the secret places of its heart--for it is there, beyond question. Then those communities will find something better to imitate--of course, being human, they must imitate something. Where shall these brave men be found? That is indeed a difficulty; there are not three hundred of them in the earth. If merely physically brave men would do, then it were easy; they could be furnished by the cargo. When

Hobson called for seven volunteers to go with him to what promised to be certain death, four thousand men responded--the whole fleet, in fact. Because all the world would approve. They knew that; but if Hobson's project had been charged with the scoffs and jeers of the friends and associates, whose good opinion and approval the sailors valued, he could not have got his seven.

No, upon reflection, the scheme will not work. There are not enough morally brave men in stock. We are out of moral-courage material; we are in a condition of profound poverty. We have those two sheriffs down South who--but never mind, it is not enough to go around; they have to stay and take care of their own communities.

But if we only could have three or four more sheriffs of that great breed! Would it help? I think so. For we are all imitators: other brave sheriffs would follow; to be a dauntless sheriff would come to be recognized as the correct and only the dreaded disapproval would fall to the share of the other kind; courage in this office would become custom, the absence of it a dishonor, just as courage presently replaces the timidly of the new soldier; then the mobs and the lynchings would disappear, and--

However. It can never be done without some starters, and where are we to get the starters? Advertise? Very well, then, let us advertise.

In the meantime, there is another plan. Let us import American missionaries from China, and send them into the lynching field. With 1,500 of them out there converting two Chinamen apiece per annum against an uphill birth rate of 33,000 pagans per day, it will take upward of a million years to make the conversions balance the output and bring the Christianizing of the country in sight to the naked eye; therefore, if we can offer our missionaries as rich a field at home at lighter expense and quite satisfactory in the matter of danger, why shouldn't they find it fair and right to come back and give us a trial? The Chinese are universally conceded to be excellent people, honest, honorable, industrious, trustworthy, kind-hearted, and all that--leave them alone, they are plenty good enough just as they are; and besides, almost every convert runs a risk of catching our civilization. We ought to be careful. We ought to think twice before we encourage a risk like that; for, once civilized, China can never be uncivilized again. We have not been thinking of that. Very well, we ought to think of it now. Our missionaries will find that we have a field for them--and not only for the 1,500, but for 15,011. Let them look at the following telegram and see if they have anything in China that is more appetizing. It is from Texas:

The negro was taken to a tree and swung in the air. Wood and fodder were piled beneath his body and a hot fire was made. Then it was suggested that the man ought not to die too quickly, and he was let down to the ground while a party went to Dexter, about two miles distant, to procure coal oil. This was thrown on the flame and the work completed.

We implore them to come back and help us in our need. Patriotism imposes this duty on them. Our country is worse off than China; they are our countrymen, their motherland supplicates their aid in this her hour of deep distress. They are competent; our people are not. They are used to scoffs, sneers, revilings, danger; our people are not. They have the martyr spirit; nothing but the martyr spirit can brave a lynching mob, and cow it and scatter it. They can save their country, we beseech them to come home and do it. We ask them to read that telegram again, and yet again, and picture the scene in their minds, and soberly ponder it; then multiply it by 115, add 88; place the 203 in a row, allowing 600 feet of space for each human torch, so that there be viewing room around it for 5,000 Christian American men, women, and children, youths and maidens; make it night for grim effect; have the show in a gradually rising plain, and let the course of the stakes be uphill; the eye can then take in the whole line of twenty-four miles of blood-and-flesh bonfires unbroken, whereas if it occupied level ground the ends of the line would bend down and be hidden from view by the curvature of the earth. All being ready, now, and the darkness opaque, the stillness impressive--for there should be no sound but the soft moaning of the night wind and the muffled sobbing of the sacrifices--let all the far stretch of kerosened pyres be touched off simultaneously and the glare and the shrieks and the agonies burst heavenward to the Throne. There are more than a million persons present; the light from the fires flushes into vague outline against the night the spires of five thousand churches. O kind missionary, O compassionate missionary, leave China! come home and convert these Christians!

I believe that if anything can stop this epidemic of bloody insanities it is martial personalities that can face mobs without flinching; and as such personalities are developed only by familiarity with danger and by the training and seasoning which come of resisting it, the likeliest place to find them must be among the missionaries who have been under tuition in China during the past year or two. We have abundance of work for them, and for hundreds and thousands more, and the field is daily growing and spreading. Shall we find them? We can try. In 75,000,000 there must be other Merrills and Beloats; and it is the law of our make that each example shall wake up drowsing chevaliers of the same great knighthood and bring them to the front.

Mark Twain was ahead of his time. His writings on race are as true today as they were when he wrote them over 100 years ago, but his advice would not be heeded. Mob rule would continue to rule the country and dictate the fate of African Americans, in the 1900's and into the 21st century.

CHAPTER 7

EARLY 1900'S RACE RIOTS

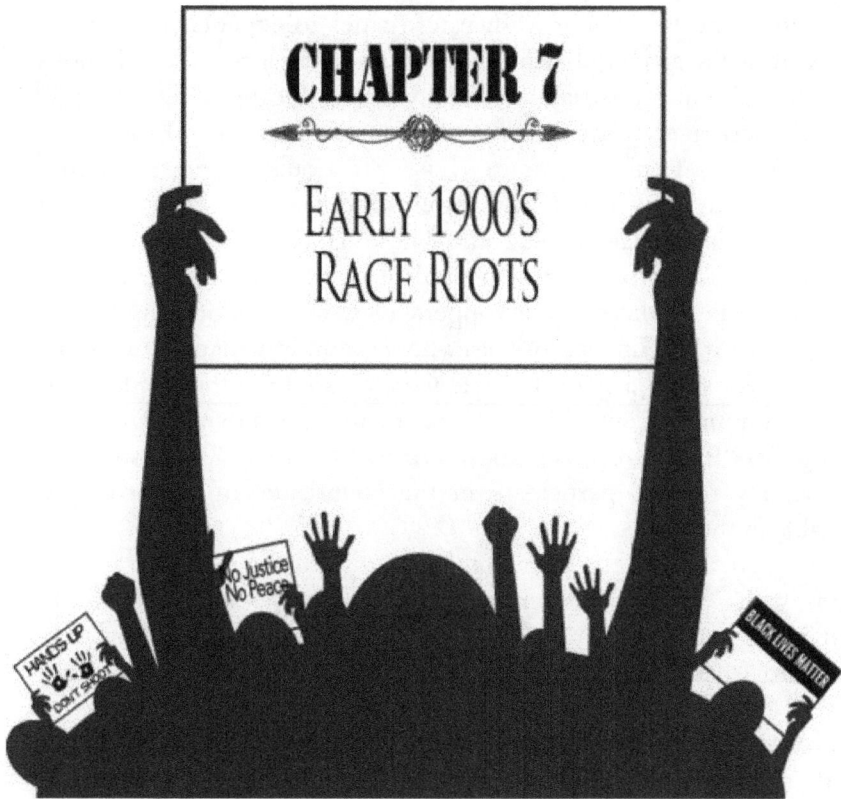

When World War One began in 1914 the number of immigrants emigrating to America from Eastern Europe to work in U.S. manufacturing plants began to dramatically decline, but the factories were still producing munitions for the government, garments for the clothing industry and materials for manufacturing at an exponential rate each year and companies continued to need large numbers of unskilled laborers to fill their workforce.

Between 1871 and 1915 over twenty five million Europeans came to the Untied States to find work. They made up over twenty-five percent of the nation's workforce. European immigrants accounted for nearly 1 million new workers each year for the manufacturing industry in the U.S., but when the inflow of new immigrant job seekers got cut off by the war, northern American factories looked to the south to fill the void. The black exodus from the southern states began.

One of the first major Midwestern cities to experience the mass influx of newly arriving black inhabitants was East St. Louis, Illinois; a residential and industrial community that is located directly across the Missouri river from downtown St. Louis Missouri. Prosperous cities like St. Louis, Missouri, East St. Louis, Illinois, Detroit, Michigan and many other Midwestern and northern cities evolved during the industrial revolution. These cities were the envy of southern blacks who had grown tired of working on the farm fields as poorly paid workers, sharecroppers, or worse. As other industrial cities similar to St. Louis arose elsewhere around the nation, an ample supply of jobs and a good lifestyle were created for the residents of those communities, and blacks began to make a move to the north during this "First Great Migration," from 1901 to 1930. It was their opportunity to also participate in the abundance of opportunities available in the north.

In 1910 there were 8 million African Americans in the United States, with 7 million of them living in the south, below the "Cotton Curtain." Southern workers were severely underpaid, earning only two-thirds of the salary of workers in the northern and midwestern states. Further, working conditions in the north were pleasant compared to the grueling conditions of working the farm fields in the south, so the thought of relocating to a northern state was the dream of many minorities. unfortunately, it was out of reach for most of them, until free travel and accommodations were offered by northern businesses to induce the southern workers to move to the north for work and a better life.

When the influx of European workers subsided, job recruiters from companies in the north came south to find unskilled workers to fill the factories. Free train tickets were offered to those who wanted to relocate to the north to find work. Black newspapers advertised the jobs and wrote personal stories of black families who already relocated to the north and who were living a good life in cities like St. Louis and New York City. The stories described a plethora of job opportunities and excellent living conditions.

The ads sparked a fever of interest from the southern blacks who were eager to find more work and better wages far away from the reminders of southern slavery.

The great migration of blacks moving from the south to northern states dramatically increased the number of minorities in these communities in a way that wasn't expected. From 1910 to 1920 the black population in New York increased by 66%, Chicago rose by 148%, Philadelphia rose by 500% and Detroit rose by 611%. Detroit's tremendous rise in population is partly due to Henry Ford's "experiment" to see if he could train African Americans to be productive assembly line workers for his automobile company. In 1910 there were only 600 black automotive workers in the U.S. but by 1929 the number had grown to 25,000.

On one day in Chicago during The Great Migration, over 600 blacks applied for housing when only fifty-three units were available. This same scene played out in most northern cities during this period. Since blacks were being confined to certain areas in the inner city that did not have adequate housing facilities, these newcomers were forced to live in overcrowded and deplorable conditions, and thus confirmed and reinforced the beliefs by whites that the blacks would turn any neighborhood they lived in into a slum.

White workers began to become hostile when the black workforce moved in to replace them at the factories, and began accepting lower wages for work the whites wanted. An unskilled worker would make $2,50 per day of work in Alabama but an unskilled worker in Illinois was making $4.25 per day. When the black workers arrived in northern cities and began to undercut the hourly wage of white workers, the white workforce reacted. Violently.

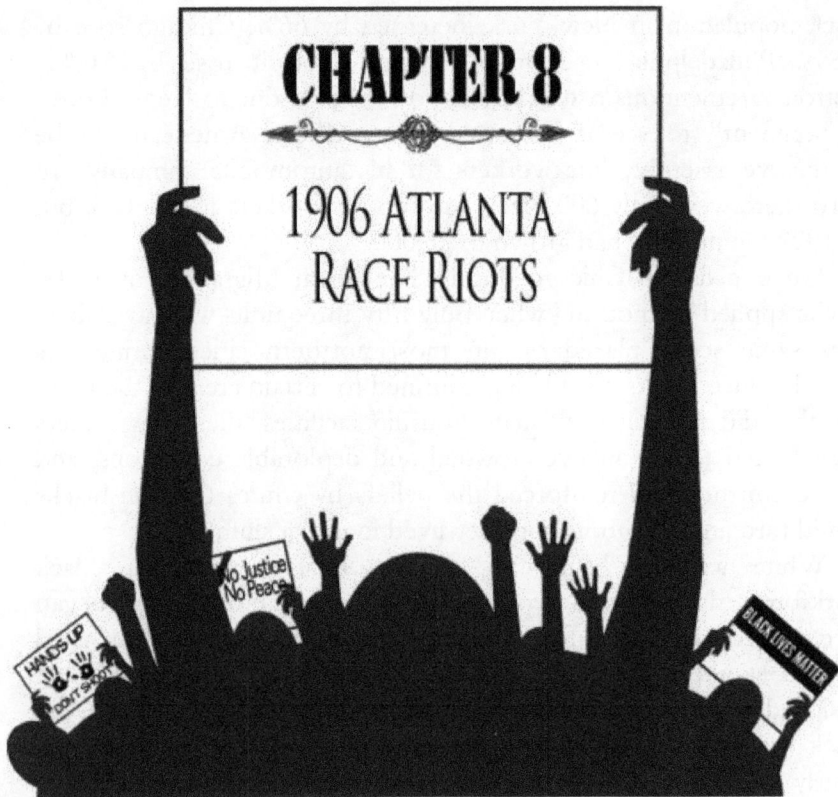

CHAPTER 8

1906 ATLANTA RACE RIOTS

Atlanta Georgia was considered the capital of the "New South" in the early 1900's. The city was thriving, largely due to the cheap Negro workforce. Atlanta businesses boasted about their cheap and obedient labor pool of ex-slaves. It was claimed that blacks were not interested in, or knowledgeable about, union organizing, a problem that plagued northern companies. As money flowed in from the north to build factories and businesses that relied on inexpensive labor, more and more blacks moved to Atlanta to take advantage of the abundance of jobs.

With cheap labor and ample other resources Atlanta became a booming metropolis and a promising place for families to work and live, but in 1906, with opposing Democratic Governor candidates race-bating and debating in public how each of them could best keep the Negros from voting, the city turned violent. Over-sensationalized news reports of lynchings, white women being attacked by black males and the need for a new Ku Klux Klan organization to control blacks, were stories being written daily in the newspapers. This helped push the white inhabitants of Atlanta past their breaking point and propelled some of them into a frenzied mob of killers. On Saturday, September 22nd, a gang of ten thousand angry white assassins armed with pitch forks, guns and knives roamed the city streets and began attacking and killing any blacks that could be found. The mob violence continued for four days in the Five Points district of downtown Atlanta.

Evelyn Witherspoon, a 10-year old girl at the time of the Atlanta riots recounted what she witnessed: "I woke somewhere around midnight and could feel tension in the room. My mother and her sister were kneeling in front of the window, looking out into the street. I got up and said, 'What is it?' They said, 'Go back to bed.' But I knew something was going on, and I came to the window and knelt down between them. And there I saw a man strung up to the light pole. Men and boys on the street below were shooting at him, until they riddled his body with bullets. He was kicking, flailing his legs, when I looked out."

Local leaders covered up the crimes so they could preserve Atlanta's image. Members from the black and white communities began to have meetings together after the riots, to begin a dialogue and mark a beginning of interracial cooperation between the races, but it wouldn't take long for another massacre to occur that would take race rioting to whole new level – in East St. Louis.[6]

[6] Century-Old Race Riot Still Resonates in Atlanta – www.npr.org

CHAPTER 9

EAST ST. LOUIS MASSACRE OF 1917

Throughout the 20th century the African American population of the United States has been moving steadily from rural areas to urban cities and from Southern to Northern states. In 1910, 91 percent of the nation's 9.8 million African Americans lived in the South and only 27 percent lived in cities of 2,500 persons or more.

One of the most affluent and pristine neighborhoods in the Midwest in the early 1900's was in East St. Louis, Illinois; a city in easy proximately for workers to commute to jobs in the inner city of St. Louis, Missouri or work in the plethora of factory jobs that were available in East St. Louis, Illinois. It was a white-only enclave until a surge of southern blacks moved into the community to seek-out the American Dream of having a good job, a good home and a happy family.

During the early 1900's when new industries were arising in the north and blacks were fleeing the farm jobs of the south, East St. Louis was a town on the upswing, and full of opportunities, for whites as well as for blacks. It was located in a strategically important location in Illinois, across the Mississippi river from downtown St. Louis, Missouri (and only 14 miles from Ferguson). Further, with a population of over 500,000 inhabitants, the city of St. Louis Missouri was the forth-largest city in the United States, behind only New York, Philadelphia, and Chicago. Its location directly across the river from East St. Louis afforded both cities an ample supply of workers for the factories, and customers for the stores. The city of St. Louis housed over 400 stores, 200 schools, 95 hotels, 40 hospitals, 30 factories, 6 daily newspapers and 27 breweries, including world famous Budweiser. Although only 1 out of 5 people owned their own home, a 4-bedroom house could be purchased for only $2,000. It was at a time when a quarry worker would make only $2 per day but a women's dress would cost only $3.00. Lodging was $1 per week. A men's suit was $11. Round trip tickets to San Francisco were $47. Horse drawn buggies were $30. And straw hats cost only $1.

East St. Louis, Illinois, was initially called Illinoistown after its inception in 1859, but soon changed its name to represent its affiliation and geographical proximity close to downtown St. Louis, Missouri, and a short walk across the Eads bridge, which was the longest arched bridge at the time, with a length of 6,442 feet. The bridge was so long and unusual when it was built in 1874 that an elephant was used in a publicity stunt to prove to people that the bridge would not collapse, even under the weight of an elephant. The new bridge was a monumental technological advance, which led to larger steel projects around the United States. Andrew Carnegie provided the highly refined steel for the bridge which helped launch his company into what would become the largest steelmaker in the world. When JP Morgan bought him out for $480 million, Andrew Carnegie became the richest man in the world, and his first large construction project was the Eads bridge, connecting St. Louis to East St. Louis.

East St. Louis bragged of having the cheapest coal in the country, due to the city's close proximity to Illinois coal mines. Cheap energy, along with large numbers of unskilled workers willing to work long hours in the manufacturing plants, induced factories to develop in, or relocate to, the area.

With such a large number of factories in the greater St. Louis area, it was ripe for union participation and recruitment. There were more than 120 unions located around St. Louis which sought better working conditions for workers at some of the largest employers in the area. These large employers, at the time, included the Standard Oil Refinery, the American Steel Foundry, the Republic Iron & Steel company, and the Aluminum Ore Company.

When the supply of Eastern European workers waned, the factories sent recruiters to Louisiana to spread the word that there were good paying jobs and plenty of opportunities to the North. This recruitment of black farm workers led to a mass exodus of blacks from southern plantations leaving Louisiana for the city streets of East St. Louis.

In January of 1917, newspaper advertisements in the south proclaimed *"Millions to Leave the South. Northern Invasion will start in spring - Bound for the Promised Land."* These ads sparked the full-scale exodus of blacks from the south to the factories in the north. East St. Louis, Illinois was the destination of choice for many of the newly liberated black farm workers. The ads offered reduced or free train fare and cheap accommodations. The trips to the north were scheduled to begin on May 15th, 1917. For the blacks, their opportunity had arrived.

Many southern blacks took the bait of the factory recruiters and left Louisiana for East St, Louis. Once there, they were met with hostility and hatred from a population that was 98% white. The African Americans arrived at a time when the local factories were fighting unionization. It was the Spring of 1917. Unions were gaining momentum as a political force in America with a loyal membership of active and angry manufacturing workers, who were mainly white, and of European decent.

The exodus of southern blacks from the farm felids of Louisiana to the manufacturing cities in the north and in the midwest caused two major problems. These were: The loss of workers for the farms in Louisiana and an influx of new black residents into the white neighborhoods of East St. Louis. Both Louisiana Plantation owners and the voters of East St. Louis called upon East St. Louis Mayor Fred Moflman to find a way to keep the blacks from leaving Louisiana, and keep his constituents in East St. Louis content in knowing that no more blacks were going to move into the community and take their jobs.

Louisiana farmers wrote letters to their Governor, to newspapers, politicians and the New Orleans Board of Trade to try to find a way to convince the black population in Louisiana, to stay in Louisiana. The residents of East St. Louis urged the Mayor to do something to preserve their jobs and their way of life. Their Mayor traveled to New Orleans to meet with plantation owners and trade organizations and tried to find a way to keep the blacks contained in the south. His political career depended on it.

Even the railroads were pressured, by political and corporate forces, to keep the blacks from traveling to the north. The railroad companies complied, as much as they could, but they could not stop the flow of jobless blacks fleeing from southern oppression.

On April 26th, 1917, a month before the East St. Louis massacre, East St. Louis Mayor Fred Moflman took a trip to Louisiana to talk to New Orleans Mayor Martin Behrman about their mutual problems associated with the back exodus from the south.

He also met with the Louisiana Farmers and Board of Trade and promised to do all he could to discourage blacks from going to East St. Louis. He declared that southern Negros were arriving in St. Louis at a rate of 2,000 per week and disrupting life and labor conditions in Midwest industrial cities. He promised that he would do what he could to keep the black farm workers in Louisiana, which would also preserve the white jobs of East St. Louis factory workers, and preserve his own job.

The growing resentment of the "black invasion" pushed the residents of East St. Louis to a breaking point. Union leaders demanded that City Hall "get rid" of the newcomers, and they did. In 1917, workers at the Aluminum Ore processing plant went on strike. The company responded by hiring 470 mainly African Americans workers to replace the mainly white workers who went on strike. The Union fought back and provoked their members to take action to eradicate all of the African Americans in East St. Louis. During union meetings in the spring of 1917, the "Negro problem" became the major issue. The white residents of East St. Louis saw their financial and family lives being ruined by the new influx of minorities and they thought they had to put an end to it, immediately, to preserver their jobs and their all-white way of life.

On May 28th, immediately following a city council meeting that was held so white workers could file formal complaints about black workers taking their jobs, a rumor spread across town that a black man had attempted to rob a white man. A mob formed quickly and tore through downtown East St. Louis, attacking every African American that could be found. Trolley cars were stopped and black riders were pulled from them and savagely beaten. The National Guard was eventually called-in to contain the rioters and restore peace. When the National Guard was ordered out of the city on June 10th, a high state of racial tension remained.

The white residents of East St. Louis had become emboldened by the lack of repercussions for the May 28th rioting, looting and beatings of blacks so when they had the opportunity to strike again, they did. The witness accounts of what happened next would be concealed as "confidential Information" by the U.S. government until 1986, to prevent another civil war, or a race war within America. Congress thought the people of the United States were not ready to hear the true fact about what happened during the East St. Louis Massacre. It's a story you won't want to believe.

On July 1st, 1917, a car drove through the black section of East St. Louis with several white occupants shooting randomly into black homes. A black mob then formed and fired their weapons at the next car that came through their neighborhood with white occupants. They unfortunately shot and killed two plain clothed policemen who were "reportedly" coming to investigate the earlier shootings.

The following day, on July 2nd, after a heated union meeting, white union members became enraged about the killing of the white police officers and also about loosing their jobs to the blacks, and they decided to get rid of "The Black Problem" once and for all. City residents rushed from their meeting and attacked every African American they could get their hands on. The mob screamed, "get a nigger" then chanted, "get another" and systematically went to every black occupied house in the city and burned it to the ground, forcing the inhabitants to come outside and meet their fate. The ones who were smoked-out of their homes were beaten to death in the street. Some who witnessed the atrocities occurring to their black neighbors decided to stay inside and to burn with their possessions, rather than being beaten to death by the marauding white crowd. Thousands of blacks fled across the Eads Bridge to downtown St. Louis. City police officers harassed the media who were trying to cover the event and also participated in some of the attacks on African Americans, along with the National Guard.

Carlos Hurd, a famous reporter for the St. Louis Post Dispatch newspaper, who interviewed the first surviving passengers of the Titanic sinking in 1912, witnessed the East St. Louis riot firsthand. He wrote, "For an hour and a half last evening, I saw the massacre of helpless negroes at Broadway and Fourth Street, in downtown East St. Louis, where a black skin was a death warrant."

The ethnic cleansing that occurred in East St. Louis in 1917 caused 312 buildings to be burnt to the ground and at least 39 deaths. There were estimates that the actual death toll was more than 300, with the police and the National Guard participating in the brutality, but the death toll was probably much higher. Many of the bodies were thrown into the Mississippi river and buried in mass graves on the outskirts of town.

Following is a July 8, 1917 speech given by Marcus Garvey, a powerful black political leader at the time and a person who is considered a prophet for the Rastafarian religion and the Nation of Islam. He painted a picture of the East St. Louis Riots that's hard to imagine, unless you read his words. Marcus Garvey stated:

The East St. Louis Riot, or rather massacre, of Monday July 2nd, will go down in history as one of the bloodiest outrages against mankind for which any class of people could be held guilty. This is no time for fine words, but a time to lift one's voice against the savagery of a people who claim to be the dispensers of democracy. I do not know what special meaning the people who slaughtered the Negroes of East. St. Louis have for democracy of which they are the custodians, but I do know that it has no literal meaning for me as used and applied by these same lawless people. America, that has been ringing the bells of the world, proclaiming to the nations and the peoples thereof that she has democracy to give to all and sundry, America that has denounced Germany for the deportations of the Belgians into Germany, America that has arraigned Turkey at the bar of public opinion and public justice against the massacres of the Armenians, has herself no satisfaction to give 12,000,000 of her own citizens except the satisfaction of a farcical inquiry that will end where it begun, over the brutal murder of men, women and children for no other reason than that they are black people seeking an industrial chance in a country that they have laboured for three hundred years to make great. For three hundred years the Negroes of America have given their life blood to make the Republic the first among the nations of the world, and all along this time there has never been even one year of justice but on the contrary a continuous round of oppression. At one time it was slavery, at another time lynching and burning, and up to date it is wholesome wholesale butchering. This is a crime against the laws of humanity; it is a crime against the laws of the nation, it is a crime against Nature, and a crime against the God of all mankind.

Somewhere in the book of life we are told that "God created of one blood all nations of men to dwell on the face of the earth," and after mankind, in scattered groups, had for thousands of years lived in their own spheres without trouble or molestation, promoting in their own way the course of peace and happiness, the white race, a party of this group, went out to enslave, conquer and rob the rights of the Peaceful. Through that system of enslavement, conquest and robbery, the black man was taken into this country where he was forced against his will to labor for the enrichment of the white man. Millions of our people in the early days of slavery gave their lives that America might live. From the labours of these people the country grew in power, until her wealth to-day is computed above that of any two nations. With all the service that the Negro gave he is still a despised creature in the eye of the white people, for if he were not to them despised, the 90,000,000 of whites of this country would never allow such outrages as the East St. Louis massacre to perpetuate themselves without enforcing the law which provides justice for every man be he black or white.

The black man has always trusted the white man. He has always clung to him as a brother man, ever willing to do service for him, to help him, to succor him, yet with all this the white man has never found it convenient to live up to the principles of brotherhood which he himself teaches to all mankind. From the time of Livingstone to the present day the black man has always been kind to the white man. When there was no white man in Africa to help the sickly and dying Livingstone, the black man, ever true, even as Simon the Cyrenian was true, in bearing the cross of the despised Jesus, came to the rescue of the suffering Englishman, and when he was dead, faithful as they were, they bore his body for hundreds of miles across the desert and plains of Africa until they deposited his remains at a place where other white men could reach him to convey him to England and inter his bones in the Cathedral of Westminster Abbey. The Negro in American history from the time of Crispus Attucks at Boston, the 10th Cavalry at San Juan Hill which saved the day for Roosevelt, up to the time when they stuck to Boyd at Carrizal, has demonstrated to the American Nation that he is as true as steel. Yet for all his services he receives the reward of lynching, burning and wholesale slaughter. It is even strange to see how the real American white people, the people who are direct descendants from the Pilgrim Fathers, allow the alien German, the Italian and other Europeans who came here but yesterday to lead them in bloody onslaught against the Negroes who have lived here for over three hundred years. When I say that the Aliens are leading the descendants of the Pilgrim Fathers against the Negroes in this country I mean to support it with as much facts as possible.

Mayor Mollman of East St. Louis, if not himself a German, descendant of German immigrants, he is the man to be blamed for the recent riots in East St. Louis. I say so because I am convinced that he fostered a well arranged conspiracy to prevent black men migrating from the South much the loss of Southern Farmers who for months have been moving heaven it seems to prevent the exodus of the labor serfs of the South into the North.

Two months ago I was in New Orleans completing a lecture tour of the United States, and on the 26th of April Mayor Fred W. Moflman arrived in the city on a trip from St. Louis. In New Orleans he was met by Mayor Behrman and the New Orleans Board of Trade. For months the Farmers of Louisiana were frightened out of their wits over the everyday migration of Negroes from great farming centers of the State. They wrote to the papers, they appealed to the Governor, the Mayor and the Legislature and the Board of Trade to stop the Negroes going away, but up to the 26th of April nothing was done to stop the people excepting the Railway Companies promising to use certain restraint on the rush of people obtaining passages on the trains by Railway orders sent to them from the North. At this time Mayor Mollman arrived and the Farmers and Board of Trade met him and asked his help in discouraging the Negroes from going North and especially to East St. Louis. In an interview given out to the New Orleans press he said that the Negroes from the South were reaching St. Louis at the rate of 2,000 per week, and that they were creating a problem there. He said that some of the largest industries in the country were established in East St. Louis and there were strikes for the last few months. He believed the labor conditions in East St. Louis were responsible for the number of Negro laborers going to that city. When the strikes started, he said, United States District Judge Wright issued an injunction restraining the strikers from intimidating the laborers who took their places. This order prevented uprisings and riots. 'Conditions are very bad in East St. Louis,' he said, 'because many plants are suffering for the want of labor. However, our city is growing and we have a population of 85,000 persons. During 1916 we gained 1,600 in population.' His interview did not make pleasant reading for the Farmers and others interested in labor in New Orleans and Louisiana so that the very next day he appeared at the Board of Trade where he met the Farmers and others and in discussing the labor exodus with them, he promised that he would do all he could to discourage Negroes from Louisiana going into East St. Louis as the city did not want them. His interview on the first day was an encouragement to the Negroes to go to East St. Louis, as there was work for them, owing to the inability of the various plants to get labor. On the second day when he was approached he said East St. Louis did not want the Negroes, and he then promised to do all in his power to prevent them going there. His remarks to the people whom he met were published under big headlines in the newspapers, so that the Negroes could read that they were not wanted in East St. Louis, but that did not deter the blackmen of Louisiana who were looking for better opportunities in the land of their birth going about the country looking for better conditions than the South offered with lynching and Jim Crowism. The Negroes still continued their migration North. The Mayor of East St. Louis returned to the city after making his promise to the Farmers, Board of Trade and others who were interested in Negro labor.

On the 5th of May the New Orleans Board of Trade elected Mr. M. J. Sanders its president, and Mr. W. P. Ross as delegates to attend a transportation conference at St. Louis to be held on May 8-9. You will remember that Mayor Mollman appeared before the Board of Trade on Friday the 27th of April where he made his statement of promise. The transportation conference was held at St. Louis on the 8th and 9th of May at which several prominent men interested in the labor condition of the South were present as also Messrs. Sanders and Ross, from New

Orleans. It isn't for me to suggest that Mayor Mollman met these gentlemen again; it is for you to imagine what further transpired while these gentlemen from the South who were so deeply interested in keeping the Negro below the Mason and Dixon line said and did among themselves while in that vicinity where Mayor Mollman held sway so much so as to be able to make a promise to keep out citizens of the United States who were not born in Germany, but in the Southland. One thing I do know; the first riot started on May 28 after a conference of labor leaders with Mayor Mollman. On that day, May 28, crowds of white men after leaving the City Council stopped street cars and dragged Negroes off and beat them. Then the night following three Negroes and two white men were shot. An investigation of the affair resulted in the finding that labor agents had induced Negroes to come from the South. I can hardly see the relevance of such a report with the dragging of men from cars and shooting them. The City authorities did nothing to demonstrate to the unreasonable labor leaders that they would be firmly dealt with should they maltreat and kill black men. No threat was offered to these men because Mayor Mollman himself had promised to do all he could to drive the Negroes out of East St. Louis, and to instill fear in the hearts of the people in the South so as to prevent them coming North. On the 29th of May, a day after the first disturbance, and when three Negro men had been killed, Mayor Mollman sent a dispatch to Governor Pleasant of Louisiana advising the Negroes of Louisiana to remain away from East St. Louis. This news item from the 'Call' of May 31 which I will read will speak for itself. I have not seen the Louisiana papers that published that order but you, can imagine for yourselves how the papers made prominent news of it so as to bring home to the Negroes of the State the very discouraging situation which the Mayor of East St. Louis helped to create. Because nothing was done to crush the originators and leaders of the first riot the Negro haters of East St. Louis took fresh courage and made their final attack on our defenseless men, women and children on Monday July 2nd and which resulted in the wholesale massacre of our people. When we read in the white press a report like what I will read to you, we can conjure to our own minds the horror of the whole affair.

Newspapers reported:

East St. Louis, July 2nd. Negroes are being shot down like rabbits and strung up to telegraph poles.

The official police estimate at 9 o'clock put the number of dead at 100. They reach this total partly through reports that many victims have been pursued into creeks and shot, burned in buildings or murdered and thrown into the Mississippi. The exact number of dead will probably never be known. Six Negroes were hanged to telegraph poles in the south end of the town. A reliable white man reports having counted nineteen Negro corpses on a side street. "A reign of terror prevails. The police and the tow companies of the National Guard are powerless. The companies of soldiers were powerless as they had orders not to shoot. The whites took their rifles from them telling them they might hurt some one whilst these very whites took the rifles and shot Negroes." The whole thing my friends is a bloody farce, and that the police and soldiers did nothing to stem the murder thirst of the mob is a conclusive proof of conspiracy on the part of the civil authorities to condone the acts of the white mob against Negroes. In this report we further read that as the flames of fire would drive a Negro man, woman or child from a dwelling, their clothes burning, the mob would set up a great shout and rifles and pistols would be fired. So far no Negro was known to escape as the whites had a merciless net about the Negroes, and the cry was "kill 'em all." Negro faces were seen at frames of windows and when they say what happened to those who flew from the burning structures, they dropped back into the fire rather than tempt a similar fate. An example of what the guardsmen encountered, and themselves enjoyed, was the beating of colored women by white girls. This sort of thing was common. It resulted in the death of several Negro women. Six girls, according to the report pursued a colored girl around the main railway station. A mob formed behind the girls who were screaming frantic epithets at the terrified black girl. "Send them back to Africa." "Kill them all." "Lynch them," shouted the young amazons. Suddenly the crowd swept from the trail of the girl. A yell then arose. "There is one." It was a Negro walking on the railroad track. Before he realized his peril he was killed. Half a dozen pistols cracked and the man dropped without a chance to run. Two white girls, neither more than 17 years old, the report said, were cheered when they dragged a colored girl from a street car, removed her slippers and beat senseless with the sharp wooden heels. Some reports said black women were stripped by white women for the amusement of the crowd.

The mob and entire white populace of East St. Louis had a Roman *holiday. They feasted on the blood of the Negro, encouraged as they were by the German American Mayor who two months ago went to New Orleans and promised to keep the Negroes out of East St. Louis. That this man did absolutely nothing to let the people know that the law would be enforced to preserve order and ensure the peaceful lives of the black people is amply demonstrated by a report which comes from East. St. Louis, and was published in the "New York Tribune" of Saturday, July 7. Under the caption: "Citizens Blame Long Reign of Lawlessness for Riots" the paper published this bit of news. "Resignation of Chief of Police Payne of East. St. Louis and of Cornelius Hickey Night Chief of Police will be demanded of Mayor Mollam by the citizens' committee of the Chamber of Commerce. This determination is a result of the race riots here Monday in which thirty-seven persons lost their lives. Maurice Joyce, vice-president of the Chamber of Commerce, declared today the rioting was the direct result of the long reign of lawlessness in East St. Louis. We have a police department that is incompetent and inefficient if not worse. Not only was the word sent out that law would not be rigidly enforced but the impression was allowed to spread that law violations would be winked at." This gallant vice-chairman of the Chamber of Commerce who knew this even before one Negro was shot, never said a word and did nothing to bring the delinquent Mayor who rules the city to a realization of these facts until great property damage was done to the Southern Railway Company, when their warehouse of over 100 car loads of merchandise was consumed by the flames causing a loss to the company of over $500,000, and a white theatre of over $100,000 was destroyed. It was not until property was destroyed in which the Chamber of Commerce was most interested, that the officers of the body let the Mayor know that he must do his duty. It was not through over-population or through scarcity of work why East. St. Louis did not want Negroes. It was simply because they were black men. For Mayor Mollman himself said months ago that East St. Louis was badly off for laborers as many of the plants could not get hands to operate them.*

I can hardly see why black men should be debarred from going where they choose in the land of their birth. I can not see wherefrom Mayor Mollman got the authority to discourage black men going into East St. Louis, when there was work for them, except he got that authority from mob sentiment and mob law. It was because he knew that he could gain a following and support on the issue of race why he was bold enough to promise the white people of Louisiana that he would keep Negroes out of East. St. Louis. He has succeeded in driving fully 10,000 in one day out of the city, and the South has gone wild over the splendid performance in so much so that the very next day after the massacre the Legislature of Georgia sent out the message that their good Negroes must come home as they will treat them better than East St. Louis did. Can you wonder at the conspiracy of the whole affair? White people are taking advantage of black men today because black men all over the world are disunited."

Author James Patrick wrote an article immediately after the riots entitled, "The Horror of the East St. Louis Massacre." It highlights some of the atrocities that occurred during the race riot of 1917. James Patrick wrote:

The horror of the East St. Louis massacre of July 2,1917 is told in the eyewitness accounts of over fifty people interviewed by Mrs. Ida B. Wells-Barnett and the eyewitness accounts of white news reporters. What follows is a brief synopsis of a report entitled 'History of the East St. Louis, Illinois, Riot' written by Mrs. Ida B. Wells-Barnett.

This report was held under seal by the U.S. Government as 'classified information' and the U.S. Government did not de-classify this report until 1986. The first three stories were told to Mrs. Wells-Barnett as she traveled back and forth from East St. Louis to St. Louis. Taking women with trunks of their wearing apparel, which they were able to salvage from their ransacked and burned out homes in East St. Louis, Illinois. Mrs. Emma Ballard said, men and boys were in the street hollering, 'come out, n_____s' as they roamed up and down in the African American district. They shot and beat every African American found on the streets Monday night. She saw fourteen men beaten and two killed.

Mrs. Mary Howard said, that during the riot a young fellow whom she had sent to the grocery to get a chicken, was knocked off his wheel by the mob. Then the mob took his wheel and struck him on the side of his head with a brick and knocked a hole in it. His name was Jimmie Eckford, eighteen years old and he roomed at her house. He ran into the nearest yard which happened to be that of white people. When the mob said they would burn this house down if they didn't make Mr. Eckford come out, the tenants picked him up and threw him out in the street to the mob.

Where he was kicked and stamped on and beaten till they knocked his teeth from his head and killed him. The street cars ran right along in front of Mrs. Howard's house, and she saw white women stop the street cars and pull African American women off and beat them. One woman's clothes they tore off entirely, and then took off their shoes and beat her over the face and head with their shoe heels. Another woman who got away, ran down the street, with every stitch of clothes torn off her back, leaving her with only her shoes and stocking on. Mrs. Howard saw two men beaten to death.

She had escaped all excepting having rocks thrown at the house, until this solider humiliated her by coming into her house and arresting her and the other women there, because they couldn't find any guns concealed. In the Chicago Herald, July 4, 1917, a white reporter wrote that the National Guards were lax and cruelly good-natured. In one instance a corpulent African American woman brought up the rear of a procession and for several blocks a white boy, one of the gang of stone-throwing mischief-makers, who followed every squad, was beating her with an iron bar at intervals of a few yards.

She did not dare to protest or to resist. She was even too frightened to scream. At last a white man, probably a nonresident of East St. Louis, called the attention of a guardsman to the outrage, and he laughingly drove the boy off. The square block from Broadway and Eighth streets was burned to an ash heap. On that corner stood an African American commercial building containing a grocery and barber shop. The vanguard of the rioters invaded these stores and found an African American crouching timorously in each.

The armed invaders drove the two African Americans out through the back doors and there they were shot down and left to be burned alive. The shots were fired from militia rifles by khaki-uniformed men.

Dozens of men who saw it done today loudly proclaimed it so, slapped their thighs and said the Illinois National Guard was alright. Another white newspaper said, boys 13, 14, 15 and 16 were in the forefront of every felonious butchery. Girls and women, wielding bloody knives and clawing at the eyes of dying victims, sprang from the ranks of the mad thousands. Another eyewitness, Mr. Carlos F. Hurd of St. Louis, Mo., a white staff reporter, wrote and published a part of what he saw in the St. Louis Post-Dispatch on July 3, 1917.

For an hour and a half on July 2,1917, Mr. Hurd saw the massacre of helpless African Americans at Broadway and Fourth street, in downtown East St. Louis, where a black skin was a death warrant. Mr. Hurd saw man after man, with hands raised, pleading for his life, surrounded by groups of men; men who had never seen him before and knew nothing about him except that he was African American; and saw them administer the historic sentence of intolerance, death by stoning.

Mr. Hurd saw one of these men, almost dead from a savage shower of stones, hanged with a clothes line, and when it broke, hanged with a rope which held. Within a few spaces of the pole from which he was suspended, four other African Americans lay dead or dying, another had been removed dead, a short time before. Mr. Hurd saw the pockets of two of these African Americans searched, without the finding of any weapon. Mr. Hurd saw one of these men, covered with blood and half conscious, raise himself on his elbow, and look feebly about, when a young man, standing directly behind, lifted a flat stone and hurled it directly upon his neck. This young man was much better dressed than most of the others. He walked away unmolested.

Mr. Hurd saw African American women begging for mercy and pleading that they had harmed no one, set upon by white women of the baser sort, who laughed and answered the cource sallies of men as they beat the women's faces and breasts with fists, stones and sticks. "Get a n_____r," was the slogan, and it was varied by the recurrent cry, "Get another." It was nothing so much as the holiday crowd, with thumbs turned down, in the Roman Coliseum, except that here the shouters were their own gladiators, and their own wild beasts.

The sheds in the rear of African American houses, which were themselves in the rear of the main buildings on Fourth Street, had been ignited to drive out the African American occupants of the houses. And the slayers were waiting for them to come out. It was stay in and be roasted, or come out and be slaughtered. A moment before Mr. Hurd arrived, one African

American had taken the desperate chance of coming out and the rattle of revolver shots, which Mr. Hurd heard as he approached the corner, was followed by the cry, "they've got him," and they had. He laid on the pavement, a bullet wound in his head and his skull bare in two places. At every movement of pain which showed that life still remained, there came a terrific kick in the jaw or the nose, or a crashing stone, from some of the men who stood over him.

At the corner, a few steps away, were a Sergeant and several guard men, the Sergeant approached the ring of men around the prostrate African American. 'This man is done for,' he said. "You better get him away from here." No one made a move to lift the blood-covered form, and the Sergeant walked away, remarking, when Mr. Hurd questioned him about an ambulance, he said, 'that the ambulances had quit coming.' However, an undertaker's ambulance did come 15 minutes later, and took away the lifeless African American, who had in the meantime been further kicked and stoned.

The mob then turned to see a lynching. An African American who had his head laid open by a great stone-cut had been dragged to the mouth of the alley on Fourth Street and a small rope was being tied about his neck. It broke when it was pulled over a projecting cable, letting the African American fall. A stouter rope was secured. Right there Mr. Hurd his most sickening sight of the evening. To put the rope around the African American's neck, one of the lynch men stuck his fingers inside the gaping scalp and lifted the African American's head by it. 'Get hold and pull for East St. Louis,' called a man with a black coat and a new straw hat on as he seized the other end of the rope, and lifted the body seven feet from the ground, and left it hanging there.

A mob of white men formed and burned all the African American houses on Bond Avenue between Tenth and Twelfth Streets, 43 houses being destroyed. In the fire zone at Sixth and Broadway two African Americans are reported to have burned to death. At Fifth and Railroad, another death by fire was reported. One of the mid-afternoon killings was at 4 o'clock, at Broadway and Main Street. An African American was shot down.

One of those firing on him being a boy in short trousers. The driver of the first ambulance that came was not permitted to remove this body, and it layed for an hour beside the street car tracks seen by the passengers in every passing car. At 9:30 that morning an African American still living, but in critical condition, was found in a sewer manhole at Sixth Street and Broadway. He was beaten by the mob with paving bricks 13 hours before and thrown in. The two-year old African American child who was killed was the daughter of William Forest of 1118 Division Ave..

The following stories were told to Mrs. Ida B. Wells-Barnett after she met with Illinois Governor Lowden on July 9,1917. He told her to return to St. Louis to get him the names of people who would testify. John Avant said, he worked at the C.B.&Q.. He was with about twenty-five other African Americans who got off of work on Tuesday morning. They were sitting or standing around the restaurant where they usually ate, when six soldiers and four or five policemen came upon them suddenly and shot into the crowd, wounding six. One of the number has since died.

They also were searched and even had their pocket knives taken from them. One of the shots fired took off an arm of a woman who was working in this restaurant. One of the half dozen men standing around, told Mrs. Well-Barnett that he saw a woman and two children killed, also her husband. That they were going across the bridge and the mob seized the baby out of her arms and threw it into the river. Frank Brown said, he saw a man hit an African American with a piece of iron and shoot him four times in the stomach.

Mrs. Mary Lewis said, she saw the mob kill a man a few doors away. The mob had broken windows in her house and set it on fire, shooting into it. Her sister was in the house, but escaped, being shot, and was badly stoned. Her husband, though shot, got up and ran about 40 feet before they finished him. William Lues, an employee of the Wabash R.R.CO., was on his way home from work, sitting between his employer and his employer's son in the street car, when the mob grabbed him, shot him to pieces and then put a rope around his neck and dragged him in the streets.

James Taylor said, the mob started at 2:30. At 4:15 they hanged two African Americans who were coming from work, to a telegraph pole and shot them to pieces. He saw them rush to cars and pull women off and beat them to death, and before they were quite dead, Stalwart men jumped on their stomachs and finished them by trampling them to death. This was at the corner of Broadway and Collinville. The cars were crowded and moving, yet they jumped on and pulled them off.

Others they stuck to death with hat pins, sometimes picking out their eyes with them before they were quite dead. An old African American woman between 70 and 80 years old who had returned to her house to get some things, was struck almost to death by women, then men stamped her to death. An African American store keeper at Eighth and Broadway with his family was shot and wounded. The store was set on fire and they burned to death. George Launders and Robert Mosely were burned to death at the Library Flats at Eighth and Walnut.

African American men had their fingers cut off by the mob and their heads split open with axes. Will Morgan, employed at the B.&O. Roundhouse, saw the mob make the African Americans swim into the Cahokia River, then shoot them, one being killed instantly. The others managed to struggle back to shore, only to be stoned to death by children. Mr. Buchanan said, he saw them beat men down with revolvers and clubs; white men knocked African American women down, and then the white women would finish by beating them to death or nearly so.

Every African American man that he saw get out of Black Valley alive, the soldiers would march them to the police station, badly beaten though they were, and scarcely able to walk, with their hands raised in front of them and afraid to turn their heads. The mob threw bricks at their heads and bodies, because the soldiers had their bayonets pointed at either side of them. They did the women the same way, excepting their hands were not raised in front of them.

They were dodging around the soldiers to keep the mob from hitting them with bricks, stones and sticks. Their clothing badly torn. An Associated Press dispatch of July 10, 1917, from East St. Louis had the following: 'A man arrested by Capt. O.C. Smith, F Company, police, ostensibly 'on order of the state's attorney.' Captain Smith asserted that he heard the man say, 'I've killed my share of Negroes today. I have killed so many I am tired and somebody else can finish them.' When Capt. Smith went to the police station yesterday to file a formal charge he found that the prisoner had been released.

This was just a small part of the horror of the racial massacre which occurred on July 2,1917 in East St. Louis, Illinois. It's estimated that from 40 to 150 African Americans were killed and that 6,000 African Americans were driven from their homes, that were indiscriminately burned. All the impartial witnesses agree that the police were indifferent or encouraged the barbarities, and that the major part of the Illinois National Guard was indifferent or inactive. No organized effort was made to protect the African Americans or disperse the murdering groups. [7]

Newly arriving black workers from the south found out how dangerous life in East St. Louis could be and it strengthened their resolve to begin to arm themselves in preparation for more potential massacres in the future. More than 6,000 residents were permanently removed from East St. Louis during the 1917 riots, and left homeless, with no possessions. Some of those families probably relocated to Ferguson. The East St. Louis riots spawned a wave of white on black violence that resulted in mass rioting across the country--known as the Red Summer of 1919. [8] [9]

---

[7] http://www.usd116.org/profdev/ahtc/lessons/PollockFel10/4chorrorESL.pdf

[8] http://www.epi.org/publication/making-ferguson/#_ref5

[9] http://www.blackpast.org/aah/east-st-louis-race-riot-july-2-1917

CHAPTER 10

RED SUMMER OF 1919

When World War 1 ended in 1919, American soldiers came home to find fierce competition for jobs and also found African Americans employed in many of the positions they wanted. The job climate had changed from 1917 when jobs were plentiful. In 1919, with the influx of returning troops from the war, jobs were scarce.

Unions were becoming popular social organizations and a tool to pressure employers to offer better working conditions, and pay, but when white workers went on strike, black workers replaced them, and worked at a cheaper labor rate, which infuriated the white workforce.

Whites were seeing their livelihoods being taken from them, fast, so they struck back, in the summer of 1919, in cities all across America, in an all-out-effort to put "uppity niggers" back in their place as second class citizens, and force them out of the labor pool.

In America, after the war, racial tension were at a breaking point. Then citizens snapped.

In the course of 6 month, from May through October, white rioting broke out against African Americans in over 27 cities across America, in the states of South Carolina, Texas, Tennessee, California, Arizona, Nebraska, Mississippi, Louisiana, Illinois, Kentucky, Alabama, Connecticut, Delaware, Virginia, Georgia, Florida and Washington D.C., in an all-out-effort to kill, humiliate and humble African Americans.

On July 7th, 1919, Chicago Illinois was hot and children were looking for ways to cool off. The Lake Michigan beach off 29th street was a favorite destination for white kids but black kids also swam at the beach--but only in a designated "Negro" area. When one of the black youths, Eugene Williams, floated on his raft into the designated white-only swimming area, he was quickly spotted and subsequently stoned by the angry white bathers, and drowned. A small group of African Americans gathered at the beach to protest the killing and force the police to arrest the perpetrators, but the police chose to let the suspects loose, without charging them with any crimes and instead they arrested a black protester. When the black mob began to riot in retaliation, a larger white mob merged on them from all parts of Chicago and proceeded to beat, kill and burn as many blacks as they could catch, for 13 consecutive days, leaving over 1,000 African Americans homeless, more than 500 injured and over 50 killed.

On July 19th, 1919, based on rumors that a black man rapped a white woman, a mob of angry white residents formed, and for four days, they tried to beat the blacks into submission, but in Washington D.C., the blacks began to fight back and fend off their attackers. The New York Times conceded their was a problem with post war blacks, by writing, "There had been no trouble with the Negro before the war when most admitted the superiority of the white race."

The African American community was proud, probably for the first time, that their people were fighting back against oppression. A southern black women explained when she heard that blacks were beginning to fight back, "The Washington riot gave me a thrill that comes once in a lifetime. At last our men had stood up like men. I stood up alone in my room and exclaimed aloud, 'Oh I thank God, thank God.' The pent up horror, grief and humiliation of a lifetime was being stripped from me." In all, 4 whites and 2 blacks were reported to be killed in the melee.

One of the most intense riots to occur in 1919 broke out on October 1st in Arkansas after a black sharecroppers union meeting of the *Progressive Farmers and Household Union of America* was broken up by two white police officers, who claimed they were looking for a bootlegger, but who were probably there to break up the meeting as a favor to the local white farmers who were not happy about the blacks forming a farming union. One of the police officers was shot during the meeting and the other one was wounded when they exchanged gunfire with the black crowd. The county sheriff called-out for community members throughout Arkansas and into Mississippi to come to his aid and "to hunt Mr. Nigger in his lair."

Hundreds of vigilantes came to the county and tried to kill every black they came across, saying "if it was black and moving, it was target practice." Witness Frank More saw the massacre occur first hand and reported, "The whites sent word that they was comin down here and kill every nigger they found. There were 300 or 400 more white men with guns, shooting and killing women and children." Over the 3 day carnage, twenty-five blacks were confirmed killed, but before it was over it is believed that over 200 bodies were also dumped into the Mississippi River, to be forgotten about forever.

The Federal Government sent in troops and restored order, but order was hard to establish in the middle of a race war.

The most outrageous act of rioting in 1919 happened In Omaha, Nebraska when a 19-year-old white girl named Agnes Loeback accused Will Brown, a black warehouse worker, of rape. He was arrested and held in jail until a mob formed and demanded that he be released to them. When the police refused to turn over the prisoner, the residents of the town set the police station on fire and then stormed in to the building after the judge passed a note out the 4th floor window agreeing to release the Negro and asked for the mob to save the white prisoners who escaped to the roof.

The mob had grown to over 5,000 people by the time the mob stormed the courthouse. The Mayor tried to stop the Lynching but the frenzied mob turned on him and hung him by the neck from a light pole before he was cut loose and saved by his guards.

Once Will Brown was removed from the courthouse, the crowd beat, burnt, hanged and shot him hundreds of times, then dragged his corpse through the streets of downtown Omaha, on display.

After the lynching, white rioters paraded themselves to the black neighborhoods of Omaha, to attack more minorities. The looters broke windows and burned much of the black owned properties and businesses.

The city was placed under Marshal law and 1,500 National Guard troops were called in to stop the violence. 100 rioters were arrested but none were charged. A Grand Jury declined to file charges against anyone involved.

Actor Henry Fonda was 14 years old when he witnessed the Omaha race riots from his fathers printing company across the street from the court house. He stated, "It was the most horrendous sight I'd ever seen. We locked the plant, went downstairs, and drove home in silence. My hands were wet and there were tears in my eyes. All I could think of was that young black man dangling at the end of a rope."

Although the Red Summer of 1919 produced a record number of racial incidents around the country, they couldn't compete with the carnage that occurred in Tulsa, in 1921. [10] [11]

---

[10] http://www.historicomaha.com/riot.htm

[11] http://www.pbs.org/wnet/jimcrow/stories_events_red.html

CHAPTER 11

1921 TULSA RACE RIOTS

Oklahoma was originally intended to be a state comprised of minorities, including both Indians and African Americans, who had no place else to go, or who were forced to go to outlaying U.S. territory by the U.S. Government. Perhaps the best-known travelers on this, "Trail of Tears," were the Cherokee, Muscogee, Seminole, Chickasaw, and Choctaw Indian nations which were forced, by the Indian Removal Act of 1830, to abandon their ancestral lands and to move into an area once known as "Indian Territory," later constituted as the State of Oklahoma. One third of the people who traveled this infamous "Trail" between 1830 to 1842 were African Americans. The Indians were persuaded to move to "Indian Territory," to free up 25 million acres of profitable land that could then be developed by white industrialists. This forced migration would finally drive the remaining Indian "savages" to the fringes of the United States. An additional benefit of the Act was that it gave

African Americans someplace else to go, far away from white Americans.

The original settlers of Tulsa were granted land by the Federal Government, as an inducement to relocate to the barren outpost of Oklahoma, and as reparations for forcibly displacing them from their communities in the Midwest. Many of these forced or willful immigrants to Oklahoma later became wealthy, after the "Glenn Pool" oil deposit was found under and around Tulsa. The oil discovery was reputed to be the "richest small oil field in the world." It turned Tulsa into a land of opportunity for the Indians, and for some of the African Americans who took a chance on coming to Oklahoma seeking a better way of life. Tulsa had a reputation as "a place where fortunes could be made, lives could be rebuilt, and a fresh start could be had."

Tulsa was a boom town in the early 1900's. In 1910 the city held 10,000 residents, but by 1920 the population had grown to more than 72,000 people. Oil was the main catalyst of economic growth in the area, but it created a demand for all types of ancillary businesses. In addition to the four-hundred oil and gas companies that had offices in Tulsa, the oil industry also created business opportunities for oil field supply companies, pipeline companies, refineries and a plethora of other supporting businesses. Tulsa was known as the "Oil Capital of the World." The 72,000 residents of Tulsa also needed clothing, food, shelter and all of the other necessities of everyday living. Tulsa businesses provided all that was needed, for both whites, and blacks. Of the 72,000 Tulsa inhabitants, 11,000 of were black. They also needed supplies and services. They found them in the all-black community of Greenwood.

Greenwood:

Greenwood was a thriving black community located on the fringes of Downtown Tulsa. It was the envy of African Americans throughout the country after they heard about the black-owned mansions, and the upscale black boutiques that lined the city streets. The community preached nepotism and believed that African Americans had to take control of their own destiny, provide for themselves, and maintain a militia to fend off the white enemy, when and if needed.

In 1905 an African American entrepreneur O.W. Curley, began the development of Greenwood when he built a house and commercial building on the outskirts of the downtown Tulsa business district, across the San Francisco & St. Louis Railroad tracks, known as the Frisco tracks. Blacks, at that time, were usually relegated to areas of major cities that were "on the other side of the tracks" from the white area. Tulsa was no exception. White Americans established downtown Tulsa on the south side of the tracks and African Americans established their own town north of the train tracks. Curley decided to develop Greenwood as a self-sustained, black owned and operated business district that would rival the white business districts of downtown Tulsa and other major American cities. It became a downtown within the shadows of a downtown; one for whites and one for blacks. Hotels, grocery stores, theaters, drug stores, restaurants, barber shops, tailors, bars, repair shops, rooming houses, jewelry stores, pawn shops, doctors, lawyers, banks, busses, churches, and any other business that could be found in a white business district, were found in Greenwood. Every range of economic appetite could be satisfied from the stores and shops in the Greenwood business district. It was the envy of blacks everywhere - and also the envy of whites within Tulsa.

Although Greenwood was one of many black communities that sprang up in and around Tulsa at the time, Greenwood stood out as the best. It was one of the most affluent black cities in America. Blacks called it "Black Wall Street," and also "Black Beverly Hills," but the white community knew it as "Little Africa."

More than 600 businesses occupied the 36 blocks of the Greenwood business and residential district. The money that came into Greenwood usually stayed in Greenwood. In 1921, a dollar would circulate 36 to 100 times in Greenwood, and sometimes would take over a year to leave the community, as opposed to 1995 when a dollar took only 15 minutes to leave an average black community.

The wealth in Greenwood was unheard of among African Americans. Six residents had their own airplanes. One resident was reported to be making $500 per day, an unimaginable sum for anyone to earn in 1921, especially an African American. It shocked their white neighbors, who had grown more bitter every year that passed.

As in almost all other communities in the country which have a large tax base, schools and educational facilities for the children in the community are usually the first to receive funding and resources. Greenwood was no different. The priority of the residents was to educate every child. Students would go to school in suit and tie to demonstrate the respect they had for education and to show-off their good moral upbringing. Neighbors could count on each other in Greenwood. It was typical that, if a resident's home was accidentally burned down, it would be rebuilt within a few weeks by the neighbors. It was a fanciful place to live for African Americans in 1921, but on Memorial Day of that year, a nineteen-year-old black teenager from Greenwood, would provoke a race war that would lead to the destruction of the entire community.

Diamond Dick:

Jimmie Jones was a black teenage shoe-shine boy from Tulsa, Oklahoma in 1921 when he was arrested for attempting to rape a white girl who was operating an elevator in the all-white business district of Tulsa. The incidents that followed would lead to what historians would later call "The American Holocaust."

Before moving to Tulsa, Jimmie Jones grew up as a homeless orphan. He was living on the street in Vinita Oklahoma, begging for food at the age of eleven. A neighborhood African American woman named Damie Ford took pity on him, brought him into her home, and raised him as her own son. When Ford moved to Tulsa, Oklahoma, to be near her extended family, whose last name was Rowland, Jimmie came with her, and unofficially adopted her family's last name as his own. His favorite first name was "Dick," so he chose the name Dick Rowland for himself, although he was known by the nickname of "Diamond Dick."

While living in Tulsa, the young "Diamond Dick" dropped out of high school to become an apprentice shoe shiner. It was a lucrative trade for anyone who could get a foothold in the business. Dick was a smooth talker. He used that skill to get himself a job in the white district, shining, mending and tending to shoes for his white patrons. Since blacks were not allowed to use the restroom facilities strictly reserved for whites, Dick had to use a bathroom designated for blacks in a public building near his work. The bathroom was on the third floor of the four-story Drexel building, and was accessible by an elevator, manned by a white girl named Sarah Page. Although the job of operating elevators in Tulsa, at the time, was mainly a black woman's occupation, some white women were still employed as elevator operators. Sarah Page was probably employed out of pity, since she too was an orphan. Newspapers later reported that Sarah was working in the elevator to pay her way through business college.

Memorial Day weekend parties were in progress throughout Tulsa on May 30th, 1921. Both Diamond Dick and the white female elevator operator were working all day, since there were many patrons who needed shoes shined or elevator rides. During the afternoon of May 30th, 1921, Diamond Dick entered the Drexel building to relieve himself in the third-floor restroom. During the ride in the elevator something occurred which made Sarah Page scream and left her looking as though she had been assaulted. A nearby businessman rushed to the scene to see Diamond Dick fleeing out the back door of the building, and a disheveled young white girl in distress.

Some accounts of the incident suggest Dick might have tripped when going into the elevator and fell into Page, which made her scream when he grabbed onto her arm. Others say Sarah Page screamed over a lovers quarrel between the two, and some others claim that Diamond Dick attempted to rape her. Regardless of the cause of the initial incident, the police were quick to point the finger at Diamond Dick, who they knew often used the elevator to take a restroom break. Dick was arrested at his mother's home the following morning and taken to the County Courthouse to await a hearing.

Media Hate Mongering:

In the early 1900's, newspapers often wrote embellished stories of crimes committed by blacks against whites in an attempt to acquire more subscribers and create a need to know the news. The Tulsa Tribune was quick to come out with a story about the rapist, Diamond Dick. The paper generally approved of lynchings as appropriate acts of deterrence when law enforcement became ineffective in preventing crime. Many articles were printed in support of lynching. Crime was a big issue in Tulsa at the time. The Tulsa Tribune began an anti-crime campaign in the city, "to clean it up," just prior to Memorial Day of 1921. The African American community was the target of the articles. The added tension created by those articles might have brought Tulsa to the brink of its breaking point.

The afternoon following the alleged assault by Diamond Dick, the Tulsa Tribune printed a sensationalized story of the incident and encouraged whites to go to the courthouse to kidnap and lynch the "nigger rapist," that night. The Tribune's front page headline on May 31st was "Nab Negro for Attacking Girl in Elevator." The article stated:

A Negro delivery boy who gave his name to the public as 'Diamond Dick' but who has been identified as Dick Rowland, was arrested on South Greenwood Avenue this morning by Officers Carmichael and Pack, charged with attempting to assault the 17-year-old white elevator girl in the Drexel Building early yesterday. He will be tried in municipal court this afternoon on a state charge.

The girl said she noticed the Negro a few minutes before the attempted assault looking up and down the hallway on the third floor of the Drexel Building as if to see if there was anyone in sight but thought nothing of it at the time.

A few minutes later he entered the elevator she claimed, and attacked her, scratching her hands and face and tearing her clothes. Her screams brought a clerk from Renberg's store to her assistance and the Negro fled. He was captured and identified this morning both by the girl and the clerk, police say.

Tenants of the Drexel Building said the girl is an orphan who works as an elevator operator to pay her way through business college.

Another article in the paper that day was entitled "To Lynch Negro Tonight." It encouraged white residents of Tulsa to kidnap Dick from the courthouse and lynch him in a public execution. The paper referred to Greenwood as "Little Africa." Black businessmen, while walking to work, could hear newspaper boys yelling the morning headlines while selling their papers. The headline being chanted on May 31st, 1921, was, "A Negro assaults a white girl."

Dr. Blaine Waynes, an African American physician, reported that after the Tulsa Tribune was issued that day, "rumors of the intended lynching of the accused Negro spread so swiftly and ominously that even the novice and stranger could readily sense the fast-approaching chain of events that was about to unfold."

A white mob finally formed at the Tulsa County Courthouse after the rumors spread about a possible lynching. The event was mainly advertised through articles in the Tulsa Tribune, namely, "a lynching tonight." The white crowd responded to the newspaper's pronouncement and began chanting "Let us have the nigger," at the steps of the county courthouse. At approximately 8:20 p.m., three white men entered the courthouse and demanded that the sheriff turn over Diamond Dick.

The Sheriff convinced the would-be kidnappers to leave the courthouse, and then positioned several of his officers on the rooftop with weapons. They disabled the building elevator and put barricades around the building and waited for a possible assault on the courthouse.

As the white mob grew larger, word spread through the black community that the black youth was about to be lynched. A group was quickly convened in Greenwood to discuss if anything should be done to try to save Diamond Dick. Three black members of the community had successfully fended off a mob of lynchers two years previously when another black man was arrested, so the black leaders of Greenwood thought that an even stronger showing of force and armed resistance would drive the white mob away from the courthouse and back to their homes. After a short discussion, a vocal black leader stood up and stated sternly, "We're not going to let this happen. We're going to go downtown and stop this lynching. Close this place down." A group of twenty-five armed black business men and veterans of World War One drove out of Greenwood for a 7 mile journey to the Tulsa courthouse, to save young Diamond Dick from the lynch mob, Once there, the Sheriff told them to go away. He assured the armed group that the prisoner was safe and would not be harmed. The group went back to Greenwood to regroup.

By 9:30 p.m., the white mob outside the courthouse had swollen to nearly two-thousand people. They started to become unnerved, shocked and then outraged by the sight of minorities coming into downtown Tulsa, armed.

By 10:00 p.m., the Chief of Police had left the courthouse to hunker-down at the police headquarters.

After 10 p.m., rumors began to spread in Greenwood that the courthouse was about to be overrun. In response, a of over seventy-five black armed members of the Greenwood group drove off in their cars to confront the white mob at the courthouse. Groups of black men drove through downtown Tulsa, displaying their guns so the white residents understood that the blacks were going to fight back, with violence, to prevent the kidnapping and lynching of Diamond Dick. Many members of the white mob thought the African Americans were beginning a "Black Uprising," which needed to be put down quickly and with absolute and overwhelming force.

The armed black militia offered their protection services to the authorities at the courthouse once again, but were rebuffed. As the group of black armed men were leaving the courthouse, a white man yelled out to a black veteran who was carrying a military-issued pistol, "Nigger, what are you doing with that pistol?" The black veteran replied, "I'm going to use it if I need to." The white man replied, "No you're not." The argument escalated into a heated battle over the gun. The white man yelled, "You give it to me," and then tried to grab the gun. The black veteran said, "Like hell you will," and a struggle ensued for the gun. The gun accidentally discharged, but the next shots were purely intentional. Members of the white mob opened fire on the group of black protectors, who themselves returned fire. The gunplay left about a dozen dead, both black and white. The blacks made a hasty retreat to Greenwood, with a white mob in hot pursuit. Greenwood residents quickly realized they had no chance against an armed mob of two-thousand angry white men, that outnumbered them twenty-to-one. As the blacks retreated, the whites pursued them, all the way into Greenwood. Physician George Miller came across a dying black man in the street who was surrounded by a white mob. He said he tried to offer assistance but knew there was nothing he could do. He stated, "I went over to see if I could help him, as a doctor, but the crowd was gathering around him and wouldn't even let the driver of the ambulance, which just arrived, to even pick him up. I saw it was an impossible situation to control, that I could be of no help. The crowd was getting more and more belligerent. The Negro had been shot so many times in his chest, and men from the onlookers were slashing him with knives. Many of the rioters were holding a rifle or shotgun in one hand, and grasping the neck of a liquor bottle with the other. Some had pistols stuck into their belts." He said he decided to drive off and go home.

While some of the white mob were chasing the black militia back to Greenwood, others went to the police station to get assistance in assassinating the African Americans. Approximately five-hundred white Tulsa residents, who had just recently been part of the lynch mob, pleaded with the Sheriff to make them "Special Deputies." The white mob was "officially" deputized, and given the directive by police officers to "Get a gun and get a nigger."

The white mob swept through downtown Tula looting sporting goods stores and pawn shops for weapons and ammunition, and anything else they could use to kill or drive away the blacks. The owner of J.W. MeGee Sporting Goods store testified that he witnessed police officers handing out weapons they stole from his store. After the mob was armed, they went looking for victims. A white moviegoer at the Rialto Theater named William R. Holway, remembered someone running into the theater and yelling, "nigger fight, nigger fight." He said, "Everybody left that theater. We went out the door and looked across the street, and there was Younkman's drug store with those big pillars. There were two big pillars at the entrance, and we got over behind them. Just got there when a Negro ran south of the alley across the street, the minute his head showed outside, somebody shot him. We stood there for about half-an-hour watching, which I shall never forget. He wasn't quite dead, but he was about to die. He was the first man that I saw shot in that riot."

After the initial shooting at the courthouse, approximately 400 white men stormed the National Guard armory in an attempt to arm themselves--to put down the "black uprising." A National Guardsman recounted the threats he received from the angry white mob. He stated:

Grabbing my pistol in one hand and my belt in the other I jumped out of the back door and running down the west side of the Armory building I saw several men apparently pulling at the window grating. Commanding these men to get off the lot and seeing this command obeyed I went to the front of the building near the southwest corner where I saw a mob of white men about three or four hundred strong. I asked them what they wanted. One of them replied, 'Rifles and ammunition,' I explained to them that they could not get anything here. Someone shouted, 'We don't know about that, we guess we can.' I told them that we only had sufficient arms and ammunition for our own men and that not one piece could go out of there without orders from the Governor, and in the name of the law demanded that they disperse at once. They continued to press forward in a threatening manner when, with drawn pistol, I again demanded that they disperse and explained that the men in the Armory were armed with rifles loaded with ball ammunition and that they would shoot promptly to prevent any unauthorized person entering there. The mob was thusly dispersed.

In the Royal Theater, Police Officer William Phillips recounted what he witnessed. He said, "The mob action was set off when several white men chased a Negro man down the alley in back of the theater and out onto Fourth Street where he saw the stage door and dashed inside. Seeing the open door the Negro rushed in and hurried forward in the darkness hunting a place to hide. Suddenly he was on the stage in front of the picture screen and blinded by the bright flickering light coming down from the operator's booth in the balcony. After shielding his eyes for a moment he regained his vision enough to locate the steps leading from the stage down past the orchestra pit to the aisle just as the pursuing men rushed the stage. One of them saw the Negro and yelled, "there he is, heading for the aisle." As he finished the sentence, a roaring blast from a shotgun dropped the Negro man by the end of the orchestra pit.

As the riots raged on in downtown Tulsa, word began to spread that a movement was taking shape to attack Greenwood. Once the threat was realized by Glenwood residents, they armed themselves and took positions around their neighborhoods to protect their borders and defend Greenwood from the approaching white enemy.

As evening descended further into darkness, the white mob began to forget about Diamond Dick. They instead set their sights on decimating the entire town of Greenwood.

Fires began to erupt at about 1:00 a.m.. The first was started at the home of an elderly black couple who were preparing for bed. Tulsa resident Walter White reported, "Many are the stories of horror told to me - not by colored people - but by white residents. One was that of an aged colored couple, saying their evening prayers before retiring in their little home on Greenwood Avenue. A mob broke into the house, shot both of the old people in the backs of their heads, blowing their brains out and spattering them over the bed, pillaged the home, and then set fire to it."

Some African Americans saw the writing on the wall and fled the black district in the middle of the night, to hide out in the country until things cooled down in Tulsa. Irene Scofield told the "Black Dispatch," "I and about forty others started out of the town and walked to a little town about fifteen miles away." Others were less fortunate. Billy Hudson, who left Greenwood the night rioting broke out, was attacked and killed in his wagon while trying to get out of town.

Throughout the evening skirmishes flared up between the blacks and whites in Greenwood and in downtown Tulsa. Firefighters were prevented from putting out the flames so that homes that were set on fire burned to the ground. Groups of white gangs made plans to invade Greenwood in the morning and eradicate the blacks once and for all.

In the morning of June 1st, there were thousands of white invaders waiting to take over Greenwood. The roads in and out of town were protected by patrols of white gangs. Up to ten thousand rioters were reported to have surrounded Greenwood, waiting for the morning directive to descend on the city.

At 5:08 a.m., a medley of sirens, horns and whistles went off at almost the same time, to signal the assault on Greenwood. A machine gun that had been mounted in a grain elevator overlooking Greenwood opened fire down the main roadway of Greenwood. The barrage of gunfire from the machine gun into downtown Greenwood set-off the beginning of the Tulsa race war. Swarms of white rioters rushed across the train tracks that divided the white and back towns, and headed into downtown Greenwood. Each house in Greenwood was ransacked, looted and burned. The inhabitants were removed from their homes, by force, and then marched to internment camps where they were imprisoned "for their own protection." Any black man who was found with a weapon was shot and killed.

At least seven airplanes were used to fire upon black men, women and children, and to drop nitroglycerin bombs on the brick buildings of Greenwood, to ensure their destruction. Tulsa physician Dr. R.T. Bridgewater, described what he saw from the air. He said, "Shortly after we heard a whistle blew. The shots rang from a machine gun located on Standpipe Hill near my residence and aeroplanes began to fly over us, in some instances very low to the ground. A cry was heard from a women saying, 'Look out for the aeroplanes, they are shooting upon us.'"

There are reports that turpentine and nitroglycerin bombs as well as sticks of dynamite were dropped from the planes on homes and businesses within Greenwood. An eyewitness to the carnage stated, "Then, I saw aeroplanes, they flew very low. To my surprise, as they passed over the business district, they left the entire block a mass of flame."

The invasion of Greenwood seemed to be perfectly planned and executed to eradicate the blacks in one quick battle. Some members of the white mob took off work to participate in the rioting, calling it "Nigger Day," claiming they were "going out to hunt niggers."

By 11:00 a.m. June 1st, martial law was declared and the National Guard was mobilized, but they did little to prevent the rioting. They were there to contain the "Negro Uprising." One National Guardsmen was heard referring to the African Americans as the "enemy." The local chapter of the American Legion loaned the National Guard their antique machine gun, which the Guard mounted onto a truck and stationed it between the border of the white and black townships--the so-called "skirmish line." Once the National Guard was deployed, they began to go to each black home and business, to round-up the remaining blacks and jail them in containment camps with the minorities who were captured earlier.

Reports of killings were widespread. One witness recalled seeing an elderly and crippled African American man being tortured and then killed. The witness claimed, "I was downtown with a friend when they killed that good, old, colored man that was blind. He had amputated legs. His body was attached at the hips to a small wooden platform with wheels. One leg stub was longer than the other, and hung slightly over the edge of the platform, dragging along the street. He scooted his body around by shoving and pushing with his hands covered with baseball catcher mitts. He supported himself by selling pencils to passersby, or accepting their donations for his singing of songs."

The death toll is impossible to know. There are reports of 37 confirmed deaths to over 300, or possibly more that have been buried in mass graves around Tulsa. Politicians and the police, to this day, have decided to leave those bodies buried rather than uncover the true death toll. The night's carnage left more than 1000 injured and over 600 successful businesses lost. Among these were 21 churches, 21 restaurants, 30 grocery stores and two movie theaters, plus a hospital, a bank, a post office, a library, schools, law offices, a half dozen private airplanes and even a bus system. 36 city blocks were left in ruins, including over 1,200 homes.

Nearly 9,000 residents of Greenwood were left homeless and penniless. Greenwood was gone. The community slowly tried to rebuild, without the cooperation of the Tulsa City Commission, who 6 days after the riot, passed a fire ordinance that was crafted to prevent the commercial district from being rebuilt. The ordinance was eventually deemed to be unconstitutional but the damage had already been done. Greenwood would never return to its former glory as the Black Beverly Hills. Those who remained had to endure a cold winter in a tent on the site of their former homes.

African Americans living in Tulsa would learn how unjust the justice system was for them when they heard the verdict of the Grand Jury that was convened to investigate the Tulsa riots. The final report of the Tulsa Grand Jury concluded:

We find that the recent race riot was the direct result of an effort on the part of a certain group of colored men who appeared at the courthouse on the night of May 31, 1921, for the purpose of protecting one Dick Rowland then and now in the custody of the Sheriff of Tulsa Country for an alleged assault upon a young white woman. We have not been able to find any evidence either from white or colored citizens that any organized attempt was made or planned to take from the Sheriff's custody any prisoner; the crowd assembled about the courthouse being purely spectators and curiosity seekers resulting from rumors circulated about the city.

There was no mob spirit among the whites, no talk of lynching and no arms," the report added, "The assembly was quiet until the arrival of armed Negroes, which precipitated and was the direct cause of the entire affair.

One white Tulsa publication, the "Exchange Bureau Bulletin," later listed "niggers with money" as one of the so-called causes of the catastrophe. In the end, while a handful of African Americans were charged with riot-related offenses, no white Tulsan was ever sent to prison for the murders, lootings, burnings and beating of blacks on May 31, and June 1, 1921, in Tulsa Oklahoma.

The "1921 Tulsa Race Riot Commission" was established by the Oklahoma Legislature in 1997 to investigate what happened, to seek-out survivors and to make reparations, if necessary. Their report was completed in 2000. In terms of survivors the Commission report stated, "As the commission submits its report, 118 persons have been identified, contacted, and registered as living survivors of the 1921 Tulsa Race Riot. Another 176 persons also have been registered as descendants of riot victims. They lived everywhere from California to Florida, one in Paris, France!"

The Commissioners of the 1921 Tulsa Race Riot Commission recommended making reparations to the survivors and descendants of victims of the Tulsa Race Riot. The report stated:

> *There are members of this commission who are convinced that there is a compelling argument in law to order that present governments make monetary payment for past governments' unlawful acts. Because we must face it: There is no way but by government to represent the collective, and there is no way but by reparations to make real the responsibility. The Tulsa race riot can be about something else. It can be about making two Oklahomas one — but only if we understand that this is what reparation is all about. Because the riot is both symbolic and singular, reparations become both singular and symbolic, too. Compelled not legally by courts but extended freely by choice, they say that individual acts of reparation will stand as symbols that fully acknowledge and finally discharge a collective responsibility.*

In a February 7th, 2000 letter to Oklahoma Governor Keating, the Commission wrote about the need for reparations, stating:

Dear Governor Keating:

The Tulsa Race Riot Commission, established by House Joint Resolution No. 1035, is pleased to submit the following preliminary report.

We have seen a continuous pattern of historical evidence that the Tulsa

Race Riot of 1921 was the violent consequence of racial hatred institutionalized and tolerated by official federal, state, county, and city policy. And Whereas, government at all levels has the moral and ethical responsibility of fostering a sense of community that bridges divides of ethnicity and race. And Whereas, by statute we are to make recommendations regarding whether or not reparations can or should be made to the Oklahoma Legislature, the Governor of the State of Oklahoma, and the Mayor and City Council of Tulsa. That, we, the 1921 Tulsa Race Riot Commission, recommend that restitution to the historic Greenwood Community, in real and tangible form, would be good public policy and do much to repair the emotional as well as physical scars of this most terrible incident in our shared past.

The Commission also recommended reparations for the victims and their survivors. The Suggested Forms of Restitution in Priority Order, are:

1) Direct payment of reparations to survivors of the Tulsa Race Riot.
2) Direct payment of reparations to descendants of the survivors of the Tulsa Race Riot.
3) A scholarship fund available to students affected by the Tulsa Race Riot.
4) Establishment of an economic development enterprise zone in the historic area of the Greenwood District.
5) A memorial for the reburial of any human remains found in the search for unmarked graves of riot victims.

The "Report by the Oklahoma Commission to Study the Tulsa Race Riot of 1921" directed most of their ire at law enforcement, whom the Commission claimed were responsible for committing many of the atrocities that occurred during the Black Holocaust of 1921. The Commission also chastised government officials who were complicit in pushing Tulsans to their breaking point. The Tulsa Race Riot Report stated:

The systematic disfranchisement of the black electorate through constitutional amendment in 1910. Add to that the constitution's segregation of Oklahoma's public schools, the First Legislature's segregation of its public transportation, local segregation of Oklahoma neighborhoods through municipal ordinances in Tulsa and elsewhere, even the statewide segregation of public telephones by order of the corporation commission. Do not forget to include the lynchings of twenty-three African Americans in twelve Oklahoma towns during the ten years leading to 1921. Stand back and look at those deeds now.

In some government participated in the deed.
In some government performed the deed.
In none did government prevent the deed.
In none did government punish the deed.

That riot proclaimed that there were two Oklahoma's; that one claimed the right to push down, push out, and push under the other; and that it had the power to do that.

In the Tulsa Race Riot Report, Commissioners realized how unimaginable the occurrence of the 1921 riots were, so they tried to dispel any doubts. The Commissioners reaffirmed: "These things are not myths, not rumors, not speculations, not questioned. They are the historical record." [12] Diamond Dick was released from jail in September, 1921 after Sarah Page sent a letter to the county prosecutor declining to press any charges. After being exonerated, Diamond Dick moved to Kansas City, Missouri, and disappeared.

[12] http://digital.library.okstate.edu/ENCYCLOPEDIA/ENTRIES/T/TU013.html

CHAPTER 12

ROSEWOOD MASSACRE

Rosewood Florida was a small town 113 miles south of Gainesville, on Highway 24 near the gulf city of Cedar Key. It was abandoned in 1923 after its black inhabitants were driven off their properties by a gang of not so neighborly neighbors evicted them over a lie that was started by a white girl named Fanny Taylor who claimed to have been beaten and raped by a black man, to conceal a relationship with a white man she had been having an affair with.

Rosewood was named after the rich red lumber that the local trees would produce, and which manufacturing plants turned into pencils. It was founded in 1845 by a mixture of black and white residents. Rosewood had three churches, a school, a masonic lodge, several homes, two stores (one white and one black) and a baseball team. The largest employer in the area was the lumber Mill, which employed most of the town. In 1890, when deforestation caused the pencil company to move out of town, so did most of the white workers, leaving Rosewood to become an all black community, between the white cities of Sumner and Cedar Key.

On January 23 of 1923 Fanny Taylor, from Sumner, made the claim that she was raped and beaten by a Negro. Men from Sumner and the surrounding communities gathered together to raid Rosewood to find and kill the rapist and run off all remaining Negros from the area.

Fanny Taylor's maid, Sarah Carrier, came forward to claim that Taylor was having an affair with a white man named John Bradley, who was really the one who had beaten her, and had then fled to Rosewood to hide.

A mob of approximately 400 KluKluxKlan members marched on Rosewood to find the perpetrator and eradicate "The Africans." They beat, lynched and burned Aaron Carrier at his home and stole his belongings for souvenirs. The mob then went to other black homes to kill any black they could catch. The African American residents fled to the swamps to hide-out and wait to be saved, but over a span of 4 days the mobs came back to Rosewood to find and kill more blacks, picking them out of the swamps for a summary execution.

The refugees who escaped the carnage were taken to Gainesville, by train, with the help of a white Rosewood merchant who contacted the railroad company to make clandestine pick-ups of the remaining black residents of Rosewood, but no men were accepted on the train. Only women and children where allowed to go to Gainesville, leaving some families who survived the carnage to never be reunited.

A predominantly white grand jury heard from 25 mainly white witnesses and ruled that there was insufficient evidence to charge anyone with a crime for the looting, arson and killing of any of the black inhabitants of Rosewood, but in 1994 the Florida Legislature passed Bill 591 to award survivors of Rosewood with $2.1 million in compensation. Only one empty lot remains in Rosewood today, with a sign of condolence to commemorate the town that no longer exists.

The Rosewood sign states:

Racial violence erupted in the small and quiet Rosewood community January 1-7, 1923. Rosewood, a predominantly colored community, was home to the Bradley, Carrier, Carter, Goins, and Hall families, among others. Residents supported a school taught by Mahulda "Gussie" Brown carrier, three churches, and a masonic lodge. Many of them owned their homes, some were business owners, and others worked in nearby Sumner and at the Cummer Lumber Mill. This quiet life came to an end on January 1, 1923 when a white Sumner woman accused a black man of assaulting her. In the search for her alleged attacker, whites terrorized and killed Rosewood residents. In the days of fear and violence that followed, many Rosewood citizens sought refuge in the nearby woods. White merchant John M. Wright and other courageous whites sheltered some of the fleeing men, women and chidden. Whites burned Rosewood and looted livestock and property: two were killed while attacking a home. Five blacks also lost their lives; Sam Carrier, who was tortured for information and shot to death on January 1: Sarah Carrier; Lexi Gordon; James Carrier; and Mingo Williams. Those who survived where forever scarred. Haunted by what had happened, Rosewood residents took a vow of silence. Lived in fear and never returned to claim their property. That silence was broken seventy one years later. In 1994 survivors, including Minnie Lee Langley, Arnett Turner Goins, and Wilsom Hall filed a claims bill in the Florida Legislature. A Special Master, an expert appointed by the Speaker of the House, ruled that the state has a "moral obligation" to compensate survivors for the loss of property, violation of constitutional rights, and mental anguish. On May 4, 1994, Governor Lawson Chiles signed a $2.1 million compensation bill. Nine survivors received $150,000 each for mental anguish, and a state university scholarship fund was established to compensate those Rosewood families *who could demonstrate property loss. This historic marker was dedicated by Governor Jeb Bush in May, 2004.*

CHAPTER 13

DETROIT MICHIGAN RIOTS OF 1943

Called Detroit's Great Rebellion, the 1943 Detroit Michigan race riots turned the tables on white dominated rioting and looting. Blacks were beginning to become the aggressors.

Racial tension had risen to a level where fighting between the races was commonplace in and around Detroit. Hostilities grew out of control when a fight between white and black youths at a recreation area on the Detroit River grew out of control and expanded into a full scale citywide riot, in which blacks were pulled from streetcars and beaten, as usual, but this time the blacks began to fight back. They pulled white passengers off the streetcars and beat them, in the same manner as the blacks had being pulled of streetcars and beaten in the past. White rioters looted and burned black owned businesses and blacks looted and burned white owned businesses, tit for tat. 6,000 federal troops were called in to contain the rioting but before the smoke cleared there were at least twenty five blacks and nine whites who were killed. 17 of the blacks were killed by police. It signaled a resolution by the black community to fight back with violence when white rioters came to their towns to do them harm. Poet Claude McKay wrote about being a militant negro. He said, "If We Must Die: If we must die, let it not be like hogs: hunted and penned in an accursed spot! If we must die; oh let us nobly die, dying but fighting back."

African Americans realized how useful rioting and looting could be for their own political and personal purposes and when racial tensions got out of control in the 1960's, it was the black community that revolted, by looting and burning buildings. Rioting in America. after World War II, would change from white on black aggression to black on white aggression. Police forces in white America felt they had to become more militarized, to fight the growing threat of a race war within America, which could lead to a full-scale civil war.

Although race relations were already strained in America in the early 1900's much of the blame of the racial rioting in America after 1934 can be placed on the Federal Housing Administration and the governmental mandates that separated the races into segregated communities, and deprived most minorities of the American dream of home ownership, and liberty.[13]

---

[13] http://www.pbs.org/wgbh/americanexperience/features/general-article/eleanor-riots/

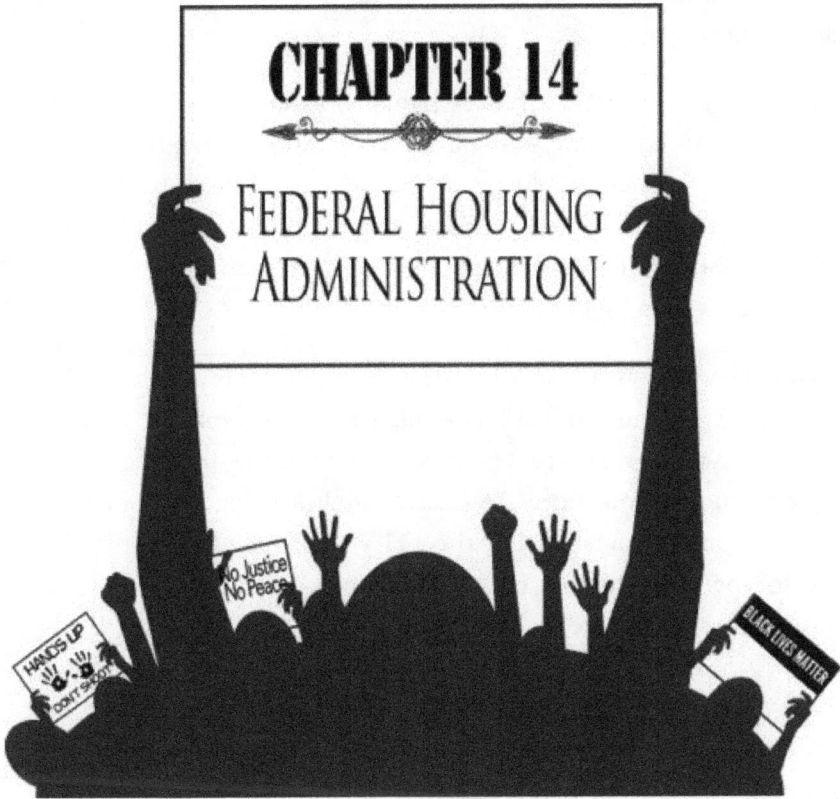

CHAPTER 14

FEDERAL HOUSING ADMINISTRATION

The negative racial ramifications of the governmental housing policies of the past cannot be over-emphasized. These practices led directly to the inequalities between the races that are evident today, in Ferguson and in almost every other large city, and surrounding suburbs, all across the country.

The housing stock in the United States was developed in a way that would purposefully and systematically separate the races and deny minorities the American Dream of home ownership through a practice of deed restrictions, zoning rules and other strategic barriers that were put in place by politicians, real estate developers and bankers in the early 1900's to prevent race mixing and preserve property values in all-white communities, while relegating African Americans to the inner-city ghettos of the city-planed and federally financed slums.

The biggest offender of civil rights violations in America can probably be traced to the Federal Housing Administration (FHA). Its guidelines created a blueprint for developers and bankers to follow in order to establish black inhabited ghettos and white inhabited suburbs all across the country, to keep the races segregated and property values high.

The FHA was created in 1934 after the Great Depression of 1929 devastated American families' retirement accounts, and the housing market. It was formed to encourage more home-building, more mortgage-lending and more American families living the American dream of home ownership, but the FHA only intended on offering loans for people who played by their rules of racial segregation. Although the FHA increased home ownership from 40% in 1920 to 70% in 1970, by providing low interest rates and long term mortgage loans, it came with a cost, and African Americans would pay the price. When the Federal Housing Administration was formed, the regulations contained in the home loan underwriting manual prevented minorities from buying properties in white neighborhoods because the FHA considered minorities to be "adverse influences," and would cause property values to decline in areas where they resided. Applications were denied for reasons that would be illegal today. Property appraisers were required to decrease values on homes that were black owned or in areas where minorities were residing. It was also FHA policy to increase loan interest rates for black home buyers, or flat out decline loan requests for minorities, since it was a common belief that minorities would bring crime and slum conditions to communities that allowed them in.

The FHA's restrictive racial covenants pressured developers, real estate agents and property owners, through subsidies and low interest loans, to keep minorities out of areas the federal government wanted to be kept all-white. The 1934 FHA manual explains that the most important consideration to preserving property value is to protect against "adverse influences." The FHA also claimed that the appeal of a residential neighborhood results from "the kind and social status of the inhabitants." In the updated 1935 manual the FHA defined the factors, which are considered "adverse influences" in a neighborhood, such as the "infiltration of inharmonious racial or nationality groups." The agency warned their appraisers to be on the lookout for signs that minorities might be moving into an area being appraised. The FHA concluded, "Some adverse influences may be immediately noticeable while others arise gradually or are destined to occur after a certain number of years. The estimated time of such occurrence must, therefore, be compared to the life of the mortgage to arrive at a proper rating." The most important among the adverse influential factors was the 'ingress of undesirable racial or nationality groups.'

The FHA made recommendations to municipal governments to help them keep minorities out of their communities. The FHA manual stated, "The Protection against some adverse influences is obtained by the existence and enforcement of proper zoning regulations and appropriate deed restrictions." The FHA pointed out that geographical features, like rivers and mountains or other impediments to travel can be used to prevent "adverse influences" from infiltrating a neighborhood. The manual further stated, "The natural geography of a neighborhood may be such that adverse influential factors are kept out. City planning affords some assistance in preventing the occurrence or growth of adverse influences. Sometimes a neighborhood may be so completely built up and well planned that although no zoning regulations or deed restrictions exist, the adverse influences against which such controls protect may be absent or of remote probable occurrence. The natural geography of a neighborhood may also present effective barriers against some adverse influences."

Loan qualification guidelines put pressure on real estate developers and city planners to build infrastructure projects and approve housing development that were in-line with Federal lending policies, or they would get cut off from financing. Cities and real estate developers who played by the rules got rewarded with low interest loans and higher approval ratings. The manual stated, "All mortgages on properties in neighborhoods protected against the occurrence or development of unfavorable influences, to the extent that such protection is possible, will obtain a high rating. The absence of protective measures will result in a low rating or, possibly, in rejection." The FHA manual was revised on November 1, 1936. The revision expanded the racist doctrine of the 1935 Federal Housing Administration policies. It warned that the "mixed" neighborhood in competition with the "homogeneous" neighborhood would suffer, and that "the chances are that within a comparatively short period of time a lower grade of social occupancy will exist." The FHA manual advised property appraisers to investigate areas surrounding a loan applicants property location to "determine whether or not incompatible racial and social groups are present, to the end that an intelligent prediction may be made regarding the possibility or probability of the location being invaded by such groups." The FHA concluded, "If a neighborhood is to retain stability it is necessary that properties shall continue to be occupied by the same social and racial classes. A change in social or racial occupancy generally leads to instability and a reaction in values."

Section 266 of the 1936 manual recognized the critical role that public schools could play in determining the racial and ethnic characteristics of a neighborhood, to determine the direction of property values in those neighborhoods. The FHA manual stated:

The social class of the parents and of children at the school will in many instances have a vital baring. Thus, although physical surroundings of a neighborhood area may be favorable and conducive to enjoyable, pleasant living in its locations, if the children of people living in such an area are compelled to attend school where the majority or a goodly number of the pupils represent a far lower level of society or an incompatible racial element, the neighborhood under consideration will prove far less stable and desirable than if this condition did not exist. In such an instance it might well be that for the payment of a fee children of this area could attend another school with pupils of their same social class. The question for the Valuator to determine is the effect created by the necessity for making this payment upon the occupants of the location. Under any conditions the rating could not be as favorable as if the desirable school were available without additional cost. In many instances where a school has earned a prestige through the class of pupils attending, it will be found that such prestige will be a vital element in maintaining the desirability of the entire area comprising the school district.

The updated 1938 FHA manual stated:

Natural or artificially established barriers will prove effective in protecting a neighborhood and the location within it from adverse influences. Usually the protection from adverse Influences afforded by these means includes prevention of the infiltration of business and industrial users, lower class occupancy and inharmonious groups. Areas surrounding a location are investigated to determine whether incompatible racial and social groups are present, for the purpose of making a prediction regarding the probability of the location being invaded by such groups. If a neighborhood is to retain stability, it is necessary the properties shall continue to be occupied by the same social and racial classes. A change in social or racial occupancy generally contributes to instability and a decline in values.

Section 1014 of the 1938 FHA manual even suggested investigating the social relationships of loan applicants to make sure they were of proper moral character to acquire a loan. Underwriters were required to examine "the type of people with whom the borrower associates socially, rather than those with whom he is associated in business activities. The highest rating could hardly be ascribed in cases where the borrower's chosen associates are other than substantial, law-abiding, sober-acting, sane-thinking people of acceptable ethical standards."

On December 16th, 1949 the FHA, responding to civil rights complaints, amended its underwriting manual to clearly state that race may not be used as a factor in property valuation by the FHA anymore, and removed all references to race contained in the manual. The FHA also announced that it would ignore all "racial covenants" in deeds and loan instruments executed before February 1950, and would not insure mortgages on properties subject to racial restrictive covenants filed after February 1950. The new "equal opportunity" policy of the FHA was a first step on the long road of reversing the damage that had already been done and intertwined into the banking system and real estate industry in America. The new FHA policy stated, "Underwriting considerations shall recognize the right to equality of opportunity to receive the benefits of the mortgage insurance system in obtaining adequate housing accommodations irrespective of race, color, creed or national origin. Underwriting considerations and conclusions are never based on discriminatory attitudes or prejudice. Determinations which adversely affect the eligibility for mortgage insurance, the degree of mortgage risk, or the valuation of the property to be insured shall be supported by observable conditions, precedent or experience directly applicable to the subject case."

On November 20, 1962, President Kennedy signed Executive Order 11063 (Equal Opportunity in Housing), which "prohibits discrimination because of race, color, creed or national origin in the sale or rental of residential property owned or operated by the federal government, or provided with the aid or loans or grants made by or insured by the federal government." the Executive Order prohibited discrimination in all federally-assisted housing projects. Although the FHA eventually reversed its discriminatory housing policies, its rules remained in place in cities across America, intertwined in the customs and practices of municipal governments into the future. Municipalities enacted restrictive zoning rules, such as only allowing large homes on large lots, which most minorities could not afford, city boundary lines were established that separated white neighborhoods from minority neighborhoods, minority housing developments were built in industrial areas, and other local ordinances were put in place that prevented race mixing and segregated the races into separate communities.

Urban redevelopment projects were the chosen plan of action by federal and municipal governments in 1960's and 1970's to respond to racial rioting, to clean up the slums, to reacquire valuable land for parks or redevelopment and to encourage minorities to disperse and move-on, elsewhere. The St. Louis Housing Authority began providing minority residents of the inner city slums with financial assistance that allowed them to relocate out of downtown and into surrounding suburbs like Kinloch, Dellwood, Jennings, Ferguson and other St. Louis cities that were put in transition by the forced relocation of minorities out of the downtown slums and into the sections of the white suburbs, which allowed "section 8" government rent subsidies, which inevitably became suburban slums.

The St. Louis Arch was constructed on land at the western bank of the Mississippi river on valuable land that was originally a black slum, on the site where the city was founded. City officials condemned the site and demolished the housing developments despite protests from the city residents who considered it a boondoggle and waste of taxpayer money. The people who once lived there were displaced to other areas around St. Louis, and a park and an Arch were put in place of the previous black enclave.

In the 1960's blacks were abandoning the inner cities, due to their own desires and with the prompting of governmental forces and rent subsidies. Those who could afford to leave, escaped to the suburbs, but those that stayed in the inner city slums began to fight back against the oppression they felt, in the same manner in which whites rioted against blacks in the early 1900's, through looting, burnings and beatings.

CHAPTER 15

1960's RIOTS

In the 1960's racial rioting reversed, from being perpetrated by whites against blacks, as in the past, to being perpetrated by blacks against whites, up until the present.

The riots of the early 1900's were due mainly to the mass influx of black workers into northern cities and in retaliation for minorities moving into white neighborhoods and taking white jobs. In contrast, during the 1960's and thereafter, racial rioting has been caused mainly by blacks fighting back against the police or governmental agencies that have often been viewed as their oppressors.

In the 1960's, inner cities were crumbling from over-population and lack of maintenance. Blacks began to fight back against the oppression they felt, the only way they knew, using the same tactics that were used against their forefathers; namely - looting, beatings and burning businesses and government property. Although some civil rights leaders renounced violence, most minorities seemed to feel that violence and rioting were a justifiable means to redress racial discrimination and retaliate against their perceived oppressors.

Only two weeks after President Lyndon B. Johnson signed the Civil Rights Act prohibiting discrimination of all kinds based on race, color, religion or national origin, riots broke out in Harlem New York after a white police officer shot and killed a 15-year-old black boy. It was the first incident to spark a wave of violence in the 1960's that span across the country and provoked looting, beatings and burning businesses in 750 American cities, by the hands of black protesters.

Harlem, New York City, New York:

The Harlem riot on July 16, 1964 grew over a period of six days, from a protest rally of 300 friends of a black boy who was killed by a mob, to over 4,000 black New Yorkers who joined forces to attack the police department and to vandalize Harlem and Bedford-Stuyvesant.

Rochester, New York:

Racial tensions in New York, and elsewhere around the country, were at a breaking point. Only two weeks after the Harlem riot, a police officer in Rochester, New York arrested a 19-year-old black youth for public intoxication at a neighborhood block party of about 200 people. The crowd grew violent after hearing rumors of a child being attacked by a police dog and a black woman being slapped in the face by a white officer. The crowd quickly grew to 400 protesters and then to 2,000, and then began looting businesses and burring buildings with Molotov cocktails. The police called in all available law enforcement officers from the state but the protesters were overwhelming. When Police Chief William Lombard urged the protesters to disperse, he was spat upon, had bricks and stones hurled at him and had his car overturned. In response, Chief Lombard ordered his officers to use riot weapons, declared a state of emergency, and then called in the National Guard to help "weary local and state police" control the rioting. City manager Porter Homer ordered all liquor stores to be closed in Rochester and adjoining towns, and issued a nightly curfew at 8:00 PM to quell the violence. Over 1,000 rioters were arrested.

Philadelphia, Pennsylvania:

On August 28th of 1964, Odessa Bradford's car stalled at the corner of 23rd Street and Columbia Avenue, in Philadelphia. Two police officers arrived to investigate and told her to remove the car from the roadway. An argument ensued after she told them that she could not start the car. When the officers tried to forcibly remove her from her automobile a bystander stepped in to fend off the police. They were both arrested. Rumors quickly spread around north Philly that a white officer had beaten and killed a black woman, which provoked angry black mobs to roam around Philadelphia, looting and burning white owned businesses for the next two days. Instead of confronting the rioters head-on with violence, the police responded by pulling back and deescalating the tensions without force. Regardless of this restraint, nearly 225 white-owned businesses were burned. [14]

Watts, Los Angele, California:

When the Civil Rights Act of 1964 was passed, some states tried to wiggle around the national law. California passed Proposition 14 which was aimed at blocking the "fair housing" section from having any force in the state. Prop 14 angered many inner city minorities who felt that they had been denied justice, again, though a "Jim Crow" type of law. On August 11, 1965, the residents of the South Central section of Los Angeles were at a breaking point. Over 35,000 black rioters from Watts L.A. would descend on the city to loot and burn its buildings after a two black youths were stopped by the police under suspicion of drunk driving. The police beat the youths with their batons and then arrested them and their mother when she arrived to protest their arrest. A black mob formed to protest the police brutality, and grew into a frenzied mob of thousands of rioters who took over the city for 6 days of looting and burning of buildings resulting in the destruction of approximately $100 million in property and leaving over 1,000 people wounded. The police arrested 4,000 of the rioters. California Governor Pat Brown created a commission to investigate the Watts riots. The commission concluded that the Watts riots were not merely the act of thugs, but "symptomatic of much deeper problems: the high jobless rate in the inner city, poor housing, and bad schools."

---

[14] http://www.pbs.org/independentlens/july64/timeline.html

Detroit, Michigan:

The worst race riot of the 1960's was in Detroit Michigan on July 23rd, 1967. It was in direct response to an incident involving police brutality but the underlying cause of the inner city tensions was a lack of adequate housing, poor education facilities, high unemployment and an over-oppressive police force. When the police raided an after-hours bar called the "Blind Pig" and arrested its 87 occupants, the residents in the community became outraged and began looting and burning buildings through their neighborhood, and then the violence spread to other parts of the city. All the usual steps were taken to try to end the rioting. Businesses were shut down, alcohol and firearm sales were restricted and a curfew was put in place to try to stop the violence. More than 2,000 weapons were stolen by the mob from stores which were looted and ransacked for their weapons. Over 10,000 people participated in the riots.

U.S. Representative John Conyers tried to regain control of the city by driving through the community with a loudspeaker to try to talk some sense into the growing black gang. He got on the roof of his car and proclaimed, "We're with you! But, please! This is not the way to do things! Please go back to your homes!" The rowdy crowd was not interested in hearing his sermon so they pelted the Representative's car with bottles and stones as he drove off.

Michigan Governor George Romney requested the assistance of the state police, National Guard and U.S. Army Paratroopers to contain the outbreaks of riots that sprang up in Detroit, Flint, Grand Rapids, Pontiac and Saginaw.

In total, 360 police officers, 800 state troopers, 8,000 national guardsmen and 4,700 U.S. Army Paratroopers were deployed to halt the insurrection, which started in Detroit, and caused over 2,500 stores to be looted, 483 fires, 43 deaths, 1,189 injured and 7,200 people to be arrested during the melee. The city has never recovered. Whites fled to the outer suburbs, or elsewhere. Although the white exodus of the inner city had already begun by the summer of 1967, after the riots, the whites wanted out - fast. In 1966 only twenty two thousand people left the inner city of Detroit, but after the 1967 riot, the whites fled, in droves. In 1967 sixty thousand people fled the city and in 1968 eighty thousand people moved out of Detroit, looking for peace and safety in the white-only suburbs.

Dr. Martin Luther King commonly spoke out and protested about the many civil rights violations that were occurring in the

1950's and 1960's. His speeches sparked a movement that galvanized African Americans to stand up for equal rights and for their freedom, but he frightened white Americans. During his May 5th, 1966 speech to the Planned Parenthood Federation King seemed confounded by the lack of resources being devoted to the racial divide in America. King stated:

Recently, the press has been filled with reports of sightings of flying saucers. While we need not give credence to these stories, they allow our imagination to speculate on how visitors from outer space would judge us. I am afraid they would be stupefied at our conduct. They would observe that for death planning we spend billions to create engines and strategies for war. They would also observe that we spend millions to prevent death by disease and other causes. Finally they would observe that we spend paltry sums for population planning, even though its spontaneous growth is an urgent threat to life on our planet. Our visitors from outer space could be forgiven if they reported home that our planet is inhabited by a race of insane men whose future is bleak and uncertain.

There is no human circumstance more tragic than the persisting existence of a harmful condition for which a remedy is readily available. Family planning, to relate population to world resources, is possible, practical and necessary. Unlike plagues of the dark ages or contemporary diseases we do not yet understand, the modern plague of overpopulation is soluble by means we have discovered and with resources we possess. What is lacking is not sufficient knowledge of the solution but universal consciousness of the gravity of the problem and education of the billions who are its victims.

King was becoming a powerful force in the civil rights movement. During his appearance at the 1963 "March on Washington for Jobs and Freedom" he gave his famous "I have a dream" speech at the steps of the Lincoln Memorial, in Washington D.C., to a crowd of over 250,000 supporters and onlookers who gathered around the reflecting pool to hear him pronounce his views on peaceful civil disobedience, and then, at the suggestion of one of his aides during the speech, added an ad-lib parable about "his dream." He stated:

I say to you today, my friends, so even though we face the difficulties of today and tomorrow, I still have a dream. It is a dream deeply rooted in the American dream.

I have a dream that one day this nation will rise up and live out the true meaning of its creed: 'We hold these truths to be self- evident: that all men are created equal.'

I have a dream that one day on the red hills of Georgia the sons of former slaves and the sons of former slave owners will be able to sit down together at the table of brotherhood.

I have a dream that one day even the state of Mississippi, a state sweltering with the heat of injustice, sweltering with the heat of oppression, will be transformed into an oasis of freedom and justice.

I have a dream that my four little children will one day live in a nation where they will not be judged by the color of their skin but by the content of their character.

I have a dream today.

I have a dream that one day, down in Alabama, with its vicious racists, with its governor having his lips dripping with the words of interposition and nullification; one day right there in Alabama, little black boys and black girls will be able to join hands with little white boys and white girls as sisters and brothers.

I have a dream today.

At the time, the March on Washington for Jobs and Freedom was the largest gathering of protesters in Washington, D.C.'s history. King's "I have a dream" speech rocketed him to stardom and solidified his position as the leading civil rights leader in America.

In a 1965 interview for Playboy magazine, King made some radical remarks that provoked the ire and fear of white taxpayers when he claimed that the federal government should pay $50 billion in compensation for the historical wrongs committed against "disadvantaged Americans," to help close the economic gap between racial groups. Other proclamations by King would be silenced when he was assassinated in Memphis Tennessee just prior to the biggest civil rights event of his career, scheduled to take place in Washington

D.C.

A new national occupation rally in Washington, D.C., was being organized by King and planned to take place in 1968, to be called "The Poor People's Campaign." It was gaining momentum to become even larger than the "March on Washington for Jobs and Freedom" from 1963, but a bullet to his jaw ended Kings life and his career as a civil rights organizer, before he could deliver what could have been his most important revelations about race relations in America.

On April 3, Martin Luther King gave his last speech; "I've Been to the Mountaintop," at a union rally in Memphis Tennessee to a congregation from the Church of God in Christ. He was alerted to possible assassination attempts against him but he continued his quest for equality regardless of the risks. He was even delayed in getting to Tennessee due to a bomb threat against the plane he was traveling on. King referenced the threats against his life during the closing remarks of the Memphis speech the day before his death. He stated:

And then I got to Memphis. And some began to say the threats, or talk about the threats that were out. What would happen to me from some of our sick white brothers? Well, I don't know what will happen now. We've got some difficult days ahead. But it doesn't matter with me now. Because I've been to the mountaintop. And I don't mind. Like anybody, I would like to live a long life. Longevity has its place. But I'm not concerned about that now. I just want to do God's will. And He's allowed me to go up to the mountain. And I've looked over. And I've seen the promised land. I may not get there with you. But I want you to know tonight, that we, as a people, will get to the promised land. So I'm happy, tonight. I'm not worried about anything. I'm not fearing any man. Mine eyes have seen the glory of the coming of the Lord.

The next day, on April 4th at 6:01 PM, Dr. Martin Luther King Jr. was shot in the face on the balcony of his hotel room in Memphis Tennessee and died from his wounds. His legacy would live on but his fight for freedom would die with him. Although other civil rights leaders have tried to fill his shoes, nobody has garnered the support of their followers as much as Martin Luther King.

Over the few days following Kings assassination, More than 110 cities across America were looted and burned in one of the worst acts of widespread civil disobedience the country had ever seen. More than 34,000 national guard members and 22,000 federal troops were deployed around the country to prevent further rioting. In Chicago, Mayor Richard Daley told reporters that he had ordered police "to shoot to kill any arsonist or anyone with a Molotov cocktail in his hand, and to shoot to maim or cripple anyone looting any stores in our city." [15]

Many of the burned buildings in the looted neighborhoods were bulldozed and left abandoned for decades. Although the racial riots of the 1960's helped promote public attention and garner some funding for the plight of minorities, it came at a cost. The riots left many inner city communities destitute and destined for further dilapidation once businesses and homeowners moved away and took their tax base with them to safer communities, thereby dooming these neighborhoods to decay and worsening conditions.

The outbreak of riots in the 1960's frightened white America and compelled President Lyndon B. Johnson to create the National Advisory Commission on Civil Disorders to investigate the causes and seek-out solutions to prevent rioting from occurring in the future. [16] [17]

---

[15] http://www.chicagotribune.com/

[16] http://www.yale.edu/ynhti/curriculum/units/1979/2/79.02.04.x.html

[17] http://www.latimes.com/books/jacketcopy/la-et-jc-reading-ferguson-books-on-race-police-protest-and-us-history-20140818-story.html

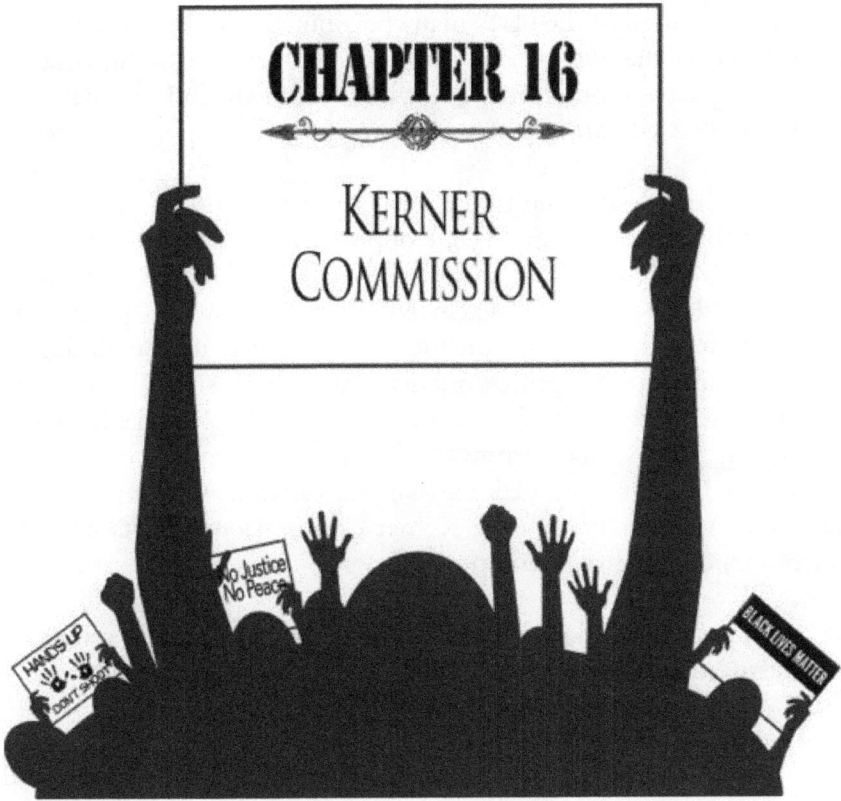

CHAPTER 16

KERNER COMMISSION

In response to the mass riots of the late 1960's, President Lyndon B. Johnson created the National Advisory Commission on Civil Disorders (Kerner Commission) to investigate the causes of the racial discord in the country and try to find a solution for mutual peace and cohesiveness between the races.

The Commission was created in July of 1967, while rioting continued throughout the country and Detroit was still smoldering. The commission consisted of "prominent Americans" included Illinois Senator Otto Kerner. The commission was called the Kerner commission in his honor.

After extensive discovery of evidence and examination of witnesses, the Kerner Commission concluded in February of 1968 that conditions in the slums were deplorable, unbearable and must be addresses immediately.

The Kerner Commission also concluded that governmental housing discrimination, discriminatory police practices and attempts toward emasculation of the black man contributed to the mass rioting that occurred in the 1960's, and suggested the nation was "moving toward two societies, one black, one white – separate and unequal." It warned, "If we are heedless, none of us shall escape the consequences."

In the period leading up to the 1960's race riots, police brutality, lack of opportunity and an overall oppressive culture led African Americans to feel powerless and disenfranchised. Many minorities felt they had been largely excluded from meaningful political representation and economic prosperity, which led to the rioting across the country that crippled American cities in the sixties.

After the race riots of 1965, 1966 and 1967 President LBJ realized that racial discontent was growing too strong to ignore anymore so he commissioned the national investigation into race relations in America through the Kerner Commissions and its panel of 11 prominent politicians and public figures.

The Kerner commission was to answer three main questions that President Johnson wanted answered about the race riots:

1. *What happened?*
2. *Why did it happen?*
3. *What can be done to prevent it from happening again?*

The "Kerner Report," also called "The Report of the National Advisory Commission on Civil Disorders" was released to the public on February 29th, 1968. It was a scathing rebuke of the racist principles and policies of the United States government and corporate America. Reverend Martin Luther King said at the time that the 426 page report was a "physician's warning of approaching death, with a prescription for life."

The report blamed federal, state and local governments for a failed housing scheme that created poor education facilities and caused lackluster social and civil services for minorities. It also pointed out that the media "has long basked in a white world looking out of it, if at all, with white men's eyes and white perspective," and should take some responsibility in provoking racial tensions.

The report recommended hiring a more sensitive police force. It also called for the creation of new jobs for underprivileged youth and the investment of billions in a national effort to construct new residential communities across the country, to desegregate housing in to smaller clusters of black housing developments instead of the previous policies of grouping minorities in massive inner city slums. The report stated, "we believe that the emphasis of the housing program should be changed from traditional publicly built slum based high rise projects to smaller units on scattered sites."

The report also contained the top 12 grievances of the minority community that were most responsible for the rioting. Their ranking in order of importance were:

1. Police practices.

2. Unemployment and underemployment.

3. Inadequate housing.

4. Inadequate education.

5. Poor recreation facilities and programs.

6. Ineffectiveness of the political structure and grievance mechanisms

7. Disrespectful white attitudes.

8. Discriminatory administration of justice.

9. Inadequacy of federal programs.

10. Inadequacy of municipal services.

11. Discriminatory consumer and credit practices.

12. Inadequate welfare programs.

The Kerner report concluded that the overall effects of the racial prejudices in the United States has caused "Pervasive discrimination and segregation in employment, education and housing, which have resulted in the continuing exclusion of great numbers of Negroes from the benefits of economic progress."

The report warned, "A new mood has sprung up among

Negroes, particularly among the young, in which self-esteem and enhanced racial pride are replacing apathy and submission to 'the system'. The police are not merely a 'spark' factor. To some Negroes police have come to symbolize white power, white racism and white repression. And the fact is that many police do reflect and express these white attitudes. The atmosphere of hostility and cynicism is reinforced by a widespread belief among Negroes in the existence of police brutality and in a 'double standard' of justice and protection—one for Negroes and one for whites." The Kerner report stated:

> *Segregation and poverty have created in the racial ghetto a destructive environment totally unknown to most white Americans. What white Americans have never fully understood—but what the Negro can never forget—is that white society is deeply implicated in the ghetto. White institutions created it, white institutions maintain it, and white society condones it. It is time now to turn with all the purpose at our command to the major unfinished business of this nation. It is time to adopt strategies for action that will produce quick and visible progress. It is time to make good the promises of American democracy to all citizens—urban and rural, white and black, Spanish, American Indian, and every minority group. To pursue our present course will involve the continuing polarization of the American community and, ultimately, the destruction of basic democratic values.*

The Report of the National Advisory Commission on Civil Disorders also gave some hope for healing, if the nation changed its course quickly. It stated, "This deepening racial division is not inevitable. The movement apart can be reversed. Choice is still possible. Our principal task is to define that choice and to press for a national resolution. In the summer of 1967, we have seen in our cities a chain reaction of racial violence. If we are heedless, none of us shall escape the consequences."

The Commission believed there was a grave danger of indiscriminate and excessive uses of force on the citizens of a community by their own police force. The Commission wrote:

> *The harmful effects of overreaction are incalculable. The Commission condemns moves to equip police departments with mass destruction weapons, such as automatic rifles, machine guns and tanks. Weapons*

which are designed to destroy, not to control, have no place in densely populated urban communities. The abrasive relationship between the police and the minority communities has been a major and explosive source of grievance, tension and disorder. The blame must be shared by the total society. The police are faced with demands for increased protection and service in the ghetto. Yet the aggressive patrol practices thought necessary to meet these demands themselves create tension and hostility. The resulting grievances have been further aggravated by the lack of effective mechanisms for handling complaints against the police. Special programs for bettering police-community relations have been instituted, but these alone are not enough. Police administrators, with the guidance of public officials, and the support of the entire community, must take vigorous action to improve law enforcement and to decrease the potential for disorder."

The Commission made the following recommendations to the government, and to the police:

* Review police operations in the ghetto to ensure proper conduct by police officers, and eliminate abrasive practices.
* Provide more adequate police protection to ghetto residents to eliminate their high sense of insecurity, and the belief of many Negro citizens in the existence of a dual standard of law enforcement.
* Establish fair and effective mechanisms for the redress of grievances against the police, and other municipal employees.
* Develop and adopt policy guidelines to assist officers in making critical decisions in areas where police conduct can create tension.
* Develop and use innovative programs to ensure widespread community support for law enforcement.
* Recruit more Negroes into the regular police force, and review promotion policies to ensure fair promotion for Negro officers.

Ominous warnings persisted throughout the report of what could happen to racial tensions in America if changes were not made to public policy, and address the police problem, immediately. The report warned:

The first choice, continuance of present policies, has ominous consequences for our society. The share of the nation's resources now allocated to programs for the disadvantaged is insufficient to arrest the deterioration of life in central city ghettos. Under such conditions, a rising proportion of

Negroes may come to see in the deprivation and segregation they experience, a justification for violent protest, or for extending support to now isolated extremists who advocate civil disruption. Large-scale and continuing violence could result, followed by white retaliation, and, ultimately, the separation of the two communities in a garrison state.

To continue present policies is to make permanent the division of our country into two societies; one, largely Negro and poor, located in the central cities; the other, predominantly white and affluent, located in the suburbs and in outlying areas.

The second choice, ghetto enrichment coupled with abandonment of integration, is also unacceptable. It is another way of choosing a permanently divided country. Moreover, equality cannot be achieved under conditions of nearly complete separation. In a country where the economy, and particularly the resources of employment, are predominantly white, a policy of separation can only relegate Negroes to a permanently inferior economic status. We believe that the only possible choice for America is a policy which combines ghetto enrichment with programs designed to encourage integration of substantial numbers of Negroes into the society outside the ghetto.

One of the witnesses that was invited to appear before the Kerner Commission was Dr. Kenneth Clark, a distinguished scholar in race relations. Referring to other Commission reports of previous race riots in America, Dr. Clark stated:

I read the report of the 1919 riot in Chicago, and it is as if I were reading the report of the investigating committee on the Harlem riot of '35, the report of the investigating committee on the Harlem riot of '43, the report of the McCone Commission on the Watts riot. I must again in candor say to you members of this Commission--it is a kind of Alice in Wonderland--with the same moving picture re-shown over and over again, the same analysis, the same recommendations, and the same inaction.

The Commission concluded their report with a passionate plea to lawmakers to make change. It stated:

We have provided an honest beginning. We have learned much. But we have uncovered no startling truths, no unique insights, no simple solutions. The destruction and the bitterness of racial disorder, the harsh polemics of black revolt and white repression have been seen and heard before in this country. It is time now to end the destruction and the violence, not only in the streets of the ghetto but in the lives of people.

Even though recommendations were made to improve race relations, billions were invested to break up the inner city slums and laws were changed to open up America to African Americans, the policies that created the grid-work of housing developments, subdivisions and suburbs across the country has been so embedded in America's culture that it will be impossible to really ever reverse it.

Martin Luther King was murdered one month after the release of the Kerner report, in April of 1968. Over 100 cities across America broke out in riots to protest Kings killing. Was his prescription for peace too radical for the time? [18] [19]

---

[18] http://www.law.umaryland.edu/marshall/usccr/documents/cr114sa2l.pdf

[19]

https://www.stlbeacon.org/#!/content/20593/living_apart_despite_decades_of_court_cases_st._louis_remains_one_of_the_most_segregated_cities

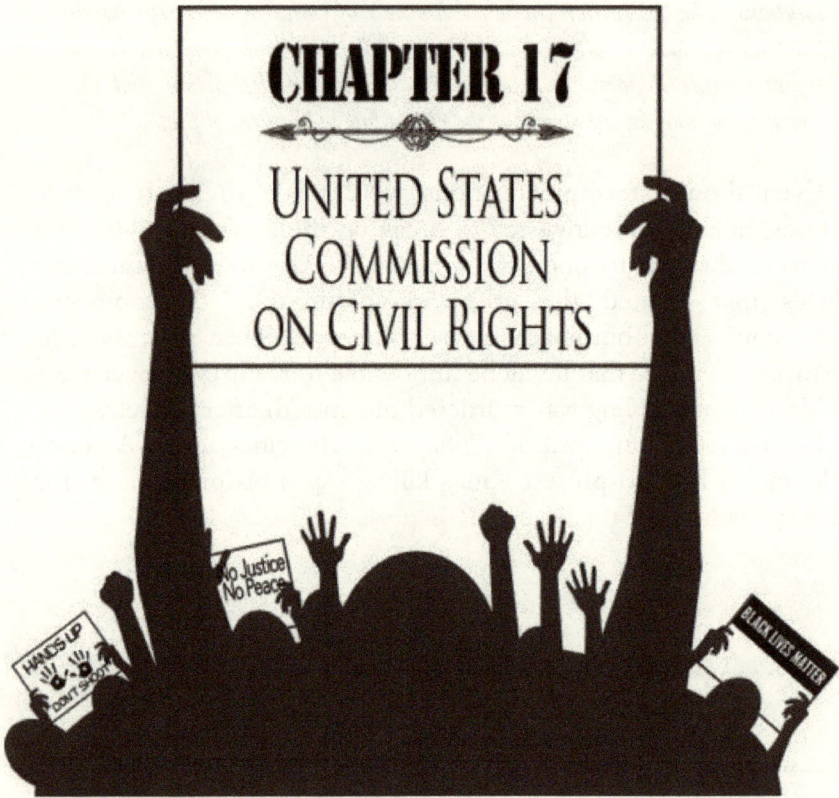

CHAPTER 17

UNITED STATES COMMISSION ON CIVIL RIGHTS

The U.S. Commission on Civil Rights was convened in 1970 to investigate the racial divide in the United States and propose solutions to curtail the ongoing strife between the races.

The U.S. Commission on Civil Rights was created in 1957 with the passage of the Civil Rights Act, as a fact-finding, bipartisan, independent commission of the U.S. federal government that's responsible for investigating and making recommendations concerning civil rights issues that face the nation.

Their mission is to "inform the development of national civil rights policy and enhance enforcement of federal civil rights laws," by "studying alleged deprivations of voting rights and alleged discrimination based on race, color, religion, sex, age, disability, or national origin, or in the administration of justice." The Commission plays a vital role in "advancing civil rights through objective and comprehensive investigation, research, and analysis on issues of fundamental concern to the federal government and the public."

During the 1970 testimony to the United States Commission on Civil Rights, witnesses were called upon to testify about their experiences with racial profiling and discrimination. One witness was Adel Allen, a black engineer from Witchita Kansas who was hired by the McDonnell Space Center in 1962. Allen became so disenchanted by what he found while relocating to Missouri that he was ready to quit his job and move back to Witichta after realizing that St. Louis policies relegated him, and other minorities, to the ghettos of downtown St. Louis.

The only way Allen was able to finally purchase a property in a St. Louis suburb was to have a white person make the purchase on his behalf, as a straw buyer, to hide his true identity. Even though Allen's income was higher than most of his white neighbors and he was one of only a few people in the neighborhood to have a college degree, he was an outcast.

When he eventually purchased his home in the suburbs there were 30 white neighbors and two black residents along the same street but soon after Allen moved in, for sale signs sprang-up all around the block as white families finally realized that a black incursion was manifesting. Whites fled to the outer suburbs, hoping to sell fast before their property values declined. Eight years after Allen moved in, the demographics of the street had changed. Instead of having 30 white families and two blacks, the street had 30 back families and only two white families.

When Allen first moved to the all white neighborhood he reported to the commission that he couldn't understand all of the police protection he was receiving around the clock. He testified:

I don't know if the police were protecting me or protecting someone from me. We had patrols on the hour. Our streets were swept neatly, monthly. Our trash pickups were regular and handled with dignity. The street lighting was always up to par. The streets were cleaned when there was snow.

But he reported that soon after he and other blacks moved into the community it had been abandoned by local officials and left to decay, and to eventually become a slum.

Allen stated to the Commission:

We now have the most inadequate lighting in the city.... Now we have the people from the other sections of town that now leave their cars parked on our streets when they want to abandon them.

What they are making now is a ghetto in the process. The buildings are maintained better than they were when they were white but the city services are much less. Other sections of the city I believe are being forced to take sidewalks, for example. We are begging for sidewalks. Other portions of the city are being forced to get curbs. We can't even get them to come out and look at the curbs.

When the Commission asked if Allen had ever been stopped by the police, he answered:

Yes. I don't think there's a black man in South St. Louis County that hasn't been stopped at least once if he's been here more than 2 weeks. There's an almost automatic suspicion that goes along with being black. There is an obvious attempt toward emasculation of the black man. I've been stopped, searched, and I don't mean searched in the milder sense, I mean laying across the hood of a car.

The staff attorney for the The U.S. Commission on Civil Rights, Conrad Smith, gave some startling details about the inner city slums of Baltimore Maryland in his August 1970 testimony to the commission.

Smith stated to the commission that the white population of Baltimore has been making a move to the suburbs while blacks continue to fill the inner cities, which has strained its resources and depleted its tax base. He stated:

In contrast to the rapid growth of the white population in Baltimore County, the city of Baltimore has experienced a substantial loss in its total population and a steady rise in its black population. In the past two decades, the city has lost over 55,000 residents, but the city's black population has grown from 226,052 in 1950 to an estimated 410,000 in 1970.

The commission staff report indicated that black people in the Baltimore area have substantial problems with respect to earning adequate incomes, obtaining employment, and securing decent housing. They determined, "In 1967, in the predominantly black neighborhoods of Mt. Royal, Central Business District, and West Baltimore, the median family income was $6,300, $5,200, and $5,100 respectively. By contrast, in Baltimore County in the predominantly white neighborhoods of Towson and Pikesville, median family incomes were $12,000 and $10,500 respectively."

The commission was also concerned with the flight of inner city businesses to the suburbs which has deprived minorities of those jobs, stating:

One of the factors affecting blacks in the Baltimore inner-city has been the movement of industry from the city to suburban areas. During the decade from 1955 to 1965, 82 firms left the city of Baltimore for the surrounding counties. Sixty-five of these firms, employing over 4,000 persons, relocated in Baltimore County. Only six firms, employing only 248 persons, moved from Baltimore County to Baltimore City. The movement of these firms, together with the failure of job growth in the city to match that of the county, contributes to the high unemployment rates in the city among black workers. In some predominantly black census tracts in the city, for example, unemployment rates range as high as 27 percent. While black workers encounter serious unemployment problems in the city, employment opportunities in the counties surrounding the city have been expanding at a rapid rate. Between 1948 and 1968, jobs in the city increased by 11 percent, but during the same period jobs in the counties surrounding the city increased by 245 percent.

Although The United States Commission of Civil Rights, the National Advisory Commission on Civil Disorders, and other agencies of the government all concluded that institutionalized discrimination was pervasive in America, and provided solutions that could have been taken to mend relations between the races, most of the recommendations were ignored. Instead, more federal money was poured into urban redevelopment projects, forcing more minorities into the suburbs and causing racial tensions to increase exponentially. After the riots of the 1960's subsided, there was relative peace between the races, but hostilities were building, and when Rodney King was beaten by Los Angeles police in 1992, rioters took to the streets in an unprecedented showing of force, and violence. [20]

---

[20] http://www.law.umaryland.edu/marshall/usccr/chrolist.html.

CHAPTER 18

RODNEY KING

There was relative peace between the races for a few decades following the riots of the 1960's, but when black motorist Rodney King was pulled over in 1992 after leading officers on a high speed chase through Los Angeles, he was severely beaten, while being recorded on amateur video tape. The community demanded that the officers be charged with assaulting King. Although several police officers were eventually charged with assault with a deadly weapon, a mostly white jury failed to convict them, which set-off a racial riot that consumed Los Angeles for days, led to white motorist Reginald Denny being pulled from his truck, badly beaten and smashed in the head with a brick. Rodney King made an appeal to the rioters after the third day of rioting, stating: "People, I just want to say, can't we all get along? Can't we all get along?"

Over 9,500 protesters and looters were arrested, 2,000 people were injured, 50 were killed and more than $1 billion in damages were caused by the L.A. riots. The United States Department of

Justice filed suit against the officers involved in Kings beatings and two of them were found guilty of violating King's civil rights. Both of them were sentenced to 30 months in prison. King was awarded $3.87 million by the city of Los Angeles in a civil suit over his injuries. The city paid the fine, the police chief resigned, and all was forgotten--until Ferguson. [21]

---

[21] http://www.biography.com/people/rodney-king-9542141#beating-by-lapd.

CHAPTER 19

FERGUSON

Ferguson Missouri is located 12 miles west of downtown St. Louis. It began as a railroad town when William B. Ferguson swapped 10 acres of his land with a railroad company, while retaining naming rights, to create a railway depot called Ferguson Station. Ferguson was later incorporated into a city in 1894 and then bloomed into a residential community close to St. Louis city jobs, but far enough away from the downtown slums for white residents to feel safe and secure in their new suburb.

Ferguson was like many other suburbs near downtown St. Louis, and almost all other suburban communities circling inner cities throughout America in the early to mid-1900's. It was an almost all white community with manicured lawns, nicely built homes, good schools and plenty of city services. It was one of many other similar small towns around the city of St. Louis that swelled with white blue-collar workers fleeing the inner city to escape the "great migration" of black workers coming from the south to find jobs in Midwestern and Northern factories.

Once minorities arrived in the inner cities, the whites moved out, to form an outer-laying ring of towns known as "the suburbs." In the 1970's, when the federal government provided funding to relocate inner city minorities to "the suburbs" and desegregate schools and housing, blacks moved to the inner circle of suburbs--to towns like Ferguson. Once African Americans began to move into an area, the whites would move out, to form newer communities in areas farther away, where new barriers were put in place to prevent the encroachment of minorities into these outer layer of suburbs.

Many minority residents of downtown St. Louis aspired to one day live in the pristine suburbs, like Ferguson, but minorities were not entitled to loans in those areas and realtors could lose their licenses if caught selling properties to blacks in all-white neighborhoods. Further, restrictive covenants prevented homeowners from selling to black buyers, so they were precluded entirely from some areas of town and only allowed to purchase properties is designated "black zones." Such zones were usually in industrial areas, or areas that minorities had already infiltrated, which were then zoned for commercial/industrial/multi-family use once they became "mixed."

Although African Americans thought they were escaping the poor schools, violence and terrible living conditions of the ghetto by moving out of the inner cities, the reality of relocating to the suburbs usually meant their families would be confined to suburban ghettos, and continue to live in poor neighborhoods, with high crime rates and inadequate schools and neighborhood facilities.

Several suburbs surrounding Ferguson had already been transformed into slums. An example is Kinloch, a community of black residents that was, and still is today, feared for the violence and deplorable living conditions of its inhabitants.

Ferguson and surrounding property owners tried desperately to keep the Kinloch residents from entering the city, and from being out past dark. Ferguson officials blocked the main roadway leading between Kinloch and Ferguson and created curfews that prevented blacks from being "out" at night, but their efforts were not enough to keep them out. As minorities slowly became more integrated into Ferguson, whites slowly moved out to other communities even further from St. Louis, such as, St. Charles and St. Peters, which were across the Missouri river and far away from Ferguson and Kinloch.

Ferguson's bordering city of Berkeley was incorporated specifically to separate its white residents from the neighboring town of Kinloch and its all black population. Berkeley thrived after it was formed. With a large all-white tax base, the city could afford to build the best schools and hire the best teachers. Public services were well funded and the community was kept clean. Berkley's annexation from Kinloch caused the Kinloch community to become even more dilapidated and the decreased tax base reduced funding for education and public services even further.

In 1975 the federal courts forced Ferguson, Berkeley, Kinloch, and other segregated cities, to integrate their schools and begin mixing their white students with those of black communities. In the 1970's and 1980's, after desegregation of housing and schools facilitated movement of minorities from the inner cities. St. Louis, and other major cities across the country, began to lose a large part of their minority population to their outlying suburban communities. Those who could leave the city of St. Louis did, and they moved out fast. The population of St. Louis was 622,734 in 1970 but it declined to 517,671 by 1977, a loss of 17%.

After Berkley and Ferguson were ordered to desegregate their schools, white parents began to move their families away--and as far away from Kinloch as they could go.

Black enrollment in Ferguson schools rose from 2,537 in 1970 to 4,930 by 1978, a change in enrollment of 2,393 black students (94% increase), further illustrating the mass exodus of black families from the inner cities to the suburbs. In Ferguson the black population was only 1% in 1968 but by the 1980's it had grown to 14%, then to 25% by the 1990's and in 2000 the black population in Ferguson was 52%. The minority population in Ferguson has continued to steadily increase and by 2010, 67% or the residents of Ferguson were black. However, the white political power structure still remains.

During the time between the 1960 riots and the Ferguson riots, blacks became entrenched in the inner ring of suburbs surrounding St. Louis, while many young, white professionals moved back to the inner city as part of a nationwide movement to redevelop inner cities for "Yuppies," (Young Urban Professionals). The St. Louis downtown area went from 36 percent white in 2000 to 44 percent white in 2010. Whites are now a solid majority in some inner-city neighborhoods. Each year more whites move to downtown St.

Louis, and more blacks move to the next "ring" of suburbs, like Ferguson. This migration subsequently forces more whites to flee to the even more distant suburbs, and a "donut ring" forms with three concentric layers, with blacks "sandwiched" between two layers of whites. Soon there may be nowhere to go to escape the "other race," and a race war may ensue. The Ferguson riots may have been a prelude.

The sandwich effect has pushed the races closer together so stricter police enforcement was thought to be the only recourse for city administrators to keep their swelling ranks of minority citizens under control and off the streets. A strong police presence is the last line of defense for most communities which feel they have lost the battle to prevent African Americans from encroaching into their neighborhoods.

Richard Rothstein, a research associate of the Economic Policy Institute and senior fellow of the Chief Justice Earl Warren Institute on Law and Social Policy at the University of California School of Law, in Berkley, wrote a detailed report describing the housing policies that precipitated the Ferguson riots. It's a telling tale that sums-up how Ferguson became the epicenter of racial tensions in America in the 21st century, and how other cities around the United States have evolved, in the same manner as Ferguson, and are also nearing their breaking point. Richard Rothstein wrote:

In 1916, the St. Louis Real Estate Exchange, the city's Realtors' association, sponsored an organization to draft and campaign for a ballot referendum to prohibit blacks from moving onto blocks where at least 75 percent of existing residents were white (and whites from moving onto blocks where at least 75 percent were black). The referendum passed, but before it could have much effect, the U.S. Supreme Court overturned a similar ordinance in Louisville, Kentucky. The court's 1917 decision didn't rely primarily on a claim that a racial zoning ordinance violated equal protection principles, but rather that it infringed on property owners' rights to sell to whomever they wished.

Some other cities, mostly in the South, ignored the court's ruling and continued to enforce racial zoning ordinances, but St. Louis, like many others, took a different approach. Before the court's ruling, it had begun to develop zoning rules that defined boundaries of industrial, commercial, multifamily residential, and single-family residential property. It developed these new rules with racial purposes unhidden, although race was not written into the text of the zoning rules themselves.

St. Louis appointed its first City Plan Commission in 1911 and hired Harland Bartholomew as its full-time planning engineer in 1916. His assignment was to supervise a survey of every building in the city to determine into which of the property types it fell and then to propose rules and maps to prevent future multifamily, industrial, or commercial development from impinging on single-family neighborhoods. A neighborhood filled with single-family homes whose deeds prohibited black residence or prohibited resale to blacks was almost certain to receive a "first residential" zoning designation that prohibited future construction of multifamily, commercial, or industrial buildings.

According to Bartholomew, a St. Louis zoning goal was to "preserve the more desirable residential neighborhoods," and to prevent movement into "finer residential districts ... by colored people." He noted that without a previous zoning ordinance, such neighborhoods have become run down, "where values have depreciated, homes are either vacant or occupied by colored people." The survey Bartholomew supervised prior to drafting the new zoning rules collected, among other information, the race of occupants of each residential building in the city, and Bartholomew estimated the future direction of African American population expansion so that the zoning ordinance could attempt to direct and circumscribe it. The Bartholomew Commission's first zoning ordinance was adopted in 1919, two years after the Supreme Court banned explicit racial zoning, but the St. Louis ordinance, with no explicit mention of race, was apparently in compliance. The new ordinance designated zones for future industrial development if they were in or adjacent to neighborhoods with substantial black populations.

Once the first zoning ordinance was adopted, City Plan Commission meetings were consumed with requests for variances. Race was an important consideration. One meeting in 1919 was devoted to a proposal to reclassify a single-family property from first residential to commercial, because the area to the south had been "invaded by negroes." Bartholomew persuaded the commission to deny the variance because, he said, keeping the first residential designation would preserve homes in the area as unaffordable to blacks, and thus stop the encroachment. On other occasions the commission changed an area's zoning from residential to industrial if black families began to move into it. In 1927, violating its normal policy, the commission placed a park and playground in an industrial, not residential area, in hopes that this placement would draw black families to seek housing nearby.

Similar policy continued through the middle of the 20th century. In a 1942 City Plan Commission meeting, commissioners explained that they were zoning an area in a commercial strip as second residential (multifamily) because it could then "develop into a favorable dwelling district for Colored people." In 1948, commissioners explained that they were designating a U-shaped industrial zone to create a buffer between black residences inside the U and white residences outside it.

In addition to promoting segregation, zoning decisions contributed to degrading St. Louis's African American neighborhoods into slums. Not only were these neighborhoods zoned to permit industry, even polluting industry, but taverns, liquor stores, nightclubs, and houses of prostitution were permitted to locate in African American neighborhoods, but prohibited as violations of the zoning ordinance in residential districts elsewhere. Houses in residential districts could not legally be subdivided, but those in industrial districts could be, and with African Americans restricted from all but a few neighborhoods, rooming houses sprung up to accommodate the overcrowded black population. Once the Federal Housing Administration (FHA) was established during the New Deal, these zoning practices rendered African American homes ineligible for mortgage guarantees, because FHA underwriting principles considered "inharmonious uses" of neighboring properties to threaten the security of property value. But such homes were eligible a quarter century later for slum clearance with urban renewal funds, zoning practices having made them unfit for habitation.

Urban zoning set patterns for subsequent zoning in the suburbs. Jurisdictions farthest from the city of St. Louis typically zoned for single-family homes with large lots only. Communities closer to the city were more likely to have zones for multifamily residences. Some inner-ring suburbs, like Ferguson, were initially zoned only for single-family homes, though without requirements for large minimum lot sizes that would make them unaffordable to working and lower-middle-class families. During the World War II housing shortage, Ferguson and towns like it allowed some multifamily construction, although when Ferguson revised its zoning ordinance a decade after the war, it eliminated any provision for multifamily units. Other inner-ring suburbs, however, increasingly permitted apartment development because of the increased tax revenue the higher assessment on such properties would bring.

Suburban zoning rules were on their face race-neutral, and the communities using them did not have nationally prominent planners like Harland Bartholomew to boast about their racial implications. In a few cases, scholars have unearthed suburban planning documents with similarities to Bartholomew's public pronouncements about race. In 1940, for example, officials in Kirkwood (the town to which Adel Allen later moved) prepared a document referring to "several scattered Negro developments" and recommending that this be "corrected" in the city plan. Urging that ways be found to shift black families back to the city of St. Louis, the planning document stated it was "much more desirable for all of the colored families to be grouped in one major section where they could be provided with their own school and recreational facilities, churches, and stores."

A 1963 planning document in Webster Groves, a suburb between the city of St. Louis and Kirkwood, identified commercial and multifamily zones as "100% Negro or very close" and took steps to prevent enlargement of a "developing ghetto" across a rail bed it termed the "Great Divide."16 Such documents were exceptions to suburban zoning plans that were apparently racially innocuous. But it is difficult to consider St. Louis County's exclusive suburban zoning as merely an expression of economic snobbishness if we keep in mind the racial motivation behind the earliest urban zoning policies, both in St. Louis and elsewhere.

Segregated public housing

Zoning rules in St. Louis could affect future development, but had little impact on previously integrated neighborhoods. To eliminate these, federal and city officials employed early public housing development to increase and solidify the city's segregation.

At the beginning of the New Deal, Congress adopted a public housing program to simultaneously put Americans back to work and address

121

a national housing shortage. Part of the National Industrial Recovery Act, the Public Works Administration (PWA) housing efforts were headed by a confidante of President Franklin D. Roosevelt, Harold Ickes, who specified a "neighborhood composition rule": Public housing projects could not alter the racial composition of neighborhoods in which they were located. Projects located in white areas could house only white tenants, those in black areas could house only black tenants, and projects in integrated neighborhoods could be integrated. Going further, the PWA segregated projects even in neighborhoods where there was no such previous pattern. As Roosevelt's biographer James MacGregor Burns concluded, cities "in which prewar segregation was virtually unknown ... received segregated housing, starting a new 'local custom' still in force many years later." In its segregation policy, the PWA was consistent with other New Deal agencies. The Works Progress Administration, for example, segregated its work crews in St. Louis and elsewhere in the nation.

At first, the PWA attempted to enlist private developers to build federally subsidized but privately owned nonprofit housing. It was not successful because few builders could be induced to provide housing for low-income families, even with subsidies. Only seven of these "limited dividend" projects were built nationwide, one of which, Neighborhood Gardens, was placed in St. Louis. Each of the seven was reserved for whites only, and Neighborhood Gardens was no exception, designed to provide housing for white workers who could walk from the project to jobs in the downtown garment district.

Following the failure of nonprofit subsidies to spur a housing boom, the PWA changed its approach to publicly financed and publicly owned housing. In 1934, the city of St. Louis proposed to raze the DeSoto-Carr area, a racially integrated low-income tenement neighborhood on the near-north side whose population was about 55 percent white and 45 percent black. The city said it would construct in DeSoto-Carr a whites-only low-rise project for two-parent families with steady employment. When the PWA objected to the city's failure to accommodate African Americans, St. Louis proposed an additional blacks-only project removed from the white one, but also in the previously integrated area. This met the federal government's conditions, insisted upon by liberals and civil rights leaders, for nondiscriminatory funding.

Bureaucratic obstacles delayed construction until 1940. During the interim, public housing needs grew as thousands of rural black and white workers flocked from the Ozarks to take jobs in St. Louis's rapidly growing armaments industry. War workers packed themselves into already crowded tenements in central St. Louis, subdividing apartments, converting them to rooming houses, or simply taking in boarders. In some cases, the federal government placed segregated Quonset huts near defense plants as dormitories for workers. The apartment vacancy rate in St. Louis during World War II fell below one percent.

The city revised its public housing plans and designated the DeSoto-Carr project (renamed Carr Square Village) for African Americans only, with the separate project designated for whites (called Clinton-Peabody) moved south of downtown. The area cleared for Clinton-Peabody was also integrated, but with fewer African Americans than the DeSoto-Carr area had contained. The segregated projects were opened in 1942 with initial preferences for war workers and then, later, for veterans.

With a continuing critical nationwide civilian housing shortage after World War II, newly elected President Harry Truman proposed a massive public housing effort. Republican opponents of the bill proposed a "poison pill" amendment to prohibit racial discrimination in public housing. They knew that if their amendment were adopted, southern Democrats who otherwise supported public housing would kill the legislation. Liberal proponents, led by Illinois Senator Paul Douglas, had to choose between enacting a segregated public housing program or no program at all. On the Senate floor, Douglas said: "I should like to point out to my Negro friends what a large amount of housing they will get under this act.... I am ready to appeal to history and to time that it is in the best interests of the Negro   race that we carry through the housing program as planned, rather than put in the bill an amendment which will inevitably defeat it."

The Senate and House each then considered and defeated the poison pills and the 1949 Housing Act, with its provisions for federal finance of public housing, was adopted. It permitted local authorities to design separate projects for blacks and whites, or to segregate blacks and whites within projects. The federal government did not require segregation, but neither did it require integrated projects. It financed each, respecting local policy.

St. Louis then applied for and received federal funds for segregated public housing under the new program. In 1952, a second project for whites only, the John J. Cochran Garden Apartments, was opened on land that, like Carr Square and Peabody-Clinton, had been cleared of both black and white residences.

As Joseph Heathcott, a scholar of the St. Louis urban landscape, has observed (referring to Carr Square Village and Clinton-Peabody), "The City Plan Commission, the St. Louis Housing Authority, the mayor's office, and the Board of Aldermen conspired to transform two multiethnic mixed-race neighborhoods – one on the north side and one on the south side – into racially homogenous projects."

Several African American World War II veterans (with other low-wage workers) sued the St. Louis Housing Authority when they were denied placements solely because of their race in the more desirable whites-only Clinton-Peabody and Cochran Garden apartments. In 1955, a federal judge concluded that the conspiracy to segregate public housing extended beyond these local officials: "The limitation of the Clinton-Peabody Terrace Project and the John J. Cochran Project to white occupancy was approved by the [federal government's] Public Housing Administration, conditioned upon the provision of [separate] facilities for non-white occupancy." The judge ordered the St. Louis Housing Authority to cease segregating its projects by race and to admit qualified black families to the two white projects. But the ruling came too late. By the 1950s, federal policy to move working-class whites to homeownership in the suburbs was in full swing. Clinton-Peabody and Cochran Gardens gradually increased their share of African Americans as white residents departed, many with mortgages guaranteed by the FHA or Veterans Administration (VA), for suburbs from which blacks were excluded.

In the early 1950s, St. Louis began construction of the Pruitt-Igoe towers and other high-rises to house the African American poor. Pruitt had been intended for blacks and Igoe for whites, but by the time the projects opened in 1955–56, few whites were still interested in urban public housing; there were so many inexpensive options for them in south St. Louis and in the suburbs. Igoe then filled with black families as well.

By the 1960s, Pruitt-Igoe became a national symbol of dysfunctional public housing, high-rise towers packed with welfare-dependent families, frequently headed by single mothers. Youth gang activity was pervasive. The Housing Authority's neglect of maintenance and facilities exacerbated matters. The Pruitt-Igoe vertical ghettos discredited the entire national public housing program, giving the lie to Senator Douglas's promise that it would be in the "best interests of the Negro race that we carry through" with a segregated housing program. The combination of deteriorating social conditions and public disinvestment made life in the projects so untenable that the federal government evicted all residents and dynamited the 33 towers, beginning in 1972.

Restrictive covenants

When St. Louis leaders developed zoning rules to control black population movement in the second decade of the 20th century, private real estate agents and individual white homeowners began to attach clauses to property deeds and adopt neighborhood contracts to prevent African Americans from moving into their environs. Called "restrictive covenants," the first in St. Louis was recorded in 1910. Later, covenants were promoted nationwide by the National Association of Real Estate Boards, which provided model language. In St. Louis, the Real Estate Exchange provided a "Uniform Restriction Agreement" for neighborhood associations to use. By 1945, about 300 neighborhood covenants were in force.

The legal instruments took two forms. In one, homebuilders attached clauses to property deeds committing the first and subsequent buyers of a house never to sell that property to an African American or permit the property to be occupied by one. Exceptions were typically made for live-in domestic servants. In the other, associations of homeowners in particular neighborhoods signed mutual agreements that no member of the association would sell to, or permit occupancy by, an African American – again, with a similar exception. The second form was easier to enforce, because any signatory had standing to compel compliance. The Real Estate Exchange itself was typically a signatory, and it frequently initiated litigation to prevent a breach.

Courts in Missouri and elsewhere supported this segregation by consistently ordering the cancellation of sales made in violation of such agreements. But if initial sales in an all-white neighborhood proceeded without challenge, courts frequently refused to prohibit subsequent sales because the all-white character of the neighborhood had already been lost, and the intent of an association to preserve segregation could no longer be fulfilled by enforcing the covenant. This legal theory required the Real Estate Exchange and other white activists to be perfectly vigilant, something rarely achieved. Once sales to African Americans proceeded without challenge, neighborhoods bordering overcrowded ghetto areas quickly flipped from white to black.

Public policy was deeply entangled in restrictive covenants, and not only because Harland Bartholomew's City Plan Commission considered their existence to be a factor supporting a neighborhood's first-residential classification. The federal government also became entangled in racial covenants because so many of them were promoted by institutions subsidized by the government with tax exemptions and tax deductibility.

As the U.S. Supreme Court found in an unrelated case in 1983, the Internal Revenue Service has the power to revoke the tax favoritism of institutions practicing racial discrimination. Although that case involved a seemingly tangential aspect of the institution's mission and practice (Bob Jones University banned interracial dating by its students), the court found this sufficient to justify the IRS revocation. The court did not reach the question of whether the IRS is compelled by the Constitution and law to withhold tax exemption from institutions that are heavily involved in promoting racial discrimination, but such an interpretation seems to follow. The court observed that the Internal Revenue Code intends that "an institution seeking tax-exempt status must serve a public purpose and not be contrary to established public policy." IRS regulations specifically authorize charitable deductions for organizations that "eliminate prejudice and discrimination" and "defend human and civil rights secured by law."

Inasmuch as the right of African Americans to purchase residential property without discrimination had been secured by law since 1866, it follows that granting tax-exempt status to churches or other institutions promoting restrictive covenants constituted improper federal support, as it violated established public policy.

The government, however, never questioned the prominent involvement of tax-exempt churches, hospitals, and universities in enforcing segregation.

If church leaders had to choose between their tax-exemptions and racial exclusion, there might have been many fewer covenants blanketing white St. Louis and other cities.

Although the Supreme Court had upheld the legality of covenants themselves in 1926, it found in 1948 that state courts could not enforce them without violating the 14th Amendment to the Constitution. The decision came in Detroit and St. Louis cases (although many similar cases had been pursued elsewhere, in Los Angeles with the greatest frequency) and the decision has come to be known by the St. Louis case, Shelley v. Kraemer. And this case was particularly interesting because of the role played by tax-exempt institutions.

The case arose from the objections of a white St. Louis homeowner, Fern Kraemer, to the purchase of a home near hers by the African American Shelley family. The area had been covered by a restrictive covenant organized by a neighborhood group, the Marcus Avenue Improvement Association. The association, including 2,000 property owners, was sponsored by the Cote Brilliante Presbyterian Church, whose trustees provided funds from the church treasury to finance Ms. Kraemer's lawsuit to enforce the covenant. Another church, the Waggoner Place Methodist Episcopal Church South, was also a signatory to the covenant; its pastor had defended the covenant in court in an earlier (1942) case.

Restrictive covenants also became an expression of public policy when, in the early New Deal, the Federal Housing Administration subsidized suburbanization and made the existence of racial covenants an important condition of mortgage insurance. Beginning in 1934, and continuing thereafter, FHA underwriting manuals stated that "protection against some adverse influences is obtained by the proper zoning and deed restrictions that prevail in a neighborhood" and elaborated that "the more important among the adverse influential factors are the ingress of undesirable racial or nationality groups." As public housing helped define the north side of St. Louis as black, and the south side as white, this FHA policy began a half-century of federal government effort to move St. Louis's white families to newly growing exclusively white suburbs.

Subsidization of suburban development for whites only

The FHA not only insured individual mortgages of white homeowners.

127

Perhaps even more important, it effectively financed the construction of entire segregated subdivisions by making advance commitments to builders who met FHA construction standards for materials used, lot size, setback from street, and location in a properly zoned neighborhood that prohibited industry or commercial development threatening home values. Aware that the Supreme Court had prohibited explicit racial zoning, the FHA took the position that the presence of African Americans in nearby neighborhoods was nonetheless a consideration that could threaten FHA insurability and that racial exclusion in the insured subdivision itself could be accomplished if deeds in the subdivision included mutually obligatory clauses prohibiting African Americans from residence.

Subdivision developers who obtained such commitments could use them to persuade bankers to issue low-interest construction loans. Developers could then also assure potential (white) buyers that their homes were FHA-approved and that FHA (and later VA) mortgages would be available at low interest rates and with no or limited down payments. The FHA's policy was to prefer homebuilding priced for lower-middle- to middle-class buyers.

At its peak in 1943 when civilian construction was limited, the FHA financed 80 percent of all private home construction nationwide. During the postwar period, it dropped to one-third. But even when subdivisions were not built with advance FHA commitments, individual homebuyers needed access to FHA or VA insured mortgages, so similar standards for new construction pertained. Subdivisions throughout St. Louis County were developed in this way, with FHA advance commitments for the builders and a resulting whites-only sale policy.

The FHA's suburban whites-only policy continued through the postwar housing boom that lasted through the mid-1960s. In 1947, the FHA sanitized its manual, removing literal race references but still demanding "compatibility among neighborhood occupants" for mortgage guarantees. "Neighborhoods constituted of families that are congenial," the FHA manual explained, "…generally exhibit strong appeal and stability." This very slightly sanitized language suggested no change in policy, and the FHA continued to finance builders with open policies of racial exclusion for another 15 years.

These practices of the FHA were once well known, but have now mostly been forgotten, although their effects persist. In 1959, the United States Commission on Civil Rights' annual report summarized how the suburban landscape, by then firmly established, was created:

Nonwhite home buyers and renters have not, however enjoyed the benefits of FHA mortgage insurance to the same extent as whites. According to testimony given before this Commission, less than 2 percent of the total number of new homes insured by FHA since 1946 have been available to minorities. Most of this housing has been all-Negro developments in the South....

Although the relatively low participation of nonwhites has in part been due to their lower incomes, FHA bears some responsibility. Of great significance in this respect are FHA's policies with regard to the discriminatory practices toward Negroes of real estate boards, home builders and lending institutions.

For the first 16 years of its life, FHA itself actually encouraged the use of racially restrictive covenants. It not only acquiesced in their use but in fact contributed to perfecting them. The 1938 FHA Underwriting Manual, which contained the criteria used in determining eligibility for receipt of FHA benefits, warned against insuring property that would be used by "inharmonious racial groups," and declared that for stability of a neighborhood, "properties shall continue to be occupied by the same social and racial classes." The Manual contained a model restrictive covenant which FHA strongly recommended for inclusion in all sales contracts. Furthermore, FHA instructed land valuators that among their considerations should be a determination as to whether "effective restrictive covenants are recorded against the entire tract, since these provide the surest protection against undesirable encroachment and inharmonious use. To be most effective, deed restrictions should be imposed upon all land in the immediate environment of the subject location."

FHA continued this practice of encouraging racially restricted housing developments until 1950, despite mounting pressure from civic organizations, State and local antidiscrimination commissions and other groups to abandon the practice. The only change made by FHA during this period was a softening of the wording in the Underwriting Manual in 1947. This change in language amounted to no real change in policy, however....

While the unenforceability of racial restrictive covenants [following the Supreme Court's 1948 Shelley ruling] has undoubtedly increased Negro participation in FHA's insurance programs by making available to them additional existing housing, it has done little in the way of new housing or of apartment units in suburban and outlying areas. There the discriminatory practices of the real estate business, home building industry, and financial institutions continue for the most part unabated. FHA insurance remains available to builders with known policies of discrimination. With the help of FHA financing, all-white suburbs have been constructed in recent years around almost every large city. Huge FHA-insured projects that become whole new residential towns have been built with an acknowledged policy of excluding Negroes.

In the St. Louis metropolitan area as well as elsewhere, the FHA and VA continued to promote racial restrictions in their loan insurance programs until the 1960s.

The FHA seal of approval guaranteed that a subdivision was for whites only. Advertisements for suburban subdivisions like those from 1952 were commonplace in St. Louis (and nationwide). The two advertisements were among those collected in a booklet for home seekers, published and distributed by the Home Builders Association of Greater St. Louis. By marketing an "FHA Financed" subdivision in Ferguson, and an "FHA approved" Peaseway subdivision in Kirkwood, these ads signal the development's whites-only character. Other advertisements in the booklet tout a "Veterans' Preference" subdivision called Woodson, located in Overland (a few towns south of Ferguson); and "FHA terms" for houses in Webster Groves.

In that era, the St. Louis-area builder with the most liberal attitudes on racial matters was Charles Vatterott, a devout Catholic(and brother of the Ferguson subdivision builder in the advertisement reproduced here). Charles Vatterott obtained FHA guarantees for St. Ann, a subdivision (later an incorporated town) he started building in 1943. Vatterott intended for St. Ann to be a community for lower-middle-class Catholics, particularly returning war veterans, although he did not prohibit sales to non-Catholic whites, but only to blacks, as the FHA expected. As was conventional for FHA-financed subdivisions in St. Louis County, deeds on St. Ann homes stated that "no lot or portion of a lot or building erected thereon shall be sold, leased, rented or occupied by any other than those of the Caucasian race."

Vatterott's limited liberalism was expressed in an insistence, over residents' opposition, that the golf course he built as part of the St. Ann development be open to nonresident African Americans. And he built a separate, lower-quality subdivision for African Americans – De Porres in the town of Breckenridge Hills, a few miles away (but not adjacent to) St. Ann. The buyers had incomes and occupations – from truck drivers to chemists – similar to those of St. Ann buyers. Had they been permitted to do so by the FHA and its merchant builders, they could have purchased homes in St. Ann or in any of the many other subdivisions that were built for whites in St. Louis County in the postwar period.

Vatterott could not get FHA financing for De Porres because it was intended for African Americans. As a result, many of the homes were rented, and Vatterott set up a special savings plan by which residents could put aside money towards a purchase of their homes without an FHA or VA mortgage. The De Porres development for African Americans also lacked the full community facilities – parks and playgrounds – that Vatterott had built into the St. Ann subdivision.

As noted earlier, the federal and local governments in 1952 were still operating public housing projects restricted to lower-middle-class white families. The option of these families to remain in public housing was an impediment to suburban home sales. The Home Builders Association booklet denounced public housing (because it "shackles private builders who can't compete with the government's half-price product") and included a barely disguised racial appeal: "IN YOUR OWN HOME you can pick your own neighbors, IN PUBLIC HOUSING ... the government picks them for you." On its face, the claim was clearly false – homeowners could not pick their own neighbors because they had no control over the identities of those buying homes nearby. The only way in which they could pick their neighbors was to purchase their homes in subdivisions that, with government approval, excluded a class of buyers, specifically, African Americans.

The Home Builders' 1952 warning was accurate that the government picks one's neighbors in public housing, so there was always the threat that the St. Louis Housing Authority would end its segregation policy and assign African Americans to white projects. In fact, as noted earlier, only three years later, a federal court ordered the authority to do so. The only plausible explanation for the Home Builders' warning about the government picking neighbors is that if families remained in public housing, they might experience racial integration.

Each of the subdivisions in the advertisements described here is in St. Louis County. The farther south and west in the county a suburb is, the more distant it is from the north St. Louis black ghetto. The suburban developments in the advertisements were all-white, with FHA approval, when constructed; by the 2010 census, Ferguson was only 29 percent white, and then, going south and west, Overland was 73 percent white, Webster Groves was still 90 percent white, and Kirkwood was 89 percent white.

This governmental policy of segregation, though now more than a half-century distant, has had enduring consequences. It contributed mightily not only to our present-day residential segregation, but to all aspects of black-white economic inequality. For example, as shown in the Kirkwood subdivision advertisement, homes were marketed as selling to white FHA buyers for "$8,100 up" in 1952. In that year, such home prices were about twice the national median family income of $3,890, and easily affordable to lower-middle or middle-class African Americans, especially to veterans if they could have benefitted from VA mortgage guarantees. A decade later, when assistant principal Larman Williams and engineer Adel Allen were looking for homes in integrated middle-class suburban neighborhoods, those homes were still affordable. Today, however, houses in Kirkwood sell for about $400,000, more than six times national median family income, and mostly unaffordable to working- and middle-class families. But for whites permitted to buy in Kirkwood 50 years ago, the advantages they've been able to bequeath to their children have been considerable, relative to those of blacks who were denied similar opportunities.

Even accounting for home improvement investments that owners of these homes have made since 1952, the capital gain for white homeowners, and their heirs, endures. The federal government's support for residential segregation in the mid-20th century is largely responsible for the fact that while the median family income of African Americans is now about 60 percent of whites' income, the median household wealth of African

Americans is only about 5 percent of whites' wealth. This enormous difference translates into differences between blacks and whites in the security and comfort of retirement (and in the obligations of adult children to divert their incomes to support elderly parents), in the ability of young people to attend college, and in the selectivity of the colleges they can afford to attend.

In small ways, local government also worked closely with private agencies to encourage whites to leave the city and move to suburbs to escape proximity to African Americans. A 1947 pamphlet of the Social Planning Council of St. Louis and St. Louis County, a federation of public and private social welfare agencies, rated every neighborhood by, among other characteristics, the "presence of negroes" and concluded, "People Who Can, Move Away." Of 70,000 housing units built in the city of St. Louis and in St. Louis County between 1947 and 1952, fewer than 35 were available to African Americans, whether because of FHA policy, restrictive covenants, or the policy of the real estate industry.

Denial of adequate municipal services in ghettos

As restrictive covenants and zoning rules barred the growing African American population from most areas of the city and county in the early and mid-20th century, black ghettos formed on the north and northwest sides of the city, becoming increasingly hemmed in, overcrowded, and run down. City services like trash collection, street lighting, and emergency response were less adequate than in white neighborhoods. African Americans paid higher rents than whites for similar space – about 25 percent more, according to one postwar estimate – because their demand for apartments, relative to supply, was greater and because less adequate city fire protection led to higher insurance rates for landlords. With FHA mortgages mostly unavailable, families bought homes with mortgages having very short repayment periods, or with contracts that permitted no accumulation of equity. Late installment payments could trigger repossession. To make the higher rent or contract payments, black families took in boarders, or subdivided and sublet their homes or apartments, exacerbating the overcrowding. With higher housing costs, African Americans with good jobs were less able to save than were whites with similar incomes – reduced savings made leaving the ghetto for better surroundings more difficult.

Whites observed the black ghetto and concluded that slum conditions were characteristic of black families, not a result of housing discrimination. This conclusion reinforced whites' resistance to racial integration, lest black residents bring slum conditions to white communities. Thus, to the extent we attribute segregation of the contemporary St. Louis metropolitan area to white flight, government policy bears some responsibility for creating conditions that supported the racial stereotypes fueling such flight.

Annexation, spot zoning, expulsive zoning, incorporation, and redevelopment

White jurisdictions deterred the possible integration of their neighborhoods in myriad ways. This can be seen in the fate of several isolated clusters of black residents in suburban St. Louis County in the early and mid-20th century.

In some cases, white communities surrounding black neighborhoods devised methods to expel their black populations, sometimes with barely disguised racial motivation. In other cases, white towns adopted new zoning rules, brazenly designed to prevent African Americans from settling. And in yet other cases, towns annexed unincorporated land or incorporated it independently to maintain segregated housing patterns.

One tool used nationwide by suburbs pursuing segregation was invoking eminent domain – the power to condemn and seize land for public purposes. In 1959, Howard and Katie Venable, an African American couple, purchased a residential lot in the mostly white St. Louis suburb of Creve Coeur. The Venable's applied for, and the town approved, the necessary permits to build a home, and construction had begun when town residents discovered that the purchasers were black. A hastily organized citizens committee raised contributions to purchase the property, but could not pressure the couple to sell. The city then condemned the property for use as a park and playground. The couple challenged the condemnation, but a Missouri appeals court ruled that courts could not inquire into the motives for a condemnation, provided its purpose was for a public use, which a park and playground surely were.

Fifteen years later, Creve Coeur again forestalled the possibility of integration when it ousted its one small black neighborhood, characterized by small homes on small lots that had been deeded before the city's zoning law required much larger ones. The city harassed the homeowners with code violations and denied building permits for remodeling. The city itself even bought up lots in the neighborhood through a straw party, as the Creve Coeur mayor allowed that he "personally did not want any colored in there." The neighborhood was razed and is today the Malcolm Terrace public park and neighborhood, one of the more affluent in Creve Coeur.

In 1969, a Methodist church-sponsored nonprofit organization proposed to construct a racially integrated and federally subsidized development for moderate- and low-income families in Black Jack, an all-white suburb in unincorporated St. Louis County. In response, Black Jack rapidly incorporated and adopted a zoning ordinance prohibiting more than three homes per acre, making development of new moderate-income housing impossible (although some already existed within the new city boundaries). Several African American residents of the city of St. Louis sued. They claimed they had been unable to find decent housing outside the ghetto and therefore had little access to employment that was increasingly suburban. The incident attracted national attention, and the Nixon administration deliberated for many months about whether to file its own suit to enjoin the zoning ordinance.

Eventually it did, and a federal appeals court ordered Black Jack to permit the development to proceed. The court observed that opposition to the integrated development was "repeatedly expressed in racial terms by persons whom the District Court found to be leaders of the incorporation movement, by individuals circulating petitions, and by zoning commissioners themselves." The court continued: "Racial criticism of [the proposed development] was made and cheered at public meetings. The uncontradicted evidence indicates that, at all levels of opposition, race played a significant role, both in the drive to incorporate and the decision to rezone."

Citing similar cases from elsewhere in the country, the court concluded that Black Jack's actions were "but one more factor confining blacks to low-income housing in the center city, confirming the inexorable process whereby the St. Louis metropolitan area becomes one that 'has the racial shape of a donut, with the Negroes in the hole and with mostly Whites occupying the ring.'"

However, by the time the court order was obtained, the Methodist group had lost its financing, interest rates had climbed, and, according to urban historian Colin Gordon, the federal government was "lukewarm" about proceeding with the integrated development. The lawyers for the integrated project said that, despite the court ruling, "no developer in his or her right mind" would proceed with the project in the face of such hostility. It was never constructed.

In 1981, an almost identical series of events transpired in Affton, a white suburb south of the city of St. Louis. A religious order offered to sell a parcel of land to a developer who planned to build low-density subsidized housing. Groups that had originally formed to protest court-ordered school busing for racial integration flooded a meeting of the St. Louis County Planning Commission. The groups demanded that the parcel be rezoned to prohibit multifamily housing. A councilman who was one of the leaders of the rezoning proponents, probably with Black Jack in mind, admitted that "I think we'll get sued" for this rezoning, but the county council nonetheless voted 6 to 1 to ban multifamily construction. There were no lawsuits, however, perhaps because the lesson of Black Jack was that winning a lawsuit is not the same as winning the fight for integration.

As years have passed, public officials and citizens generally have learned to be less explicit about racial animus. Other predominantly white areas in southern and western St. Louis County have incorporated to adopt exclusionary zoning ordinances, but support was expressed in terms of desires to keep out low-income families and to preserve uniform single-family lots throughout the communities, not in terms as racially explicit as the court found in Black Jack.

Nationwide, beginning in the 1970s, public housing authorities have demolished their physical projects and substituted subsidies to eligible families for rental of privately owned and operated housing. The subsidies, now known as "Section 8" vouchers, permit low-income families to rent market-rate apartments that would otherwise be unaffordable. The vouchers could, in theory, be used to promote integration, although this would not be possible in communities with exclusionary zoning ordinances. But in the St. Louis County suburbs and unincorporated areas where working class whites were living in multifamily units, the likelihood of housing Section 8 voucher recipients increased as the city of St. Louis demolished more of its projects.

To forestall this growing threat, in 1995 alone two white suburban areas in St. Louis County incorporated to be able to adopt zoning ordinances preventing multifamily buildings accessible to Section 8 voucher holders. One, Wildwood, encompassed all the unincorporated area in western St. Louis County, an area equal in size to the city of St. Louis itself. As of the 2010 census, this new city remained 92 percent white and less than 2 percent African American. It has managed to prevent development of housing affordable to most African Americans. Wildwood's median family income is over twice the national median and its poverty rate is less than 2 percent. The other, Green Park in southern St. Louis County, also incorporated to prevent the construction of apartments that could house Section 8 voucher holders. It remains 93 percent white and 1 percent African American, despite its solidly middle-class character. Green Park's median family income is close to the national median, while the town's family poverty rate is also less than 2 percent.

Urban renewal and redevelopment programs:

In 1950, Olivette in St. Louis County annexed a portion of the adjacent unincorporated community of Elmwood Park. Twenty years later, the chairman of the Olivette Land Clearance and Redevelopment Authority asserted that the annexation was needed simply to "straighten" the city's boundaries. Olivette was an all-white, solidly middle-class community where nearly two-thirds of residences were single-family; apartment dwellers in the balance were socioeconomically similar. Adjacent Elmwood Park, in contrast, was very poor, African American, with 37 dilapidated homes, subject to frequent flooding from the River Des Peres, and without paved roads or sewers. Elmwood Park had been settled after the Civil War by laborers, formerly slaves on nearby farms.

The area was bisected by railroad tracks; Olivette annexed the portion north of the city and south of the tracks, creating a physical boundary between the expanded city and unincorporated Elmwood Park. Olivette was under no legal obligation to notify affected Elmwood Park residents of the annexation, and it did not do so. After the annexation, Olivette provided no services to its new Elmwood Park neighborhood and erected a barbed-wire fence between the neighborhood and the nearest white subdivision. (Even after 1954 when schools were integrated, school buses did not come into the annexed neighborhood, so black children had to walk around the perimeter of the white subdivision, rather than taking a direct route across it, to board their school bus.) Olivette did mail tax bills to the newly annexed residents, but few Elmwood Park homeowners apparently understood the implication of these bills. Most were not aware of the annexation until 1955, when Olivette began to auction off their homes for nonpayment of taxes and other fees.

The actual aim of Olivette officials was almost certainly not to "straighten boundaries" but to force Elmwood Park residents to abandon their homes (or have them seized) so the area could be redeveloped with industry, both to increase Olivette's tax revenue and to reinforce the barrier between Olivette and the remaining African American community in unincorporated Elmwood Park.

By 1960, however, a decade after the annexation, Olivette had not succeeded in driving most Elmwood Park residents away. Most had scraped up enough money to pay their back taxes. So Olivette applied for and obtained federal urban renewal funds, enabling it to condemn the land and attract industrial development. Olivette then informed Elmwood Park residents that their homes were too dilapidated to rehabilitate and would be demolished. It rezoned Elmwood Park as industrial, condemned the African American residents' properties, and began charging them rent to live in homes they had previously possessed clear of mortgages.

Although federal urban renewal policy required Olivette to relocate the displaced residents within Olivette, the federal government initially refused to enforce that requirement, and Olivette instead offered housing either in a public housing project being constructed in unincorporated Elmwood Park or in the city of St. Louis. Responding to protests, the government eventually required Olivette to build 10 residential units in the industrial zone, which the city separated from its middle-class areas by a park. Most of the original residents of the annexed neighborhood relocated to St. Louis, to the all-black suburb of Wellston, or to a black neighborhood in another suburb, University City. Once constructed, Olivette's new public housing development in the industrial zone was also all-black, separated from the rest of the city.

Meanwhile, St. Louis County also declared the unincorporated area of Elmwood Park a redevelopment zone. The homes of 170 black families there were razed in the early 1960s and the county developed industry and more expensive housing, unaffordable to the former residents. The *displaced families were given small relocation allowances, inadequate to purchase comparable housing. Many scattered to other black pockets in the county, or to the city of St. Louis's ghetto. A grand jury later concluded, too late to reverse the hardship, that because of its racial impact, the urban renewal program was "an evasion of responsibility" and nothing more than a "race clearance program."*

While suburbs with clusters of black residents were designing redevelopment projects that forced African Americans to seek public housing back in the city, St. Louis itself was pursuing urban renewal and redevelopment that forced black residents into nearby suburbs and attracted white middle-class suburbanites back to the city. Beginning in the 1950s, the city's urban renewal projects condemned and razed slum housing occupied mostly by African Americans and constructed monuments and other institutions in place of those homes. Neighborhoods were razed for the Jefferson National Expansion Memorial (which includes the Gateway Arch), a museum, a sports stadium, interstate highways (including ramps and interchanges) to bring suburban commuters into white-collar city jobs, new industry and hotels for the city, university expansion, and middle-class housing that was unaffordable to former African American residents of the redeveloped areas.

Mill Creek Valley, the community at the heart of St. Louis's African American life, was demolished beginning in 1959, displacing 20,000 residents, 95 percent of whom were black. Some 40 churches were razed as their parishioners scattered to developing ghettos in inner-ring suburbs. The Mill Creek acreage was then used for an expansion of St. Louis University, an expressway, a private market-rate housing project, and a subsidized public-private project.

In some cases, as was true elsewhere in the country, after African American neighborhoods were demolished, planners' designs for redevelopment never materialized, and the cleared land remained vacant. One early St. Louis venture, the Kosciusko Urban Renewal Project, demolished an African American neighborhood of 70 blocks and 221 acres in the early 1960s, with plans for attracting new industry. Much of it still remained vacant or with paved-over lots, 50 years later.

Some federal urban renewal laws required that displaced residents be provided with new housing, but others did not. But even for those laws with such requirements, only about half of the African Americans displaced by urban renewal in St. Louis were offered any relocation assistance. Displaced families, whether on their own or with assistance, mostly relocated to public housing or to apartments adjoining their former ghetto that were as substandard as those from which they had been displaced. Soon public housing itself became unavailable, and the St. Louis Housing Authority issued Section 8 rent supplement vouchers to eligible families. From 1950 to 1980, St. Louis assigned 7,900 family residential units either to public housing or to subsidized apartments. Of these, 94 percent were in census tracts where more than 75 percent of the residents were African American. As black families moved repeatedly to stay ahead of the urban renewal bulldozers, space in the city itself disappeared, and a wholesale movement to the northern and northwestern suburbs began.

A 1970 staff report of the U.S. Commission on Civil Rights faulted the conduct of the U.S. Department of Housing and Urban Development (HUD), concluding that:

Federal programs of housing and urban development not only have failed to eliminate the dual housing market, but have had the effect of perpetuating and promoting it.... HUD has failed to carry out [its] affirmative obligations [to prevent discrimination] and has permitted its programs to be operated in a discriminatory manner in the St. Louis metropolitan area.... As long as HUD continues to condone the discriminatory activities of the local housing and home finance industry – public and private – there is little hope of relief for black families from the existing system of separate and unequal housing conditions.

Regulatory support of policies in the real estate and financial sectors that promoted segregation

Government regulators at the local, state, and federal levels failed to halt, indeed they endorsed, discriminatory practices of the real estate and financial sectors that played significant roles in the segregation of housing in St. Louis and nationwide.

Blockbusting

Real estate speculators assisted the conversion of inner-ring suburbs from white to black by creating panic among white homeowners with the message that unless they sold quickly, their property values would deteriorate. In a systematic fashion, these real estate agents "blockbusted" neighborhood by neighborhood as African American refugees from urban renewal moved north and northwest. The blockbusting contributed to the transformation of inner-ring suburbs like Ferguson from all- white communities that excluded African Americans to today's deteriorating nearly all-black (or becoming all-black) suburbs.

In St. Louis, blockbusting began as the ghetto expanded, and then proceeded to inner-ring suburbs when St. Louis itself could no longer absorb its growing (and later, displaced) African American population. The practice was not unique to St. Louis. It was commonplace nationwide. Typically, an African American family like the Williamses or Allens found housing in a lower-middle-class neighborhood just outside the ghetto. Frequently a blockbusting real estate agent arranged this initial sale, perhaps subsidizing it himself. Once the family moved in and was visible, real estate agents solicited nearby homeowners to sell quickly before an imminent influx of black buyers caused their homes to lose value. Sometimes the agents supported their predictions by hiring black youth to drive around the neighborhood blasting music, by placing fictitious for-sale advertisements in African American newspapers (and showing copies to white homeowners), or by hiring black women to push baby carriages around, or engaging in other similar tactics.

While it was not usually necessary for real estate agents to be as flamboyant as this, such tactics were employed more than occasionally.

A 1995 St. Louis newspaper report alleged that in some cases, speculators did not have initial African American buyers but instead bought homes in neighborhoods they anticipated turning into African American communities, and let the empty houses deteriorate to depress the value of others nearby. After neighbors were sufficiently panicked, speculators bought properties at reduced prices and then resold them at inflated prices to African Americans in desperate need of housing. Agents made large profits in this way. Once a block or neighborhood had been "busted" in this fashion, agents would proceed to the next block or neighborhood, using similar tactics. Some agents did not resell homes, but subdivided and rented them to black families.

Adel Allen described how, soon after he moved into his new home, "for sale" signs went up on his block in Kirkwood (the town that zoning officials tried so hard in 1940 to keep white and where the advertisement featured earlier shows that the FHA had approved whites-only development in 1952). Allen did not mention a conspicuous role of real estate agents, but they likely were involved in his neighbors' panic selling.

Louis itself, attempted to legislate against blockbusting. But violations were and still are hard to prove, and creating a sufficiently precise definition of blockbusting for statutory purposes was and remains challenging. In 1969, St. Louis adopted ordinances prohibiting solicitation of listings by real estate agents and the placement of "open," "for sale," or "sold" signs in specific designated zones considered subject to sudden racial change. A subsequent amendment permitted such a sign if a private individual, not a real estate agent, obtained a permit from the city's Human Relations Council that could be granted only after the council made a determination that the neighborhood was not subject to rapid racial change.

In the late 1960s, the western suburb of Vinita Park adopted an ordinance prohibiting all solicitation of listings by real estate agents. Blockbusting in another suburb, University City, began as early as 1962; the suburb also banned "for sale" signs and adopted an Antiblockbusting ordinance. University City remains uniquely integrated, although within the city, black and white neighborhoods are mostly distinct. Other suburbs also took action against blockbusting, but without much impact. The only effective control over blockbusting would have been disciplinary action by the Missouri Real Estate Commission, the state agency charged with regulating the industry, but this was not forthcoming.

Racial steering

Real estate agents' practices and state action to create and support racial segregation were inseparable in St. Louis and elsewhere. Overlapping with zoning rules adopted by Harland Bartholomew's City Plan Commission in 1919, the St. Louis Real Estate Exchange surveyed its members in 1923 to define zones in which property could be sold to African Americans. City government worked hand-in-glove with the exchange, providing it with data on changing racial residential patterns so the exchange could adapt its restrictive practices accordingly. By 1930, the City Plan Commission estimated that 80 percent of the city's African American population was contained within the zones established by the Real Estate Exchange. These boundaries were revised substantially in 1941, and continued to guide real estate practice afterwards.

The Real Estate Exchange adopted a code of ethics in the mid-1920s, with language taken verbatim from the 1924 code of National Association of Realtors that stated: "A realtor should never be instrumental in introducing into a neighborhood ... members of any race or nationality ... whose presence will clearly be detrimental to property values in that neighborhood."

Both the St. Louis Real Estate Exchange and the Missouri Real Estate Commission deemed sales to African Americans in white neighborhoods to constitute professional misconduct that could result in loss of license. It could also lead to expulsion from the national as well as the local association, making it difficult for real estate agents to stay in business because they would no longer have access to multiple listing services.

In 1950, the national association amended its code so that integrating a neighborhood was no longer explicitly unethical, instead prohibiting sales that would be "detrimental to property values." real estate agents nationwide continued to interpret this rule (as it was doubtlessly intended) as prohibiting sales to African Americans in white neighborhoods and continued practices of promoting and enforcing segregation. The revised code suggested no positive obligation of nondiscrimination.

Making explicit that the revised code, despite its sanitized wording, implied no change in race policy, the St. Louis Real Estate Exchange sent this notice to all members in 1955: "No Member of our Board may, directly or indirectly, sell to Negroes ... unless there are three separate and distinct buildings in such block already occupied by Negroes.... This rule is of long standing [and is our interpretation of] the Code of Ethics of the National Association of Real Estate Boards."

In 1969, a year after enactment of the Fair Housing Act, a St. Louis real estate agent boasted to an investigator, "We never sell to colored. When they ask for a specific house, we tell them there is already a contract on that house." At that time, St. Louis real estate agents still asserted

143

they would lose their licenses if they sold homes to African Americans in white neighborhoods.

A 1953 survey by the FHA found that St. Louis had 80,000 African Americans with stable working-class and middle-class jobs who could have afforded to buy their own homes and participate in the postwar suburban boom. But few were permitted to do so (in considerable part because of the FHA's own policy) and instead were forced either to rent ghetto apartments in the city or settle in the few lower-class black enclaves (like Kinloch) in the suburbs. As Larman Williams and Adel Allen later found, until passage of the Fair Housing Act and to some extent afterwards, real estate agents openly steered black home buyers away from white neighborhoods, helping to prevent the emergence of a solid black lower middle class that could have integrated into socioeconomically similar white suburbs.

To address racial steering, the federal government had levers that it declined to use. For example, one St. Louis County employer was the Mallinckrodt Chemical Works, a government contractor that sold medical supplies to the Veterans Administration. At the same 1970 hearing of the Civil Rights Commission at which the Williamses and Adel Allen testified, Charles Swartout, vice president for personnel of Mallinckrodt, said he had difficulty attracting black professional, technical, and administrative employees to the company's suburban facility because the recruits were unable to find housing in the area. The company maintained a list of real estate agents to which it referred employees it recruited. The commission's general counsel asked Mr. Swartout whether the company might ask real estate agents on the list to agree not to discriminate. No, he replied, "I don't think we would [ask that] any more than we do [for] suppliers of chemicals or equipment." This testimony occurred two years after adoption of the Fair Housing Act making discrimination unlawful. The federal government was apparently unwilling to require its contractors to refer prospective employees only to real estate agents who agreed to obey the law.

Federal acquiescence also played a role in the case of McDonnell Douglas, a major suburban St. Louis defense contractor. The company maintained separate housing lists for white and black recruits so that employees of each race could be referred to their respective segregated communities. It merged its lists in the late 1960s, but this had little effect. By 1970 the company employed nearly 3,000 nonwhite workers. The previous year alone, some 650 new hires at the plant were nonwhite. Yet when these employees, with good and stable jobs, sought housing, real estate agents still routinely referred them to the black Kinloch suburb, avoiding the many available homes in working-class white suburban communities nearer the plant. Unlike Adel Allen, many were not in jobs paying well enough to enable them to break into a middle-class suburb like Kirkwood. In these cases, real estate agents steered African American workers away from lower-middle-class suburbs. Often these workers could find housing only far away in the St. Louis ghetto, resulting in long commutes and excessive absenteeism when carpooling arrangements failed. With public transportation, the commute took as much as two hours each way. Black workers at other industrial plants, increasingly located in the suburbs, faced similar challenges.

Heavily regulated industries as agents of the state

Should the actions of real estate agents contributing to the racial segregation of the St. Louis metropolitan area be considered private or state action? As noted above, the conventional understanding of conditions that led to the recent conflicts in Ferguson emphasizes the white flight of homeowners from inner-ring suburbs once African Americans arrived. But white flight spurred directly by real estate industry practices that were sanctioned, even encouraged, by state regulators calls for remedial public actions that account for government's role in Ferguson's transformation.

Almost every industry in the United States is regulated by government to some extent, so it would be foolish to consider the mere fact of regulation to justify a public remedy. Yet few industries are as regulated as real estate. Obtaining a real estate license in Missouri and in other states requires extensive study, testing, and recertification. Regulations cover detailed aspects of real estate practice, including not only who can show a home or how escrow funds should be handled, but the personal behavior of real estate agents in their private lives. Until late in the 20th century, however, it almost seemed that the sole area of real estate practice not subject to regulation was racial discrimination, except to the extent that real estate agents were subject to discipline if they did not discriminate. Racial steering by real estate agents had been unlawful since 1866, but Missouri's and the nation's real estate ethics rules required it.

Blockbusting on its face was a flagrant violation of the Real Estate Exchange's and the Missouri Real Estate Commission's prohibition of introducing black families into white neighborhoods, but the commission did not deem blockbusting inappropriate until 1970, two years after federal law reiterated its illegality, and even after that, enforcement was weak or nonexistent.

Insurance and banking are two industries that are even more regulated than real estate, and these also played important roles in segregating St. Louis and the nation. Until the 1960s, insurance companies openly practiced "redlining" – refusing casualty or title insurance in black neighborhoods, or making it available only at premium rates. The nation's leading insurance companies became developers themselves – of segregated apartment complexes.

For most of the 20th century banks also routinely and openly practiced redlining and refused mortgages or home improvement loans to African Americans in predominantly white neighborhoods. Federal and state regulators rarely took notice. In one recent case, however, the Department of Housing and Urban Development pursued a complaint that the First National Bank of St. Louis had avoiding making loans in predominantly minority neighborhoods. As part of its settlement of the case, the bank promised the federal government that it would open a branch in Ferguson to remedy its past failures. The branch opened in March 2012."

Kudo's to Richard Rothstein and the Economic Policy Institute for providing such a vivid explanation of the evolution of the city of Ferguson. It's an excellent segue to wrap-up Ferguson and get into the details of the Michael Brown scooting, and its aftermath.

CHAPTER 20

FERGUSON POLICE FORCE

The Ferguson Police Department employs 72 personnel including 54 police officers and 18 civilian support staff. The department has been led by Chief Thomas (Tom) Jackson since he was appointed to his position on March 10th, 2010 by the municipality's city manager John Shaw. Although the Mayor and City Council members appoint the city manager, they have no direct control of who their city manager hires or fires as police chief. The city manager of Ferguson can replace the chief of police at his or her own discretion, but even though Shaw has the only authority to remove the chief of police, the Mayor and council members could replace the city manager if he acted in a manner that displeased them. So city managers usually comply with the wishes of their political overlords.

The *Florissant Valley News* chronicled Jackson's hiring and achievements. The paper reported, "Jackson received an Associate Degree in Applied Life Science from Saint Louis Community College

(1983). He then went on to receive a Bachelor of Science in Criminal Justice Management from Tarkio College (1986), a certificate in C.J. Education from University of Virginia (2005) and is also a graduate of the 221st Session of the FBI National Academy (2005). Jackson was a member of the St. Louis Police Department for over 30 years, most recently serving as the Commander of the St. Louis County Drug Task Force. Other experiences include SWAT team supervisor, airplane and helicopter instructor pilot, undercover detective, and hostage negotiator."

Although Jackson was experienced in law enforcement tactics, he was unprepared for the rioting that engulfed his town. Ferguson city administrators were also unprepared for the resistance they received from African American members of their community, which is mainly composed of minorities.

From 1990 to 2010, Ferguson's African American population rose by more than 150 percent, but their police force remained mainly Caucasian. City officials say they are looking at ways for the community to feel "more connected" to the city leaders and the police, including developing programs to attract more African American police applicants to the Ferguson police force.

Many municipalities have found it difficult to recruit black law enforcement applicants, citing a lack of interest by African Americans in becoming police officers. Maryland Heights Police Chief Bill Carson thinks there is a stigma associated with policing that prevents many black youths from aspiring to become law-enforcement officers. He conceded that highly-qualified African American law-enforcement officers have options, and typically don't stay with small police departments. He stated, "With a lack of applicants from black candidates, it's hard to build a more diverse department. Our last hiring process we had 81 applications, and only three were African American, so it's not like we're passing over a whole bunch of quality minority applicants." Just one of the city's 79 police officers is black, although the African American population of the city is about 12 percent.

Overland Police Chief Mike Laws said, "I talked with some staff members here, and we're not even sure the last time we had an African American apply here, and I don't know what the solution is. I would jump at the chance to hire a qualified African American candidate." Hazelwood Police Department Major Henry Mansker said his department recruits candidates at job fairs and the St. Louis

Black Expo, but has not had much success with his minority recruitment program. Ferguson Police Chief Tom Jackson stated "I've been trying to increase the diversity of the department since I got here." With so many black residents receiving citations, warrants and criminal complaints in Ferguson, it's hard to imagine that many minorities in the city could pass the background check for police employment.

Despite law enforcement personal officials' claims that they are seeking-out minority co-workers to employ, the statistics suggest the police, instead of recruiting black candidates as employees, are profiling, stopping and ticketing minorities in their communities disproportionately to whites, in an effort to beef-up their budgets and keep the blacks contained.

In 2014, the budget for the Ferguson Police Department was approximately $5 million. To augment their budget and produce additional revenues for the city, Ferguson and other municipalities often impose exorbitant administrative fees and fines to cover their budgetary shortfalls. Many times these overly aggressive enforcement tactics can wreak havoc in a community, socially and financially, especially for families with limited resources, education or ability to defend themselves. Ferguson is similar to many other municipalities which are desperate for money. Taxes are increasing, fees are going up, and city services are declining almost everywhere. As city budgets get busted, fees and fines go up to fill the financial void.

Some cities in St Louis County receive almost 40% of their annual income from small infractions. Many of these violations are for traffic offenses or petty offenses such as playing loud music, uncut grass, unkempt property, saggy pants, disturbing the peace, occupancy infractions or other vague charges of lawlessness.

Former municipal court judge Frank Vatterott stated, "There are now 26 different ways you can lose your license in St. Louis County. There used to be five. You can now lose your license for things that have nothing to do with driving. We definitely have a problem with over-criminalization." Vatterott worked as a judge for St. Ann Missouri until he was fired for refusing to fine the residents of the town. He said, "I was actually let go as a municipal judge from a town because I wasn't generating enough revenue." Although St. Ann only has 12,000 residents, their police department issued 23,465 traffic tickets last year and generated $3.42 million in revenues.

Police officers have so much leeway in issuing citations that they are getting away with whatever they want, with very little oversight. Nicole Bolden was pulled over twice during the same night while traveling down a roadway in St. Louis. A St. Louis County police officer pulled her over for not using her blinker, then cited her for not having insurance, then moments later she was pulled over again, by a Florissant police officer who said he didn't like the way she was driving. He also gave her a ticket for not having proof of insurance. Bolden said, "He said I was hitting my brakes too much, so he thought I must have been hiding something."

Thomas Harvey, who represents clients in Ferguson and Florissant said:

> *Our clients haven't been accused of felonies. The fines and penalties for these violations aren't set in stone. The courts have leeway to set up payment plans and to work with people. But you need people in these positions who can have some empathy for the people in front of them, who know what it's like to have to prioritize bills, to at least know someone who knows what it's like to, say, let your car insurance expire in order to pay a medical bill. There have been instances where someone will drive to court to clear a warrant for driving with a suspended license. They'll pay the fine, get the warrant removed, and then get pulled over as they're leaving the parking lot, because a police officer in the courtroom overheard why they were there.*

Florissant Missouri provides an eye-opening example of how police departments and the courts fleece their citizenry, in Florissant and possibly in your own home-town. When the courts forced Florissant to allow the media and other observers into their courtrooms to witness what was occurring, the city responded by claiming that they did not have the room for all of the violators and also observers, so they used the court order as an excuse to fund a new courthouse. The city council now imposes a fee of $10 per each person who has to go to court, to fund the new, larger courthouse. Attorney Khazaeli was shocked at the city's response to the recent court ruling. He said, "After all the recent national attention on Ferguson, local attorneys are floored. It's just completely tone deaf. They got caught violating the law. So in response they're going to build themselves a new courthouse, and they're going to finance it on the backs of the poor. It's incredible."

In Florissant, although only 27% of the town is black, they represent an astonishing 71% of the people being arrested or receiving citations. Last year, although Florissant only has 52,000 residents, it issued 29,072 tickets and collected over $3 million in fees and fines--13% of its total annual revenue. The prosecutor for the cities of Florissant, Dellwood and Vinita Park is Ronald Brockmeyer. He also has a private criminal defense practice in St. Charles. Further, he is also a judge in Breckenridge Hills and in Ferguson. The conflict of interest is obvious and the practice of allowing someone to work as a prosecutor, practicing attorney and also a judge, all at the same time, should not be allowed.

On a 10 mile stretch of highway that passes by Ferguson, there are 16 different municipalities, each with its own sliver of the highway to patrol and write tickets from. Unfortunately for St, Louis drivers, it's a main artery into the Lambert-St. Louis International Airport, which results in a target rich environment for the issuance of tickets by overzealous police and produces huge revenues for the cities which stalk these unsuspecting drivers.

In some St. Louis cities it's hard to distinguish the cops from the criminals. In the small town of Bel-Ridge, near Ferguson, motorists were shocked to see an intersection light turn from green to red as they were driving through it, without turning yellow as it had always done before. Police were ticketing motorists with impunity until some suspicious residents complained to the Department of Transportation. A state transportation engineer investigated the allegations of fraud and found that the police were entrapping drivers by issuing citations for violations they didn't commit, by manually switching traffic signals to red, just as people were driving through the intersection.

The St. Louis Post Dispatch released a series of stories about the Bel-Ridge fraud. Reportedly, police requested that the Missouri State Department of Transportation install an override switch on their traffic lights so the police could manually turn the lights from green to red at school crosswalks, when children were crossing the street. The DOT engineer found that the police were, instead, using the switch to turn a green traffic light into a red light, prematurely without traversing through yellow, as motorists were traveling through the intersection. The police would then pull the drivers over and issue a ticket for running a red light. Two years prior to the light switch being installed, the city of Bel-Ridge generated 29 percent of it's revenues from traffic citations. The first year the switch was installed and officers began to manipulate it, traffic fines rose to account for 45 percent of the annual revenues of the city.

Red-light cameras are new tools being used by municipal governments to rip-off drivers. The Florida's Department of Transportation recently "mistakenly" sent letters to all municipal governments in the state, telling them to reduce the yellow phase of the light signal at intersections within their towns. When angry drivers across the state realized they were getting screwed and reported it to the media, the Florida Department of Transportation claimed their engineer, who instructed all Florida municipal governments to reduce their yellow light phase, was wrong to do so. Some cities which reduced the yellow phase duration saw their red-light camera revenues double. Each half-second reduction in the yellow light phase can double the number of tickets the red-light cameras issue, based on industry research reports. Red light cameras generate over $100 million in Florida per year. It's big business for the companies who supply the camera systems, and to state and local governments, who now rely on the revenues they generate.

The 2010 U.S. census found that police stops, searches and arrests in Ferguson were much more likely to happen to blacks than to whites. Of 5,384 total stops in Ferguson in 2010, 4,632 were issued to blacks (86%) and 686 were issued to white drivers (12%). At the time of the report Ferguson had a black population distribution of 63% and a white population distribution of 33%. The racial distribution of searches and arrests were:

Out of 611 searches, 563 were of blacks (92%) and 47 were of whites (8%).

Out of 521 arrests, 483 were of blacks (92%) and 36 were of whites (7%).

Performance measures are common to nearly all human endeavors these days, and police operations are no exception. A "disparity index" measures the proportion of police stops as a percentage of the population of each race within a community. A value of 1.0 represents no disparity in police stops based on race, but a value of greater than 1.0 indicates a race is over-represented. Values of less than 1 indicate under-representation. In Ferguson, in

2010, whites had a disparity index of .038 while blacks had a disparity of 1.38, indicating that blacks were being stopped disproportionately and at a much higher rate than whites.

A "contraband hit rate" is another measurement tool municipal, state and federal governments use to measure the ratio of searches that found contraband, divided by the number of searches for each race. In Ferguson, in 2010, Blacks had a contraband hit rate of 21.71 while whites had a contraband hit rate of 34.04, meaning that whites were much more likely to have contraband in their possession than blacks, although blacks seem to be the main target of police stops and searches.

Blacks had an arrest rate of 10.43 compared to 5.25 for whites, showing that blacks are arrested twice as many times as whites, based on the ratio of arrests versus stops. Whites were given citations in 10% of stops while blacks were given citations in 86% of stops. In Ferguson, in 2010, 56% of arrests were for outstanding warrants.

As of June 2013, Ferguson had just over 21,000 residents, but more than 40,000 outstanding arrest warrants. The town's aggressive approach to police operations and difficult-to-navigate court system generated $2,635,400 from fines. Court fines are Ferguson's second-largest source of revenue.

Information collected from municipal courts across Missouri show that in 2013, the city of Ferguson had the highest number of warrants issued in the state, relative to its size. As city services get more expensive to maintain, city administrators will rely more heavily on the revenues they can generate from fines and fees, at the expense of their constituent taxpayers.

CHAPTER 21

DARREN WILSON

Darren Wilson was born in Fort Worth, Texas in May of 1986 to his parents, Tonya Dee Durso and John Wilson. He has two siblings. Wilson was an honor roll student at St. Charles West High School, in Missouri, in the 9th and 10th grades, and played on the high school hockey team. Friends say he is well-mannered, soft-spoken, and likes to keep a low-profile. The Ferguson Police Chief described Wilson as a "gentle, quiet man," and "a distinguished officer." Newspapers have pointed out that Wilson's soft demeanor might have been "a reaction to a turbulent youth in which his mother was repeatedly divorced, convicted of financial crimes, and died before he finished high school in 2004."

Wilson's upbringing may have led him into a career in law enforcement. The UK Daily News wrote:

As a teenager, Darren Wilson lived in St. Peters, Mo., a mostly white city of 54,000 about 20 miles west of Ferguson, where his environment *was chaotic. He was the eldest of three children of Tonya Dee Durso, who, records show, carried out financial crimes including crimes against Sandra Lee Finney, who lived across the street and believed they were friends. Neighbors claim the policeman accused of shooting dead an unarmed teenager in St Louis had a serial con-woman for a mother. Darren Wilson's mother, Tonya Durso, won the trust of her neighbors, then cheated them out of hundreds of thousands of dollars by stealing their identities and taking out vast loans and credit card debt. At the time she committed the offenses she was on parole for similar crimes elsewhere in the state and afterwards died at the age of 35 under mysterious circumstances. Neighbors revealed how they were stunned that Wilson became a police officer after his mother behaved so deviously towards them. Mickelle Gordon, 39, a dental assistant, lived over the road from the family and said that Wilson's mother was 'charismatic' and 'charming' and first targeted her brother Jason, who lost tens of thousands including some of his pension. Gordon said: 'He used to work lots and saved all his money. She said that she was an investor and that she could help him. 'She got his social security number and stole his identity. She used it to take out loans, credit cards and went through his savings. He never got it back'. After that she fooled Gordon's mother Sandy Finney, 67, an office manager, and stole her ID too. Finney said: 'My husband and I were naive. She cleaned us out for at least $100,000 and $30,000 in cash which we didn't get back.' She explained that his mother used to intercept her mail and sent off for pre-approved credit cards that she would use herself. She got into so much debt that she had to take out one loan after another just to keep the scam afloat. Finney claimed that Wilson's mother made a copy of the key they had left by the front door to let herself in when she wanted, using the cover story that she was letting the cat back in the house. But really she was forwarding her calls from creditors to her own number so Finney had no idea how much debt she was in. The charade came tumbling down in February 2001 when Finney was told by her own bank that she could not deposit any money and the authorities were alerted. According to public records Wilson's mother pleaded guilty to six counts of forgery and one count of stealing at the 11th Judicial Court in St Louis. In 1998 she had already admitted another six counts of stealing in an unrelated matter. His mother's victims say however that she did not serve any time in jail and went into bankruptcy in October 2002. The following month she died. Finney said: 'They were not able to tell us if it was a suicide. As a victim you are not told anything'. Only afterwards did she discover that* *his mother was on probation in Washington, Missouri, for doing something similar to somebody else. Finney added: 'I'm surprised Wilson passed the background checks to become a policeman. People can change but that was a bad home. His mother was a serial conwoman'. Wilson's mother died when he would have been 16." Six years later, at 22, Wilson joined the police force.*

Sandy Finney also told The New York Times:

It's a terrible thing that has happened now, but he did have a troubled childhood. Officer Wilson's family had somewhat awkwardly stayed in the neighborhood — moving just one door down — even after his mother was convicted of stealing and forgery in 2001. After her bank informed her that it was freezing her accounts, Ms. Finney said she learned that numerous credit cards had been opened in her name. Among the purchases: tens of thousands of dollars of candles; home decorations; furniture; clothes, including some from American Eagle Outfitters, which Ms. Finney says was Officer Wilson's favorite store at the time; and hockey gear. All the while, she'd come over and sit at my kitchen table to chat and say how she would help me with this terrible thing that was happening to us. What hurt me more than all of it was what she did to those kids.

Years later, Ms. Finney said she was stunned when she saw her former neighbor appear outside the old house in a police uniform. My husband and I thought, 'How did he get to be a police officer?'"

After attending the police academy, Officer Wilson spent two years with the Jennings Police Department, before it was disbanded in 2011 because of corruption and excessive use of force by its officers. The city council shut down the police department in the midst of a federal investigation into a Jennings police lieutenant who was accused of stealing grant money to pay officers "overtime" for working "Driving While Intoxicated" checkpoints that the police department never operated.

Just prior to the Jennings police force folding, one of their officers got in trouble for shooting at a woman who was fleeing from a traffic stop. She said she fled because she was afraid of getting a ticket and going to jail. She had a baby on board and was worried her baby would be taken and put into foster care, so she drove-off. The officer opened fire, hitting the car but luckily missing the baby.

When the Jennings's Police Department closed, St. Louis County took over the duties of law-enforcement in the town, as a paid vendor to the city. All 40 Jennings police officers had to find new jobs. 12 got re-hired to work for St. Louis County but, although Officer Wilson applied for work at St. Louis County, he was not accepted. He was later hired at Ferguson, where his salary was $45,302 per year.

In testimony to the Grand Jury, officer Wilson revealed that he had also worked for the city of Pine Lawn for only eight hours, but he never explained why he left so abruptly and the prosecutors and jurors never questioned it.

Wilson reportedly spent four years with the Ferguson police department, serving a total of six years in law enforcement with the Jennings, Pine Lawn and Ferguson police departments, although Grand Jury testimony indicated that Wilson had only been with the Ferguson Police Department for two and a half years, instead of the 4 years Ferguson police had reported to the media. He was often cited as being a good cop who received a commendation for his outstanding police work, but the case in which he received his commendation doesn't appear to have been so remarkable. Apparently, Wilson was alerted to the pretense of a suspicious car in a residential driveway in Ferguson. When Wilson approached the black male who was sitting in the car, the youth stepped out, locked the door and would not open it for Wilson without a warrant. Wilson grabbed the keys and opened the car anyway. He found some "weed" and, subsequently, arrested the young man. Wilson received an award for "extraordinary effort in the line of duty," although some people claim he had no right to go into the parked, locked car, on private property, without a warrant. The victim stated that Wilson beat him during the incident, in the front yard of his grandmother's house, but Officer Wilson never showed up in court to prosecute the case, which precluded the beating from being debated. The case was dismissed, but Wilson still got the award. On his Facebook page soon after his arrest in 2013, the victim, Christopher Brook, claimed that Wilson had handcuffed him, beaten him in his front yard, and then charged him with six felonies.

In another encounter, Wilson arrested a man at his house after Officer Wilson went to the property to investigate a report of several derelict vehicles that the man had in his backyard. As officer Wilson approached, the man began video-recording the encounter with his cell phone. Wilson told the young man he couldn't record their discussion and then quickly subdued and apprehended him, cutting off the video tape recording. Wilson later confirmed that the vehicles he was investigating were not stolen. They were merely unregistered and secluded in the suspects back yard.

Although Wilson doesn't seem to be making many friends in the Ferguson community lately, his fellow officers think he's a great guy who talks with a low voice and has a mellow temper. Indicating that he's generally friendly and not overly aggressive.

28-year-old Darren Wilson, who's divorce from his first wife, Ashley Brown, was finalized on November 19, 2013, owns a $180,000 home on Manda Lane, in Crestwood, Missouri with his new bride, and former fellow Ferguson co-worker, thirty-six year-old Barbara Spradling (a dispatcher). Their Crestwood neighborhood is in a St. Louis suburb located 18 miles from Ferguson and has a population of 11,000 residents. In 2010, the U.S. Census reported that the town was 93.8% white, but new numbers indicate that Crestwood's white population percentage has been reduced to 91% over the past few years, indicating a first sign of racial "transition."

Darren Wilson has not been seen back at his home since just after the Michael Brown shooting. Before he left, he was provided around-the-clock police protection from volunteer police officers who felt his life could have been in jeopardy. The hackivist group "Anonymous" publicized Wilson's address once they became involved, which raised the level of concern from his fellow police officers. It's doubtful that Wilson will ever move back to Menda Lane. His encounter with Michael Brown has made him a marked man.

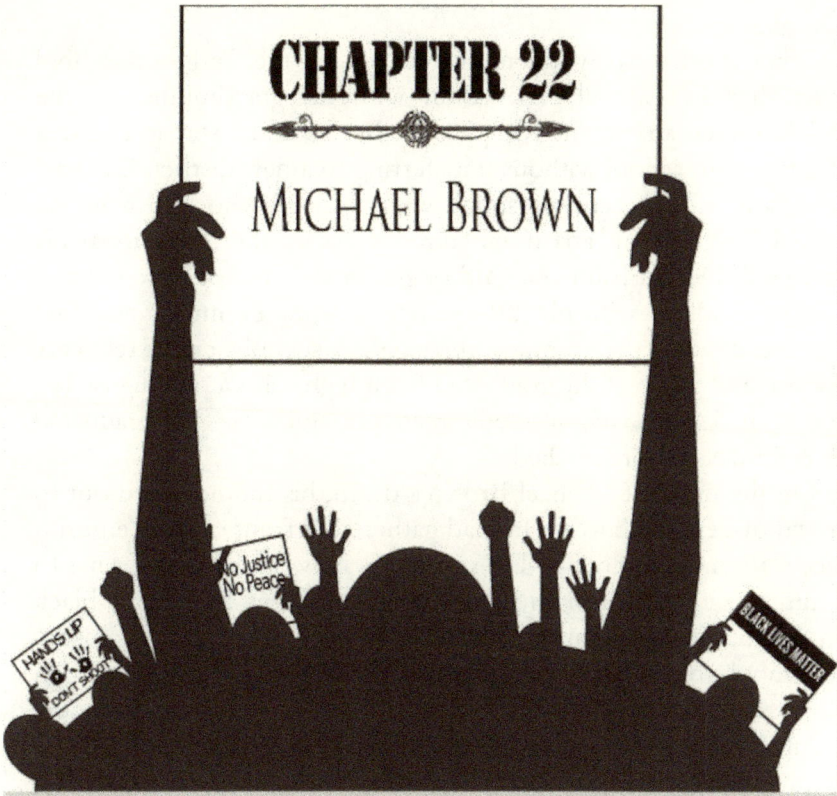

CHAPTER 22

MICHAEL BROWN

Michael Brown was eighteen years old when he passed away on August 9th, 2014. He was born to unwed teenage parents, Michael Brown Sr. and Lesley McSpadden, in May of 1996 in Florissant, Missouri. He spent most of his upbringing bouncing between the homes of his mother, father and grandmother. His parents claim Brown was a rambunctious child. He would scale his security gate as a baby and he would write on walls with pens and pencils if left unattended. His father, Michael Brown senior said, "His grades were kind of edgy. That's why I had to keep my foot on his neck to keep him on track." His mom said she relied on friends, family and a retired juvenile officer to mentor him.

After Brown was accused of stealing an iPad in the 9th grade, he left his junior high school and transferred to two other schools before enrolling in Normandy High, where he spent almost two years before graduating. Ferguson's Normandy High School was built in 1939 on the site of the old city dump. It was known as "Blizzard Hill," and said to be haunted before being leveled and developed into a school.

When Lesley McSpadden moved out of the Ferguson school district, her son initially moved in with his grandmother in the Canfield Green apartment complex so that he could stay in the area and finish high school without transferring to a new district. Michael Brown was most recently residing with a friend who also lived on Canfield Drive, in an apartment directly across the street from his new friend, Dorian Johnson. Although Brown did not have enough credits to graduate with his 2014 senior class, he eventually acquired those credits over the summer, through his school's credit recovery program, and successfully graduated from high school on August 1st, 2014, with 4 other fellow credit recovery students. He graduated only eight days before he died.

On the night of Michael Brown's death, his mother cried-out to a crowd of demonstrators who had gathered in front of the Ferguson police station. She ranted, "Do you know how hard it was for me to get him to stay in school and graduate? You know how many black men graduate? Not many." She was right, especially in Ferguson. The school that Brown had attended, Normandy/Ferguson High School, was one of the most violent schools in the state, with the absolute lowest test scores.

In September of 2012, the Missouri State Board of Education stripped Normandy High School of its state accreditation, by unanimous vote, due to low test scores and poor performance of their students. The school had been "provisionally accredited" since 2006, but it has been allowed some time to improve test scores before losing its accreditation completely. After losing their accreditation, Normandy school administrators blamed their schools poor performance on the large group of minority students who transferred to their schools the previous year from the city of Wellston, after the Wellston School District lost their state accreditation. Missouri Department of Education officials didn't give the district any credit for taking the underprivileged kids. Peter Herschend, president of the state education board, said, "No matter which way you cut it, with or without Wellston kids, the performance in the area really, really counts is at the bottom of the pile," In its annual review on school performance, Ferguson schools consistently passed only 5 out of 14 professional teaching standards. Schools need to pass at least six standards each year to maintain their state accreditation.

When the Missouri Department of Education finally stripped the Ferguson School district of their education accreditation for failing to raise test scores of their students, Ferguson Superintendent of Schools, Stanton Lawrence, called the decision to close the schools "politically obscene." He said, "I'm very disappointed, not only as a school leader but as a parent, that children -- poor, African American children -- apparently have a different standard than other children in the state of Missouri."

State Education Commissioner Chris Nicastro said the department felt the decision was necessary. He said, "The important thing here is that we focus on providing equitable, quality education for every child," Nicastro said. "It's just not acceptable to allow our kids, any of our kids, to go through a system that isn't serving their needs well, that doesn't expect high performance from them," Former president of the Normandy School Board, William Humphrey, said, "They made a mess of this. Taking away our accreditation, then taking over control. An absolute mess. I'm not sure what their plan is, if there's even one."

When Ferguson lost state accreditation, their students qualified to attend schools in other districts. Many of the Ferguson parents chose St. Charles County's Francis Howell School District for their students to be educated in, to give them a chance for a high-quality education. Francis Howell is rated as a top-performing school district in Missouri, whereas Ferguson schools are rated as the worst schools in the state, in terms of test scores, and violence.

In 2013, the St. Louis Post-Dispatch wrote an article dubbing Normandy "the most dangerous school in the area." According to the article, in 2012 the school reported 285 discipline incidents that resulted in suspensions of 10 days or more. About 60 percent of students had at least one suspension. Only one other high school in the state had a higher rate of incidents that year. Jennifer Floyd complained about the extreme violence in the Ferguson classrooms. She said, "I sent my son there to be educated, not to be assaulted or beat up." Dawn Baldesi, an English teacher at Normandy High said, "Teaching is very difficult. Teachers get cussed out, yelled out. There are so many write-ups you can't keep up."

Fires have been a constant problem at the Ferguson area schools. St. Louis Fire Chief, Quinten Randolph, says he's tired of repeatedly responding to fires set in bathrooms or trashcans at the schools. He stated, "We can't keep coming out here like this. They were setting the toilet paper on fire. They were setting the soap dispensers on fire. They were setting old papers, books on fire under the stairwells. We said, 'Hey, take some pride in your school.'"

After the school lost their accreditation, approximately 450 Ferguson students were bussed to St. Charles County each day to attend classes in the Francis Howell School District. Ferguson taxpayers were responsible for paying the tab for tuition and for bus transportation. Each student cost the city's taxpayers about $11,000 in annual tuition to transfer Ferguson students to St. Charles County for their education. This represented an annual cost of nearly $5 million. Many Ferguson residents were outraged to see their tax-dollars being spent to send black students to St. Charles instead of using that money to rebuild Ferguson schools. Parents from Ferguson began to complain that the financial drain on the district and taxpayers was hard to bear. Lola Robinson said, "While we're sending money to the districts that don't need it, our students don't have books or good computers."

To save money, Normandy laid-off teachers and closed an elementary school. William Humphrey, former president of the Normandy School Board, said, "The kids who stayed were hurt because the district didn't have resources to help them, because we're paying up for transfers."

Parents in St. Charles were so concerned about the arrival of students from Ferguson that over 2,500 moms and dads attended a meeting at the Francis Howell High School gym to protest the transfer of students from Ferguson. Jennifer Henry, a spokeswoman for the Francis Howell School District, said, "All we're saying is that kids have a right to be educated in their own community. Funds being spent to transfer a few students could definitely be better spent by improving the district." A riled-up Francis Howell parent stated, "I deserve to not have to worry about my children getting stabbed or taking a drug or getting robbed."

Ferguson parents were excited to see their children finally getting a good education. Lorrine Goodloe, a mother from Ferguson, said her daughter, Naomi, traveled 45 minutes each day to go to the Francis Howell schools. Goodloe was ecstatic about the progress she saw in her daughter, saying, "She loved it. Her reading improved and she was getting the attention she needed. She excelled in the Howell district last year — much more than if she stayed in Normandy."

Another black mother from Ferguson who was at the Francis

Howell meeting was appalled by the comments being made by the mainly white crowd. She said, "We have now gone back to 1954." She was referring to the landmark Brown vs. Board of Education decision when the Supreme Court Justices declared that the doctrine of "separate but equal" schools was illegal, which caused schools across the country to become desegregated, which also caused a widespread backlash from parents who did not want their children to be educated with minority students.

After feeling the heat from St. Charles parents, the state Department of Education quickly found a solution that would remove the minorities from the Francis Howell School District. The School Board established a new Normandy School District "collaborative" that would bring Ferguson students back home to be educated in their own city, and give the state Department of Education a little more time to figure out how to properly educate students in the new Ferguson/Florissant/Normandy education zone, or "collaborative," before low test results forced another school shutdown.

The 450 transfer students were transferred back to Ferguson, to the delight of thousands of St. Charles parents. Vice president of the Missouri Board of Education, Mike Jones, said, "We had to do something; the district was in a serious bind, we weren't going to just shutter it. That would have impacted surrounding districts. So we created the new district and gave it a clean slate."

The new Ferguson school district collaborative will have three years to prove it can maintain good test scores from their students, or they could be shut down. Sarah Potter, a spokesperson for the Department of Elementary and Secondary Education, warned, "This is the last chance to turn around Normandy." Meanwhile, parents of transferred students are suing the state to be allowed to stay at Francis Howell, saying the state acted illegally when they denied Ferguson students the ability to continue to attend classes in St. Charles. Regardless of the outcome of the lawsuit, the majority of Ferguson students are now back in Ferguson, hoping to be among the 40% of pupils who graduate from high school in that area each year.

Michael Brown's mother was excited that her son had finally graduated. She said he was enrolled to attend Vatterott College, a vocational career training school. She said he was scheduled to begin classes the week after he was killed. When asked to confirm if Brown was scheduled to attend classes in 2014, Pamela Bell, CEO & President of Vatterott college, stated, "Vatterott College has been part of the Ferguson community since the 1970s and we share in the community's grief over this young man's death and the circumstances surrounding it. As a matter of policy, we do not disclose the enrollment status of current students or those who may have plans to attend Vatterott College. Our thoughts and prayers remain with Michael Brown's family and the Ferguson community during this difficult time."

Vatterott College is accredited by the Accrediting Commission of Career Schools and Colleges. Their website claims, "All programs are industry-relevant and designed to support the Vatterott mission of providing career skills for a better life." The school programs include, diesel mechanic, cosmetologist, paralegal, commercial driver's license, culinary, personal fitness, message therapy, legal assistant, dental assistant, plumbing, web design, heating and air conditioning repair and similar programs that get people prepared for an entry level blue-collar job. Brown was planning on becoming a heating and air conditioning repairman.

Gentle Giant or No Angel:

There are two contradictory and dueling narratives regarding the temperament of Michael Brown. One is that he is a "Gentle Giant" and the other is that he is "No Angle." The truth may lie somewhere in between.

Brown's mother said, "He was my first born, sweet, loving, dedicated. He worked hard to get through high school. We were so proud of him." McSpadden described her son as a "gentle giant." She said, "He was a big teddy bear. He touched everybody. My son was the type of person that everybody flocked to him. Everybody wanted to know about Michael. Everybody wanted to be around Michael. He fixed things. He didn't create problems. He fixed things. My son was sweet. He didn't mean any harm to anybody. He wanted to be really good in visual arts and heating and cooling." She explained, "He was really good with his hands and taking things apart and putting them back together. He was almost like a healer. He was a good boy. He was a big teddy bear.

Michael Brown senior said, "He was funny, silly. He would make you laugh, and when there was any problem going on, any situation, there wasn't nothing that he couldn't solve. He could bring people back together."

Neighbors described Brown as a good boy who was never in trouble. He was "quiet and respectful" said Sharon Johnson who lives down the street from Brown. She said, "We talked about how when you turn yourself to the Lord you feel so good--and good things come your way. He had a more mature mind than a little boy's mind."

His friend, Dorian Johnson, also claimed that Brown was "a gentle giant." Johnson said, "He cared for everybody. He was loving. I loved everything about this young man." Donavan Eddington, another friend of Michael Brown, said, "It ain't true what they say about him. He didn't rob nobody. He ain't that type of person."

Michael Brown claimed to care more about others than himself. He wrote on his Facebook page before he died, "If I leave this earth today, at least you'll know that I care about others more than I cared about my damn self."

Another message he left on Facebook last August wasn't so friendly. He posted, "how yo own family don't wanna see you do good." And just a week before he was killed he posted a comment that said some of his friends treat him better than his own family.

The New York Times revealed Michael's darker side. The paper reported that he might be No Angel. Brown had been accused of stealing cigars, beating up a neighbor, drinking, smoking weed and being an overall bully, but his mother denies those accusations. When asked about rumors that her son was in the "Bloods" street gang, she replied, "You may see him on a picture with some friends that may have been in a gang. He wasn't in a gang. He just knew how to adapt to his surroundings. Michael was so cool that he could just get along with anybody." When asked if her son had a juvenile record, Ms. McSpadden said he did not, but she refused to allow his record, if there is one, to be released to the public.

The St. Louis Post Dispatch, Riverfront Times and GotNews.com have all sued to have Brown's juvenile records released. GotNews.com claims to have evidence that Michael Brown, his stepfather Michael Head and their family are in the Bloods street gang in Ferguson. GotNews.com also claimed to have proof from law-enforcement sources that Brown had an extensive criminal juvenile record that should be released, it's argued, because

Brown is dead and therefore has no right to privacy after death.

Brown reportedly weighed 289 pounds, stood six feet four inches tall, and he loved to play video games. His favorite game was Call of Duty Zombies, released in 2009. His other passion was rap music. When he wasn't writing, producing and rapping his own songs, he liked to listen to Migos, his favorite rap artist.

Brown's rap lyrics are a little rough, but he only began rapping as a serious hobby a year before his death. He uploaded his songs to Soundcloud, where they can be heard in their entirety. Here are some excerpts:

From the song "Shit Talka.": "Shit talker, shit talker, whatcha gonna do? When a real killa killa come for you? Shit talker, shit talker, whatcha gonna do? When a real nigga come for you."

From the song "Jennings Stations Roads Freestyle.": "My favorite part of killing people is when they hit the ground. Every time I call your bitch I make her cum. And when she comes I'm cumming all over her tush. I beat that pussy up. I'm smoking purple. I roll fat blunts they look just like my thumb. While I bless him with a dick on his face."

From the song "SMH Luh Vee.": "I'll be counting money by myself. I'm a rich nigga so I got that wealth. I fuck three hos by myself."

Was Michael Brown a gentle giant or a big bully? We who didn't know him will never know. He possibly left this world without ever fulfilling or realizing his destiny, but maybe his destiny was fulfilled by provoking a dialogue between the races, or by sparking a racial revolt. In a final Facebook posting the night before he died, Michael Brown wrote his last words. He said, "Everything happens for a reason, just start putting 2 n 2 together. You'll see it." [22]

---

[22] http://nyti.ms/XLP1Oc.

CHAPTER 23

DAY-1
SATURDAY
AUGUST-9

Saturday Aug. 9 (Day 1)

On the morning of Saturday, August 9th Dorian Johnson and Michael Brown met accidentally when Johnson left his apartment at around 7 a.m. to go to a neighbor's apartment where he could buy some cigars to roll a joint for his morning smoke. While outside, he saw Brown in the parking lot. The two began a conversation that resulted in them deciding to smoke some weed, hang-out and play video games. Although the day began as most other days, the events that unfolded in the afternoon would set off a worldwide debate over excessive force by police and the reality of civil rights and race relations in America in the 21st century.

During Grand Jury testimony about what happened on the day of the Michael Brown shooting, his new friend, Dorian Johnson, explained what led up to the altercation with officer Darren Wilson. Johnson told the Grand Jury that he met Michael Brown, who he called "Big Mike," only a month or two before the incident. He said Brown was living with his Grandmother, but "had to move out," so he had recently moved-in with a friend they both knew who lived across the street from Johnson's apartment on Canfield Drive.

Although Dorian Johnson admitted that he and Brown had only hung-out a couple of times, he said they got along very well. The two initially met a month or two prior when a mutual friend invited Brown over to Dorian's apartment to play video games. Dorian said that was the only time Brown was in his home, which he shared with his girlfriend, their daughter and a roommate. He mentioned that he didn't go over to Brown's grandmother's apartment, "because she was strict on who she let into her house."

Dorian said his morning routine is to get up and smoke some marijuana, but on the morning of August 9th, he needed to purchase some cigar wrappers to roll a joint. So, at 7 a.m., he left his apartment to visit a neighbor who he knew sold Cigarillo cigars, which he could fill with marijuana and smoke as a joint or "blunt," as it's commonly referred to. The two ran into each other in the apartment complex parking lot, where Brown was helping his aunt get her children into a car. They began a conversation about sports, girls, fashion and future plans.

When Dorian told Brown that he was going to a neighbor's to get Cigarillos to roll a joint, Brown said he would "match" him, which means they would each roll a joint with their own marijuana and smoke them together. Since Brown did not know the neighbor who sold the Cigarillos, he suggested that they go to the store to get them. Dorian agreed and then asked Brown to go ask his roommate if he wasted to go to the store with them. Brown checked, but his roommate said he was too tired to go.

On the way to the store, Brown and Johnson stopped to talk to a couple of construction workers who were doing some work around the Canfield apartment complex. They spoke for a short period of time, then proceeded on their way to the store. Dorian Johnson later told the Grand Jury that he couldn't hear what Brown and the construction workers were discussing, but he said "Yes" when the prosecutor asked if he overheard them talking about getting high. After one of the construction workers walked away with Brown for about 30 minutes, to apparently get high, Brown and Johnson continued on their way to the Ferguson Market. Enroute to the store, the two talked about college. Brown told Dorian that he was going to college, and Dorian responded that he had a bad experience with going to college right out of high school. He said he had attended a university for two semesters, but had left the school after repeatedly being harassed by police in the small college town. Dorian also said, while he walking to the store, that he assumed Brown had money to purchase the Cigarillos because he dressed well, and he had no indication that Brown was intending on robbing the convenience store.

When Michael Brown and Dorian Johnson walked into the Ferguson Market convenience store, Dorian claimed that Brown asked the clerk for some Cigarillos, but before the clerk could retrieve them, Brown reached across the counter and grabbed an entire box. He handed them back to Johnson and then reached across the counter again to grab a handful of unboxed Cigarillos. The clerk this time attempted to slap Brown's hand but he was too late and accidentally slapped the counter instead. His finger tips hit some of the Cigarillos and they fell on the floor. Brown bent down to pick them up, and then made a move toward the front door.

Dorian said he put the box of cigars back on the counter, since he did not see Brown pay for them. He claimed he had been to the store many times, implying that he would not want to cause any trouble there. He said to the Grand Jury, "The store clerk actually does notice me, like I said, it was a male store clerk and his daughter was there. She's looking directly at me, I'm looking at her face-to-face and she sees me actually put the box of Cigarillos back and I step back." He said the male clerk came out from behind the desk to prevent Brown from leaving with the cigars. Dorian was moving backwards and trying to get out of the way, because he didn't want any part of what was happening and he knew there were cameras in the store.

Dorian said that when the clerk tried to grab Brown, that Brown then turned and pushed the clerk backwards and said, "get back." They both then left the store, with the clerk yelling at them that he was going to call the police.

Dorian claimed that while he was walking back to the Canfield apartments with Brown he was trying to figure out what just happened. He said he felt like an accomplice to a crime. He claims he told Brown, "I don't do stuff like that. What's going on?"

Brown told him to "be calm" and "be cool," and laughed it off, but Dorian said he was uncomfortable because he knew they just committed a crime, and they were on camera.

After they left the store and were walking down West Florissant on their way home, they saw a police car coming towards them. Dorian thought to himself that he was going to go to jail for the robbery, but he said he was surprised to see the Ferguson police truck pass on by and then pulled into a McDonalds parking lot, next to the Ferguson Market. He said the police like to hang-out there. When he and Brown turned onto Canfield Drive on their way to the Canfield apartments they saw another Ferguson police truck pass by. He said that since he saw two police cars already he thought the Ferguson Market must have called the police to report the robbery but he was surprised that they just passed on by without stopping. Dorian said they walked down the middle of the road for about 30 seconds, while two or three cars passed them, but no one honked or told them to get out of the street, so he didn't feel it was a problem for anyone. They then saw officer Darren Wilson's truck coming towards them on Canfield Drive. As the officer approached the two, who were walking in the middle of the road, he rolled down his window and said "get the fuck on the sidewalk." Johnson responded by saying, We're just a minute away from our destination, I live on Canfield and we'll be off the street shortly.

Dorian told the Grand Jury:

We continued to walk and have our conversation, but almost a split second later we heard the tires screech, and the officer, he pulled back in the truck very fast to the point at an angle if we didn't hear his tires screech, the back of his cruiser would have struck one of us, if not both of us. It would have struck both of us or one of us because of the way he angles in reverse. He never drove and turned around, he reversed real fast. Why he reversed so fast on us and the angle that he did in the manner. Now we are almost not inches away from his front door, like we was right in his face. He never got out of the car, he just pulled right back on the side of us, but it is almost at an angle… When he pulled up we are face-to-face. Me and Big Mike are shoulder to shoulder now and the officer is facing us. The officer pulled back. What did you say? Very loud, angry. And Big Mike, in an instant, Big Mike was finishing saying something, his door was thrust open, he thrust his door open real hard. He was so close to the door that it hit mostly Big Mike, but it hit me on my left side and it closed back on him, like real fast. Just the same speed, boom, boom, that fast. And at that time he never attempted to open the door again like to try to get back out, but his arm came out of the window and that's the first initial contact they had. The officer grabbed ahold of Big Mike's shirt around the neck area. When the door had closed back on him, he didn't say anything, His arm almost in an instant came out the window, his left arm, I remember it was his left arm, came out the window and touched Big Mike around his neck and his throat. I watched his hands, you know, they really tightened up, so yeah, he had a good grip on it, that's what I saw first. Now, from the beginning of the grab, it is a tug of war...He never stopped us and said hey, freeze, stop right there, let me get out of my car, anything like that. I've been stopped by police before, I know there is a way that they stop or pull up on people, suspects, for committing a crime. So exactly what I said, didn't feel like he was stopping or telling us anything like we were committing a crime so much as chastising from a father to a son, like you are doing some wrong. Hey, put that down or don't touch that, it came off like that, that's how he said it.

What happened next has been widely disputed by many different witnesses. Radio calls from police dispatch provide some clues and a timeline of events:

11:48 a.m. – Ferguson Police Officer Darren Wilson responds to a call of a sick child near the Canfield apartment complex.

11:51 a.m. - Michael Brown and his friend Dorian Johnson are inside the Ferguson Market convenience store to get Swisher Sweets "Rillos" flavored Cigarillos cigars. Brown grabs a box of cigars from across the counter and leaves the store without paying. The store clerk calls out to Brown and Johnson that he will call the police while his daughter calls 911 to report the robbery.

11:52 a.m. - The Ferguson Police Dispatch calls for officers in the area to be on the lookout for a robbery suspect walking towards the Quicktrip. The call gives a description of Brown; "White shirt b/m/qt, box cigars."

11:55 a.m. - Another updated call goes out from Ferguson dispatch giving more details about the robbery suspect; "Walking N/B in a white shirt."

11:57 a.m. - An additional updated call goes out from Ferguson dispatch to give more details about the description of the suspect; "Suspect wearing red Cards cap, yellow socks, W/ another male suspect walking towards the QT at this time."

11:58 a.m. - One last call goes out through the radio from Dispatch giving details about the robbery suspects clothing; "Khaki Shorts." An officer arrived at the Ferguson Market to take witness statements and gather more information.

12:00 p.m. - Ferguson police officer Darren Wilson left the scene of a call regarding a sick child.

12:01 p.m. - Officer Daren Wilson crosses paths with Michael Brown and Dorian Johnson while driving down Canfield drive in front of the Canfield Green Apartments. Brown, Johnson and Wilson have an altercation that leaves Brown dead.

12:04 p.m. - A second officer arrives on the scene

12:04 p.m. - EMS contacted

12:05 p.m. - A Ferguson police supervisor arrives. Police secure the scene within 3 minutes of the shooting and quickly cordon off the area with yellow police-line tape. Neighbors plead for someone to give Brown CPR, but the police already know he is dead and there is no reviving him, nonetheless, no assistance was offered and the crowd seemed to have been offended by the lack of medical assistance.

12:07 - The St. Louis County Police Department was notified of the shooting.

12:10 - A paramedic from nearby Christian Hospital was driving back to the hospital from an earlier call, when he passed by the shooting scene to render assistance. His supervisor, Chris Cebollero, confirmed to reporters that his emergency medical technician took Brown's pulse and saw the wounds to Brown's head and determined that his injuries were incompatible with life, so he performed no life saving measures.

12:15 - Officers of The St. Louis County Police Department arrived at the scene.

12:16: - A Dellwood Officer arrives at the scene.

12:43 p.m. - Detectives from the St. Louis County Police Department were notified to respond to the crime scene.

1:11 p.m. - Ferguson Dispatch reports that shots were fired on Canfield.

1:12 p.m. - Ferguson Dispatch reports 4 to 6 shots were fired.

4:37 p.m. - Michael Browns body was wrapped in a tarp, removed from the street, and loaded in a truck to be transported to a morgue six miles away, about 4 and a half hours after he died. Neighbors of the Brown family were horrified by the sight of Brown laying in the middle of the street, in the sweltering summer heat, for over 4 hours after he was shot. He remained face down on the pavement, with a long visible line of blood running from his head down the street towards Officer Wilson's patrol car. This set the stage for the community rage that soon followed.

The Shooting:

Witness accounts of what happened vary. Many witnesses came out after the fact to say they saw or heard part of the altercation. Dorian Johnson, Michael Brady, Tiffany Mitchell and Piaget Crenshaw all gave interviews immediately after Brown was shot. They were all grouped together after the shooting on a grassy knoll near the site of the shooting. They were accompanied by friends and family of Michael Brown, and local activist and race-bater Anthony Shahid, who was one of the first people on the scene.

Following are the witness accounts that were made to the media immediately after the Michael Brown shooting:

Dorian Johnson

According to 22-year-old Dorian Johnson, he and 18-year-old Michael Brown, were walking back to Johnson's home from a convenience store they just left, where he admitted that Brown had shoplifted some cigars. Johnson claims the two were simply walking home in the middle of the street, when a Ferguson police officer confronted them. The officer told them to "Get the fuck out of the street." Dorian said he replied to the officer, "we are not but a minute away from our destination, and we would shortly be out of the street." The officer drove away but then abruptly puts the car in reverse and backs up rapidly. The car slants between two lanes, almost hitting the two youths. Johnson explained, "We were so close, almost inches away, that when he (the police) tried to open his door aggressively, the door ricocheted both off me and Big Mike's body and closed back on the officer."

Still in his car, the officer grabs Brown by his neck, Johnson said. Brown tried to pull away, but the officer kept pulling Brown towards him. Johnson said, "My friend, Big Mike, very angrily is trying to pull away from the officer. The officer draws his weapon. He says 'I'll shoot' or 'I'm about to shoot.' I'm standing so close to Big Mike and the officer, I look in his window and I see that he has his gun pointed at both of us. And then he fired his weapon, I moved seconds before he pulled the trigger. I saw the fire come out the barrel and I instinctually knew it was a gun. I looked at my friend Big Mike and saw he was struck in the chest or upper region because I saw blood spatter down his side."

Johnson said, "At no point in time did they struggle over the weapon because the weapon was already drawn on us." Johnson and a bloodied Mike Brown took-off running. Johnson hid behind the first car he saw. He said, "I saw the officer proceeding after my friend Big Mike with his gun drawn, and he fired a second shot and that struck my friend Big Mike, and at that time, he turned around with his hands up, beginning to tell the officer that he was unarmed and to tell him to stop shooting. But at that time, the officer fired several more shots into my friend, and he hit the ground and died."

Piaget Crenshaw

Piaget Crenshaw said she saw what happened from her apartment while waiting for her friend Tiffany Mitchell to pick her up for work. Crenshaw stated, "The officer was just trying to pull him into the vehicle – that's just what it looked like." She said, "He started chasing after the boy. I'm hearing shots fired... one did graze him... At the end he just turned around... and then was shot multiple times." Crenshaw continued, "He was running for his life and just got shot and turned around and didn't try to reach for anything. He put his hands in the air being compliant and he still got shot down like a dog."

Crenshaw can be heard on the cell phone video she took after the shooting, saying, "God bless his soul, the police shot this boy outside my apartment," When asked why she took the video she explained, "I knew this was not right. The fact that he got shot in his face, it was something that clicked in me like, no, somebody else needs to see this, this isn't right, I gotta record."

Tiffany Mitchell

Tiffany Mitchell arrived at the scene of the shooting to pick her friend up for work at the same time that Officer Darren Wilson and Michael Brown were beginning to struggle with each other. She said "I arrived whenever they were tussling through the window. It looked as if the kid was pulling away and the officer was pulling him in. I pulled out my phone to try to get a video because it just didn't look right, like I didn't know exactly what was going on but I know it didn't look right for someone to be wrassling with the police through the police window. But I didn't get the video because a shot was fired through the window so I tried to get out of the way. As I pulled onto the side, the kid, he finally gets away and he starts running. As he runs, the police gets out of his vehicle and he follows behind him shooting, and the kids body jerked, as if he was hit from behind and he turns around and he puts his hands up, like this, and the cop continued to fire until he just dropped down to the ground and his face just smacks the concrete."

When asked if it looked as if Brown was trying to grab the officer's weapon, as police have stated, Mitchell responded, "It looked as if he was trying to pull away. I saw his hand pushing up against the vehicle, as he was pulling off trying to get away from the cop." She then confirmed that she heard a gunshot, then says, "He finally gets away. He yanks away, and he runs away from the cop, away from the vehicle and the cop gets out of his vehicle and pursues him, shooting. When his body jerks, he turned around facing the cop and puts his hands in the air and that's when the cop continued to come up on him and shoot him until he fell down to the ground." After the shooting, she went to her friend's apartment and they both went to the balcony to witness the aftermath, and to call the news and her friends.

Michael Brady

Michael Brady was in his apartment across the street from the shooting. He ran to his window when he heard a commotion outside, and then ran outside to witness the final confrontation between Brown and Wilson.

Brady said, "By the time I gets outside, he's already turned around, facing the officer. He's balled-up, he had his arms under his stomach, he was half way down, like he was going down, and the officer lets off like 3 or 4 shots at him. Just like how his body is now on the ground, with his arms tucked-in - that is how he got shot." Brady claimed that Brown was falling down to the ground when he was shot. He said Brown was not running or charging the officer, but only took a couple steps towards the officer as he was going down to the ground after already being shot. Brady said he didn't see brown raise his hands over his head, as other witnesses described.

Emanuel Freeman - Live-Tweet Witness:

Twenty-nine-year-old Emanuel Freeman lives in a basement garage on Canfield Drive that overlooks the Michael Brown shooting scene. He live-tweeted what happened as it unfolded. His live tweets give a timestamp to what occurred, and when.

At 12:03 PM Emanuel Freeman, who goes by the Twitter handle "Thee Pharoah," live-tweeted the police shooting of Michael Brown that occurred right outside his basement apartment window. He tweeted, "I JUST SAW SOMEONE DIE." "I'M ABOUT TO HYPERVENTILATE." At 12:04 he tweeted, "The police just shot someone dead in front of my crib yo." At 12:05 Thee Paroah tweeted a picture of Officer Darren Wilson standing over a dead Michael Brown, with another patrol officer standing next to him. Thee Pharoah then tweeted, "Fuckfuckfuck." At 12:06 he tweeted, "its blood all over the street, niggas protesting nshit. There is police tape all over my building. I'm stuck in here omg." At 1:13 he tweeted, "Bruh, I'm so upset." When Thee Pharoah was asked why the boy was shot, he answered back at 12:14 saying, "no reason! He was running!" At 12:15 he tweeted "I saw it happen." At 12:23 Thee Paroah tweeted, "dude was running and the cops just shot him. I saw him die bruh." At 12:59 he tweeted, "he looked like 18 to 19. His parents out here tripping now." When asked if any of the shots were fired at Brown from behind, he responded at 1:01, "the first two was, the next 5 weren't, he turned around." At 1:14 he tweeted, "The first two was clear, then it was a barrage of them shits." At 2:14 Thee Pharoah tweeted a picture of an officer going by his window with an assault rifle. He said, "Nigga got an AR." At 2:36 he tweeted, "Homie still on the ground tho." When Thee Pharoah tweeted, "I AM DONE TWEETING ABOUT THE SITUATION," The No Justice No Peace coalition tweeted back to tell him, "PLEASE stay safe. You're the most important person in America right now." Another follower responded, "Lawyer up. Don't speak with media. I'm serious, brother. Please get a lawyer."

Emanuel Freeman did get a lawyer and he also eventually spoke to a reporter about the incident. In an interview with Vice News he complained about having to talk to the FBI about what he saw and having to get an attorney. When asked if he has spoken to the Brown family at all after the shooting, he said he had not, but then revealed that is would be difficult for him to do so because, he said, "I don't know if I could look his mom in the eyes without being emotionally affected."

Freedman, who is an aspiring rapper, wrote a song to express his viewpoint, saying "Song is my best form of communication so I wrote this song."

3rd Party Statement from Officer Darren Wilson:

The only account coming from Darren Wilson soon after the shooting was during a St. Louis radio show that conducted an interview with a lady who called herself "Josie." Syndicated radio show host Dana Loesch interviewed the woman who said she knew Wilson, on "The Dana Show." She claimed to be a friend of Officer Wilson's girlfriend and that she wanted to get Wilson's story out to the public so people would know his version. She claimed she was given a play-by-play recap of what happened.

"Josie" said, "It's been really, really hard to be quiet because I do know his version of the story. It seems like everyone only is talking about the other side. I understand they haven't gotten to hear this side and I have been afraid to say anything. I think we all are. I just needed to put out there his version of events so maybe people can consider them as the truth, if nothing else."

She then explained what she was told by Wilson's girlfriend. She said:

> They were walking in the middle of the street. He rolled his window down and said, 'Come on guys. Get out of the street.' They refused to and were yelling back, saying we're almost where we're going and there was some cussing involved. He just kept on rolling up and he pulled over and I believe at that point he calls for backup but I'm not sure. I know he pulled up ahead of them and he was watching them and then he gets a call about a strong arm robbery and he gets the description and he's looking at them and they've got something in their hands that looked like it could be those cigars or whatever. So he goes in reverse back to them. Tries to get out of his car, they slam his door shut violently, I think he said Michael did, and then he opens his car again, you know tries to get out, and as he stands up Michael just bum rushes him, just shoves him back into the car. Punches him in the face and then of course Darren grabs for his gun and Michael grabs the gun. At one point he's got the gun totally turned against his hip and Darren he shoves it away and the gun goes off. Michael takes off with his friend. They get to be about 35 feet away, and of you know Darren of course protocol is to pursue. So he stands up and yells, 'Freeze!' Michael and his friend turn around and Michael starts taunting him. 'Oh, what are you going to do about it? You're not gonna shoot me.' And then he said all of a sudden he just started to bum rush him. He just started coming at him full-speed so he just started shooting and he just kept coming. So he really thinks he was on something because he just kept coming. It was unbelievable. And then so he finally ended up, the final shot was in the forehead and then he fell about 2, 3 feet in front of the officer.

"Josie" said she was told this story by Wilson's girlfriend on Sunday night, August 10th, after the riots began. She also mentioned at the end of the interview, "Of course ballistics will show he wasn't shot in the back."

After the Shooting:

Michael Brown's relatives were at the scene shortly after the shooting. They were notified by a family friend who drove by the area of the shooting and recognized Brown's body lying in the street. When Michael's mother and extended family arrived, they were cordoned off by the police and refused any access to Michael's body or any information about what happened. Brown's mother stood behind a yellow police tape line, wondering what happened, and wishing her son would be covered up, taken off of the street and shown a little more respect. Mr. Brown's stepfather, Louis Head, said he was kept away from the body and denied any information about the shooting. He was outraged. "Nobody came to nobody and said, Hey, we're sorry," he said. "Nobody said nothing." Mr. Brown's uncle, Bernard Ewing, ducked under the yellow police-line tape to get a closer look but he was immediately ejected by a cop who screamed at him to get back, and then quickly ran over to escort him away from the body. Ewing later stated in an interview, "I went up to it. I seen the body, and I recognized the body. That's when the dude grabbed me." He said he pleaded with the officer for information about what happened to his nephew but the police wouldn't say. Mr. Ewing remembers asking the police officer who was escorting him; "A cop did this?" but he received no reply, except for a warning to not go near the body again.

Michael's grandmother, Desiree Harris, saw her grandson walking through the neighborhood while she was driving home just a few moments before he was shot. When she arrived home she heard a commotion and then went outside to see her grandson dead on the ground.

Police eventually placed a white sheet over the corpse, and then placed an orange car-crash partition around him, but it was too late to appease the crowd. Too many people had arrived, witnessed what occurred, taken pictures and video, and now activists and the media were beginning to arrive. The mayhem was about to begin.

Even though the St. Louis County Police Department was on the scene shortly after the incident occurred, it took their homicide detectives almost one and a half hours to arrive. The Police Department waited 40 minutes to call the detectives and dispatch them to the crime scene. An investigator from the Medical Examiners Office would take an additional hour to arrive. It took until about 2:30 in the afternoon for both investigators to be on the scene and begin to process the corpse. The investigation cannot proceed until both officers are at the scene. Michael Brown died at 12:01. His body lay in the street, in front of the crowd, for over two hours before detectives and the medical examiner began doing their investigation. The body was not removed from the street for over four hours from when Brown was shot. This was one of the issues that provoked so much outrage and community resentment, and also allowed the antagonists in the crowd to ramp-up their rhetoric.

Patricia Bynes, a committeewoman from Ferguson, said, "The delay helped fuel the outrage, It was very disrespectful to the community and the people who live there. It also sent the message from law enforcement that 'we can do this to you any day, any time, in broad daylight, and there's nothing you can do about it.'"

The Mayor of St. Louis confirmed that the city has a very specific policy on how to deal with a dead body. He said, "About 80 percent of the time, the body is generally taken away immediately, and if the body remains at the scene, we'll block off the area. We'll cover the body appropriately with screening or tents, so it's not exposed to the public. We do the investigation as quickly as we can."

Dr. Michael Baden, The medical examiner who was later hired by the Brown family to do their own impartial autopsy, believed it was a mistake for the police to leave the body in the street for such a long time. Dr. Baden is a former New York City chief medical examiner who had performed over 20,000 autopsies in the past. He said, "In my opinion, it's not necessary to leave a body in a public place for that many hours, particularly given the temperature and the fact that people are around." He said. "There is no forensic reason for doing that."

Ferguson Police Chief Tom Jackson thought the delay was justified. He stated, "You only get one chance at that crime scene." Jackson said authorities also were concerned about gunfire they could hear from a nearby building, which might have delayed the investigation.

Police added additional fuel to the fire by desecrating the makeshift memorial that Brown's mother erected for him on the spot of his death. Missouri State Representative Sharon Pace, whose district includes Ferguson, said she went to the scene of the shooting to comfort the parents. She helped Brown's mother place candles and flowers on the ground where Brown had died. "They spelled out his initials with rose petals over the bloodstains," but soon after the memorial was constructed the police closed Canfield Drive and then let one of their police dogs urinate on the memorial, in plain view of all of the bystanders. Then, police cars repeatedly drove over the memorial in what the crowd believed was an overt act of aggression against the community. Protesters began to walk into the street to block the police cars from further desecration of Michael Brown's memorial.

One community activist summed-up the feelings of many of the Ferguson residents. He said, "the people in the community saw the way Brown's body was handled as a deliberate act of intimidation, echoing the slavery era, when somebody was beaten or lynched and they made everybody come out and watch. The Ferguson police force has a us against them attitude, and they care nothing at all about the people who pay their salaries and that they have sworn to serve and protect."

County police spokesman Officer Brian Schellman claims St. Louis county police tried to process the crime scene right away. He said the investigators "usually go straight to their jobs, but they couldn't do that right away because there weren't enough police there to quiet the situation and officials were contending with what they described as 'sheer chaos' on Canfield Drive, where bystanders, including at least one of Mr. Brown's relatives, frequently stepped inside the yellow tape, hindering investigators."

National Association for the Advancement of Colored People (NAACP) Reaction:

The NAACP was quick to put out a statement about the death of Michael Brown. In a written statement the day of Brown's death, St. Louis County NAACP President Esther Haywood said:

We are hurt to hear that yet another teenaged boy has been slaughtered by law enforcement, especially in light of the recent death of Eric Garner in New York who was killed for selling cigarettes. We plan to do everything within our power to ensure that the Ferguson Police Department as well as the St. Louis County Police Department releases all details pertinent to the shooting.

The Grassy Knoll:

After Michael Brown was shot, bystanders and witnesses gathered on a grassy knoll between an apartment building parking lot and the street where Brown was killed, in an area the media would soon converge on. In the crowd, immediately after the shooting, was Michael Brown's mother Lesley McSpadden, her boyfriend Louis Head, Mike Brown's uncle Calvin Swings, witness Dorian Johnson, witness Piaget Crenshaw, witness Tiffany Mitchell, and St. Louis race-baiter and police antagonist Anthony Shahid. It has been suggested that Shahid was responsible for much of the provocation that incited the initial rioting. Some people believe Shahid came-up with the slogan Hand's-up, Don't Shoot, which the witnesses then repeated to the media the day of the shooting, and thereafter. It's interesting to note that several of the "Grassy Knoll bystanders" later stated that Michael Brown was shot down like a dog. It was the same proclamation that Anthony Shahid made at the scene of the shooting and a phrase he uses quite frequently.

Police Department Protest:

In the early evening of August 9th, Michael Brown's mother, community members and activists converged on the Ferguson police department to protest the shooting. Mrs. Brown ranted into a news-crew camera, "You don't do a dog like that. You didn't have to shoot him eight times. If he was doing something to you and you was trying to stop him, where do the police shoot you? In the leg. You just shot all through my baby's body." The reporter then asked Mrs. Brown if her son had done anything wrong. She explained, "I don't know. They say he might have taken something from the QuickTrip, but I don't care, he had no gun. He throw his hands up when the police ran over to him, the boy threw his hands up. He threw his hand up. And he shot him, then the boy fell and then he shot him some more." When asked by a reporter about what she knew, Mrs. Brown responded, "They aren't telling me anything. They haven't told me anything. They wouldn't even let me identify my son. The only way I knew it was my son was from people out here showing me his picture."

CHAPTER 24

DAY-2
SUNDAY
AUGUST-10

At a 10 a.m. press conference, St. Louis County Police Chief Jon Belmar gave a statement and answered questions from a small group of reporters to explain the incident surrounding the shooting and death of Michael Brown the previous day. Chief Belmar said Brown had physically assaulted the officer, and during a struggle between the two, Brown reached for the officer's gun. One shot was fired in the car followed by other gunshots outside of the car. Mr. Brown was shot multiple times and died at the scene.

Chief Belmar began the press conference by asking the media what questions he was going to be asked, and then explained that he didn't have time for much media and he was not going to answer a lot of questions after his speech. He told the reporters to give him some sample questions "right now" so he could decide if he was going to address them in his briefing. Some of the questions from the media were: did he have a weapon, what happened, what led up to this, what led to the officer firing his weapon.

Chief Belmar then made the following statement to the press:

> *Yesterday at about noon at the 2900 block of Canfield a Ferguson police officer had an encounter with two individuals on the street. In fact, one of those individuals at the time came in as the police officer was exiting the police car and allegedly pushed the police officer back into the car where he physically assaulted the police officer. It is our understanding at this point in the investigation that within the police car there was a struggle over the officer's weapon. There was at least one shot fired within the car. After that the officer came back out of the car, he exited his vehicle and there was a shooting that occurred where the officer in fact shot the subject and they were fatal injuries.*
>
> *The entire scene from approximately the car door to the shooting is about 35 feet. There were shell casings recovered. The shell casings are all matched to one weapon, that's the officer's weapon. There were more than a few shell casing recovered. I cannot say at this time how many times the suspect was struck by gunfire. It's hard to know. It was more than just a couple but I don't think it was many more than that. The medical examiner is conducting an investigation today to determine that and please keep in mind that it will take as long as 6 weeks for the toxicologists reports to come back on this."*

Chief Belmar tried to contain any comments about leaving Brown's body in the street for 4 hours. He said:

> *I would like everybody here to appreciate that it took a very long time yesterday to process the scene. We only get one opportunity to take a look at these scenes. They are only the scene one time. There were a lot of folks down there. Their emotions were running very high. I know that we certainly understand that. I know Chief Jackson of the Ferguson police department appreciates that, but we felt like that we had to practice our due diligence down there on this scene and that is why it took as long as it did. I feel we've done a very good job regarding the investigation. The officer who was involved has been on the police department for about 6 years and I am unaware of any other issues that he has been involved in during his employment with the city of Ferguson. We also will be interviewing that officer more extensively today. We had an opportunity*

to speak with him of course yesterday but because to the dynamics of the scene we didn't get to spend as much time with him as we would have preferred so a very comprehensive interview will be conducted with that officer today, who is in fact on administrative leave. Before he comes back, Chief Jackson assures me that he will have to go through two different psychological evaluations before he will be able to return back to duty. That's basically what's going on with it. Again, the investigation is continuing. I would like to be able to answer more questions than that."

The Chief was asked whether the subject was armed with a handgun or any other weapon. He said, "The answer to that is no. It started out, the genesis of this was a physical confrontation.

The Chief then rushed out of the room without answering additional questions. During the press conference a group of protesters could be heard outside the room, either from within the building or outside on the street, chanting - "Don't shoot, Don't shoot." Chief Belmar tried not to be distracted as he gave his prepared speech to the press, but he was clearly upset at the interruption.

Benjamin Crump press release:

Civil rights activist attorney Benjamin Crump, who previously represented Treyvon Martin's family during the Sanford Orlando shooting death of the black teenager by a neighborhood watch volunteer, put out a press release stating that he would be representing the family of Michael Brown. The press release then listed the location and time of a press conference the attorney would be holding the following afternoon, in Jennings, Missouri, with the family of Michael Brown. The press release stated:

August 10, 2014

MEDIA ALERT

FAMILY OF MICHAEL BROWN RETAINS NATIONAL CIVIL RIGHTS ATTORNEY, BENJAMIN L. CRUMP, IN MISSOURI POLICE SHOOTING DEATH OF 18-YEAR-OLD MICHAEL BROWN

Who: The family of Michael Brown and their attorney, Benjamin L. Crump, Esq. of Parks & Crump, LLC.

What: Members of the Brown family along with their attorney, will share developments in the Ferguson MO police shooting death of Michael Brown and speak with members of the media.

When: Monday, August 11, 2014 at 4:00 PM CDT

Where: Jennings Mason Temple Church of God in Christ. 2120 McClean Avenue, Jennings, MO 63136.

Quicktrip Looted and Burned - Snitches get Stitches:

After a candlelight vigil that attracted thousands of supporters honoring Michael Brown, protesters streamed into the streets and began to block Florissant Road. They held their hands high in the air, chanting "We want answers" and "No justice, no peace."

As the crowd grew, they became more agitated and unruly. Some of them began banging on patrol cars as the cruisers went down the street. The police didn't confront them. They just kept on driving. Some rioters stood on top of police cars, antagonizing and taunting law enforcement. Protesters stormed the police station and repeatedly chanted "Don't shoot me." until they moved-on, out onto the streets.

At about 8 p.m., a crowd began chanting - No Justice, No Peace, and then looted, burned and destroyed at least 12 businesses, including a convenience store, check-cashing store, grocery store, sporting goods store, clothing boutique, automotive store, cellular store, beauty supply store, liquor stores and other retail businesses that the local community depended on. Bus stops were damaged, vehicles were vandalized, storefront windows were broken, merchandise was stolen and buildings were burned to the ground. The police reported sporadic gunfire throughout the night. The Quicktrip was the first business to be destroyed. It wasn't a random act of violence.

Although the police contend the Quicktrip was spontaneously looted and burned, the people in the neighborhood know it was due to rumors that Michael Brown had robbed the Quicktrip, so neighbors thought an employee at the Quicktrip called the police on

Brown and got him killed, so the Quicktrip was the first to burn. On the day Brown was killed, his mother mistakenly stated during a TV interview that Michael was coming back from "Quicktrip." The community, after becoming enflamed during the demonstrations earlier in the day took their revenge on that store, which spilled over to other businesses. On the outside wall of the Quicktrip convenience store, a message was spray-pained all across the entire side of the building. The message said, "Snitches get Stitches."

Quicktrip spokesman Michael Thornbrugh said the store is a "total loss" and that it's too early for the company to decide whether it will rebuild or not. He estimated the loss will likely total seven figures. The company is leaving all security issues to the Missouri State Highway Patrol. When asked about store security, Thornbrugh stated, "With all due respect, there's nothing left to protect."

QuikTrip also closed another store that is only 3 miles from Ferguson in fear of more violence. Quicktrip had temporarily closed a recently opened "Generation 3" super store a few miles away, as a precaution against other potential violence. Thornbrugh said, "It's a day-by-day decision. This whole situation is tragic and sad."

Ferguson's mayor, James Knowles, blamed the rioting on a few bad apples. He said, "Right now, the small group of people are creating a huge mess. We're only hurting ourselves, only hurting our community, hurting our neighbors. There's nothing productive from this. We understand people want to vent their frustrations. We understand they want to speak out. We're going to obviously try to urge calm."

The rioting was not contained in Ferguson--it began to spread across St. Louis County and throughout the rest of the country.

CHAPTER 25

DAY-3
MONDAY
AUGUST-11

5:00 a.m. - Early on Monday morning the Jennings School District, around Ferguson, cancelled their first day of classes for area elementary school students because of the rioting that occurred the previous night, and out of concern for the safety of children walking to school.

Ferguson police and city leaders report mass rioting on Sunday night and claimed they had received, through social media, a number of online death threats against police officers.

10:00 a.m. – Hundreds gather outside the Ferguson Police Department to demand justice for Brown's death. Police arrest at least seven people.

11:00 a.m. – The Federal Bureau of Investigation opened an investigation into Mr. Brown's death, focusing on whether or not the civil rights of Mr. Brown had been violated. St. Louis County police are also conducting an investigation into the shooting. Attorney General Eric Holder said the parallel FBI review "will supplement, rather than supplant," the local investigation. He said, "The shooting incident in Ferguson, Missouri this weekend deserves a fulsome review. At every step, we will work with the local investigators, who should be prepared to complete a thorough, fair investigation in their own right. Aggressively pursuing investigations such as this is critical for preserving trust between law enforcement and the communities they serve." Justice Department spokesperson Dena Iverson confirmed that Attorney General Eric Holder had already instructed attorneys in the Justice Department "to monitor developments relating to the shooting incident."

St. Louis FBI Spokesperson Cheryl Mimura said, "We have initiated a civil rights investigation. The FBI is monitoring the case and working with St. Louis County police." Mimura noted that the FBI would be investigating such a shooting regardless of the public attention.

NAACP president Cornell William Brooks released a statement from the organization saying, "The death of yet another African American at the hands of those sworn to protect and serve the community where he lived is heartbreaking."

2:00 p.m. – The St. Louis County Police Department announced that it would release the name of the officer who was accused of shooting Brown the following day, on Tuesday afternoon.

4:00 p.m. – The parents of Michael Brown spoke to the public alongside Cornell William Brooks, president of the National Association for the Advancement of Colored People (NAACP), family attorney Benjamin Crump, and St. Louis civil rights activist Anthony Shahid, in a press conference at the Jennings Mason Temple Church of God in Christ. The Brown family asked people to stop the violence, but also demanded justice for Michael.

Lesley McSpadden, the mother of Michael Brown, stood at a podium clutching a picture of her son. When she began to deliver her speech she broke down in tears and couldn't continue, so Michael Brown's father stepped in to give the opening remarks. Michael Brown Senior wore a T-shirt showing his son's baby picture silk-screened onto the front. He said, "Our son is the best son we ever had. He was funny, silly. He would make you laugh. Any problems that were going on or any situation, there wasn't anything he couldn't handle. He would bring people back together. He was a good boy. He didn't deserve any of this. We need justice for our son. We need justice for our son. I want justice for our son."

Brown's mother chimed in to say, "No violence, no violence." Then her attorney Benjamin Crump, who was standing behind her, prompted her to hold up the picture of her son.

Brown's mother held a picture of Michael above her head and told the press, "He just graduated from high school. He was on his way to college. We can't even celebrate, we've got to plan a funeral." She then broke down again and cried, and couldn't continue to speak.

Civil rights activist attorney Benjamin Crump asked Mr. Brown Sr. to speak again. Michael Brown senior told the crowd "We need answers, we need answers. If you have any information please, please give it to us."

Brown's mother interrupted to say, "He didn't deserve none of this."

Mr. Brown senior continued, "We need to know everything. We want everything. We want this done. We're going to do this right. I don't want no violence. We don't want no violence." Michael Brown's mother interrupted again, to say, "Because Michael wouldn't want no violence."

Mr. Brown then said, "He (Michael) wouldn't have wanted none of this. None of it. None of it. He would want us to do it right so that's why we're doing it right. We're going to do it the right way. But we need justice for our son."

Benjamin Crump stepped-in to launch another verbal assault on the Ferguson Police Department. He said, "The witnesses have come forward and said it did not happen as the police said it happened, and you only got their version of what happened, not the witnesses version that happened, and thanks to the NAACP, and others, they are helping secure those witnesses to turn over to the justice department. And we think it would be very clear when all this is over what really happened and how this child was executed."

Michael Brown's mother then continued her statement to the press. She said, "That's my first born son. Anybody who knew me knows how I felt about my son. I just wish I could have been there to help him. Anything. He didn't deserve that. My son." Then she broke down in tears again.

Crump quickly stepped back in front of the podium to address the press, and went into a diatribe about inequalities for blacks in America and then listed other youths across America, such as Jordan Davis, Kendrick Johnson and Eric Gardner, who have also recently been victims of police brutality. He said "it's so many situations that it's beginning to become a cliché, and to others it's a cliché, but to us, it's our children. So it's very personal."

Crump continued, "This family is very distrustful. This community is very distrustful. Brother Anthony Shahib has talked to us over and over again about the pattern that exists and why people are just frustrated. They are devastated. They are devastated that this happens again and again, and it's swept under the rug again and again. Not this time."

Crump pleaded for any witnesses to come forward to provide video tape accounts of what happened. He stated, "We want you in the public to know, if you were a witness to what happened. Don't feel intimidated. Come forward. There are people in Washington D.C. who will make themselves available to you, from the Justice Department, to give your statements without any intimidation or fear of retribution. When all the cameras go. These folks are coming in from Washington to try to help this family get answers. If you in the public have video recordings that you were concerned about giving to the local law enforcement authorities, we beg you, we beg you, to turn those recordings over, either a copy to the NAACP, the lawyers of the national bar or a family member. Just get us a copy of that video because we want to know and see exactly what happened because this family rejects what the police authorities said at their press conference about how this played out. The witnesses reject what the police said at their press conference how this played out. These parents know in their own heart and they reject what the police authorities said at their press conference how this played out. So they expect, they demand, and they will not shut-up until they get the truth, because they knew who their son was."

During interviews with reporters after the press conference, Crump continued his rhetoric. He said, "What every parent wants is simple justice. Nothing extraordinary. Nothing special. If that was your child lying on the ground shot in broad daylight, in broad daylight, wouldn't you want equal justice, due process of the law, and to get answers?"

When asked about the confrontation between Michael Brown and officer Wilson, Crump tried to deflect the answer, but the president of the National Association for the Advancement of Colored People (NAACP) stepped in to explain that "they did not want to discuss facts."

St. Louis local activist Anthony Shahid then went on a rage-filled racial rant, saying:

> *What we want to do is to make sure that the Federal government comes in, or justice department comes in, and they start working on some of these things that are happening here. When you break-out 25 dogs after a young baby who is lying on the ground for 4 1/2 hours and don't understand our pain. These people are very insensitive towards us. And this is purposely done. In the city of Ferguson alone, they have 53 police, 50 of them are white boys, only 3 blacks. And this is like this in most principalities. I'll give you a better one. City of St. Louis, they just promoted 15 white sergeants, and 16 white boy lieutenants and one black. And you want to know why we feel like we feel, because we have been shot in the street like dogs, like niggers. They have destroyed us.*

The reporter tried to pull back her mike once he said nigger, but Crump quickly told her to move the microphone back, and then continued his diatribe. He said:

> *We have been killed like niggers in the street. You all have been treating us like this in the city of St. Louis, not in Afghanistan, not in Iraq. Our problem ain't with Hamas, our problem is right here in the United States of America where you are shooting us dead like dogs and niggers.*

A reporter who was recording the post-press-conference interview pulled back her microphone and said she appreciated his time and emotion in all of this, and then cut back to the studio as quickly as she could, to get Shahid off the air.

Anthony D. Gray, another lawyer working with attorney Crump on the Michael Brown case, said he had misgivings about the objectivity of law enforcement officials in St. Louis County. He said they had conducted interviews with police officials who were on the scene when Brown was shot, but had failed to interview any of the witnesses. He said, "I believe St. Louis County lost their objectivity. There is video footage that the police confiscated. The police asked one young lady who was a witness for her phone. The police have what we think is raw footage. We're not here to indict all police officers. We have strong suspicions on this one."

6 p.m. – The NAACP hosted a prayer vigil for community members and civil rights leaders. NAACP president Cornell William Brooks released the following statement to the press:

Our prayers go out to the family and friends of 18-year-old Michael Brown of Ferguson, Missouri. The death of yet another African American at the hands of those sworn to protect and serve the community where he lived is heartbreaking. Michael Brown was preparing to begin college, and now his family is preparing to bury their child--his life cut short in a tragic encounter with the police. As the NAACP's Missouri State Conference and St. Louis Branches seek answers about the circumstances surrounding Michael Brown's death, the National office will remain vigilant until accountability and justice are served for the countless individuals who lose their lives to misguided police practices throughout the country. Even as we call for accountability by those charged with protecting the community, we call on the community to act--collectively and calmly until we secure justice for the family of Michael Brown.

Social media sites were on fire with Ferguson postings. Teens around the world began using the hashtag #IfTheyGunnedMeDown. The posts on Twitter and Instagram showed pictures of each teenager in two different looks — one smiling and one looking tough, with a caption asking which photo they would use if they were shot by police, implying that anyone could be labeled as a saint or a sinner, based on the pictures used to represent them.

CHAPTER 26

DAY-4
TUESDAY
AUGUST-11

10 a.m. – Protesters gathered at St. Louis County Police Department headquarters for a peaceful protest. A list of demands was given to law enforcement relating to the investigation of Brown's death.

Ferguson Police Chief Tom Jackson reconsidered his decision to release the name of the officer involved in the shooting of Michael Brown. He decided to withhold the officer's name due to social media threats made against the police department and city hall. Chief Jackson claimed that the department can legally refuse to release the name of an officer if they believe his safety is at risk. Otherwise they have 72 hours to release an officer's name when asked, as per Missouri's Sunshine State law. He said, "The value of releasing the name is far outweighed by the risk of harm to the officer and his family."

A group of peaceful protesters numbering several hundreds converged on the St. Louis prosecutor's office chanting, "Who do you serve? Who do you protect?" Then chanting, "No justice, no peace," before roaming down the streets of Clayton, yelling, "Hands up, don't shoot."

Citing reports from the St. Louis county police that their helicopter had been fired upon, the Federal Aviation Administration issued a temporary flight restriction, restricting aircraft from operating under 3,000 feet in the airspace around Ferguson. Officer Brian Schellman claimed the police helicopter was shot at "a couple of different times."

Noon - Rev. Al Sharpton arrived in St. Louis to speak to the family of Brown. He made his way around the St. Louis area to demand justice in the fatal shooting. Sharpton and the Brown family spoke on the Old Courthouse steps early Tuesday afternoon.

The American Civil Liberties Union (ACLU) filed a formal request with the Ferguson Police Department and the St. Louis County Police Department for a copy of the incident report naming the officer who shot Michael Brown. The requests were made under the Sunshine State law provisions which require government agencies to provide requested public information within three days after the request is made, or explain why the request cannot be complied with. ACLU of Missouri communications director Diane Balogh said the group filed the requests to find out the identity of the police officer involved in Michael Browns shooting. The Ferguson Police Department claimed they were going to release the name of the police officer on Tuesday, but decided against it because of threats to the officer. She added, "The police like their secrets." Balogh said, "If they don't follow through, we will file a lawsuit and hold a press conference. There have been other situations where we've actually had to sue the police department because they haven't fulfilled the Sunshine Law requirements."

A letter by ACLU Executive Director Jeffrey Mittman stated:

To Whom It May Concern:

This letter is a request under the Missouri Sunshine Law. Pursuant to the provisions of Chapter 610 of the Missouri Revised Statutes, we request that you provide a copy of the incident report for the shooting of Michael Brown on August 9, 2014.

If any part of this request is denied, please send a letter listing the specific exemptions upon which you rely each denial, and provide the contact information for the official to whom we may appeal. Mo. Rev. Stat 610.023.4. This request must "be acted upon as soon as possible, but in no event later than the end of the third business day following the date the request is received."

On Tuesday, St. Louis County Police Chief Jon Belmar became the target of an online attack by the hacktavist organization "Anonymous," in an attempt to pressure the Chief to release the name of the officer who shot Michael Brown. Chief Belmar's home address, phone number, and a picture of his house were posted on-line and sent out through Twitter. The hackers also posted a picture of someone inside Belmar's house who was sleeping on his couch. A caption on the image read, "He sees you when you sleep, he knows when you're awake." Another image was posted of the Chief's wife and daughter. On Sunday, the day after Brown was killed, Anonymous warned St. Louis police "there will be consequences." When their demands went unanswered, Anonymous took action and launched their "awareness campaign," which they called "Operation Ferguson." In a letter to law-enforcement preceding the release of officer Belmar's pictures and personal information, Anonymous made the following threats:

Anonymous "Operation Ferguson" Press Release:

A little over 24 hours ago in Ferguson, Missouri - USA the Ferguson Police Department shot an un-armed teen 6 times and killed him. His body was left to lie in a pool of blood in the sweltering heat for hours while the police militarized the area against protesters and attempted to concoct a reasonable story as to why they snatched this innocent student's life for no reason. The St. Louis County Sheriff Department even sealed the roads leading to Ferguson in a vain attempt to prevent protesters from reaching the city. His name was Mike Brown, he was 17 - and he would have started college next week. Instead, his family is struggling to come up with funeral costs.

The entire global collective of Anonymous is outraged at this cold blooded murder of a young teen. Not a week goes by that some young person, usually of minority ethnicity - is slaughtered by murderous police in the

USA. For this reason Anonymous will not be satisfied this time, as we have in the past - with simply obtaining justice for this young man and his family. Anonymous demands that the Congressional Representatives and Senators from Missouri introduce legislation entitled "Mike Brown's Law" that will set strict national standards for police conduct in the USA. We further demand that this new law include specific language to grant the victims of police violence the same rights and prerogatives that are already enjoyed nationwide by the victims of other violent criminals. The Equal Protection clause of the US Constitution demands nothing less.

To the good people of Ferguson, take heart - and take your streets. You are not alone, we will support you in every way possible. Occupy every square inch of your city. Open your homes and help in any way you can the protesters who will come to your city from every part of Missouri and the USA. Businesses and householders that are near protest rallies, open your WiFi routers so that live streamers and other independent journalists can use the Internet connections. Feed each other, keep each other safe - and stay in the streets until we are totally victorious in all our demands.

To the Ferguson Police Department and any other jurisdictions who are deployed to the protests: we are watching you very closely. If you abuse, harass - or harm in any way the protesters in Ferguson we will take every web based asset of your departments and governments off line. That is not a threat, it is a promise. If you attack the protesters, we will attack every server and computer you have. We will release the personal information on every single member of the Ferguson Police Department, as well as any other jurisdiction that participates in the abuse. We will seize all your databases and E-Mail spools and dump them on the Internet. This is your only warning.

The time has come for more than simple justice for these atrocities. The time has come to draw a line in the sand and say no more dead kids, no more police killings and beatings. Anonymous is drawing a line in the sand, and that line runs right down the middle of Main Street Ferguson, Missouri. Police impunity ends with the barbaric death of Mike Brown.

We Are Anonymous - We Are Legion - We Will Not Forgive - We Will Not Forget

EXPECT JUSTICE - DEMAND CHANGE

Web Site - www.OperationFerguson.cf

Twitter - twitter.com/OpFerguson

Chief Belmar had been warned that the group intended to release his personal information and gave him the opportunity to be transparent. They sent him a message stating, "Jon Belmar, if you don't release the officer's name, we're releasing your daughter's info. You have one hour." Chief Belmar refused to disclose the name of the officer, so Anonymous carried out their threat and released his home address and pictures of his house, wife and daughter. It wasn't the first attack by this group of hackers. On Sunday, they took down the Ferguson Police Department's website, Twitter account, and email delivery system, to show Ferguson they weren't fooling.

Gun sales go up:

Gun sales in St. Louis county have been on the rise since the riots erupted. Gun store owners reported a huge surge of purchases. Steven King, owner of Metro Shooting, says his sales have quadrupled. He stated, "Probably a dozen or two dozen guns to females, single mothers. We've sold to black people, white people. We've sold to Asians who have businesses on West Florissant. They're just afraid of what's going on and they're coming in to purchase either additional firearms or their first firearm." He claimed his customers have raided their savings accounts to buy weaponry and ammunitions. He said, "they feel it is worth any price to feel safe." When asked what his clients are looking for, he explained, "They're buying AR-15s, home defense shotguns, handguns, personal defense handguns something for concealed carry."

4 p.m. – In his first comments about the Ferguson rioting, President Barack Obama called for calm, saying:

The death of Michael Brown is heartbreaking, and Michelle and I send our deepest condolences to his family and his community at this very difficult time. I know the events of the past few days have prompted strong passions, but as details unfold, I urge everyone in Ferguson, Missouri, and across the country, to remember this young man through

*reflection and understanding. We should comfort each other and talk
with one another in a way that heals, not in a way that wounds. Along
with our prayers, that's what Michael and his family, and our broader
American community, deserve."*

7 p.m. – Gov. Jay Nixon, the City of St. Louis Mayor and other
area leaders, came together to speak on the Brown case. At a
separate public meeting, Rev. Al Sharpton and the Brown family
urged a peaceful fight toward justice for Michael Brown. Reverend
Al Sharpton walked hand-in-hand with the Brown family and a group
of supporters, encouraging people to attend his sermon in the
Greater St. Mark Missionary Baptist Church.

Sharpton began that sermon by railing against the
establishment. When discussing the belief that Brown had his hands
up in the air when he was shot, Sharpton said, "That's the sign you
got to deal with. Deal with the last sign he had shown. We want
answers why that sign was not respected." He went on to say, "I
know you are angry. I know this is outrageous. When I saw that
picture (of Brown's body in the street), it rose up in me an outrage.
But we cannot be more outraged than his mom and dad. If they can
hold their heads in dignity, then we can hold our heads up in dignity.
To become violent in Michael Brown's name is to betray the gentle
giant that he was. Don't be a traitor to Michael Brown."

10 p.m. – After a peaceful gathering of protesters on Tuesday
night, a crowd of unruly rioters provoked the police to respond. Law
enforcement moved-in to ban everyone from the protest site. Many
witnesses claim the police acted out-of-control and unlawfully. St.
Ann Police Lieutenant Ray Albers went berserk. He was caught on
video screaming at protesters to "Get back or I will fucking kill
you." When asked what his name was, the officer responded "go
fuck yourself."

CHAPTER 27

DAY-5
WEDNESDAY
AUGUST-12

10 a.m. – A number of community volunteers got together in the parking lot of the Baptist Church of Ferguson to hold a prayer vigil, followed by a group effort to clean up the streets and help the city start to pick up the pieces after the past few days of rioting. Erica Hampton had been helping to clean up the streets of Ferguson since rioting first tore through her town. She was concerned that the rioters had set a bad example for her son. She is trying to reverse what her son had witnessed by doing good, and giving back to the community, by cleaning up the mess the rioters had left in their wake. Hampton said, "I had to teach my son that this is just not what we do. When we want to get something done, we do it right. It's not about destroying." She claims the clean up effort began through word of mouth. As members of the community heard what she was doing, they offered to join-in and help-out. She said, "I'm all for justice and I want justice to prevail, don't get me wrong. But it's the way you go about it. We're just trying to let everyone know and

show everybody that we can do this in a positive way, keep our community clean. If we're going to do it together without destroying our community." Reggie Harris, another community clean up volunteer, echoed the sentiments of Erica Hampton. She said, "We've got to start somewhere. As long as you start somewhere. That's the beginning. You've got a lot of people who want to follow through and do the same thing. You just gotta start somewhere on a positive note."

The St. Louis County Police Department denied the public records request by Michael Hill of the Missouri American Civil Liberties Union (ACLU) for the Incident Report of the Mike Brown Shooting.

The St. Louis County Police Department Records Room sent a letter to the ACLU denying their request submitted the previous day, to release the incident report regarding the Michael Brown shooting. The handwritten letter stated:

Mr. Hill,

In ref to your request for incident report involving Michael Brown, This is an on-going investigation and we are unable to release a copy at this time.

The incident report was eventually released on August 20th, two days after a civil rights activist requested the report for a second time. His second request pointed out that the "Incident" report was distinct from the "Report of the Investigation," and that only the "Report of the Investigation" is exempt. The Incident Report that was released was created on August 19th, 10 days after the shooting incident and 1-day after it was proven that the Incident Report could not be kept from the public. Not surprisingly, the Incident Report, once it was finally released, provided no clues, except those leading to the suspicion of a whitewash by the police department. Most of the report was blank.

Afternoon - Michael Brown's body was turned-over to his family, who claim they will conduct their own, private, autopsy through a medical examiner of their choosing.

4 p.m. – The St. Louis County Prosecutor's office disclosed that Brown had no "adult" criminal background, but refused to release details of his juvenile record, other than to say that he did not have any serious criminal convictions for crimes such as murder.

GotNews editor Charles C. Johnson, filed a lawsuit to release Brown's juvenile record, after being told by several law enforcement officers that Michael Brown had a Juvenile record for second degree murder.

Johnson posted on his Twitter account, "I had two law enforcement contacts who told me #MichaelBrown had juvenile criminal record. I will be suing to get the answer." He also tweeted, "Confirmed earlier report that #MichaelBrown had juvenile arrest record involving second degree murder... Working on getting report #Ferguson."

Johnson claimed that Michael Brown was not entitled to have his Juvenile records sealed because he is no longer living, and he believed that the law only protects living juveniles.

6 p.m. – The Ferguson-Florissant School District postponed their first day of school due to safety concerns for students who walk to school. Neighborhood parents and pastors expressed concern that going to school during the protests could be unsafe. School administrators agreed and subsequently canceled the first two days of classes. The school district released the following statement:

The decision has been made to cancel school on Thursday, August 14 and on Friday, August 15, in response to concerns expressed by many about continuing unrest in our community. In order to allow additional time for the situation to stabilize and for all of our students and their families to resume normal routines, we will reschedule the first day of school for Monday, August 18. All staff members are to report to their assigned buildings. We believe that this change will help ensure a strong start to the new school year.

The school closure relieved the pressure on parents momentarily, but Monday was just five days away, and the rioting was intensifying instead of subsiding.

Ferguson Police Department proposes no protesting at night:

The Ferguson Police Department released a statement on Wednesday expressing their condolences to the Brown family and to let the community know they have heard their message. The letter stated:

The City of Ferguson mourns the loss of Michael Brown's life that occurred this past Saturday. We understand members of our community, and those nationwide, are grieving with us. We have worked diligently to provide an opportunity for our residents to both grieve and voice frustrations through prayer vigils and peaceful protests. We would like to extend our gratitude to the St. Louis County Police Department, the St. Louis City Police Department, the Missouri Highway Patrol, and numerous local law enforcement agencies for their assistance over the past several days. These officers have worked throughout the night to quell violent outbursts and restore calm to our City.

We are working to restore confidence in the safety of our community and our neighborhoods so that we may begin the healing process. We have heard the community's cries for justice and assure the public that the Ferguson Police Department will continue to cooperate fully in the investigations led by the St. Louis County Police Department, the Federal Bureau of Investigation, and the Justice Department. We ask that any groups wishing to assemble in prayer or in protest do so only during daylight hours in an organized and respectful manner. We further ask all those wishing to demonstrate or assemble to disperse well before the evening hours to ensure the safety of the participants and the safety of our community. Unfortunately, those who wish to co-opt peaceful protests and turn them into violent demonstrations have been able to do so over the past several days during the evening hours. These events are not indicative of the City of Ferguson and its residents. The City of Ferguson has been through tough situations in the past, albeit nothing to this magnitude, but will continue to display resilience and fortitude. The Mayor and City Council are committed to taking the necessary steps to rebuild and strengthen our community. We look forward to your cooperation and support.

10 p.m. – Gov. Jay Nixon announces via Twitter that he' was canceling his visit to the Missouri State Fair on Thursday to visit Ferguson.

Assault on the Media:

As night fell on Ferguson, a growing crowd of peaceful protesters became the targets of overzealous law-enforcement officers and their tactical toys. With reports of Molotov cocktails being thrown and gunshots going off in the area, police decided to end the evenings protests early and send everyone home.

Al Jazeera reporters were shot at by police, with rubber bullets and tear gas, on purpose. The news crew of four people were set-up next to their car on the side of the road, to record the night's events. Police officers from the St. Charles Country Police Department were recorded firing tear gas and rubber bullets directly at the news crew-- when there were no protesters in the area. When the Al Jazeera news crew eventually were overcome from the tear gas and ran away, a St. Charles County Police truck pulled up to the abandoned Al Jazeera video equipment and broke-down their lights, and turned the camera towards the ground, jumped into the back of their assault vehicle, and drove off. Producer Marla Cichowski said "We were clearly set up as press with a full live shot set-up. As soon as the first bullet hit the car, we screamed out loud, 'We are press,' 'This is the media.' They shined a huge floodlight at us before firing, and I can only imagine they could see what they were shooting at." AL Jazeera called the incident an "egregious assault on freedom of the press that was clearly intended to have a chilling effect on our ability to cover this important story." They said, "We believe that this situation must be investigated along with those involving our colleagues at other media outlets."

Ryan J. Reilly, a reporter with the Huffington Post, was working on his Ferguson stories and charging his cell phone at a McDonald's restaurant near the protest site when a group of heavily armed police officers came through the doors and instructed everyone to leave immediately. As Reilly was walking towards the door, he was scooped-up and hauled away to jail for trespassing. McDonalds had never told anyone to leave and the business had been a place where reporters had been allowed to congregate, while they charged their electronic equipment and filled their bellies with Cheeseburgers and hot coffee. Reilly wrote on his Facebook page that an officer in full riot gear "purposefully banged my head against the window on the way out and sarcastically apologized." Reilly said, "I'm fine. But if this is the way these officers treat a white reporter working on a laptop who moved a little too slowly for their liking, I can't imagine how horribly they treat others. And if anyone thinks that the militarization of our police force isn't a huge issue in this country, I've got a story to tell you."

Washington Post reporter Wesley Lowery was taken into custody during the same police round-up in McDonalds that ensnared Ryan Reilly. Lowery claims that the whole incident was unnecessary. He was shocked that he had been arrested for being in a public restaurant. As soon as he pulled out his camera to record what was occurring, a police officer stepped in and demanded that he "stop videotaping," even though Lowery had every right to video tape what was happening. Lowery said, "I want this to be about the community, but this arrest is in some ways an anecdote of what's going on here." Marty Baron, the executive editor of the Washington Post, was "appalled" by the actions of the police. He said, "There was absolutely no justification for his arrest."

Later in the evening, Antonio French, a City of St. Louis Alderman of the 21st Ward, was arrested for unlawful assembly while he was observing the activities of the police and the protestors. His wife tweeted when he was getting arrested, "@antonioFrench is in Ferguson jail." At 12:57 a.m. she re-tweeted, "@AntonioFrench being booked now. Not sure what the charge is yet. Was ordered out of his car and arrested because he 'didn't listen.'"

His wife disclosed that Antonio was being charged with "unlawful assembly," and said her husband expected to be detained for 24 hours. The arrest of Antonio French caused an uproar with other protestors. As the police tried to disperse a late-night crowd that had formed around the police station, the protestors began chanting, "Hell no. We won't go, until you free Antonio."

CHAPTER 28

DAY-6
THURSDAY
AUGUST-13

7 AM – City Alderman Antonio French is released from jail without being formally charged or posting bond after being "detained" the night before for sitting in his car.

Ferguson State Senator Maria Chappelle Nadel sent several profanity laden Tweets to Governor Jay Nixon after she was overcome with tear gas on Wednesday night while witnessing protests in her district. At 1:43 a.m. she Tweeted, "You don't know shit bc you never communicate. FUCK you, Governor!" One minute later she Tweeted "Get on your knees, Governor. Get ready." Eleven minutes later she Tweeted "FUCK you, Governor. I'm calling your bullshit!" She was still Tweeting at 5:04 a.m. when she posted, "proved today how disconnected he is to the Black community. He's never been to Ground Zero. This is his Katrina!"

Ferguson police chief Tom Jackson press conference:

During a Thursday morning press conference Ferguson Police Chief Tom Jackson answered questions from a hostile audience of reporters who wanted answers for the way they were treated the previous evening. In his opening remarks, The Chief stated:

What's happening now is not what any of us want. Last night we started getting rocks, bricks, bottles thrown at us and then Molotov cocktails and then gunfire went off. We need to get everyone to calm down and try to bring some peace to this. We want everybody to be able to protest. We know they are going to protest. We were going to facilitate their ability to protest because it is their constitutional right. So working with these leaders we're going to try to get the message out that they want to get out. We understand everybody's anger and their need to have questions answered. We're going to hope for the best. We are changing our tactics.

The Chief was then interrogated by the press until he fled the room. He was asked:

Question - Chief, a lot of people were saying the basic problem last night was that the police moved forward, in mass, towards the protesters. Setting off the problem?

Answer - Well we have a basic obligation to allow people to get to their homes and their businesses and to drive up and down the roadways. We can only have a part of town be closed down for so long before we have to open it back up. And we're trying to do that without physically hurting anybody and so that is why we are using these less than lethal tactics.

Question - Are you going to pull back the military styled vehicles or will they be out there again?

Answer - The tactical units will be out there. If firebombs start getting thrown, properties are getting destroyed, shots are being fired. People are being shot at. We have to respond to deadly force.

Question - They were out there before that happened?

Answer - We are going to talk about not only the tactics but the appearance. We're having conversations.

Question - Chief, there were people who were arrested who weren't shooting at police. There were people tear gassed that weren't shooting at police. Can you give us some insight into the mindset of the police. Why they approached this crowd the way that they did and what goes into making the decision to actually fire the tear gas. Why was it fired. Why did it always seem to be fired around 9 o'clock at night. Take us inside some of those decisions please?

Answer - Those decisions were made by the tactical commanders on the ground, and it was based on the threat. The threat of violence. If individuals are in a crowd that's attacking the police they need to get out of that crowd. We can't individually go in and say, excuse me sir are you peacefully protesting. Are you throwing rocks? Are you throwing a motive cocktail? It's a crowd. If the crowd is getting violent and you don't want to be violent, get out of the crowd.

Question - I'm with Al Jazeera. We were in an area last night trying to cover a story. We were in a neighborhood with no protest going on. No active protest, no one was threatening the police, yet we found ourselves as a direct target. Literally shot with rubber bullets and tear gas canisters that hit our vehicles. How would that happen and who made the decision to do that?

Answer - I don't know who made a decision to do that.

Question - Why is the media a target?

Answer - The media is not a target.

Question - Sir, what exactly is being fired?

Answer - Tear gas. Pepper balls.

Question - Why were the journalists arrested yesterday?

Answer - I don't know.

Question - We had an alderman arrested last night who said he was pulled out of his car and arrested and there were also other people who said they were getting to their car or sitting in their car and waiting to see what was going on and they were arrested. Why would that be?

Answer - All I can say, if anyone was arrested. From what I understand is that they were in an area that was being cleared by the police. Once it was declared by the commander on the scene as an unlawful gathering, because of the violence you know, and everything going, then they have to clear it.

Question - Are they actually booked or just detained temporarily?

Answer - Reporters were released at the scene and they were upset because they weren't booked. They wanted to be arrested.

Question - There are a few names circulating about this officer that was involved. We're hearing Brian Roman, Darren Wilson. Any truth to that?

Answer - We're going to have a conversation about the release of the name. I guess Anonymous put out a name this morning, Brian something. That's not the name. I haven't seen anything else.

Question - Chief the protesters who were just here announced another name. And that name, since you're giving first names, was Darren? (another reporter speaks-out to say - "Darren Wilson")

Answer - We'll I'm not going to comment about that right now.

Question - Chief, what do you think about it. Are these guys just running name after name after name after name?

Answer - I think that's probably what they are doing. They are taking the name of everybody and throwing it out there.

Question - These officers look like soldiers. The word war is being used. Are you surprised by the reaction people are having because of how these officers look?

Answer - The whole picture is being painted a little sideways from what's really happening. It's not military. It's tactical operations. It's swat teams. We're doing this in blue. Anyway, thank you very much.

That was his last response. Chief Jackson left the podium in a hurry, without answering any more questions from the media, who continued to prod him as he left the area.

11:40 a.m. – President Barack Obama addressed the nation on Ferguson and urged calm. The president called on local police to be "open and transparent" about their investigation of Brown's death. President Obama said that Attorney General Eric Holder, "should do what is necessary to help determine exactly what happened and to see that justice is done." Obama also criticized law-enforcement officers in Ferguson for what he described as excessive force during the protests. President Obama said:

> *We lost a young man, Michael Brown, in heartbreaking and tragic circumstances. He was 18 years old. His family will never hold Michael in their arms again. And when something like this happens, the local authorities, including the police, have a responsibility about how they are investigating that death and how they are protecting people in their communities. There is never an excuse for violence against the police, or of vandalism or looting. There is also no excuse for police to use excessive force against peaceful protests or to throw a protester in jail for lawfully exercising their first amendment rights. And here in the United States of America, the police should not be bullying or arresting journalists who are just doing their jobs and report to the American people on what they see on the ground. Put simply, we all need to hold ourselves to a high standard, particularly those of us in positions of authority. Now is the time for healing. Now is the time for peace and calm on the streets of Ferguson. Now is the time for an open and transparent process to see that justice is done.*

Governor Nixon turns Ferguson security over to State Troopers:

Missouri Governor Jay Nixon arrived in Ferguson to give a few speeches and turn over police operations to the State Highway Patrol. Before he arrived at the news conference, Governor Nixon visited the location where Michael Brown was shot, and then toured some of the locations of the riots. He also visited a meeting of local community leaders, business owners, and clergy. He said he intended to soften the tone of law enforcement, saying, "you all will see a much better and much different tone. We need to dim that acceleration."

3:30 p.m. - During his afternoon press conference, Nixon apologized for being late, explaining that he had been on the phone with President Barack Obama, who he said, sent "wishes of peace and justice." He then gave the following statement:

> *What's gone on here over the last few days is not what Missouri is all about. It is not what Ferguson is all about. This is a place where people work, go to school, raise their families, go to church. A diverse community. A Missouri community. But lately it has looked a little bit like a war zone. And that is unacceptable. To change that course we will all need to join hands. To rebuild the trust that has been lost and been broken and help this community regain its confidence and its stability. Literally the eyes of our nation/world are on us. In order for that important process of healing and reconciliation to begin we need to address some very immediate challenges. That is why today I am announcing that the Missouri Highway Patrol under the supervision of Captain Ron Johnson, who grew up in this area, will be directing the team that provides security in Ferguson.*

Governor Nixon encouraged the St. Louis County and Ferguson Police Departments to release the name of the officer involved in the shooting. Saying:

> *I would hope that the appropriate release of that name, with the security around it, to make sure that there is no additional violence, be done as expeditiously as possible. I think it would be an important milestone here to get that out as expeditiously as possible.*

Happy Days:

Militarized police equipment was removed from sight on Thursday night and barricades were taken down to reduce the tensions between the police and the protesters. The low-profile police presence seemed to have calmed the crowd. Kimaly Diouf, the owner of a local business, said she knows why there is peace in the street. She said, "Because they're not tear gassing us tonight." Missouri State Highway Patrol Captain Ron Johnson walked side-by-side with the protesters and held hands in solidarity. He said, "We're just starting today anew. We're starting a new partnership today. We're going to move forward today, to put yesterday and the day before behind us." Captain Johnson even posed with gang members and flashed a few hand signs for the camera--a decision he would later regret after those images went viral, leading to his nickname; "Cop Hug-A-Thug."

Thursday was the first break in violence since rioting began. People felt much better than they did the day before. They felt safer not seeing tanks in the street and heavily armed officers patrolling their neighborhoods with militarized tactical equipment. Distinguishably different than the previous days protests, on Thursday, police officers marched side-by-side with the demonstrators, intermingled with the crowd, sometimes holding their hands. It was surreal to see such a supposedly close bond between the warring factions; the protesters and the police.

Demonstrators marched in unison through the streets of Ferguson. As the march went past the burnt-out shell of the Quicktrip which was set on fire on Sunday night, other protesters who had gathered at the site joined-in and walked down West Florissant Avenue, together, and in cooperation with the police. They cheered and chanted, but they stayed in line and protested peacefully.

As a de-escalation tactic, Johnson said, he ordered police to remove gas masks from their kits before they headed out to the streets for a fifth night of protests. St. Louis Highway Patrol Captain Ron Johnson said, "It means a lot to me personally that we break the cycle of violence, heal tension and build trust. We are going to move forward from today and I would ask if we're going to critique, critique me from today." St. Louis Police Chief Sam Dotson said, "There is a sense of change," This is what communities do. What I see are people expressing their First Amendment rights. I only ask that everybody obey the law." St. Louis County Executive Charlie Dooley said he supports freedom of assembly, but not disobedience for the law. He said, "I am for justice. I am not for revenge."

Ferguson Police Chief Tom Jackson said:

We are going to try to facilitate the protests tonight and we hope the protesters will recognize that we are trying to help everybody bring the tension down. It's a powder keg, and we all recognize that. What's happening now is not what anyone of us want. We need to get everyone to calm down.

Jackson also stated that his department was prepared to respond forcibly to any act of violence if necessary, saying, "We certainly don't want to have any violence on our part. We have to respond to deadly force."

The Chief's sentiments were lost on some of the people who live in Ferguson. Sierra Smith resides in an apartment complex on Canfied Drive, the site of the Michael Brown shooting. She complained that her complex had been under siege by the police since the shooting of Michael Brown, complaining, "Every night we're tormented. The police have no respect at all for the community."

6 p.m. – Demonstrators in cities all across America joined together to hold silent vigils and respectfully remember the memory of Michael Brown. Supporters wore red ribbons and chanted "hands up, don't shoot," while listing out loud the names of black men killed at the hands of police officers. In Denver, Kenny Wiley organized a demonstration of over 100 supporters to protest "systemic inequality." He said, "It wasn't in our city, but this is our country, our world. We want to stand up and say enough is enough, and to mourn those who have lost their lives."

More than 200 followers of Reverend Jesse Jackson heard him rail against the establishment at the Peace Center for the Performing Arts, in his hometown of Greenville, South Carolina. He said, "This struggle has depth and breadth and history. And if the impact of his death wakes you up, he's made a contribution." Jackson called Brown's death "a state execution." He said, "If it's done by an official with a badge on and a gun, it is a state execution." He concluded his remarks by warning, "This is a wake-up call," he said. "I find a certain fascination with watching these young men and women be born again." Another attendee of the S.C. demonstration was automotive technician Ryan Thomas, who felt he had to take a stand. He said, "It's a problem everywhere. It's not just one city, one state."

CHAPTER 29

DAY-7
FRIDAY
AUGUST-15

Just as tensions in Ferguson seemed to be subsiding, the police, once again, riled-up the residents of the small St. Louis suburb by releasing the identity of Darren Wilson as the officer who shot Michael Brown, with a few comments about his gentle disposition. At the same time they released a 19-page police report and video of what is purported to be Michael Brown robbing a convenience store, by "strong arm" force, just moments before he was shot and killed. The inference that Brown somehow deserved to be shot because he was a suspect in a robbery just prior to his death was not lost on the media, who immediately reported that the police department was trying to assassinate the character of Brown.

Chief Jackson said that because threats had been made against the officer's life, the department "weighed the value of releasing his name against the safety factor for himself, his family and his neighborhood," and that is why the department initially decided against making his name public.

In his 8:45 a.m. Police Press Conference, Ferguson Police Chief Thomas Jackson made a very brief statement of some basic facts, then referred the media to an information package which he had brought with him. The package contained a copy of a surveillance tape which shows Brown taking cigars from a convenience store moments before his shooting. He also dropped a 19-page incident report on reporters which listed Brown as a suspect. He did not explain that the shooting was not connected to the robbery. He told the reporters that he wanted them to digest the information and then reconvene in the afternoon, and he would answer any of their questions then. The report does not name the officer who wrote the report, or contain any officer signatures. It also does not contain the address where the robbery is said to have taken place. Brown is described as being 6'4 tall and 292 pounds. He was wearing a white T-shirt, yellow socks (imprinted with marijuana leafs), khaki shorts and a red baseball cap.

Chief Jackson gave scant details about what had occurred the day of the shooting, but several times, urged reporters to review the tape. Jackson complained that he had received so many freedom of information requests that he had to release the surveillance video, and he throught it was appropriate to do it at the same time the officer involved in the shooting was identified. Chief Jackson stood in front of a small crowd of people and delivered a short speech. He said:

First of all thanks to everyone for coming out. Welcome. Sorry about being late. I know the timeline hasn't really played out like I expected it would. But as some of you are aware, I have had a lot of Sunshine law requests for information and documents about a variety of things. Some of which is not available to me.

I'm here to talk about two things. First of all the name of the officer involved in the shooting and then I've had a lot of sunshine requests* for information I'm going to be releasing about a robbery that occurred on August 9th, immediately preceding the altercation and shooting death of Michael Brown.

It is important to note that I have made contact with someone who has been in contact with someone with Browns family to make them aware of this information being released.

What we are making available today are the dispatch records and the video footage of a robbery, a strong arm robbery, with use of force, that occurred at a local convenience mart. I cannot discuss the investigation about the attempted apprehension of the suspect of that strong arm robbery. That goes to the county prosecutors office. I won't be taking any questions here. I want to give this information to you. Everybody digest it. And then later-on, sometime this afternoon, we can get together again and then I'll take questions.

So I want to give you a little timeline of what happened on August 9th. From 11:48 until noon, the officer involved in the shooting was on a sick call on Glennark. There was an ambulance present. At 11:51 there was a 911 call from a convenience store nearby. At 11:52 dispatch gave a description of the robbery suspect over the radio. A different officer arrived at the store where the strong arm robber occurred. A further description, more detail, was given over the radio and stated the suspect was walking towards the Quicktrip. At 12:01 p.m. our officer encountered Michael Brown on Canfield Drive. At 12:04 a second officer arrived on the scene immediately following the shooting. At 12:05 a supervisor was dispatched to the scene and subsequent officers arrived. There have been some questions about the calling of an ambulance. The ambulance that was on the sick case on Glenmark was coming by immediately following the shooting and they did respond to assess Michael Brown.

I'm going to have some police officers hand out packets that have all of the information that was requested and the Sunshine requests concerning the robbery. We're going to give those packets, first of all, to those agencies that have made the Sunshine requests and then anyone else who wants them, I think we have enough of them to give out. We have quite a few.

The officer that was involved in the shooting of Michael Brown was Darren Wilson. He's been a police officer for 6 years. Has had no disciplinary action taken against him. He was treated for injuries which occurred on Saturday. Again, I won't be taking any questions at this time but the package will be handed out by my officers.

Jackson then quickly left the podium and marched-off with his entourage of police officers while reporters were still asking questions about Officer Wilson.

* A sunshine request refers to a law that was originally created in the Florida state legislature, then the Missouri legislature adopted it, to require pubic disclosure and open records of government agencies. Only a court can impose penalties if it finds that the Sunshine Law has been violated, and penalties are assessed only if the violation is found to be purposeful.

The following "cover letter" was included in the "packet of information" that Chief Jackson gave to the press, to explain why they would not be providing certain information about the case that would normally be released to the public.

To: All Media Organizations and other persons submitting Requests for Records pursuant to the Missouri Sunshine Law.

From: Custodian of Records, City of Ferguson

The City has received numerous requests for records. These documents are made available pursuant to such requests and Section 610.100 R.S.Mo.

Enclosed herewith are the following documents: (i) the incident Report pertaining to the incident occurring on August 9, 2014; (ii) the dispatch logs showing the time of events commencing with the initial 9-1-1 call; and (iii) still photos of certain frames of the surveillance video showing the crime giving rise to the initial 9-1-1 call.

The store surveillance video has also been provided to those persons or organizations requesting the video.

Any report, recording, and record which constitutes an investigative report, or part thereof, is a closed record under Section 610.110 R.S.Mo.

Any 9-1-1 recordings made on August 9, 2014, are not subject to release under Section 610.150 R.S.Mo.

Personnel records, other than the name, title, salary and dates of hires of city employees, are closed records under Section 610.021 R.S.Mo.

Lastly, certain information has been redacted from the Incident Report and has been deemed closed under Section 610.100 R.S.Mo.

The contents of the police package included an incident report of the robbery of the Ferguson Market convenience store and three supplements to the original police report from the officer who responded to the robbery call, plus dispatch logs and pictures of Brown robbing the convenience store. In the police report, the name of the business that reported the robbery had been redacted with "white-out," although white-out is usually not an allowable way to redact text from a law-enforcement report. The report also indicated that the store was willing to prosecute.

Incident Report:

Ferguson Police Department
222 S. Florissant Road, Ferguson, MO 63135
Complaint No.: 14-12388
Report date: 08/09/2014
Type of incident: 2nd degree strong-arm robbery - convenience store
Received Date / Time: 08/09/2014, 11:51
Dispatch Date / Time: 08/09/2014, 11:53
Call Received Via: Radio
Arrival Time: 08/09/2014, 11:54
Departed Date / Time: 08/09/2014, 1854
Item(s) stolen: 1 box of Swisher Sweets Cigars, valued at $48.99

Suspect 1 - Michael Brown
DOB: 05/20/1996 - age 18
6 feet 4 inches tall, 292 pounds
Michael Brown had an expired drivers permit. Expired 09/18/2013

Suspect 2 - Dorian J. Johnson

DOB: 1/15/1992 - age 22
5 feet 5 inches tall, 120 pounds
No drivers license. Only state ID, expires 1/15/2016

Statement of Officer:

On 08/09/2014 at approximately 1151 hours, while on a call in the Park Ridge Apartment complex, immediately located behind _____, I received a call for a stealing in progress at _____(____W Florissant Ave). I responded to that location and was given a description by dispatch of a BM in a white t-shirt that was walking northbound on W Florissant toward Quicktrip. I did not see the suspect in the area, so I returned to _____ on the parking lot, who continued to point up W Florissant toward Quicktrip and said, "He went that way." He was indicating with his hands toward his chest and then north on W Florissant. I still could not see the suspect on W Florissant, and _____. I went inside to contact a _____ clerk who was not identified at the time, and _____, and _____ patron, who was not identified at that time, who advised the suspect took cigars and pushed _____ on his way out. He was wearing a white t-shirt, khaki longer shorts, yellow socks, and a red cardinals baseball cap. They also stated that another B/M was with him, but gave no further description on that suspect. I gave out this information over the radio and drove northbound on Florissant, to try to find the suspects. I did not locate the suspects.

Supplement 1:

8/11/2014, 11:31 AM

Pursuant to the original report, the following information is pertinent. On Monday, 08/11/2014 @ 0900hrs, I was assigned to this investigation.

_____ had just come out of the restroom and returned to the counter where she observed Brown tell _____ that he wanted several boxes of cigars. As _____ was placing the boxes on the counter, Brown grabbed a box of Swisher Sweet cigars and handed them to Johnson who was standing behind the counter.

_____ witnessed _____ tell Brown that he had to pay for those cigars first. That is when Brown reached across the counter and grabbed numerous packs of Swisher Sweets and turned to leave the store. _____ then calls "911". Meanwhile _____ comes out from behind the counter and attempts to stop Brown from leaving. According to _____, _____ was trying to lock the door until Brown returned the merchandise to him. That is when Brown grabbed _____ by the shirt and forcefully pushed him back in the display rack. _____ backed away and Brown and Johnson exited the store with the cigars.

I then had the opportunity to review a copy of the video surveillance footage which captured the following events. The date and time stamp correspond to the video footage provided. The entire incident takes place on Saturday, 08/09/2014 between 11:52:58hrs and 11:54:00hrs.

The video reveals Brown enter the store followed by Johnson. Brown approaches the register with Johnson standing behind him. _____ can be seen in the background walking from the restroom to behind the counter. Brown hands a box of Swisher Sweets to Johnson. An apparent struggle or confrontation seems to take place with Brown, however it is obscured by a display case on the counter. Meanwhile, Johnson sets the box he was handed back on the counter. Brown turns away from the counter with another box of Swisher Sweet cigars and walks towards the exit door. _____ then comes out from behind the counter, with what appears to be a set of keys in his hands. _____ then stands between Brown and the exit door. Brown, still holding a box a Swisher Sweets in his right hand, grabs, _____ by his shirt with his left hand, Brown aggressively pulls _____ in close to him and then immediately pushes him back in to a display rack. Johnson continues out the door and out of camera frame. _____, no longer between Brown and the door, stops and watches Brown as he walks towards the exit door. Brown then abruptly turns back around and advances on _____. Brown towers over _____ appearing to intimidate him. Brown then turns back around and walks out of camera view.

It is worth mentioning that this incident is related to another incident detailed under Ferguson Police Report #2014-12391 as well as St. Louis County Police Report #2014-43984. In that incident, Brown was fatally wounded involving an officer of this department. I responded to that scene and observed Brown. After viewing Brown and reviewing this video, I was able to confirm that Brown is the primary suspect in this incident. A second person, also at the scene, identified himself as being with Brown. That person was later identified as Dorian Johnson. After observing Johnson and reviewing the video, I confirmed he is the second suspect in this incident.

A disc containing the 911 call made by _____ was obtained from police communications.

Supplement #2:

Date: 8/12/2014, 11:38 AM

On 08/10/2014, I contacted _____ and received a copy of their surveillance video disc of the incident. I was unable to view the disc as our computer system would not read it. The disc was entered into evidence.

Supplement #3:

Date: 8/12/2014, 11:48 AM

On 08/10/2014, I returned to _____, to contact the witnesses from the original incident and obtain written statements. Neither witness was present in the store. I left witness statement forms to be completed and instructed them to call when they were completed, for pickup.

Police dispatch radio calls before Brown's death:
11:52:53 - White shirt b/m/qt, box cigars
11:55:06 - Walking N/B in a white shirt
11:57:47 - Suspect wearing red Cards cap, yellow socks, W/ another male suspect walking towards the QT at this time.
11:58:04 - Khaki Shorts

Police dispatch radio calls after Brown's death:
12:04 - EMS contacted
12:16:23 - Dellwood Officer at scene
14:11:36 - Shots fired on Canfield
14:12:34 - 4 to 6 shots
14:13:01 - 2939 Canfield 22 and 25
14:14:33 - EMS staging

The day bore some startling revelations, such as there being four calls that went out about the robbery at the convenience store, with descriptions given of Brown and Johnson, but no officers were able to find them. Officer Wilson and two other police patrol cars drove past the suspects as they were walking back to their apartment complex, without noticing that the two youths matched the identity of the robbery suspects that the police were looking for.

It's also interesting to note that in Supplement #1, the reporting officer's name and ID number are blank, and most of the page has been redacted to hide what was written on it. Supplement #2 also seems a little suspicious. The reporting officer indicated that he was unable to view the convenience store video when he got it back to the police station. He stated, "I was unable to view the disc as our computer system would not read it." If that is true, the Ferguson police department might want to update their computer equipment and make sure their employees know how to use it.

In Supplement #3 the police officer reported, "I returned to _____, to contact the witnesses from the original incident and obtain written statements. Neither witness was present in the store. I left witness statement forms to be completed and instructed them to call when they were completed, for pickup."

The two "witnesses" to the Michael Brown stealing are the store clerk and his daughter. The police would not have gone back to the Ferguson Market four days after the robbery, expecting to still find the lone customer who was in the store during the theft. The store clerk's daughter called 911 to report the robbery as soon as Michael Brown and Dorian Johnson left the convenience mart.

The fact that the clerks daughter called the police is contrary to reports by the store owner and his attorney that no one from the store called 911 to report the robbery. Some versions of the convenience store surveillance tape are longer in duration than most of the clips that the media have shown. In the longer version, a

222

female is seen coming out of the bathroom and then going back behind the counter, where her father was also working. The police incident reports states:

_____ had just come out of the restroom and returned to the counter where she observed Brown tell _____ that he wanted several boxes of cigars. As _____ was placing the boxes on the counter, Brown grabbed a box of Swisher Sweet cigars and handed then to Johnson who was standing behind the counter. _____ witnessed _____ tell Brown that he had to pay for those cigars first. That is when Brown reached across the counter and grabbed numerous packs of Swisher Sweets and turned to leave the store. _____ then calls "911". Meanwhile _____ comes out from behind the counter and attempts to stop Brown from leaving.

The officer who wrote the report confirmed that the "witness" was the girl seen on the video tape who had come out of the restroom and then went back to behind the counter at the same time Brown was attempting to steal the Cigarillos from her father. The indecent report stated:

_____ can be seen in the background walking from the restroom to behind the counter.

It's curious why the St. Louis County Police would need a warrant to get a copy of the convenience store surveillance tape. The Ferguson Police Department already had a copy of it, and they got it without needing a warrant. Perhaps a warrant would make it appear as if the store hadn't already given up a copy of the tape to the police without requiring a warrant.

After the video of the Ferguson Market was released to the public, the store owners knew that the community would target them, just like as Quicktrip was targeted once rumors spread that Quicktrip had called the police on Brown. Ferguson Market quickly coordinated a news conference, through their attorney, to put their spin on the 911 call.

Through the store's attorney, Jake Kanzler, they made a statement to the public which claimed that neither the store owners nor any of their employees called the police to report a theft at the store prior to Michael Brown being killed. Kanzler stated that it was a "customer" who witnessed the robbery from within the store, and claimed that it was he who called 911.

Kanzler continued his apparent lies and propaganda to the public after stating that the convenience store owners "do not wish to be wrapped up in the middle of this. They are simply complying with police orders." He repeatedly emphasized that the 911 call did not come from the owners or any employee of the store and that "the market has been in the community for a long time and they hope to continue serving this community. They had nothing to do with this investigation. It's not about them. They didn't call the police. They didn't ask the police to come and take the video. They just want to comply and let the process take it's course, and they will because they have to."

A question may arise as to the propriety of an attorney lying to the public on behalf of his client, especially in such an important case where transparency and truth should prevail above all else, even over special interests. Purposeful lies make the process of getting to the truth more murky and difficult to achieve. Lying to the public seems to be a violation of the "good moral character" clause lawyers need to abide by in order to keep their law license.

The residents of Ferguson, and the activists who had gathered there, were outraged by the manner in which the police released the information about Michael Brown, and the obvious implication that he somehow deserved to be shot because he was involved in a strong-arm robbery before his confrontation with officer Darren Wilson. The morning press conference by Ferguson Police Chief Tom Jackson escalated the tension between protesters and the police, which caused some consternation among the law-enforcement agencies and the Governor.

11 a.m. – In a morning press conference, Missouri Governor Jay Nixon, with Highway Patrol Colonel Ron Rapola and Captain Ron Johnson, spoke to an unruly crowd about the aggressive police tactics and the way the Ferguson Police Department released the surveillance tape and incident report on Michael Brown, while at the same time releasing the name of the officer who shot Brown. Governor Nixon rambled through his prepared script, trying to reassure his constituents and the press that the investigations' focus remained on finding out how and why Brown was killed. He then quickly turned the microphone over to the Colonel of the Missouri

Highway patrol, who quickly read through a prepared speech, then hastily passed the torch to their front-man, Captain Ron Johnson, A.K.A. - Officer Hug-A-Thug.

Missouri Governor Jay Nixon stated, "We just finished an initial overnight security briefing. I want to thank those folks for giving that. Clearly as we've seen over the last 18 to 20 hours we've made progress. Work continues to ensure both the safety and the freedom of people to assemble and to express their views while respecting property and staying safe. I want to thank all of law enforcement for their work last night and their continuing work today. Moving forward our goal is to make sure we keep the peace while these parallel investigations are going on, to get done, and continue until justice is served. As we saw this develop a couple days ago we worked on a number of things. One of the things I did was to make sure that we're going to get security in a situation here where folks felt secure and willing and able to express their opinions while these important investigations about this horrific tragedy are carried out. In that sense I ordered the colonel of highway patrol to begin both the planning and execution of that. Let me turn it over to the colonel who will go through a couple of very small matters and turn it over to Captain Johnson for a daily briefing. Thank You. Colonel Ron Rapola."

Highway Patrol Colonel Ron Rapola proclaimed, "Thank you for your leadership over the last couple of days. The governor called me and said he wanted us to take control of the security situation and I needed to pick a commander for that job. We have a lot of resources that we can bring to the table but I can assure you the best resource that the Highway Patrol has is its personnel and the best resource that I could bring to this situation in Ferguson, Missouri was captain Ron Johnson. And I think you've seen the tremendous job that he's already done here in this community over the evening. So I would like to introduce him, for him to update you on the events that occurred last night and what's ahead for today. So captain Johnson."

Highway Patrol Capt. Ron Johnson tried to go into the crowd to talk among the people, but the press and the protesters told him to get back behind the microphone. He abandoned his attempt to "mingle and connect" with the people of the community, and got behind the podium, in embarrassment, to deliver his speech. He said:

The people of our community need to hear what I'm saying. They've got questions and I've invited them here. This isn't about Ron Johnson. This isn't about the highway patrol. Saint Louis County. Saint Louis City. It's about the people that live in our community. When this day is over a lot of people will be gone. The people behind you will be here and I'll be here. OK. So I'll answer your questions. Last night was a great night. It was a great night. There was no calls for service. We did not deploy tear gas. We did not have any road blocks. We did not make any arrests. It was a good night. People were talking. People were inspiring each other. People were getting their voice out, and we were communicating a lot better, and they were communicating a lot better with us. We had many leaders and activist out there yesterday that were helping keep the road open and informing the crowd what I expect to continue throughout this event. Our department along with Saint Louis County, Saint Louis City, had a great night. Myself and Chief Belmar went down to the Quicktrip yesterday and walked and shook hands and talked to people and listened and promised that we're going to communicate better and were going to give answers to their needs and we're going to continue to do that each and every night, you're going to see me walking down there this morning when I came it was the first thing that I did before I even came up here and got a briefing from our officers here at the command post. I went down there so I could get a briefing from the people that are living in this community so I could come back and have a proper conversation here at the command post.

Captain Johnson responded to several questions from the audience.

Question: Does the release of the officer's name and also security footage showing the suspect possibly involved in a strong-armed robbery change the dynamics, and any new challenges on that?

Ron Johnson: I think the relationship of the name is what was requested by the community, and they've gotten it. I have not seen the video. I was watching the news this morning when I heard that it came out, so I've not seen that so it would be hard for me to comment on that.

Question: How do you anticipate the impact of what we saw last night? A lot of people are in this open wound once again. They're angry once again?

Ron Johnson: Why I can tell you that today I will meet with the Chief of Ferguson and talk about how that was released and try to get a copy or be able to analyze the packet that they have, and this afternoon I will be walking back down to the QuikTrip and I will talk to the people there and explain what I see in the packet and some of the questions that maybe unclear in the presentation this morning. I will try to make those clear but I can tell you our task here is to ensure the safety of the citizens of Ferguson to help with the businesses and Ferguson, but also to ensure that the people of Ferguson have their voice, their right to speech, their right to gather is maintained, and that's what we will continue to do.

Question: Is there any concern about security with this name release? Is he being protected and are you concerned about his safety?

Ron Johnson: I have not talked to chief Tom Jackson and so I'm unaware of any of the things he has in place.

Question: On the picture they have showing it's Mike Brown. On the video that they released this morning, the young man in the picture looks like him, but the picture, If you look closely at the details. Look down at his feet. Low white socks on. There's Nike flats on. In the picture of Mike Brown laying in the middle street he had long striped socks on with black and white tennis shoes. So if they're saying that that is Mike Brown in that picture that is just so unfair to his parents. You got to look at the whole picture, from head to toe.

Ron Johnson: And I have not seen that but I guarantee that I will look into that packet and I will look at that and that's why I'm down there so I can get this kind of information.

Question: Did the locals mishandle the tragedy?

Ron Johnson: Like we've talked before I am going to talk about yesterday and I think yesterday we handled it just right. We shook hands and we hugged and we had a great time. We're going to talk about last night and move forward today and I can tell you what happened last night is what's going to happen here forward.

Question: Is there now a strained relationship between the state and the law?

Ron Johnson: No there's not. I've talked to Chief Belmar last night. You see their officers here, officers riding hand in hand, and no there's not.

Question: How do you explain the timing of these releases. The community has been asking for the name of this officer to be released for a longtime now and it comes on the very same day where there's footage believed to be Michael brown in some kind of robbery. What's behind the timing of this?

Ron Johnson: I really can't tell you what the timing is because I saw it on the news this morning along with everybody else. Highway patrol is not involved in the investigation. Highway patrol is tasked with security. The governor wants to make sure the people of Ferguson are safe and that they have a right to protest and speak their mind and so that's what he's tasked us to do and that's why we're here.

Question: They're talking about you anticipating you releasing more information about what happened in the car. A lot of people are really suspicious.

Ron Johnson: The highway patrol is not involved in the investigation. The Governor has tasked us to provide security. He wants to make sure that people of Ferguson are safe. And that they have a right to protest and speak their mind. And that is what he has tasked us to do and that's why we're here.

Question: Can you talk about how law enforcement approaches suspects and what you try to do to make sure such shootings don't occur?

Ron Johnson: You know yesterday you saw me out there talking, communicating, understanding and respecting, and that's our task.

That's what this uniform stands for. When you look at a lot of the mission statements for law enforcement, it talks about respect, and service, so that's number one. I can't speak about the incident there. I wasn't there and I think it would be unfair to speak on something I don't know about, but the things I do know about is what I will speak to, the things that are questions I could get answers to I will give to you, and I promise you that and I will continue to do that.

Question: What about being consulted before they released the information of the convenience store robbery and images from the surveillance security camera. Should you have been consulted?

Ron Johnson: I would have liked to have been consulted.

Question: A lot of the criticism has been about the local police and have used heavy-handed tactics and have deployed very militarized units on the street. What will we see from your department?

Ron Johnson: Were you here last night? Alright you're going to see a bunch of smiles, a bunch of hugs, a bunch of conversation, so that's what you're going to see from me.

Question: As a young black man that lives in this community, whites harass us in this community all the time and I was one of the ones that sat back and said hold up let's wait and hear what the official word is. I took a lot of pressure for saying hold up, wait and let's see what the official word is. Those were my thoughts when you were appointed to this position, but now to come out this morning, and I took off work to come up here because I was concerned, that now the official word comes out, it comes out like it did, with the release of the officers name, following immediately or including all of the other B.S. about it possibly being Mike Johnson. Then to hear you say that you weren't included in the release of this information although you have this high-profile position. I find it utterly disgusting and now I don't know how I can go back to my community and say hey, I asked you all to hold up and wait for official word, they gave you as a head person, they gave this as their official position, what am I supposed to go back and tell the people, because you are not being included in the conversation. This looks like it's a figurehead position. This is all the stuff Jay Nixon was accused of doing." This is all figurehead stuff. What do you have to say about that?

Ron Johnson: Well I can say that's not the case, and I can tell, you and I are meeting each other for the first time, and I can tell this is going to be a serious conversation when I leave here and I'll tell you when you see me tonight down there I think you'll get the tone of my conversation is going to change, but I can also tell you this inner anger, we have to make sure we don't burn down our own house. That we don't go down there and vandalize our own buildings. We can stand on the sidewalk and we can talk about our issues we can talk about what we want and what we need and a conversation that needs to happen and we can make that happens but what I don't want is us to go down there and burn our own neighborhood. That does not prove a point. That does not solve an issue. That hurts this community, and that is what I don't want.

Question: There appears to be a direct link between the release of information and how the community is reacting. You're in charge of securing the community, keeping the peace, other agencies are in charge of releasing the information. Apparently the two sides have not met and gotten together to coordinate that effort. Do you think this is something, a conversation that's going to be had so that you're in the loop with the release of the information so you can react accordingly to the public?

Ron Johnson: I guarantee there is going to be a conversation. It's not going to be a conversation that I am going to have over the phone.

Question: Do you want to clarify about the County Prosecutor, Bob McCulloch, and the County police. Is the release of this video linked to that strain about Bob McCulloch objecting to the Highway Patrol being in charge?

Ron Johnson: This release came from the Ferguson Police Department and Chief Tom Jackson.

Question: How are you going to make your own community,

especially the black community, feel safe and protected around here again? I mean after many incidents over the last three days here and all across the United States. This is the one with the biggest outrages, especially internationally. What are your exact actions to make black young people and black families feel safe in their own communities?

Ron Johnson: Because yesterday we saw what it should be, we saw what it could be, and we saw what it will be.

Question: How do you feel about body cameras for police officers on duty? The reports about officers that stepped over their power decreased by 60%. Is this something that you would push for, or no, to prevent incidents like where a young boy looses his life?

Ron Johnson: I believe in cameras. Every Missouri patrol car is equipped with cameras.

Question: You talked about the scaled-back presence last night. But we're already seeing threats on social media of riots tonight even in the city of St. Louis. What's the plans security-wise tonight to make sure this doesn't get out of hand?

Ron Johnson: You're telling me what social media is telling you. I want to see what the people are telling me.

Question: Have you noticed a change in the protesters mood since these pictures were released this morning?

Ron Johnson: Yes I have. It's unclear. It's unclear. We need to state the facts. And there has been a change in my attitude since that was released.

Gov. Nixon then stepped-in to prevent Johnson from going any deeper about his feelings about the release of the surveillance video. After a few minutes of continued questions by reporters and community members, the police and Governor left the stage and retreated to their command center.

12:30 p.m. - The family of Michael Brown released a statement saying they are "beyond outraged" by how the information was released in a way to "assassinate the character of their son," tying him to the robbery. The statement read:

Michael Brown's family is beyond outraged at the devious way the police chief has chosen to disseminate piecemeal information in a manner intended to assassinate the character of their son, following such a brutal assassination of this person in broad daylight.

There is nothing based on the facts that have been placed before us that can justify the execution style murder of their child by this police officer as he held his hands up, which is the universal sign of surrender.

The prolonged release of the officer's name and then the subsequent alleged information regarding a robbery is the reason why the family and the local community have such distrust for the local law enforcement agencies.

It is no way transparent to release the still photographs alleged to be Michael Brown and refuse to release the photographs of the officer that executed him.

The police strategy of attempting to blame the victim will not divert our attention, from being focused on the autopsy, ballistics report and the trajectory of the bullets that caused Michael's death and will demonstrate to the world this brutal execution of an unarmed teenager.

Benjamin Crump, an attorney for Brown's family, told USA TODAY the release of the officer's name alongside a robbery report naming Brown as a suspect was "smoke and mirrors." Crump said:

There was nothing based on the facts that have been placed before us that would justify this execution style murder by this police officer in broad daylight. It's not enough that they assassinated him in broad daylight in the middle of the street. They also have to assassinate his character to try to get away with it. Police only releasing photos of the robbery suspect and not Wilson shows that the department will not be transparent.

Crump additionally told TheBlot magazine:

The reports of the Ferguson Police Chief's deliberate misleading account about the basis for his release of the video tape is very troubling to Michael Brown's family. It follows a disturbing pattern of behavior by the Ferguson Police Department since this tragedy occurred. This simply serves as another example of why many in the Ferguson community lack trust in all of the local law enforcement officials and the grand jury process, in general, and Chief Jackson, in particular.

Brown family attorney Anthony Grey complained about the family not being allowed to view the video tape before it was released to the public. He said:

They were appalled by it. They saw it for the first time – a glimpse of it — on nationwide TV. They had requested an opportunity, through the attorneys, to see any video footage before it was released. That request was not honored."

Regarding the timing of the police releasing the video, Grey stated:

The family feels that that was strategic, they feel that it was aimed at denigrating their son. It was a character assassination. Do not take the bait from anybody who is trying to character assassinate Mike. Don't take that.

3:00 p.m. - Afternoon press conference. Ferguson police chief Thomas Jackson delivered a statement to the press to seemingly exonerate himself and his police department from the immediate backlash they received for releasing the videotape of Michael Brown allegedly robbing a convenience store at the same time the police released the name of Officer Wilson.

When asked pointedly by a reporter covering the news conference if Officer Wilson knew that Brown was involved in a robbery when he confronted him in the street, Chief Jackson begrudgingly stated, "No. It had nothing to do with the stop. They were stopped because they were walking down the middle of the street blocking traffic. That was it."

When asked about the condition of Officer Wilson, the Chief said "The side of his face was swollen." He then continued to speak highly of officer Wilson: "We had no complaints. He was a gentle, quiet man. He was a distinguished officer." He then repeated the same lines a few moments later about Wilson, as if the compliments were part of the talking points. He said Wilson was a gentleman, a quiet officer, an excellent officer, and that he never "intended" for any of this to happen.

When asked more direct questions from reporters about why he was releasing the video of the robbery at the same time he released the name of the officer involved in the shooting, the Chief got visibly flustered and then blurted out, "All I did was release the video tape to you because I had to. I had been sitting on it, but too many people put in a FOI request for that thing and I had to release that tape to you."

The Chief stated:

> *So I gave you a lot of information this morning and I wanted to give you a chance to let you go over it. We've had some questions that have been coming in to our Twitter and so forth so were going to address some of those. There have been some questions about the timing of the release of the tape. So we've had this tape for a while. We had to diligently review the information that was in the tape to determine if there was any other reason to keep it or any other person to be charged with a crime. We determined that that was not going to be the case. We got a lot of freedom of information request for this tape. At some point it was just determined we had to release it. We didn't have good cause absent any other reason to not release it under the FOI and decided at the same time it wouldn't be prudent to release that information which, you know, could be a little bit, I don't know, well we needed to release that at the same time we would release the name of the officer who was involved in the shooting so that we could just keep open and give you all the information we have. We have pretty much given you every bit of information we have now. I don't think there is anything else that we have to give out. Regarding the second suspect that was in the store in the tape, Dorian Johnson. We have determined that he did not commit a crime, he was not complicit in the crime.*

Question - Have we heard any information yet Chief that would justify the use of deadly force particularly outside of the car?

Answer - OK, I understand that, and these are questions that have to go to the investigation and I don't think anything from the investigation is going to be released.

Question - Chief, when a weapon is discharged is there paperwork that needs to be filled out under protocol?

Answer - There is a use of Force report that we have but all reports that are going to be written on this are going to be written by St. Louis County. All I did. What I did was, uh, was release the video tape to you because I had to. I've been sitting on it. Too many people put in FOI requests for that thing and I had to release that tape to you.

Questions - Can I read you a statement. Michael Brown's family is beyond outraged by the devious way the police chief has chosen to decimate, in piecemeal, information in a manner intended to assassinate the character of their son. What is your response to that?

Answer - My response to that is first my heart goes out to the family I can't imagine what they are going through. We have given you everything that we have now. And everything we can give you, so from our police department, you have everything we've got. There is nothing else I can give you.

Question - It seems like you are only answering questions that demean the character of Mike Brown. When we ask you guys questions about how you are handling the case, you say it is under investigation. You just put more citizens in trouble by releasing that video and now they have to be protected because their stores and businesses have been placed in the media. You say you are concerned about our safety but you seem to be more concerned about your officers?

Answer - I am absolutely concerned about the safety of my community.

Question - Can you tell us anymore about the officer?

Answer - He was a police officer for 6 years. Two of those years were with Jennings and for four years with us.

Question - Was the officer involved in the shooting aware of the

235

robbery call?

Answer - I don't know. I don't know what came out in the interview. I know his initial contact was not related to the robbery.

Question - You're telling us, that when the officer stopped Michael Brown for the first time he was not aware that Brown was a suspect in a robbery?

Answer - No. He was just coming off a sick case which is why the ambulance was there so quickly.

Question - What are you saying? Did he know that he was a suspect in a case or did he not know?

Answer - No. He didn't.

Question - Did it have anything to do with the stop?

Answer - No. It had nothing to do with the stop.

Question - Why did he stop Michael Brown?

Answer - Because he was walking down the middle of the street blocking traffic.

Question - Can you describe this officer to us?

Answer - He had no complaints. He was a gentle, quiet man. He was a distinguished officer. He was a gentleman. He was a quite officer. He is, has been an excellent officer for the police department.

Question - How has he been effected by this?

Answer - He's been devastated. Absolutely devastated. He never intended any of this to happen.

Question - If the murder and the robbery did not come together why did the video come out of the robbery if they're not related?

Answer - Because the press asked for it.

Question - Earlier in the day you said the officer was responding because a description of a robbery suspect had gone out and that description matched Michael Brown. Now you're saying he only stopped Michael Brown because he was blocking traffic?

Answer - No, no, no. I don't think I said he went there because of a robbery call. He was in the area following a robbery call because he was on a sick case.

Question - If the robbery had nothing do with the stop, then why would you release the video of the robbery?

Answer - Because you asked for it. You asked for it. I held it for as long as I could.

Question - Did you let Captain Johnson know you were going to release that video because it appears as if he knew nothing about it?

Answer - Captain Johnson and I just spoke about our communication breakdown. I talked to Chief Belmar about this. We talked to the command post up there but I did not personally call him and I should have done that. I'm still in the county-being-in-charge mode.

Thank you very much. Appreciate your time.

The Chief retreated from the podium and hastily left the scene before being asked any more pointed questions.

Following is a written statement from the Ferguson City Attorney regarding FOI requests about the surveillance video:

Within days of the tragic events on August 9, the City of Ferguson began receiving multiple requests for information and documents. While some of these requests were made in writing, many requests were made verbally due to the fact that the City's website and email were down at several points during that week. City personnel cataloged all requests and treated them in the same manner as it would any Sunshine Law request. (The "Sunshine Law" is Missouri's equivalent of the federal Freedom of Information Act).

Several reporters, news organizations and others asked for documents specifically pertaining to Michael Brown. One such request was made by the St. Louis Post Dispatch. On August 12, 2014, the paper requested "all documentation concerning the events leading up to and including the shooting of Michael Brown" which shall include "incident, arrest and investigative reports, 911 audio, photos and video retained by the police department." Another request, made on August 14, 2014, by Judicial Watch, requested all records relating to Michael Brown, dated between August 1, 2013, and August 9, 2014.

The Sunshine Law dictates that Governmental entities must respond to both general requests and specific requests and release all documents that are responsive to the those requests, unless those documents are otherwise closed.

The Ferguson police department retained the incident and investigative report of the store robbery which occurred less than 10 minutes before the shooting. The reports, which included the surveillance video, concerned Michael Brown. Under the Sunshine Law, the police department had no reason to close these records and withhold them from the public.

By the date of August 15, the City, having reached its statutory deadline to respond to the information requests, released the store robbery reports, including the surveillance video.

The Department of Justice was aware that the Ferguson Police Department were in procession of the convenience store surveillance tape and were worried that they would release the tape to the public to defame Brown, so the DOJ told the Chief to not release the video out of fear that the footage would spark more violence and further unrest in Ferguson. He complied on Thursday, but on Friday he defied their wishes and released the video of Brown robbing the convenience store, telling reporters that he had no choice because the media requested the release under the Freedom of Information Act, although it was later confirmed that no Freedom of Information Request was ever made for the surveillance tape of the robbery.

ACLU Lawsuit:

The American Civil Liberties Union, after their initial FOI request was denied, filed a lawsuit against the St. Louis County Police Department to get access to the "Incident Report" of the Michael Brown shooting. Anthony Rothert, from the Missouri ACLU said, "from what we can tell right now it looks like the Ferguson Police Department never did an incident report, which would be contrary to their policy, it would be contrary to the law, and quite suspicious, not to take even an initial statement from someone who's killed another person." He continued, "When this incident happened in Ferguson, the ACLU had several concerns, among them being the First Amendment rights of protesters, and the militarized police response, but one of the pieces of it was transparency in the investigation." Rothert felt the police response was not unusual. He said, "I don't think it's unique to this story that police departments often operate with lack of transparency, and that really deteriorates the trust that the community has in the police departments. So you have a pretty good law in Missouri, on paper, the Sunshine Law requires incident reports to be made public, and arrest records to be made public, right away, and requires investigative reports to be made public at conclusion of investigations. But time and again police departments do not release those records unless it is favorable to them."

The ACLU lawsuit was filed after their request for the Incident was denied. The police department responded to the initial Request for Information on August 13th, stating, "In ref to your request for incident report involving Michael Brown, This is an on-going investigation and we are unable to release a copy at this time. St. Louis County Record Room."

Circumstances in which law-enforcement can deny access to incident reports:

Under Missouri state statute 610.100.3 and 610.100.4, a governmental agency has the authority to withhold the disclosure of records that may otherwise be subject to disclosure under two circumstances. First, if the agency has an articulable concern over the safety of a victim, witness, or other person if the record is revealed. Second, disclosure is not necessary if the criminal investigation is likely to be jeopardized. However, the agency may need court approval for withholding the information.

Early evening – Reverend Jesse Jackson linked arms with protesters in Ferguson as he led a precision of supporters to the site where Michael Brown died, urging them to ""turn pain into power," while fighting back non-violently. Jackson gave a short sermon and then made a few statements to the press. When asked if he could comment on the change of police tactics in handling this protest, Jackson replied:

> *There are several tactics aside from shooting an unarmed man multiple times. They have said nothing for 7 days except having a police riot with canisters of tear gas. They released the police name today and then released a discrediting tape about Michael. No matter what might have happened in the store it had nothing to do with him being shot down on Saturday afternoon in this place, in front of these people. The police do not have the power to be judge, jury and executioner. The police are still trying to cover their flanks. We need a full and thorough investigation. And given the abundance of unemployment here. Poverty is a weapon of mass destruction. There must be some kind of urban policy of reconstruction. Closing public housing and foreclosing private housing. People need a way out of this. And this is the situation in almost every urban center around the nation. In Chicago, there's Memphis, there's East St. Louis, there's St. Louis. We as Americans deserve better.*

When asked what his message was for the folks in Ferguson, Jesse Jackson stated:

> *Don't surrender their hope and don't self destruct. You can reshape an iron while it's hot but don't burn yourself. Don't destroy yourself in the process. We should have a massive door-to-door campaign for voter registration. Only those who are registered can serve as jurors. Jurors can elect mayors. Jurors can determine the fate of killers. With votes you can determine the mayor. Mayors determines the police chiefs. They can elect judges. They have power. And they must turn this image into that kind of political power."*

Evening Riots:

Friday night descended into chaos just before midnight when a small group of rioters began to throw rocks and bottles at the police. The police pulled-back "for safety" and left the Ferguson Market and other local businesses abandoned. Once the police moved-out, the looters moved-in. Their first target was the Ferguson Market. A location the police promised to protect. Although the police were not able to prevent the looting and burning of businesses because they were too afraid of the teenage vandals, they appeared to be completely capable of dispersing an earlier peaceful protest of clergy and elderly protesters with their arsenal of tactical equipment.

CHAPTER 30

DAY-8
SATURDAY
AUGUST-16

What began as an evening of peaceful protesting, soon descended into another night of chaos when a small element of protesters broke off from the main crowd and turned violent. Police claimed they had bottles thrown at them when they asked people to leave the area. This assault on police required them to move in and try to disperse the entire group through intimidation tactics. Although law-enforcement mobilized their tactical vehicles and riot squad, the looters were not intimidated. They continued to break into stores and loot businesses, as police stood by and watched the destruction. The police pleaded through a distant loudspeaker, for the rioters to go home, repeating the threat, "You must disperse immediately or you will be subject to arrest." However the officers seemed unwilling to risk their own personal safety to protect the stores and disperse the marauding gang.

After realizing that the police were not going to intervene, peaceful protesters stepped-in and risked their own safety to protect the stores. In one instance of bravery, protesters formed a line of bodies in front of a business, chanting "Hands up, don't shoot!" to fend off five kids who had smashed the storefront windows and were running-off with the merchandise. Once the looters were confronted, they moved-on to loot unprotected businesses.

Eighteen-year-old Marqueise Gordon, witnessed a meat-market being looted, and said, "I think it's pretty stupid, to be honest. The same store that people are breaking into is the same store people are going to go into to buy whatever. It doesn't make sense." Although Gordon seemed to be upset by the thievery and violence of the evening, he did admit that the bottle of liquor in his hand was given to him by a looter who was leaving a ransacked store.

Feel Beauty Supply store lost most of their merchandise. They had been closed-down for the past week after earlier riots had decimated their store, and had just reopened the previous day. One witness said, "They tried to get into the cash register, stole hair items and some jewelry. I'm just frustrated because these people are not understanding how this affects others when they come with this foolishness. There was a tragedy, yes, but this is not how you deal with a tragedy." Store employees were concerned that the store would be closed again, and perhaps would not reopen. A frustrated store employee stated, I'm crushed. This is my living! I have to take care of my family. This is not good. It's not fair. People are not looking at this as a positive thing, they're looking at it as a rage, and it's not about raging. Raging gets you nowhere." Store manager Tanya Littleton confirmed that the store would shut down. She said, "It's not worth it. Right now our safety is more important than anything. She doubts she will reopen, saying that the owners are scared for their lives, and simply want out.

Another Ferguson resident wasn't so upset about the violence and looting. Twenty-nine-year-old Kevin Brankley claimed he knew Brown before he died. He blamed the police for the rioting, explaining that the police started the hostilities by firing tear gas into the intersection, which provoked a few members of the crowd to fired their guns into the air, in response. He said of the police, "The more worse they act, the more worse we'll act."

Saturday afternoon -- Peaceful protesters gathered outside of the Ferguson Police Station to hold a silent vigil in remembrance of Michael Brown. During the hour in which Brown died the previous week, the demonstrators quietly lifted their hands in the air to symbolize the hands-up don't shoot slogan.

Governor declares a curfew for Ferguson:

In response to Friday evening's riots, Missouri Governor Jay Nixon announced that he was ordering a curfew for the city of Ferguson, "beginning immediately," to last from Midnight to 5 a.m. the following morning, until further notice. The curfew was enforced by the Missouri State Highway Patrol, who had operational control of security in Ferguson. Activist leaders were worried that the curfew would spark more unrest and lead to more confrontations between the police and protesters. Captain Ron Johnson tried to downplay the curfew. He said, "We won't enforce it with trucks, we won't enforce it with tear gas, we will enforce it with communication. We will be telling people, It's time to go home." Captain Johnson also claimed the curfew would be enforced through conversations, and not by tanks and tear gas. He said, "We will survive this and will make a change."

In his 3 p.m. speech, Governor Nixon blamed the curfew on the rioters and then called for peace. He said, "If we are going to achieve justice, we must first have and maintain peace. This is a test. The eyes of the world are watching. I'm committed to making sure the forces of peace and justice prevail."

Margaret Huang of Amnesty International disagreed with the Governor. She responded to his comments, saying, "It's clear that the community doesn't feel heard. It's hard to build trust when the Governor won't meet with community members and restricts their movements with a curfew. The people of Ferguson should not have their rights further restricted."

Civil rights leader Jesse Jackson joined a loud but peaceful crowd that marched in the middle of the street carrying signs saying, "Mike Brown is our son" and "The whole world is watching Ferguson." They chanted "Hands up, don't shoot" and "Hey hey, ho ho, killer cops have got to go."

CHAPTER 31

DAY-9
SUNDAY
AUGUST-17

Riots erupted after midnight early Sunday morning, after police took a stand against the remaining rioters, who decided to test the police resolve to enforce a curfew. Community leaders tried to convince the demonstrators to go home before midnight, and to abide by the Midnight to 5:00 a.m. nightly curfew the Governor had enacted the day before, but several dozen of the remaining rioters were not willing to leave. They were reported to be mainly from out of town, and considered by police to be "troublemakers." Although the evening rain drove off many of the earlier demonstrators, the ones who remained were determined to provoke a confrontation with the police, which they hoped would be witnessed and recorded by the media.

Leading up to midnight, the rioters and the police squared-off in the middle of Ferguson Avenue. Several people parked their cars on Florissant Avenue, between the protesters and the police, in hopes of preventing a confrontation, but the police and the protesters were both ready to rumble, and determined to clash.

As law-enforcement personnel were preparing to disperse the crowd, several youths stripped off their shirts and laid down in the street. The youths told reporters, "I'm staying here because this is bigger than me. I'm sacrificing myself for the cause. We're ready to die." Another man was more confrontational. He said, "They armed. We armed. Let's do this."

When a protester shot a bottle rocket into the air, which exploded with a bang, the police used the opportunity to disperse the crowd, claiming shots had been fired.

The police announced over a loudspeaker "You must disperse the area. You are in violation of the state-imposed curfew. This is no longer a peaceful protest. You must leave the area." Moments later, the police line moved forward toward the rowdy group of remaining rioters and launched an assault on the crowd. With flash bang grenades going off, tanks rolling down the streets, and tear gas canisters exploding, it was a scene eerily similar to war-torn Iraq or Afghanistan. In response, an angry mob hurled Molotov Cocktails at officers, creating an even more dramatic scene, reminiscent of a war-zone. In the end, seven people were arrested for "failing to disperse," and one person was hospitalized for a gunshot wound to their head. Police reported hearing at least thirty gunshots and witnessing three Molotov Cocktails. Papa John's and Imo's pizzerias were both looted. Captain Ron Johnson of the Highway Patrol said the aggressive police force he used during the demonstrations was a "defensive measure," because the crowd was getting violent. He gave an example of a report he received about a man who brandished a handgun in the middle of the road, earlier in the day, to prove that some of the protesters had weapons. He said some people also hurled bottles at police, so "fearing for the safety of officers" he was forced to deploy smoke canisters and tear gas to clear the streets. Johnson claimed that multiple gunshots were fired throughout the night, and a patrol car was fired upon, although it was apparently not hit. During a 3 a.m. news conference, Johnson told reporters that his response to the "threat" was "proper" and "not related to the enforcement of the curfew." He also mentioned that he was disappointed, but his disappointment didn't extend to the Governor. Missouri Governor, Jay Nixon, said he thought the curfew was actually effective in helping to maintain peace. He extended the curfew for an additional night.

Attorney General Eric Holder announced that a Federal Medical Examiner would conduct an independent autopsy of Michael Brown. The decision was due to "extraordinary circumstances" in the case. The autopsy will be part of the FBI investigation. In all, three autopsy's will be performed on Michael Brown's body. One by the St. Louis County Medical Examiner, one by the Brown family, and one by the Justice Department.

Private Autopsy Released:

Dr. Michael Baden, who conducted a pro-bono private autopsy at the request of the Brown family, revealed on Sunday that, according the preliminary report, Michael Brown's wounds to his head and brain were the likely cause of death. Dr. Baden said, "There were at least six entry wounds, there might have been seven, but we'll have to correlate that with what was found in the first autopsy." Two head shots made several bullet holes in Brown's face, and an additional hole in his neck. The last shot that hit Brown was to the crown of his head and stayed in his body. That was the kill-shot, but the other head shot entered brown's head directly above his hairline, on the right side of his face. The bullet came out of Brown's right eye and then went through his jaw. The bullet then reentered his body at his neckline. Dr. Baden also stated that there was no gunshot residue on Brown's body, inferring that the shots might not have been fired at close range, but he could not tell without testing Brown's clothing.

The doctor could not find any marks on Browns body that would indicate that he was involved in a physical altercation before being shot. He concluded that Brown was shot at least 6 times with all bullets seeming to be fired from the front, but also indicated that one wound Brown had on his forearm could have possibly come from behind. The last shot to the top of Browns head was the kill-shot. Dr. Baden felt that Michael Brown could have survived the other gun shot wounds. Three bullets were recovered from Brown's body.

Al Sharpon Unity Rally:

Reverend Al Sharpton organized a community event at 3 p.m. on Sunday, calling it the "Unity Rally for justice for Michael Brown." It was held at the Greater Grace Church, in Ferguson, to bring the community together and hear the spoken words of Al Sharpton,

Martin Luther King III and other notable civil rights orators. Michael Johnson, the CEO of the Dane County Boys and Girls Club and a past vice-president of the St. Louis NAACP, also spoke at the Unity event. He said, "I think what's bothering me is I'm not seeing unity among our African American leaders here." He said. "There's a lot of good groups here trying to do the right thing, but they're not coordinated as well as they should be. I'm also disappointed in the police that they're continuously using tear gas. I think the current police department is culturally incompetent. You look at what happened in the 1960s, it's a direct mirror of what happened during the Civil Rights era. You don't sic German Shepherds on African Americans. This is the United States. This is not Syria, this is not China. We shouldn't have military vehicles driving up and down our streets." During the Unity Rally for justice for Michael Brown, Johnson presented the Brown family with a college scholarship for the three siblings of Michael Brown, which was donated by a university president, who wished to remain anonymous. Johnson complained about the lack of proper educational facilities for African American youths. He said, "I've had an opportunity to visit other cities in the last couple of weeks, and I'm just tired of seeing boarded-up school buildings and resources being taken away from our public schools. When you don't properly educate kids, they're going to grow up and have challenges." State Highway Patrol Captain Ron Johnson also gave a short speech. He told the mostly-black congregation, "I should stand up and say, I'm sorry," He told the press and parishioners that the violence has left his heart heavy, with "tears to my eyes and shame to my heart."

CHAPTER 32

DAY-10
MONDAY
AUGUST-18

Riots in Ferguson reached a new level of violence on Sunday night and Monday morning as the police stepped-up their riot control efforts. Two men were reportedly shot during the night as tear gas, rubber bullets, fires and live gunfire filled the evening sky and the streets of Ferguson. The police reported that thirty-one people were arrested the previous night, and many of these individuals resided in states other than Missouri, mainly California and New York. Six reporters were "detained."

In an early morning press-conference, Governor Jay Nixon canceled the curfew and called up the National Guard after protesters shot at police, threw Molotov Cocktails, looted local businesses, and carried out a "coordinated attempt" to block roads and overrun the police's command center. It was the worst night of violence since the death of Michael Brown. The Governor refused to answer questions relating to how many soldiers were being deployed to Ferguson or how long they would be there, but he tried to emphasize that the

Guard would have "limited responsibilities," in securing the area. The Governor pointed out, "Last night, Ferguson, Mo., experienced a very difficult and dangerous night as a result of a violent criminal element intent upon terrorizing the community. As long as there are vandals and looters and threats to the people and property of Ferguson, we must take action to protect our citizens,"

Greg Mason of the Missouri National Guard said, "We have well-trained and well-seasoned soldiers that will be assigned to protect the joint command headquarters here." Many people were concerned about how the National Guard would be used. History has proven that sometimes the National Guard contributes to violence in riot situations. President Obama addressed those concerns. He said, "I'll be watching, over the next several days, to access whether, in-fact, it is helping rather than hindering progress in Ferguson. There is no excuse for excessive force by police or any action that denies people the right to protest peacefully. Ours is a nation of laws. For the citizens who live under them, and for the citizens who enforce them."

Missouri Highway Patrol Captain Ron Johnson said, "Peaceful protests will be allowed in the city of Ferguson. We will not allow vandals and criminal elements to impact the safety and security of this community. We will not allow those elements to disrupt or impact the sole of this community." Later in the day, the state Highway Patrol and local police began enforcing an unconstitutional no standing policy, that made it illegal for anyone to stand still, illustrating the fact that the police ran out of legitimate tactics to use to disperse the crowds of protesters.

9:45 a.m. – In another morning news conference, Michael Baden, the Brown family's hired pathologist, who performed a private autopsy on Brown's body, said his results could be consistent with the police or witnesses accounts of how Brown died. "From a scientific point of view, we can't determine which witness is most consistent," Baden said at a news conference.

3:30 p.m. – In his second and longest speech on Ferguson, President Obama announced that he was going to dispatch Attorney General Eric Holder to monitor the unrest in Ferguson. Obama called on the citizens of America to address "the gulf of mistrust" that exists between minorities and law enforcement. He called for law-enforcement organizations across the country to review their policies on the use of military equipment and tactics on protesters during riot situations. Obama claimed the violence in Ferguson was caused by "a small minority" of crowd members who threw Molotov Cocktails at police. He said, "They are damaging the cause. They are not advancing it." He made a plea to the Ferguson community and to protesters, stating, "Let's seek to heal rather than to wound each other."

Obama gave the following speech to the White House Press Corps:

I want to address the situation in Ferguson, Missouri.

Earlier this afternoon, I spoke with Governor Nixon as well as Senators Roy Blunt and Claire McCaskill. I also met with Attorney General Eric Holder.

The Justice Department has opened an independent federal civil rights investigation into the death of Michael Brown. They are on the ground and along with the FBI, they are devoting substantial resources to that investigation. The Attorney General himself will be traveling to Ferguson on Wednesday to meet with the FBI agents and DOJ personnel conducting the federal criminal investigation and he will receive an update from them on their progress. He will also be meeting with other leaders in the community who's support is so critical to bringing about peace and calm in Ferguson.

Ronald Davis, the director of the DOJ's Office of Community-Oriented Policing Services, or COPS, is also traveling to Ferguson tomorrow to work with police officials on the ground. We've also had experts from the DOJ's community relations service, working in Ferguson since the days after the shooting to foster conversations among the local stake holders and reduce tensions among the community.

So, let me close just saying a few words about the tensions there. We have all seen images of protesters and law enforcement in the streets. It's clear that the vast majority of people are peacefully protesting. What's also clear is that a small minority of individuals are not.

While I understand the passions and the anger that arise over the death of Michael Brown, giving into that anger by looting or carrying guns, and even attacking the police only serves to raise tensions and stir chaos. It undermines rather than advancing justice.

Let me also be clear that our constitutional rights to speak freely, to assemble, and to report in the press must be vigilantly safeguarded: especially in moments like these. There's no excuse for excessive force by police or any action that denies people the right to protest peacefully.

Ours is a nation of laws: of citizens who live under them and for the citizens who enforce them. So, to a community in Ferguson that is rightly hurting and looking for answers, let me call once again for us to seek some understanding rather than simply holler at each other. Let's seek to heal rather than to wound each other.

As Americans, we've got to use this moment to seek out our shared humanity that's been laid bare by this moment. The potential of a young man and the sorrows of parents, the frustrations of a community, the ideals that we hold as one united American family.

I've said this before. In too many communities around the country, a gulf of mistrust exists between local residents and law enforcement. In too many communities, too many young men of color are left behind and seen only as objects of fear. And through initiatives like My Brother's Keeper, I'm personally committed to changing both perception and reality. And already, we're making some significant progress, as people of good will of all races are ready to chip in. But that requires that we build, and not tear down. And that requires we listen, and not just shout. That's how we're going to move forward together -- by trying to unite each other and understand each other, and not simply divide ourselves from one another. We're going to have to hold tight to those values in the days ahead. And that's how we bring about justice, and that's how we bring about peace.

So, with that, I've got a few questions I'm going to take.

QUESTION: The incident in Ferguson has led to a discussion about whether it's proper to militarize the nation's city police forces. And I'm wondering whether you wonder, or if you think that -- you see that as a factor regarding the police response in Ferguson. And also, do you agree with the decision by the governor to send in the National Guard?

ANSWER: Well, I think one of the great things about the United States has been our ability to maintain a distinction between our military and domestic law enforcement. That helps preserve our civil liberties. That helps ensure that the military is accountable to civilian direction. And that has to be preserved. After 9/11, I think understandably a lot of folks saw local communities that were ill-equipped for a potential catastrophic terrorist attack. And I think people in Congress, people of good will, decided we gotta make sure they get proper equipment to deal with threats that historically wouldn't arise in local communities. And some of that's been useful. I mean, some law enforcement didn't have radios that they could operate effectively in the midst of a disaster. Some communities needed to be prepared if in fact there was a chemical attack, and they didn't have hazmat suits. Having said that, I think it's probably useful for us to review how the funding has gone, how local law enforcement has used grant dollars, to make sure that what they're -- what they're purchasing is stuff that they actually need. Because, you know, there is a big difference between our military and our local law enforcement, and we don't want those lines blurred. That would be contrary to our traditions. And I think that there will be some bipartisan interest in reexamining some of those programs. With respect to the National Guard, I think it's important just to remember, this was a state-activated National Guard, so it's under the charge of the governor. This is not something that we initiated at the federal level. I spoke to Jay Nixon about this, expressed an interest in making sure that if in fact the National Guard is used, it is used in a limited and appropriate way. He described the support role that they're gonna be providing to local law enforcement. And I'll be watching over the next several days, to assess whether, in fact, it's helping rather than hindering progress in Ferguson.

Afternoon – Getty Images photographer Scott Olson was arrested on Monday afternoon while working in Ferguson, apparently for reporting from outside the police-designated "media reporting area." Fellow journalist Rob Crilly, of The Telegraph, said Olson was arrested for "not getting out of the way fast enough." A cell phone video of the arrest recorded Olson complaining to other reporters, "I'm being arrested because they said the media is required to be in a certain area." Olson's colleague, Joe Raedle, was lucky to elude arrest, and captured a picture of Scott Olson, with his hands bound behind him with zip-ties, being placed in a tactical police truck before being hauled off to jail. Olson's boss, Pancho Bernasconi, vice-president of news at Getty Images said of Olson's arrest:

> *Getty Images staff photographer Scott Olson was arrested this afternoon in Ferguson, Missouri, while on assignment documenting the events there. We at Getty Images stand firmly behind our colleague Scott Olson and the right to report from Ferguson. Getty Images is working to support his release as soon as possible. We strongly object to his arrest and are committed to ensuring he is able to resume his important work of capturing some of the most iconic images of this news story." When he was finally released, Olson told his boss at Getty Images, "I want to be able to do my job as a member of the media and not be arrested for just doing my job.*

Trayvon Martin's mom, Sybrina Fulton, wrote a heartbreaking letter, published in TIME magazine, to the family of Michael Brown. Fulton said she wished she could say "it will be alright" but the truth is she can only "pray." Their "lives are forever changed." The letter reads:

> *To The Brown Family,*
>
> *I wish I had a word of automatic comfort but I don't. I wish I could say that it will be alright on a certain or specific day but I can't. I wish that all of the pain that I have endured could possibly ease some of yours but it won't. What I can do for you is what has been done for me: pray for you then share my continuing journey as you begin yours.*
>
> *I hate that you and your family must join this exclusive yet growing group of parents and relatives who have lost loved ones to senseless gun violence. Of particular concern is that so many of these gun violence cases involve children far too young. But Michael is much more than a police/gun violence case; Michael is your son. A son that barely had a chance to live. Our children are our future so whenever any of our children — black, white, brown, yellow, or red — are taken from us unnecessarily, it causes a never-ending pain that is unlike anything I could have imagined experiencing.*
>
> *Further complicating the pain and loss in this tragedy is the fact that the*

killer of your son is alive, known, and currently free. In fact, he is on paid administrative leave. Your own feelings will bounce between sorrow and anger. Even when you don't want to think about it because it is so much to bear, you will be forced to by merely turning on your television or answering your cell phone. You may find yourselves pulled in many different directions by strangers who may be well-wishers or detractors. Your circle will necessarily close tighter because the trust you once, if ever, you had in "the system" and their agents are forever changed. Your lives are forever changed.

However with those changes come new challenges and opportunities. You will experience a swell of support from all corners of the world. Many will express their sympathies and encourage you to keep fighting for Michael. You will also, unfortunately, hear character assassinations about Michael which I am certain you already have. This will incense and insult you. All of this will happen before and continue long after you have had the chance to lay your son to rest.

I know this because I lived and continue to live this. I have devoted my life to the comprehensive missions of The Trayvon Martin Foundation – including providing support to families that have lost a young child to senseless gun violence regardless of race, ethnicity or gender. I will support you and your efforts to seek justice for your Michael and the countless other Michaels & Trayvons of our country. The 20 Sandy Hook children. Jordan Davis. Oscar Grant. Kendrick Johnson. Sean Bell. Hadya Pendleton. The Aurora shooting victims. The list is too numerous to adequately mention them all. According to The Children's Defense Fund, gun violence is the second leading cause of death for children ages 1-19. That is a horrible fact.

Facts, myths, and flat out lies are already out there in Michael's case. Theories, regardless of how ridiculous, are being pondered by the pundits. My advice is to surround yourselves with proven and trusted support. Through it all, I never let go of my faith, my family, or my friends. Long after the overwhelming media attention is gone, you will need those three entities to find your 'new normal.' Honor your son and his life, not the circumstances of his alleged transgressions. I have always said that Trayvon was not perfect. But no one will ever convince me that my son deserved to be stalked and murdered. No one can convince you that Michael deserved to be executed.

But know this: neither of their lives shall be in vain. The galvanizations of our communities must be continued beyond the tragedies. While we fight injustice, we will also hold ourselves to an appropriate level of intelligent advocacy. If they refuse to hear us, we will make them feel us. Some will mistake that last statement as being negatively provocative. But feeling us means feeling our pain; imagining our plight as parents of slain children. We will no longer be ignored. We will bond, continue our fights for justice, and make them remember our children in an appropriate light. I would hate to think that our lawmakers and leaders would need to lose a child before protecting the rest of them and making the necessary changes NOW...

With Heartfelt Support,

Sybrina D. Fulton

9 p.m. – Ferguson-Florissant School District cancels school for the rest of the week amid safety concerns for students. The district's first day was set for Aug. 14, but continued unrest led to a postponement. Ferguson School District officials said, "We believe that closing schools for the rest of this week will allow needed time for peace and stability to be restored to our community and allow families to plan ahead for the additional days that children will be out of school."

Soon after President Obama gave his afternoon speech to the press, Attorney General Eric Holder sent out a press release, entitled, "Attorney General Statement on Latest Developments in Federal Civil Rights Investigation in Ferguson, MO." The following Monday, after briefing President Obama on the latest developments in the investigation, he released the following statement:

FOR IMMEDIATE RELEASE

Monday, August 18, 2014

As I informed the President this afternoon, the full resources of the Department of Justice are being committed to our federal civil rights investigation into the death of Michael Brown.

During the day today, more than 40 FBI agents continued their canvassing of the neighborhood where Michael Brown was shot. As a result of this investigative work, several new interviews have already been conducted.

Moreover, at my direction, an additional medical examination is being performed on the body of Michael Brown. This autopsy is being performed today by one of the most experienced medical examiners in the United States military. I am confident this additional autopsy will be thorough and aid in our investigation.

In addition to updating the President on these developments, I informed him of my plan to personally travel to Ferguson Wednesday. I intend to meet with FBI investigators, and prosecutors on the ground from the Civil Rights Division and U.S. Attorney's Office officials about the ongoing investigation.

I realize there is tremendous interest in the facts of the incident that led to Michael Brown's death, but I ask for the public's patience as we conduct this investigation. The selective release of sensitive information that we have seen in this case so far is troubling to me. No matter how others pursue their own separate inquiries, the Justice Department is resolved to preserve the integrity of its investigation. This is a critical step in restoring trust between law enforcement and the community, not just in Ferguson, but beyond.

In order to truly begin the process of healing, we must also see an end to the acts of violence in the streets of Ferguson. Those who have been peacefully demonstrating should join with law enforcement in condemning the actions of looters and others seeking to enflame tensions.

To assist on this front, the Department will be dispatching additional representatives from the Community Relations Service, including Director Grande Lum, to Ferguson. These officials will continue to convene stakeholders whose cooperation is critical to keeping the peace. Furthermore, as the President has announced, Ron Davis, our Director of the COPS office will arrive on the ground in Ferguson Tuesday. Ron has been in touch with local and state officials since last week, providing technical assistance on crowd control techniques and facilitating communications between Missouri officials and other law enforcement officials whose communities have faced similar challenges in the past.

Also on Monday, the National Bar Association announced their filing of a lawsuit for information related to the shooting death of Michael Brown. The National Bar Association was founded in 1925. It claims to be the nation's oldest and largest national network of predominantly African American attorneys and judges, representing the interests of approximately 60,000 lawyers, judges, law professors and law students. In a press release, the National Bar Association release the following letter:

FOR IMMEDIATE RELEASE

August 18, 2014

The National Bar Association has Filed a Lawsuit Against the City of Ferguson and the Ferguson Police Department Seeking Pertinent Information Related to the Shooting:

WASHINGTON, DC — Earlier today, the National Bar Association filed a lawsuit against the City of Ferguson, MO and the Ferguson Police Department seeking any and all incident reports, investigative reports, notes and memorandums prepared by Ferguson Police officers, in-dash camera video, photographs, cellphone video and recordings in connection with the shooting death of Michael Brown.

The National Bar Association also sent a Preservation of Evidence Notice to both entities, requesting that they preserve the police officers' raw notes of all statements, observations, and data collected from the scene of the incident, specifically including the officer involved and all responding officers, officer detail logs from the crime scene, and video & photographic evidence related to the August 9, 2014, fatal shooting of Michael Brown and subsequent arrests of protestors in the City of Ferguson.

"There can be no full, fair and accurate accounting in any state or federal criminal or civil action unless any and all footage is carefully preserved," stated Pamela J. Meanes, President of the National Bar Association. "We want to ensure the family of Michael Brown and the residents of St. Louis understand correct measures are being taken to protect evidence regarding this tragic incident."

Monday evening's protests began peacefully, but then turned violent again, as scores of protesters clashed with police in another night of late-night rioting. Many Ferguson residents were growing worried about Ferguson's future, and began to express their concern, and their desire to leave town. Jodie Robinson said that she's not going to take any more chances. She said, "I'm moving to Atlanta or Houston." Others in the community were more reserved and understanding about the rioting. Barber Shop owner Antonia Henley, who claims his employees are too afraid to come to work, still believed the protesting had merit. He said, "You do have to go through some rough times to get change."

CHAPTER 33

DAY-11
TUESDAY
AUGUST-19

After another evening of unrest on Monday, community members got up early to clean the roadways and sidewalks of the debris and trash the protesters left behind. Police erected a metal fence around the burnt-out shell of Quicktrip to prevent any further protests at the convenience store parking lot.

7 a.m. – Michael Brown's father and mother, Lesley McSpadden, gave an interview on the Today Show with Matt Lauer, calling for peace and praying for justice for her son. Later she was asked the following questions:

Question - Mrs. McSpadden, what will bring peace to the streets of Ferguson?

Answer - Justice. Justice will bring peace, I believe.

Question - Only if that justice results in the arrest or charges being filed against officer Wilson. Is that what it's going to take?

Answer - Yes--him being arrested. Charges being filed, and a prosecution. Him being held accountable for what he did.

Question - Mr. Brown, do you have faith in the system, in the matter?

Answer - Yes I do.

Question - Do you think it's worked so far?

Answer - No

Question - So what gives you the faith that is will work eventually?

Answer - Eventually justice will prevail.

Question - I want to ask you about the autopsy that was conducted on behalf of your family by Dr. Boden. We do know that he was shot at least six times. Did you learn what you think you needed to know from that autopsy to give you a clearer picture of what happened to your son that night?

Answer. - No.

Question - What else do you need to know?

Answer - Why. Why. What was the cause for that. Excessive force. Nobody deserved that.

Question - Let me ask you about that force, and Ben (Crump) let me bring you in on this one. The St. Louis County Prosecutor, Mr. McCulloch, said police shootings are different than other shootings because officers, by law, are authorized to use force. Ben, based on what you saw in that autopsy by Dr. Boden, are you convinced it was excessive force?

Answer from Brown family attorney Ben Crump - "I think clearly this was excessive force Matt. In fact, you look at the autopsy, you look at the witness accounts, when he put his hands up and surrendered and all the witness accounts say the police continued to shoot. It's going to be an issue that comes before this prosecution praying that he is arrested. That the jury is going to have to decide what is the amount of necessary force to use, because all of the witnesses said it seemed like an execution style murder and that is why there is so much unrest. To say, you can't do this to our children in broad daylight."

Question - Mrs. McSpadden and Mr. Brown, you say you are looking for justice for you son. I ask you, do you think this continuing violence, in the street of Ferguson, night after night, runs the risk of overshadowing that search for justice. In some ways, does it detract from justice for your son?

Mr. Brown Answers - No.

Mrs. McSpadden answers - I think that is does somewhat,

because it is a distraction, but we won't let it distract us to the point where we lose focus. We have to remain focused and we have to remain strong and the violence needs to stop. When justice is prevailed then maybe they will regain their trust in the locals, but right now it is really out of control." Mr. Brown interrupted to say, "We need to keep the focus on Michael Brown Jr. That's who we need to keep the focus on, Michael Brown Jr."

1 p.m. – A twenty-three year-old man was fatally shot by two police officers in north St. Louis, just four miles from Ferguson. Authorities said the suspect threatened officers with a knife after begging them to kill him. The incident did not appear to be related to the unrest in Ferguson.

In a police press conference that same afternoon, St. Louis Police Chief Sam Dodson stated:

A gentleman entered a convenience store nearby and walked out carrying two energy drinks. When he was asked to stop he walked out and the store owners let him walk out. A few minutes later he came back into the store front, took what was described as a package of muffins, or pastries. The store owner walked out with him, and asked him, hey, can you please pay for those before you leave. The suspect tossed them into the street. And then he continued walking. The suspect, who is described right now as a twenty-three-year-old African American was business owner, an Alderman in the City of St. Louis, noticed the behavior and also contacted the police department. The store owner and the Alderwoman said the suspect was armed with a knife, acting erratically, pacing back and forth in the street, talking to himself. As officers arrived, the suspect turns towards the officers and started walking towards them clutching his waistband. He then pulled out a knife in what we describe as an over hand grip, and told the officers shoot me now, kill me now. As he walked towards the officer, the officers began giving him verbal commands. Drop the knife. Step back. Drop the knife. At which time the suspect stopped as he was approaching the driver and then turned his attention on the officer in the passenger seat. Both officers are out of the car. When they initially got out of the car they did not have their weapons drawn. When the suspect displayed his knife, they drew their weapons. The officers are giving the suspect verbal commands, stop, drop the knife. Stop. Drop the knife. The suspect moved towards the passenger, the police officer that was seated in the passenger side of the vehicle, at which time he came within three to four feet of the officer, and the officer shot. Both officers fired their weapons, striking the suspect, and the suspect is deceased.

A cell phone video that caught the entire scene of the shooting, from start to finish, was released soon after the police press conference. The video showed the suspect acting erratically, and mainly confirmed what the police stated at the time, except the video does not show the suspect holding a knife in an overhand grip, contradicting what the police initially reported.

The suspect had his hands down by his side when he was shot, and he was further away than the three to four feet the police had claimed. When asked about these discrepancies, Chief Dodson said that even though the suspect had his hands down, he was still advancing towards the officers with a knife when he was shot. He said, "The officers did what I think you or I would do, they protected their life in that situation." In an interview with Chris Cuomo on CNN, Chief Dodson was asked why a less lethal form of force wasn't used, such as a Taser. The Chief responded, "Certainly a Taser is an option that's available to the officers, but Tasers aren't 100 percent. So you've got an individual with a knife who's moving towards you, not listening to any verbal commands, continues, says, 'shoot me now, kill me now.' Tasers aren't 100 percent. If that Taser misses, that individual continues on and hurts an officer. In a lethal situation, they use lethal force.

Chief Dodson claimed that the erroneous information he gave out in the press conference was based on "witness accounts" and not by any information he was given by the police officers involved in the shooting. It is not clear what witnesses Dodson was referring to, since the cell phone video which showed the shooting also showed the police telling all witnesses to leave the area, and a witness yelling back at officers that they were running off their witnesses.

To their credit, The St. Louis Police Department immediately released the two 911 calls about the suspect, and also the dispatch recordings from police. Dozens of people began to protest at the site where the man was shot, waving signs and chanting, "Hands up! Shoot back!" Fearing possible looting and rioting in the area, at least one store owner backed-up a U-haul to his business and took away the store's valuables.

The relative calm on Tuesday afternoon descended into chaos soon after Missouri Highway Patrol Captain, Ron Johnson, made an effort to mend fences with the protesters. Johnson explained, "Our peaceful protesters are not the enemy. Tonight we closed the roadway. We allowed those who come in peace to walk the roadway," Some members of the crowd did not want to hold hands with the police. They demanded justice for Michael Brown and clashed with law-enforcement personnel into the evening. Police reported being under heavy gun fire, and responded by making 78 arrests. Highway Patrol Captain Johnson praised law-enforcement personnel for their "restraint." He said they, "acted with restraint and calm." Johnson also claimed that even though officers were shot at, they did not discharge their firearms. He then pleaded for safety, saying, "I don't want anyone to get hurt. I don't want an officer to get hurt. I don't want a citizen to get hurt. We have to find a way to stop it."

CHAPTER 34

DAY-12
WEDNESDAY
AUGUST-20

Missouri Highway Patrol Captain Ron Johnson stated in a morning news conference that protests were less confrontational on Tuesday night and into Wednesday morning than they have been in previous days, although he claimed threats were made to kill a police officer, and law-enforcement still had to arrest 47 people. One of those arrested was an activist who laid down in the middle of the street and refused to move until officers pulled him to his feet and took him to jail.

Ferguson Mayor James Knowles pleaded for peace. He said, "Let's have a night that we can completely separate those good people exercising their First Amendment rights from those who are trying to co-opt this horrible situation into something to meet their own needs."

Even though the police had asked activist organizations to refrain from holding demonstrations in the evening, a few dozen stalwarts stayed into the night to confront law-enforcement. One group chanted "We young, we strong, we marching all night long," but when the clergy asked the group to go home, many of them left, except for the extremists, who began throwing bottles at police. At one point in the evening, the police announced over a loudspeaker, "Leave the area immediately! Media get out of our way. We're trying to do a job." Then law-enforcement moved-in with a quick and aggressive response that cleared the streets, for a while, until the group re-formed and then began to attack local businesses. Violence broke out again, at 1 a.m., when a McDonald's came under attack by a mob of young rioters who broke windows, threw bottles and taunted the police, provoking an immediate and aggressive tactical response that allowed law-enforcement to clear the streets again and arrest the agitators.

Attorney General Eric Holder arrived in St. Louis on Wednesday to meet with community leaders and federal investigators. His first speaking engagement was at the Florissant Valley Community College in North St. Louis. In his fifteen-minute prepared speech, Holder told about 50 students and community members that he had assigned his, "most experienced agents and prosecutors to investigate the Michael Brown shooting." He continued, "We have seen a great deal of progress over the years, but we also see problems and these problems stem from mistrust and mutual suspicion."

Kiyanda Welch, a student at the community college, told reporters that Holder told them, "Change is coming." The students felt Holder truly cared about their plight, One student stated that Holder, "specifically wanted to know how we feel about the police department." He said, "I really felt he was listening to us and took heed of what we were saying."

In the community meeting, Holder tried to find some solidarity with blacks who are harassed by the police. He said, "I am the Attorney General of the United States, but I am also a black man. I can remember being stopped on the New Jersey turnpike on two occasions and accused of speeding. Pulled over. ... 'Let me search your car' ... Go through the trunk of my car, look under the seats and all this kind of stuff. I remember how humiliating that was and how angry I was and the impact it had on me." Holder continued, "The eyes of the nation and the world are watching Ferguson right now. The world is watching because the issues raised by the shooting of Michael Brown predate this incident. This is something that has a history to it, and the history simmers beneath the surface in more communities than just Ferguson."

After his speech to the students at the community college, Eric Holder visited the Missouri office of the FBI for a briefing on the status of their investigation. He told reporters that his civil rights investigators and prosecutors are "very experienced."

On his last stop of the day, Eric Holder sat down with the parents of Michael Brown at the U.S. attorney's office, in a private, twenty-minute-long meeting. The family had a chance to ask the Attorney General about the upcoming investigation and took the opportunity to tell him about their son. Holder reportedly promised the Brown's that the inquiry into the death of their son would be, "fair and independent," but he added that his investigation would be different than the local police investigation. He said, "We're looking for possible violations of federal civil rights statutes."

The St. Louis Post Dispatch published an opinion editorial article (Op-Ed), that the Attorney General wrote, to coincide with his visit to Ferguson. His Op-Ed said:

Since the Aug. 9 shooting death of Michael Brown, the nation and the world have witnessed the unrest that has gripped Ferguson, Missouri. At the core of these demonstrations is a demand for answers about the circumstances of this young man's death and a broader concern about the state of our criminal justice system. At a time when so much may seem uncertain, the people of Ferguson can have confidence that the Justice Department intends to learn -- in a fair and thorough manner--exactly what happened.

Today, I will be in Ferguson to be briefed on the federal civil rights investigation that I have closely monitored since I launched it more than one week ago. I will meet personally with community leaders, FBI investigators and federal prosecutors from the Justice Department's Civil Rights Division and the U.S. Attorney's Office to receive detailed briefings on the status of this case.

The full resources of the Department of Justice have been committed to the investigation into Michael Brown's death. This inquiry will take time to complete, but we have already taken significant steps. Approximately 40 FBI agents and some of the Civil Rights Division's most experienced prosecutors have been deployed to lead this process, with the assistance of the United States Attorney in St. Louis. Hundreds of people have already been interviewed in connection with this matter. On Monday, at my direction, a team of federal medical examiners conducted an independent autopsy.

We understand the need for an independent investigation, and we hope that the independence and thoroughness of our investigation will bring some measure of calm to the tensions in Ferguson. In order to begin the healing process, however, we must first see an end to the acts of violence in the streets of Ferguson. Although these acts have been committed by a very small minority -- and, in many cases, by individuals from outside Ferguson -- they seriously undermine, rather than advance, the cause of justice. And they interrupt the deeper conversation that the legitimate demonstrators are trying to advance.

The Justice Department will defend the right of protesters to peacefully demonstrate and for the media to cover a story that must be told. But violence cannot be condoned. I urge the citizens of Ferguson who have been peacefully exercising their First Amendment rights to join with law enforcement in condemning the actions of looters, vandals and others seeking to inflame tensions and sow discord.

Law enforcement has a role to play in reducing tensions, as well. As the brother of a retired law enforcement officer, I know firsthand that our men and women in uniform perform their duties in the face of tremendous threats and significant personal risk. They put their lives on the line every day, and they often have to make split-second decisions.

At the same time, good law enforcement requires forging bonds of trust between the police and the public. This trust is all-important, but it is also fragile. It requires that force be used in appropriate ways. Enforcement priorities and arrest patterns must not lead to disparate treatment under the law, even if such treatment is unintended. And police forces should reflect the diversity of the communities they serve.

Over the years, we have made significant progress in ensuring that this is the case. But progress is not an endpoint; it is a measure of effort and of commitment. Constructive dialogue should continue -- but it must also be converted into concrete action. And it is painfully clear, in cities and circumstances across our great nation, that more progress, more dialogue, and more action is needed.

This is my pledge to the people of Ferguson: Our investigation into this matter will be full, it will be fair, and it will be independent. And beyond the investigation itself, we will work with the police, civil rights leaders, and members of the public to ensure that this tragedy can give rise to new understanding -- and robust action -- aimed at bridging persistent gaps between law enforcement officials and the communities we serve. Long after the events of Aug. 9 have receded from the headlines, the Justice Department will continue to stand with this community.

As we move forward together, I ask for the public's cooperation and patience. And I urge anyone with information related to the shooting to contact the FBI by dialing 800-CALL-FBI, option 4."

Grand Jury Investigation:

A Grand Jury was convened to determine if there was enough evidence to charge officer Darren Wilson with the murder of Michael Brown. They were responsible for determining whether there was probable cause to believe the accused committed a crime.

In Missouri, 12 jurors are appointed to a three-to-four month term on the Grand Jury. At least 9 jurors need to agree that there is sufficient evidence to indict a suspect and charge that subject with a crime. Each juror receives $18 per day, plus reimbursement for car mileage. It's normal to have two alternate jurors sit through all of the testimony, but the Darren Wilson Grand Jury excluded alternates.

Prosecutors have a lot of discretion in determining if a person will be charged with a crime, or not. If a prosecuting attorney believes a crime has been committed, they then have the ability to file charges themselves, independently. In cases where it is less obvious that a crime has been committed, a Grand Jury is often used to see if there is enough evidence to arrest a suspect and send the case to trial.

The jurors for the Darren Wilson Grand Jury had been appointed since May, for a four month commitment. Their term was scheduled to end in September, but the Attorney General extended their service through January, to give them the time they might need to hear all of the evidence and witnesses that would be presented to the jurors in the Darren Wilson case.

When a police officer is involved in a fatal shooting, he/she is automatically put on paid administrative leave until an investigation can be concluded, either vindicating the officer or finding enough evidence to pursue an indictment. If an officer is vindicated, he/she must attend counseling before returning to duty.

The duration of a Grand Jury investigation varies. It can end in a day or it could last for months. The duration depends on the amount of evidence to be presented, and the ability of the jurors to agree on a verdict. Prosecutor McCulloch said, "Our target date is hopefully by the middle of October."

Two assistant prosecutors on Attorney General McCulloch's staff presented evidence in the case. Prosecutor Kathi Alizadeh, is a white woman who has worked as a homicide prosecutor for the past twenty-seven years, and Prosecutor Sheila Whirley, a black woman who has worked on Grand Jury investigations for eighteen years, were the chosen prosecutors for the Darren Wilson investigation. Governor Jay Nixon had been putting soft pressure on Attorney General Bob McCulloch to recuse himself from the case after reporters pointed out that McCulloch's father was a police officer who was shot and killed by a black man, and people questioned his impartiality in a case against a police officer who killed a black man. Governor Nixon had the power to replace McCulloch himself, but that would have been a risky political move, so he hoped that McCulloch would step-down, by himself. Governor Nixon's lack of support for McCulloch was obvious to everyone, including McCulloch. He said of the Governor, "Just make a decision. Stand up, man up. Either say 'I am not removing McCulloch,' or 'I am removing McCulloch.' And let's get on with this." McCulloch stated, "This is one distraction he can put to rest. Others are demonstrating and calling for my removal. I understand that but they need to express it to the guy who can do it." He went on to say, he had "absolutely no intention of walking away from my duties and responsibilities. I've done it for twenty-four years and, if I say so myself, done a very good job of being fair and impartial." McCulloch complained that the Governor's inability to make a clear decision of who was going to prosecute the case "undermines everything except the cover that he's pulled over his head."

Shooting incident report - finally released - August 20th:

The St. Louis County Police Department finally released the incident report of the Michael Brown shooting. The two-page report offered few details, since most of the information that it should have contained was either redacted or not included in the report. The Incident Report was created on August 19th, 2014, ten days after the incident occurred. The report was not approved until August 20th, 2014. Some of the scant details listed in the report were the name of the victim, Michael Brown, and the nature of the incident, which lists "homicide." The few other details the report provided were the name of the officer involved, Darren Wilson and the address in which the shooting occurred. All other information about what occurred was either redacted or left out of the Incident Report entirely.

CHAPTER 35

DAY-13
THURSDAY
AUGUST-21

Ferguson police and protesters enjoyed a night of relative calm. By 12:30 early Friday morning, many of the 150 protesters who had paced back and forth on Ferguson's West Florissant Avenue, had gone-home after an evening rainstorm made protesting uncomfortable. Police showed a more relaxed approach to policing than they had shown before, and it seemed to help decrease tensions between police and protesters. Buses were back in service and people from the community could be seen walking the streets in peace and shopping at local stores. Only seven people were arrested. Five of them were arrested for failing to disperse.

Highway Patrol Captain Ron Johnson made a statement to the media at 1.a.m. to tell the reporters how well the new police anti-tension tactics were working. He said, "Tonight was another good night. We're heading toward a sense of peace for our community. We saw a different crowd that came out tonight. Less agitators," Johnson said.

Although there was relative peace in the streets, the message from the protesters to the community, to seek justice for Michael Brown, continued, albeit more muted than they had been on previous nights, after the rain and lighting had driven off all but the most ardent activists. One of those activists was nineteen-year-old Dasha Jones, who paraded down West Florissant Avenue with a sign that read, "The Whole Damn System is Guilty." She said she was so traumatized by seeing Michael Brown's dead body laying in the middle of the street that she felt she had to do something, to tell the world what went down in Ferguson--and plea for justice for "Big Mike." She said, "I feel like that could have been any one of my family members." When asked why she was still protesting when most others had gone home, she responded, "I'm not tired because he doesn't have justice."

Police had to whisk away a white, female Darren Wilson supporter who thought it would be a good idea to carry a sign, among all of the Michael Brown supporters, that called for justice for Darren Wilson. Angry black activists surrounded the woman and began taunting and yelling at her, until the police moved in to snatch her out of the melee, before she could get mauled by the crowd.

United States Senator Claire McCaskill walked among the crowd on Thursday night, and after seeing no clashes with police, she determined that the violence that had occurred in Ferguson in the past, was over. She said, "I think it's time for a lot of the media to leave here."

National Guard Withdraws:

At 12 p.m., Governor Jay Nixon ordered the Missouri National Guard to withdraw from Ferguson, immediately, signaling that the violence in Ferguson was over and that order was restored in the small Midwestern suburb. He said the relations between police and protesters were "greatly improved with fewer incidents of outside agitators interfering with peaceful protesters and fewer acts of violence."

Governor Nixon praised the efforts of the National Guard, saying, "I greatly appreciate the men and women of the Missouri National Guard for successfully carrying out the specific, limited mission of protecting the Unified Command Center so that law enforcement officers could focus on the important work of increasing communication within the community, restoring trust, and protecting the people and property of Ferguson."

Attorney General Eric Holder said he had seen a "real fracture" in the community of Ferguson when he visited the city the previous day. He felt the people who live in Ferguson have "a desire to be seen as equals, a real desire to have healing." He said, "Out of this tragedy comes a great opportunity to reform that community,"

A national poll conducted by PEW Research concluded that whites and blacks have completely different views regarding the racial implications of the Michael Brown shooting. "Among blacks, 80% say the shooting "raises important issues about race," and 18% of blacks say "race is getting more attention than it deserves." Although "just 37% of whites polled say the case raises important racial issues, and 47% of whites say race is getting more attention than it deserves."

CHAPTER 36

DAY-14
FRIDAY
AUGUST-22

Tensions remained relaxed between the protesters and the police on Thursday night and into the early Friday morning. Law-enforcement kept most of the tactical equipment and tanks off the streets, which helped calm the crowd. While police in Ferguson were trying new tactics to reduce the hostilities between the races, other former and current police officers and government workers from a group known as "Oath Keepers" came to Ferguson and offered free security for businesses, to prevent looting and to protect the public from an over aggressive police force. The 35,000-member national organization was created in 2009 by a Yale graduate and attorney, Stewart Rhodes, to protect people's constitutional rights, including those of protesters confronted by what Rhodes considered "overly militarized police."

Oath Keepers claims to "honor our oath to defend the Constitution by acting with maximum courage, strength, and honor, to live out the spirit of the Founding Fathers, and to honor those who have come before." Oath Keepers says they are comprised of "military, veterans, and peace officers who will honor their oaths to defend the Constitution, will NOT 'just follow orders,' will stand for liberty, and will save the Republic." Their motto is: "Not on Our Watch!"

The seemingly anti-government organization had stationed armed security volunteers on rooftops all around the Ferguson business district to protect the nearby apartments and businesses from being looted and burned. Oath Keeper members were seen helping businesses board-up their storefronts, and patrolling the neighborhood in military fatigues, toting high-caliber assault weapons. Security guards on rooftops were equipped with fire extinguishers, buckets of water, emergency equipment and weapons. Oath Keepers volunteers said they had the legal right to stop arson and looting from happening, by force, if necessary.

A local apartment dweller who saw the armed security personnel on his rooftop thought it was a good idea to have more people protecting the businesses. He said, "I am in the middle of a difficult spot. I feel a lot better having those guys up on the roof." The media and local residents were wondering who the uniformed guards were. Many of them thought they were from the Ku Klux Klan.

The police interviewed Oath Keepers security guards and threatened to arrest them for operating without a license, if the group continued to provide security for the stores. Oath Keepers founder Stewart Rhodes confirmed that his group would comply, and said, "We are going to go back as protesters."

Mother Jones magazine journalists did an in-depth investigation into the Oath Keepers organizations in 2010. The magazine reported, "In the months I've spent getting to know the Oath Keepers, I've toggled between viewing them either as potentially dangerous conspiracy theorists or as crafty intellectuals with the savvy to rally politicians to their side. The answer, I came to realize, is that they cover the whole spectrum."

Oath Keepers volunteers say they have protected property and protected lives in Ferguson since they arrived. John Karriman, an Oath Keeper volunteer from Joplin, Missouri, said, "We are here to volunteer our time and make sure everybody stays safe."

With a funeral pending on Monday, demonstrators were respectful of the wishes of the Brown family--to be calm, and to keep the protesting to a minimum. Friday night was another peaceful example of what Captain Ron Johnson was trying to accomplish in the preceding week of violent protesting. It provided some hope that the rioting was over, and that normalcy would soon resume in Ferguson.

CHAPTER 37

DAY-15
SATURDAY
AUGUST-23

NO JUSTICE NO PEACE

HANDS UP DON'T SHOOT

BLACK LIVES MATTER

After another night of peaceful protests, Missouri Highway Patrol Captain Ron Johnson happily announced, at a 2 a.m. press conference, that they had made it through another night of peaceful protesting, with no arrests.

The NAACP held a 2 p.m. demonstration through the streets of the Ferguson business district and surrounding neighborhoods, with approximately 400 people marching together along with Missouri State Highway Patrol Capt. Ron Johnson, Chief Sam Dotson of the St. Louis Police Department, and Jon Belmar of the St. Louis County Police Department.

During a 7 p.m. press conference, President Barack Obama announced that three White House aides would attend the funeral of Michael Brown on Monday morning. The group would include of two representatives from the White House Office of Public Engagement, and Broderick Johnson, the chairman of the "My Brother's Keeper Task Force," a program that President Obama

278

established to empower young minorities. Marlon Marshall, who attended high-school with Michael Brown's mother, was chosen as one of the representatives of the Office of Public Engagement. Obama also mentioned the need to review the tactical equipment that municipalities have been given, though military surplus programs and federal grant funding.

Protesting was kept to a minimum through the day and the evening, although a few people were arrested late at night, but violence was contained for another night.

CHAPTER 38

DAY-16
SUNDAY
AUGUST-24

In his early morning press conference, Highway Patrol Captain Ron Johnson reported that only six people were arrested, for failing to disperse, in another relatively peaceful evening.

Nearly one hundred members of the Michael Brown family gathered together for a private viewing at the Austin A. Layne Mortuary, near Ferguson, on Sunday afternoon--one day before Brown's funeral. Although Brown was shot twice in the head and sustained multiple bullet wounds to his face, there were virtually no visible signs of the shots that ended his life. His arms were laid across his chest as he lay in a gold and black casket. He was dressed in a checkered, blue-and-white button-up shirt with a navy blue sweater-vest, and a red-and-blue striped bow tie. Gospel music played in the background and pictures of Michael Brown where everywhere. Two big-screen TV's played a slideshow of pictures of Brown while he was growing up. A large black-and-white poster of Brown with his headphones on had a caption that read, "There are no goodbyes for us. Wherever you are, you will always be in our hearts." Family members who attended the viewing were wearing matching blue-and-white t-shirts, with a silk-screen image of Michael Brown and his mom, stating, "A Bond Never Broken."

Lesley McSpadden and Michael Brown Sr. had time to spend alone with their son's body before the rest of the guests were brought-in. Michael Brown's sister, fifteen-year-old Deja Brown, stood next to Brown's body for nearly an hour.

Michael Brown's uncle, Reverend Charles Ewing, gave a short sermon. He said, "Help us, Lord, to get through this. Help us to bind together in the spirit of unity and let peace prevail. Let joy prevail. Let harmony prevail. In the mighty name of Jesus, Oh father God, cover us with your blood and protect each and every one of us as we go to our respective places. Help us, Lord, those who don't know you, to keep our minds stayed on you. For you said you would keep us in perfect peace whose mind is stayed on you. There shall be glory after this."

Michael Brown senior thought the past two weeks had been like a dream. He said to his extended family, "It was a dream. It's a reality now. I can't really explain how I feel. I'm torn, hurt, upset and angry. I can't explain." He also asked protesters to take a day off during the funeral. He was hoping for a full day of focusing on Michael, without the distractions of the police and protesters clashing in the streets. He continued, "I really don't want protesters tomorrow. Our son needs to have a moment of silence for tomorrow." Brown's grandmother, Desuirea Harris, was inconsolable. She sat in a corner and cried uncontrollably.

Michael Brown's mother, Lesley McSpadden, was also dressed in a memorialized t-shirt, but her shirt was different from the others. Mrs. McSpadden's t-shirt was emblazoned with an image of her son in a high-school graduation cap, along with a picture of her looking sad. The text on the t-shirt read, "He was special 2 me," on the front, and on the back it said, "To my children, if I had to choose between loving you and breathing--I would use my last breath to tell you I love you." After the viewing, McSpadden stated, "They say tomorrow is going to be the hardest day, but I think today was--just seeing my baby laying there, cold."

Sunday's St. Louis Peace Fest was an annual event near Ferguson. It was already scheduled to be a day of festivities and for promoting peace, but this year, in the wake of the death of Michael

Brown, the event coordinator decided to make it about race relations. The festival ran all-day Sunday, from 8 a.m. until 8 p.m., and drew hundreds of attendees who braved the 98-degree heat to encourage peace over violence, and to have some fun.

The families of Trayvon Martin, Oscar Grant and Michael Brown, who have all lost children to police violence, were in attendance to participate in the "Peace Fest," and speak to the crowd about their loss. Michael Brown Sr. asked for protesters to suspend their protests until after his son's funeral. He said, "All I want is peace while my son is being laid to rest."

In the evening, a small group of protesters walked along Florissant Avenue, in Ferguson's business district, to continue to get the message out, and to bring justice to the Brown family. The violence that erupted in the past, seemed to be in the past, or at least the protesters were abiding by the wishes of the Brown family to be respectful leading up to the funeral.

As the day ended, protesters, police and the Brown family prayed for peace the following day.

CHAPTER 39

DAY-17
MONDAY
AUGUST-25

The Funeral:

There was standing room only, and not much of that, at the Monday morning funeral of Michael Brown at the Friendly Temple Missionary Baptist Church, in St. Louis, Missouri. Friends, family and strangers said goodbye to Brown on a sweltering summer day. The twenty-five hundreds seats in the church's main auditorium filled up quickly, and so did the two-thousand seat overflow rooms, so the rest of the mourners had to stay outside, in 100 degree heat, waiting for a chance to get a glimpse of the Brown family, Jesse Jackson, Al Sharpton, Spike Lee or any of the other notable celebrity speakers and attendees.

The Brown family was led to the funeral by a motorcycle procession of uniformed police officers. The church was filled with flowers and images of Michael Brown. A large projection screen TV replayed a slideshow of Brown's best photo's, and a full-band and choir also accompanied the performances of some of the speakers.

None of those speakers was Governor Jay Nixon, who's office put out a statement earlier in the day, stating, "The governor has communicated to attorneys representing the family of Michael Brown that he will not be attending today's funeral out of respect for the family, who deserve time to focus on remembering Michael and grieving for their loss."

Al Sharpton would not have missed the funeral for anything. It was his moment of glory, when all eyes were on him. He said some nice words about Michael Brown and his family, but he was not so friendly in his comments about law-enforcement, nor to some African Americans who, he suggested, were part of the problem. In Sharpton's eulogy, he said:

To the Brown family, to all of the ministers, to all of the officials that have gathered, I want to go to the book of Micah, sixth chapter, eighth verse. 'He has shown you, o men, what is good. What does the lord require of you but to do justice and to love kindness and to walk humbly with your God?' There has been a lot said in the last few days. This afternoon, Leslie and Michael Sr. will have to do something that is out of order. They will have to lay their son to rest. Order says that children bury their parents. It is out of order for children to be buried by their parents.

We should not sit here today and act like we are watching something that is in order. In all of our religious and spiritual celebration, let us not lose sight of the fact that this young man should be doing his second week in college.

Religion ought to affirm what we are doing, not being an escapism from what is done. And some of us are so heavenly bound that we're no earthly good. Before you get to heaven, before you put on your robes, before you walk down the street, you've got to deal with the streets in Ferguson, in St. Louis. God is not going to judge you by your behavior in heaven. He's going to judge you by what you do on earth. He will not judge you by what Moses did at the Red Sea. He will not judge you by what Joshua did at the Jordan. He will say what Michael Brown, 18-year-old boy, laid out in the street, hour and a half before the detective came. Another hour or so before they came to remove his body. Family couldn't come to the ropes. Dogs sniffing' through. What did you do? What did I require of you?

We sit like we have no requirements. Like it's somebody else. But all of us are required to respond to this. And all of us must solve this.

I watched as it went back and forward. I got a call from the grandfather, Reverend Tomb. Called me and said there's a man, Mr. McSpadden on the phone. Said his grandson was killed in Ferguson, Missouri. I said, 'Where is Ferguson, Missouri?' He says, Right outside of St. Louis. He said, 'You have your iPad with you?' He told me what to punch in. And when I saw Michael lying there, I thought about how many of us were just considered nothing. How we were just so marginalized and ignored. Whatever the circumstance an investigation leads to, to have that boy lying there, like nobody cared about him. Like he didn't have any loved ones, like his life value didn't matter. I told his grandfather, I don't care what happened, but whatever we can do I'll be there to do it.

That night violence started. We were here Tuesday. And we went in front of that old courthouse with Big Mike and the mother, and they had to break their mourning to ask folks to stop looting and rioting. Can you imagine? Their heartbroken. Their son taken, discarded and marginalized. And they have to stop mourning to get you to control your anger, like you're more angry than they are. Like you don't understand that Michael Brown does not want to be remembered for a riot. He wants to be remembered as the one that made America deal with how we gonna police in the United States.

This is not about you! This is about justice! This is about fairness! And America is going to have to come to terms when there's something wrong that we have money to give military equipment to police forces, but we don't have money for training, and money for public education, and money to train our children!

America. How do you think we look when the world can see you can't come up with a police report, but you can find a video? How do you think we look when young people march nonviolently asking for the land of the free and the home of the brave to hear their cry, and you put snipers on the roof and pointed guns on them? How do we look?

How do we look when people that support the officer – and they have a right to do, and an obligation if they feel that – but if they support him, they're 'supporters,' but if we come to support the family, we're dividing the country?

What does God require of us? In three weeks, we saw Marlene Pinnock, a woman in Los Angeles, laid out on the freeway, a California highway patrolman hit her 15 times on video, with no weapon in her hand, nothing, no threat to her. Right after that, a man, they said he had loosie cigarettes, and they put an illegal chokehold on him — a man videoed it, eleven times he said he couldn't breathe – and the policeman wouldn't let him go. Later that week, we see Michael lying on the ground. America, it's time to deal with policing! We are not the haters, we're the healers!

What does it require of us? We can't have a fit; we've got to have a movement. A fit you get mad and run out for a couple of nights. A movement means we've got to be here for the long haul, and turn our chants into change, our demonstration into legislation, we have got to stay on this so we can stop this. We need the Congress to have legislation about guidelines in policing. We need to have a fair, impartial investigation. Those that are compromised will not be believed. And we need those that are bad cops – we are not anti-police, we respect police – but those police that are wrong need to be dealt with, just like those in our community are wrong need to be dealt with.

Let us be real clear: The only thing, if you have a bushel of apples, the only thing that messes up good apples is if you don't take the rotten apples out the bushel. We are not the ones making the cops look bad; it's the bad apples that you won't take out the bushel.

What does God require? We've got to be straight up in our community, too. We have to be outraged at a 9-year-old girl killed in Chicago. We have to be outraged by our disrespect for each other. Our disregard for each other. Our killing and shooting and running around gun-toting each other. So that they are justifying trying to come at us because some of us act like the definition of blackness is how low you can go. Blackness has never been about being a gangster or thug. Blackness was no matter how low we was pushed down, we rose up anyhow.

Blackness was never surrendering our pursuit of excellence. It was when it was against the law to go to some schools, we built black colleges and learned anyhow. When we couldn't go downtown to church we built our own AME church, and our church of God and Christ. We never surrendered, we never gave up, and now we get to the 21st century, we get to where we got some positions of power. And you decide it ain't black no more to be successful. Now you wanna be a nigga and call your woman a ho, you lost where you come from.

We've got to clean up our community so we can clean up the United States of America! Rev. Al, you don't understand what they doin' to us. I understand. But I understand that nobody gonna help us if we don't help ourselves. Sitting around feeling sorry for ourselves won't solve our problems. Sitting around having ghetto pity parties rather than organizing and strategizing and putting our differences aside. Yes, we got young and old. Yes, we got things that we don't like about each other, but it's bigger than our egos. It's bigger than everybody. We need everybody because I'm gonna tell you, I don't care how much money you got. I don't care what position you hold. I don't care how much education you got. If we can't protect a child walking down the street in Ferguson, and protect him, and bring justice, all you got don't matter to nobody but you! We are required to leave here today and change things. Michael Brown must be remembered for more than disturbances. He must be remembered for this is when they started changing what was going on. Oh yeah, there had been other times in history that became seminal moments. And this is one of those moments. And this young man, for whatever reason, has appealed to all of us, that we've got to solve this. And not continue this. This man, this woman, their spouses, their family, are going to go through some real trials and tribulations. They're going to call them all kinds of names but their target is all of us. If we cannot focus and do what the lord requires of us, we'll be right back here again.

Let me say this in closing. The policies of this country cannot go unchallenged. We cannot have aggressive policing of low-level crimes and can't deal with the higher level. Something strange that you can get all these guns into the hood, but you run around chasing folks selling loosie cigarettes and walking around in the middle of the street. There's something crazy about that kind of policing.

Policeman are human. Yes they are. But they also have a different kind of commitment because once you put on that state badge and that gun that is state backed-up, you cannot react like another citizen. You're supposed to be trained above that, and we should expect that in our community like they get it in any other community. No community in America would tolerate an 18-year-old boy laying in the street four and a half hours and we not going to tolerate it either. Whatever happened, the value of this boy's life must be answered by somebody.

I want to say to the family, you got some difficult days. Won't be long before the crowds'll be gone. These cameras will go on to another story. But I want you to know that there is a God. A God that I'm told Michael believed in. And he requires of you to believe in him. And if you trust him, he'll give you strength that you didn't know you had. There's a God that sits high, and he ain't looking at no good bishops and pontiffs up here. God loves those that love mercy and do justice and walk humbly before him. God will make a way. God will guide your feet. How do I know? Because he's done it for me.

The challenge from here is that you must be committed. That for whatever reason God chose you, and chose Michael. Michael's gone on to get his rest now. We're required in his name to change the country.

I sat and thought about this, Bishop Jakes, and thought about where and what was the meaning of all of this. As I was sitting in the room in St. Louis last week, I was trying to figure out what made sense. There was violence; there were peace rallies; some of the preachers were mad other preachers were in town; all this backstabbing and backbiting. More folk worried about getting on the program than developing a program. But I remembered an old preacher, told me a story that tied it together for me. He said, Al, 'I was reading a novel one night. The more I read the more I couldn't put it down.' He said, 'It was time for me to go to bed, but I couldn't, because I had to deal with the plot of the story and I couldn't figure the plot out.' He said, 'I looked at the clock, and it was 12 midnight and I wanted to put it down, but I couldn't figure out the plot. He said, 'So, Al, I cheated. I turned to the end of the book and I saw how the story ended, and that's how I got my rest.'

I want you to know Michael Sr., I want you to know, Leslie, I cheated. I sat up in the hotel and I took out my Bible, and I turned to the end of the book. I don't know how long the investigation will be. I don't know how long the journey's going to be. But I know how this story gonna end. The first will be last. The last will be first. The lion and lamb gonna lay down together. And God will! God will! God will make a way for his children! I been to the end of the Book. Justice is gonna come! Justice is gonna come! Justice gon' come!

Michael Brown's stepmother, Cal Brown, gave a heartfelt speech in which she said Michael prophesied about his own death, but Michael thought his dreams were about his grandmother. She said:

I feel really privileged to stand here to talk about such a dynamic young man. I met mike-mike 3 years ago, and he truly became my best friend. We spent so much time together just talking about God. He was truly curious about what God had to offer. About a month ago we both completed the first book of Genesis and Revelations. That truly opened his heart and his mind to God. The week that Mike-Mike was killed, I was admitted in the hospital and Mike-Mike called, on a Tuesday, and I was out for testing. And he talked to his dad, and he asked where I was, and his dad said that I was out for testing, and he said Dad I got something I want to tell you, and he said well what son, he said. 'I don't think that Cal is going to make it.' His dad got upset and he hung up the phone, and when I came back in the room his dad was upset, and he said, 'your son has ticked me off again,' And I said well what did Mike-Mike do now, and he didn't want to share it with me, but I got it out of him, and he said Mike-Mike said he didn't think that you were going to make it. And I said, is that all that he said. He said 'I don't know because I hung up the phone.'

The day that I was getting discharged, Mike-Mike was the one that called me, within moments of me getting my discharge papers, and he said, hey mom, I said hey son, how are you doing. He said, I'm doing good. I been wanting to talk to you for a few days but haven't been unable to. And he said, I think daddy is upset with me, and I said well why. He said because I didn't think you were going to make it. And I say why did you say that Mike-Mike, and he said, I have been dreaming of death. I've been seeing pictures of death. He said I see bloody sheets hanging on the clothes line. And it truly touched my heart, and when I went out there, and I saw Mike-Mike, that's exactly what he was laying up under, so he pretty much prophesied about his own death and didn't even realize it. The day that Mike-Mike graduated, we went to the graduation, and then we took him out to lunch and his entire talk was about God. He said, Cal, I feel like I am God. I got so much going inside of me and I just know that the world is some day going to know my name. He said, 'I am going to shake the world.' And I promise you that he has. If I had the time to tell you all that Mike-Mike shared with me it wouldn't be an empty seat in here. Mike-Mike is an awesome man. I have to say that because I met him three-years ago and he evolved into a man. A good man, and he just wanted so much. He wanted to go to college. He wanted to have a family. He wanted to be a good father, but God chose differently, and I am at peace about that, because he is not a lost soul. His death is not in vain. And I just want to say to Mike-Mike that I love you and I wish I could hold you and kiss you, but I know he would say, 'Cal, we don't do that gay stuff.'

The "program guide" that explained how the funeral would progress also included Michael Brown's obituary and a message from his parents.

Michael Brown Obituary:

Michael O.D. Brown was born on May 20, 1996, to Michael Brown and Lesley McSpadden in St. Louis, MO.

Michael departed this life suddenly in Ferguson, MO, on August 9, 2014. Michael was preceded in death by his grandfather, Lubie Brown, his great-grandmothers, Para Lee Ewings, Eldora Forston and Lillie Carpenter.

Michael accepted Christ at an early age and joined Original Friendship Baptist Church where he attended with his parents.

Michael was educated in the St. Louis Public School System. He graduated from Normandy High School on May 23, 2014. Michael was in the process of getting ready to attend Vatterott College.

Michael was an avid lover of music, computers and sports. During his young life he played football. He loved to Rap about life and was so good at it that he was asked to write a song for a friend. He was a very friendly, gentle giant who loved his family very much. Michael enjoyed playing PS4 and X Box games.

Message from Michael Brown senior:

To My Son.

Dear Son,

I don't understand why you were chosen by God. I know He knows what He is doing because God Almighty doesn't make mistakes. So that's why you were called home. I think of you day and night. Just wish I was there to save you from harm. I always told you I will never let nothing happen to you. And that's what hurt soooooooo much that I couldn't protect you. But we love you. I will never let you die in my heart. You will always live forever. Your dad and best friend. Your old dude, that's what you called me. -- Michael Brown Sr.

Message from Michael Brown's mother, Lesley McSpadden:

To My Son,

I never want this to go unsaid. There are no words to express how much you mean to me. A son like you, I thought could never be. Because the day you were born, I just know, God sent me a blessing -- and that was you. For this I thank Him every day. You are the true definition of a son, in every way. Becoming a mom has shown me a new sense of being. I want you to know that you were the purpose in my life. Out of everything I did--it was you that I did right. Always remember that I know how much you care. I can tell by the relationship that we share. For a son like you there could be no other. And whether we are together or apart please, don't forget, you will always be in my heart.

Love, Lesley

In his evening press conference, Captain Ron Johnson, of the Missouri Highway Patrol, seemed happy to announce how chaos has turned to calm, in Ferguson. He praised the police for deploying no smoke devices, no tear gas, or mace. He said the police did not fire a single bullet or need to respond to any calls for assistance. Johnson stated, I believe the citizens of Ferguson have spoken for peace, and I am happy for Ferguson tonight.

CHAPTER 40

AFTER THE FUNERAL

Ferguson descended into chaos after the funeral of Michael Brown, and continued during the days that followed. Activists used protests, rioting, looting and all sorts of civil disobedience techniques to promote the message "black lives matter."

On September 10th, at 3:00 p.m., the Justice for Michael Brown Leadership Coalition orchestrated a shut-down of Interstate highway 1-70, a part of the transcontinental Interstate system that passes by Ferguson. Activist attorney Eric Vickers explained to reporters that the shut-down of the highway was a result of Missouri Governor Jay Nixon's refusal to appoint a special prosecutor in the Darren Wilson murder investigation. During a press conference, Vickers said, "We are taking this direct action on the tenth because we are using the means of civil disobedience that Doctor Martin Luther King used to affect change. It is going to cause people some discomfort. It is going to cause inconvenience to people. That is a small price to pay to change the conditions suffered by African American youth, and it's a very small price to pay to bring justice to Michael Brown." The 1-70 sit-in (or lay-down) was similar to many other interstate shut-downs across the country. Protesters knew that the surest way to get on TV and into the newspapers was to cause wide-scale disruption to people's everyday lives. Shutting down the roadways in America has turned into an effective tool for activists to use to receive free, or "earned" media exposure, such as in Selma Mississippi, in 1965, when Dr. Martin Luther King closed the roads during his Selma-to-Montgomery March for voting rights. On a day that became known as "Bloody Sunday" 600 protesters attempted to walk from Selma Alabama to the state capital in Montgomery, to demand equal voting rights for African Americans. They made it to the Edmund Pettus Bridge, six miles from where they started, before being beaten back by a police force who were determined to keep them out of the Montgomery court house. The marchers were beaten with Billy-clubs and attacked with dogs and tear-gas until they fled back to Selma. Eventually, Dr. Martin Luther King would lead a march of supporters that began as a group of 3,200, but swelled to 25,000 vocal marchers by the time they arrived at the state capital in Montgomery Alabama, on March 25th, 1965. Although the march caused wide-scale disruption to mass transit, the closure of U.S. Route 80 by the walking protesters was found to be Constitutionally allowable. It was determined that the right to protest was more important than a motorist's right to travel on the roadway.

In a 1956 decision from a lawsuit filed by twenty-seven-year-old Martin Luther King, Federal District Court Judge Frank Johnson made a ruling in favor of the demonstrator's right to march, over motorist's right of mobility. Judge Johnson ruled, "The law is clear that the right to petition one's government for the redress of grievances may be exercised in large groups, and these rights may be exercised by marching, even along public highways."

Moral Monday:

After weeks of relatively peaceful protests and toned-down rioting, "Moral Monday," would become a day that would require a national police effort to quell the crowds, especially in and around Ferguson. It was the beginning of mass rioting that spread throughout the nation, to protest the killing of Michael Brown, Eric Gardner and other victims of police brutality. Moral Monday was launched on Monday, October 20th, in cities all across America, to fill jail cells and cause a nationwide crisis to overburden police departments with protesters who demanded to be arrested. The day-long series of civil disobedience began in Ferguson, but reached cities around the country. A National Football League game was crashed by protesters who held-up banners throughout the stadium, stating, "Black lives matter," and other activist slogans. The City of St. Louis City Hall was invaded and so were police departments all over America. The Saint Louis University clock tower was over-run by hundreds of protesters who said they intended to stay, laying on the floor, in a position resembling a dead-man, then reading the names of black youths killed by police. The school's president didn't want to elevate the situation, so he let them stay and protest in peace, in a demonstration known as a "dead-in," which also spread to other cities. Universities in the area, such as Washington University, in Saint Louis, were also targets of the protests. Student Samantha Pitz described the scene. She said, "It was a powerful image. I noticed that there were multiple tours going on so I think it shows that the Wash. U. community is very active, and the demonstration will show prospective students that we are involved in the community and there isn't necessarily a Wash. U. bubble." Washington University junior Max Lyons was not as optimistic. He said, "I sympathize. I agree with their message, but I'm pessimistic about their chances of having a real effect,"

In Ferguson, the clergy and civil rights leaders, including Harvard-educated professor and civil rights leader, Cornell West, who orchestrated the demonstration, confronted police and chanted, "Black lives matter! All lives matter!" Protesters purposefully pushed, prodded and provoked the police until they were arrested, thereby filling-up the jail cells, as per the day's mandate for Ferguson protesters and other activists across the nation.

Governor's Independent Commission:

Missouri's Governor Jay Nixon announced the formation of an independent commission, he said, "to study and make specific recommendations for how to make progress on the issues raised by events in Ferguson." The Governor suggested conducting a wide-ranging examination of the challenges that were exposed and exacerbated by the death of Michael Brown and its aftermath, and offer specific recommendations for overcoming them. Governor Nixon said, "Throughout the history of our nation, we have struggled to treat all our citizens as equals. Too often we have fallen short of the guiding principles on which our great democracy was founded. For too many, the promise of unalienable rights of life, liberty and the pursuit of happiness, rings hollow. Some people would tell you that the choice is one thing or the other: Trust or force. Speech or silence. Black or white. It is far more complicated than that. Legitimate issues are being expressed by thoughtful voices that must be heard. People yelling past one another will not move us to where we need to go. We need to solve these problems ourselves, we need to solve them together, and we need to act now."

The Governor tasked the committee with three goals.

1. Conduct a thorough, wide-ranging and unflinching study of the underlying social and economic conditions underscored by the unrest in the wake of the death of Michael Brown;

2. Tap into expertise needed to address key concerns identified by the Commission -- from poverty and education, to governance and law enforcement;

3. Make specific recommendations for making the St. Louis region a stronger, fairer place for everyone to live.

Police chief apologizes:

Ferguson Police Chief Tom Jackson released a video tape apology to the family of Michael Brown, on September 26th, to express his sorrow for the loss of their son. Chief Jackson said:

As many of you know, my name is Tom Jackson, and I'm the chief of police of the city of Ferguson. The events of the past few weeks have sent shockwaves, not just around the community here, but around the nation. Overnight I went from being a small-town police chief to being a part of a conversation about racism, equality, and the role of policing in that conversation. As chief of police, and as a resident, I want to be part of that conversation. I also want to be part of the solution.

But before we can engage in further discussion of the broader issues, I think it's important that we address the central issue that brought us here today, and that's the death of Michael Brown. I want to say this to the Brown family: No one, who has not experienced the loss of a child can understand what you're feeling. I am truly sorry for the loss of your son.

I'm also sorry that it took so long to remove Michael from the street. The time that it took involved very important work on the part of investigators, who were trying to collect evidence and gain a true picture of what happened that day. But it was just too long, and I am truly sorry for that. Please know that the investigating officers meant no disrespect to the Brown family, to the African American community, or the people of Canfield. They were simply trying to do their jobs.

There were many people who were upset about what happened in Ferguson, and came here to protest peacefully. Unfortunately, there were others who had a different agenda. I do want to say to any peaceful protester who did not feel that I did enough to protect their constitutional right to protest, I am sorry for that. The right of the people to peacefully assemble is what the police are here to protect. If anyone who is peacefully exercising that right is upset and angry, I feel responsible, and I am sorry."

I'm also aware of the pain and the feeling of mistrust felt in some of the African American community towards the police department. The city belongs to all of us and we all are part of this community. It is clear that we have much work to do. As a community, a city, and nation, we have real problems to solve. Not just in Ferguson, but the entire region, and beyond. For any mistakes I make, I take full responsibility. It's an honor to serve the city of Ferguson and the people who work there. I look forward to working with you in future, and once again, I apologize to the Brown family."

Attorney General Eric Holder announces guidelines for police and protesters:

Attorney General Eric Holder spoke to a congregation at the Ebenezer Baptist Church in Atlanta, a church Martin Luther King preached at, to tell the parishioners that he would soon release a report to give guidance to police departments which, he hopes, will end racial profiling by the police, "once-and-for-all." Attorney General Holder said:

In the coming days, I will announce updated Justice Department guidance regarding profiling by federal law enforcement. This will institute rigorous new standards – and robust safeguards – to help end racial profiling, once and for all. This new guidance will codify our commitment to the very highest standards of fair and effective policing.

Several people in the crowd interrupted Holder's speech by chanting "It is our duty to fight for our freedom! ... No justice, no peace," but they were quickly escorted out of the building by security, even as Holder was applauding their efforts to exercise their right to free speech and their "genuine expression of concern and involvement." He continued:

There will be a tendency on the part of some to condemn what we just saw, but we should not. What we saw there was a genuine expression of concern and involvement, and it is through that level of involvement, that level of concern and I hope a level of perseverance and commitment, that change ultimately will come. And so let me be clear, let me be clear, I ain't mad atcha, all right?"

Attorney General Holder, who is seeking to leave his position as soon as a successor can be confirmed, has made civil rights one of his highest political priorities. His guidelines for policing will probably be the last meaningful action he takes on race relations before leaving his job as America's top cop.

National Guard Mobilized Prior to Grand Jury announcement:

Missouri Gov. Jay Nixon issued an executive order to declare a state of emergency in Missouri so he could preemptively activate the National Guard in advance of the Grand Jury announcement regarding the indictment of Officer Darren Wilson. The Governor claimed the state of emergency was put in place, "to support law enforcement during any period of unrest." The State of Emergency stated:

WHEREAS, the City of Ferguson and the St. Louis region have experienced periods of unrest over the past three months; and

WHEREAS, the United States Department of Justice and St. Louis County authorities are conducting separate criminal investigations into the facts surrounding the death of Michael Brown; and

WHEREAS, the United States Department of Justice and St. Louis County authorities could soon announce the findings of their independent criminal investigations; and

WHEREAS, regardless of the outcomes of the federal and state criminal investigations, there is the possibility of expanded unrest; and

WHEREAS, the State of Missouri will be prepared to appropriately respond to any reaction to these announcements; and

WHEREAS, our citizens have the right to peacefully assemble and protest and the State of Missouri is committed to protecting those rights; and

WHEREAS, our citizens and businesses must be protected from violence and damage; and

WHEREAS, an invocation of the provisions of Sections 44.010 through 44.130, RSMo, is appropriate to ensure the safety and welfare of our citizens.

NOW, THEREFORE, I, JEREMIAH W. (JAY) NIXON, GOVERNOR OF THE STATE OF MISSOURI, by virtue of the authority vested in me by the Constitution and Laws of the State of Missouri, including Sections 44.010 through 44.130, RSMo, do hereby declare a State of Emergency exists in the State of Missouri.

I further direct the Missouri State Highway Patrol together with the St. Louis County Police Department and the St. Louis Metropolitan Police Department to operate as a Unified Command to protect civil rights and ensure public safety in the City of Ferguson and the St. Louis region.

I further order that the St. Louis County Police Department shall have command and operational control over security in the City of Ferguson relating to areas of protests, acts of civil disobedience and conduct otherwise arising from such activities.

I further order that the Unified Command may exercise operational authority in such other jurisdictions it deems necessary to protect civil rights and ensure public safety and that other law enforcement agencies shall assist the Unified Command when so requested and shall cooperate with operational directives of the Unified Command.

I further order, pursuant to Section 41.480, RSMo, the Adjutant General of the State of Missouri, or his designee, to forthwith call and order into active service such portions of the organized militia as he deems necessary to protect life and property and assist civilian authorities and it is further directed that the Adjutant General or his designee, and through him, the commanding officer of any unit or other organization of such organized militia so called into active service take such action and employ such equipment as may be necessary to carry out requests processed through the Missouri State Highway Patrol and ordered by the Governor of the state to protect life and property and support civilian authorities.

This Order shall expire in thirty days unless extended in whole or in part by subsequent Executive Order.

IN WITNESS WHEREOF, I have hereunto set my hand and caused to be affixed the Great Seal of the State of Missouri, in the City of Jefferson, on this 17th day of November, 2014. Signed, Governor Jay Nixon.

No Fly Zone:

The Federal Aviation Administration placed temporary flight restrictions over Ferguson airspace in advance of the Grand Jury announcement, after determining that is was a hazardous area. The restrictions prevent media helicopters and commercial planes from flying within 3 miles of Ferguson, under 3,000 feet. The type of flight restriction being imposed over Ferguson is, reportedly, "the strictest kind legally available to the FAA." The skies above Ferguson were also restricted soon after the Michael Brown shooting when 37 square miles of airspace was restricted to news helicopters for several weeks. The police reported shots being fired at their helicopters as an excuse to shut down the airspace, but it was revealed later that the Police and the FAA colluded together to implement a no-fly zone--to prevent the media from recording the chaos in the streets, rather than to protect aircraft from gunfire. In private emails it was revealed that the FAA had no problem with allowing aircraft to transition through the Ferguson airspace, but they said they just didn't want the media up there. The FAA claimed the flight restrictions were meant "to provide a safe environment for law enforcement activities."

Brown Family 4 1/2 minutes of silence:

The Brown family released a statement prior to the Grand Jury announcement asking for peace and requesting 4 1/2 minutes of silence to reflect on their son Michael. The statement read:

After the Grand Jury's decision, we are asking for 4 1/2 minutes of silence to remember why we lift our voices. We are not here to be violent. We are here in memory of our son. We are here for protection of all children. We are here to support justice and equality for all people. We lift our voices to ensure black and brown men, women, and children can live in this country without being devalued because of the color of our skin.

No Indictment Announced by Grand Jury:

On Monday evening, November 24th, around 8:15 p.m., Prosecuting Attorney, Bob McCulloch announced the decision of the Grand Jury to not indict Officer Darren Wilson for the murder of Michael Brown. Prosecutor McCulloch began his news conference by expressing his sympathies for the Brown family, noting that they lost a loved-one to violence. McCulloch made the following statement announcing the decision of the grand Jury:

First and foremost, I would like to extend my deepest sympathies to the family of Michael Brown. As I have said in the past, I know that regardless of the circumstances here, they've lost a loved one to violence. I know the pain that accompanies such a loss knows no bounds. On August 9th, Michael Brown was shot and killed by police officer Darren Wilson. Within minutes, various accounts of the incident began appearing on social media. Accounts filled with speculation and little, if any, solid accurate information. Almost immediately, neighbors began gathering, and anger began brewing, because of the various descriptions of what had happened and because of the underlying tensions between the police department and a significant part of the neighborhood.

The St. Louis County Police conducted an extensive investigation of the crime scene. At times, under varying, trying, circumstances, and interrupted at least once by gunfire. Continuing after that, they, along with the agents of the FBI at the direction of Attorney General Eric Holder, located numerous individuals and gathered additional evidence and information. Fully aware of the unfounded but growing concern in some parts of our community that the investigation and review of this tragic death might not be full and fair, I decided immediately that all of the physical evidence gathered, all people claiming to have witnessed any part or all of the shooting, and any and all other related matters, would be presented to the Grand Jury. A Grand Jury of twelve members of this community selected by a judge in May of this year, long before the shooting   occurred.

I would like to briefly expand upon the unprecedented cooperation of the local and federal authorities. When Attorney General Holder first announced the Federal investigation just days after the shooting, he pledged that federal investigators would be working with local authorities as closely as possible at every step of the way and would follow the facts wherever they may take us. As Attorney General Holder and I agree, we both pledged separate investigations will follow the trail of facts, with no preconceived notion of where that journey would take us. Our only goal was that our investigation would be thorough and complete, to give the Grand Jury, the Department of Justice and ultimately, the public, all available evidence to make an informed decision. All evidence obtained by federal authorities was immediately shared with St. Louis County investigators. Likewise, all evidence gathered by St. Louis County police was immediately shared by the federal investigators.

Additionally, the Department of Justice conducted its own examination of evidence and performed its own autopsy. Another autopsy was performed at request of the Brown family and this information was also shared. Just as importantly, all testimony before the St. Louis County Grand Jury was immediately provided to the Department of Justice. So although the investigations are separate, both of the local, and federal governments, have all of the same information and evidence. Our investigation and presentation of the evidence to the Grand Jury and St. Louis County has been completed. The most significant challenge encountered in this investigation has been the 24-hour news cycle and the sensational appetite for something to talk about. Following closely behind with the rumors on social media. I recognize, of course, the lack of accurate detail surrounding the shooting frustrates the media and the general public, and helps breed suspicion among those already distrustful of the system. The closely guarded details gives law enforcement a yardstick to measure the truthfulness. Eyewitness accounts must always be challenged and compared against the physical evidence. Many witnesses to the shooting of Michael Brown made statements inconsistent with other statements they made and also conflicted with the physical evidence. Some were completely refuted by the physical evidence. As an example -- before the result of an autopsy was released, witnesses claim they saw officer Wilson stand over Michael Brown and fire many rounds into his back. Others claim that officer Wilson shot Mr. Brown in the back as Mr. Brown was running away. However, once the autopsy findings were released, showing Michael Brown had not sustained any wounds to the back of his body, no additional witnesses made such a claim. Several witnesses adjusted their stories in their subsequent statements. Some even admitted they did not witness the event at all but merely repeated what they heard in the neighborhood, or assumed had happened. Fortunately, for the integrity of our investigation, almost all of the initial witness interviews, including those of Wilson, were recorded. The statements in the testimony of most of the witnesses were presented to the grand jury before the autopsy results were released by the media, and before several media outlets published information from reports they received from a D.C. government official. The jurors were therefore, prior to the time of the release of the information being public, and what followed in the news cycle. The jurors were able to have already assessed the credibility of the witnesses, including those witnesses who's statements and testimony remained consistent throughout every interview, and were consistent with the physical evidence in this case.

My Two assistants began presenting to the Grand Jury on August 20th. The evidence was presented in an organized and orderly manner. The jurors gave us a schedule of when they could make it. All 12 jurors were present for every session and heard every word of testimony, and examined every item of evidence. Beginning August 20th, and continuing until today, the Grand Jury worked tirelessly to examine and re-examine all of the testimony of the witnesses and all of the physical evidence. They were extremely engaged in the process asking questions of every witness, requesting specific witnesses, requesting specific information and asking for certain physical evidence. They met on 25 separate days in the last three months, heard more than 70 hours of testimony from about 60 witnesses and reviewed hours and hours of recordings of media and law enforcement interviews, by many of the witnesses who testified. They heard from three medical examiners and experts on blood, DNA, toxicology, firearms and drug analysis. They examined hundreds of photographs, some of which they asked to be taken. They examined various pieces of physical evidence. They were presented with five indictments ranging from murder in the first degree to involuntary manslaughter. Their burden was determined based upon all of the evidence, if probable cause exists, and that Darren Wilson was the person to commit the crime. There is no question that Darren Wilson caused the death of Michael Brown by shooting him, but the inquiry does not end there. The law allows a law enforcement officer to use deadly force in certain situations. The law allows all people to use deadly force to defend themselves in certain situations. The Grand Jury considered whether Wilson was the initial aggressor in this case, or whether there was probable cause to believe that Darren Wilson was authorized, as a law enforcement officer, to use deadly force in this situation, or if he acted in self-defense. I detail this for two reasons. First, so that everybody will know that, as promised by me and Attorney General Holder, there was a full presentation of all evidence and appropriate instruction to the Grand Jury. Second, as a caution to those in and out of the media, who will pounce on a single sentence, or witness, and decide what should have happened in this case, based on that tiny bit of information, the duty of the Grand Jury is to separate fact from fiction.

After a full and impartial examination of all the evidence involved the Grand Jury decided that evidence did not support the filing of any criminal charges against Darren Wilson. They accepted the responsibility. It is important to note, and say again, that they are the only people, the only people who have heard and examined every witness, and every piece of evidence. They discussed and debated the evidence among themselves before arriving at their collective decision. After their exhaustive review of the evidence, the Grand Jury deliberated and made their final decision. They determined that no probable cause exists to file any charges against officer Wilson and returned a "no true bill" on each of the five indictments. The physical and scientific evidence examined by the Grand Jury, combined with a witness statement supported and substantiated by that physical evidence, tells the accurate and tragic story of what happened. The very general synopsis of the testimony and the physical evidence presented to the Grand Jury follows. As I have promised, the evidence presented to the Grand Jury with some exceptions, and the testimony of the witnesses called to the grand jury, will be released at the conclusion of this statement.

At approximately 11:45 a.m. on Saturday the ninth of August, Ferguson Police Officer Darren Wilson was dispatched to an emergency involving a two-month-old infant having trouble breathing. At about 11:53 a.m., Wilson heard a radio broadcast for a "stealing in progress" at a market on West Florissant. The broadcast also included a brief description of the subject. A black male, wearing a white t-shirt and a box of swisher cigars. Officer Wilson remained with the mother and the infant until the EMS arrived. Officer Wilson left the apartment complex in his police vehicle, a Chevy Tahoe SUV. An additional description of the suspect was released at that time. He was with another male. As Officer Wilson was attending to his emergency call, Michael Brown and a companion were in a local convenience store. Michael Brown's activity in the store was recorded by the store security cameras. The video often played following his release in August by the Ferguson Police Department shows Michael Brown grabbing a handful of Cigarillos and heading toward the exit without paying. As Michael Brown and his companion left the store, somebody inside called the police. The two walked east into the middle of the street. Mr. Brown directly behind his companion. As officer Wilson continued west on Canfield, he encountered Mr. Brown and his companion walking in the middle of the street. As Wilson slowed, he told them to move to the sidewalk. Words were exchanged, and they continued walking down the middle of the street. When he passed, Wilson observed that Michael Brown had Cigarillos in his hand and was wearing a red hat. At approximately 12:02 p.m., Wilson radioed he had two individuals on Canfield and needed assistance. Officer Wilson backed his vehicle at an angle blocking their path and blocking the flow of traffic in both directions. Several cars approached from both east and west but weren't able to pass the vehicle. An altercation took place with officer Wilson seated inside the vehicle and Mr. Brown standing at the driver's window. During the altercation, two shots were fired by Officer Wilson while still inside the vehicle. Mr. Brown ran east and Officer Wilson gave chase. Near the corner, Mr. Brown stopped and turned back to Officer Wilson. Officer Wilson also stopped. As Michael Brown moved towards Officer Wilson, several more shots were fired by the officer and Michael Brown was fatally wounded. Within seconds of the final shot, the assist car arrived. Less than 90 seconds passed between the first contact and the arrival of the assist car.

During the investigation, eyewitnesses were interviewed by various news outlets. Witnesses were interviewed by local and federal law enforcement, sometimes together and sometimes separately. All the statements were provided to the other party. All previous statements of witnesses who testified before the Grand Jury were also presented to the Grand Jury whether they were media interviews or interviews by the FBI or by the County Police Department. The statements of all witnesses, civilian, law-enforcement, experts were challenged by other law enforcement, by the prosecutors and the Grand Jury themselves. A highly effective method for challenging a statement is to compare it to the previous statements of the witness for consistency, and to compare it with the physical evidence. The physical evidence does not change because of public pressure or personal agenda. Physical evidence does not look away as events unfold, nor does it block-out or add to memory. It remains constant, and is a solid foundation upon which cases are built. When statements change, witnesses were confronted with the inconsistencies and conflicts between their statements and the physical evidence. Some witnesses admitted they did not actually see the shooting or only saw part of the shooting. Only repeating what they heard on the street. Some others adjusted parts of their statements to fit the facts. Others stood by original statements even though their statements were completely discredited by the physical evidence. Several witnesses describe seeing an altercation in the car between Mr. Brown and Officer Wilson. It was described as tussling, wrestling, tug-of-war. Several other witnesses described Mr. Brown as punching Officer Wilson while Mr. Brown was partially inside the vehicle. Many of the witnesses said they heard a gunshot while Mr. Brown was still partially inside the vehicle. At least one witness said that no part of Mr. Brown was ever inside the vehicle and that the shot was fired through an open window while Mr. Brown was standing outside. The vehicle and Officer Wilson's clothing and equipment were examined by various technicians and scientists. Mr. Brown's blood and or DNA were located on the outside of the drivers door. His blood and DNA were also found on the outside of the left rear passenger door. Mr. Brown's blood and DNA were found on the inside of the driver door. The upper left thigh of Officer Wilson's pant leg, the front collar of Officer Wilson's shirt and on Officer Wilson's weapon. Additionally, a bullet fired from Officer Wilson's weapon was located inside the driver door. The shot was fired from inside the vehicle, striking the door in a downward angle, at the armrest. The second bullet was not recovered. Regarding the gunshot wounds of Mr. Brown, it should be noted that the three separate autopsies were conducted--one by St. Louis County Medical Office, one by a private pathologist, one by the Department of Defense--The result of all three autopsies were consistent with one another in all significant respects. Mr. Brown had a gunshot graze wound on his right thumb. The path was away from the tip of the hand with soot consistent with a close range gunshot. Officer Wilson also had a medical examination which indicated some swelling and redness to his face.

Almost all witnesses stated that after they heard the shots fired while Mr. Brown was at the car, he hesitated and then ran east. Most stated that almost immediately, Officer Wilson got out of his vehicle and chased after him. Some witnesses stated Wilson fired at Mr. Brown as he chased after him. At least one witness said one of the shots struck Mr. Brown. Others stated he did not fire until Mr. Brown turned and came back towards the officer. At least one witness stated that as officer Wilson got out of his vehicle, he shot Mr. Brown multiple times as Mr. Brown stood next to the vehicle. Yet another witness stated that Officer Wilson stuck his gun outside the window and fired at Mr. Brown as Mr. Brown was running. One witness stated there were actually two police vehicles. Most witnesses agreed that Mr. Brown stopped and turned around facing officer Wilson. One stated Mr. Brown did not move towards Officer Wilson at all, but was shot multiple times as he stood near the corner, with his hands raised. In subsequent interviews with law enforcement, or other testimony before the Grand Jury, many of the same witnesses said they did not actually see the shooting. Some were running for cover, some were relating what they heard from others or they said what they assumed happened in that case. Several other witnesses maintained their original statement that Mr. Brown had his hands in the air and was not moving towards the officer when he was shot. Several witnesses stated that Mr. Brown did not raise his hands at all, or that *he raised them briefly and then dropped them and turned towards Officer Wilson, who then fired several rounds. Other witnesses stated Mr. Brown stopped for a very brief period and moved towards Officer Wilson again. One describes his movement as a full charge. According to some witnesses, Officer Wilson stopped firing when Mr. Brown stopped moving towards him, and resumed firing when Mr. Brown started moving towards him again. These witnesses did not make any statements to the media. The description of how Mr. Brown's hands, raised his hands, or the position of his hands, is not consistent among the witnesses. Some describe his hands being out to his sides, some said in front of him with his palms up. Some said his hands were raised by his head or by his shoulders. Others describe his hands as being in a running position, or in fists. There are various witness statements regarding Mr. Brown's movement after he stopped and turned back towards Officer Wilson. Several witnesses said Mr. Brown never moved towards Officer Wilson and was shot near the corner. Most said the shots were fired as he moved towards Wilson. Mr. Brown's movements were described as walking, moving fast, stumbling or full charge. The varying descriptions were sometimes provided by the same witnesses in subsequent statements or testimony.*

The entire area was processed by the St. Louis County Crime Scene Unit. A total of 12 rounds were fired by Officer Wilson. Two shots at the car, 10 more farther east. Mr. Brown sustained a graze wound to his thumb while standing next to the vehicle. He sustained six or seven more gunshot wounds, depending upon whether one of the shots was an entry or reentry wound. Mr. Brown sustained a second graze wound, another graze wound, to his right bicep. He also sustained wounds to his right forearm, upper front right arm, lateral right chest, upper right chest, forehead and top of the head. The top of the head, forehead and perhaps the upper right chest were consistent with his body being bent forward at the waist. Except for the first and last wounds, the medical examiners were unable to determine the order of the shots. The graze wound of the thumb sustained at the vehicle is likely the first wound. It was the only close range shot. The shot at the top of the head was most likely the last. It would have rendered him immediately unconscious and incapacitated. Mr. Brown's body was located approximately 153 feet east of Officer Wilson's car. Mr. Brown's blood was located approximately 25 feet farther east past his body. A nearby tenant, during a video chat, inadvertently captured the final ten shots on. Ten shots on tape. There was a string of shots followed by a brief pause and then another string of shots. As I stated earlier, the evidence and the testimony will be released following the statement.

I am ever mindful that this decision will not be accepted by some, and may cause disappointment for others. All decisions in the criminal justice system must be determined by the physical and scientific evidence and the credible testimony corroborated by that evidence, not in response to public outcry or for political expediency. Decisions on a matter as serious as charging an individual with a crime cannot be decided on anything less than complete examination of all available evidence. Anything less is not justice. It is my sworn duty and that of the Grand Jury to seek justice and not simply obtain an indictment or conviction. During this extremely tense and painful time that we had, the citizens of this community should be, and are very mindful of the fact, that the whole world is watching and watching how we respond and how we react. I would urge each and every one of them with the loss that was suffered by the Brown family, no young man should ever die. This is a tragic loss regardless of the circumstances. It has opened old wounds and given us an opportunity now to address those wounds, as opposed to where they just faded away in the past. How many years have we talked about the issues that lead to incidents like this, yet time-after-time, it just fades away. I urge everybody who was engaged in the conversation, who was engaged in the demonstrations, to keep that going. Not to let that go. To do it in a constructive way, a way we can profit from this. A way that we can benefit from this by changing the structure, changing some of the issues, by solving the issues that lead to these sorts of things. I join with Michael Brown's family, the clergy, with anyone and everyone else. The NAACP. The Urban League. Every government official, private citizen, encouraging everyone to continue the demonstration, continue the discussion, address the problems, but do so in a constructive way, not in a destructive way."

Darren Wilson released a handwritten statement to his supporters after the Grand Jury announced they would not indict him for the murder of Michael Brown. Wilson wrote:

I would like to thank you all for standing up for me during this stressful time. Your support and dedication is amazing and it is still hard to believe that all of these people that I have never met are doing so much for me. I watched the CNN video we recorded at the rally on Saturday and it brought tears to my eyes.

All of you are simply amazing, and I don't know how to thank you all enough. I wish I could meet you, hug you, and personally thank you for all of your continued support, however, due to my and my families safety I am unable to. Please don't give this letter to any media or post it where they can see it. Relay the message of thanks to all and keep this letter private until the investigation is complete.

I want you all to know that I do get updates on the amount of support. Unfortunately, I don't get to see all of the comments made through social media, but overall messages are relayed to me.

Thank you from the bottom of my heart, and know that I would do the same for any of you.

Also please keep my family in blue in your hearts and prayers, they have all made a sacrifice to their own lives in order to work the excessive hours through the heat and rain to ensure that the riots and protests in Ferguson were as safe as they could be.

Thank you. P.O. Darren Wilson.

Michael Brown's parents, Leslie McSpadden and Michael Brown Sr., issued a statement soon after it was announced that no charges would be filed against Darren Wilson. The statement read:

We are profoundly disappointed that the killer of our child will not face the consequence of his actions. While we understand that many others share our pain, we ask that you channel your frustration in ways that will make a positive change. We need to work together to fix the system that allowed this to happen. Join with us in our campaign to ensure that every police officer working the streets in this country wears a body camera. We respectfully ask that you please keep your protests peaceful. Answering violence with violence is not the appropriate reaction. Let's not just make noise, let's make a difference."

In spite of the nice words written on paper, the Brown family displayed their true emotion later in the evening while at a protest at the police station. Brown's mother yelled-out to an angry mob, "You mother-fuckers think this is a joke. They think this is a fucking joke!" As the crowd began chanting, no justice, no peace, and other similar slogans, Mrs. McSpadden continued her tirade, screaming at the crowd, "Y'all know you're all wrong! Y'all know you're all wrong. And anybody out here who don't think so, I don't give a fuck. They wrong! Everybody want me to be calm--do you know how them bullets hit my son? Ain't nobody had to live through what I had to live through."

Michael Brown's stepfather, Louis Head, was recorded on video, in rage, chanting, "Burn this bitch down." He then led a procession of his supporters though the crowd, with them all yelling "burn this bitch down. Soon after Brown's step-father called for his friends and followers to burn Ferguson down, businesses in Ferguson were looted and burned.

Law-enforcement personnel had considered filing charges against the Brown family for inciting a riot, but they chose not to agitate the situation, so they let the family off the hook, although many people thought they should have been charged with a crime for provoking the crowd into a rebellious, rioting mob.

At about 9 p.m., the police tried to disperse a crowd of a few hundred protesters, who gathered around the police station. At first, the police used peaceful tactics, asking the crowd over a loudspeaker to leave the area because they were part of an "unlawful assembly." Law-enforcement repeatedly stated, "You need to stop throwing objects at the police and disperse immediately." Most of the protesters cleared-out once they were asked by law enforcement, but a few dozen "agitators," remained behind to confront the police and provoke an altercation. That altercation came about fifteen minutes later when a police line formed across Florissant Avenue and began advancing on the unruly protesters. The police shot tear gas and dispersed the crowd from around the police station. The police originally Tweeted that they had only used smoke grenades on the protesters, but later confirmed that they did indeed use tear gas when they fought back the rioters.

St. Louis County Police Chief Jon Belmar said he was grateful nobody was killed, but he was also disappointed by the amount of damage that occurred. Belmar explained to reporters at an early morning news conference, what they already knew. He said "there was nothing left in Ferguson," along Florissant Avenue. "What I've seen tonight is probably much worse than the worst night we ever had in August, and that's truly unfortunate. Frankly, I'm heartbroken about that," he said. Belmar claimed that, as far as he knew, that no shots were fired by police, but he said he personally heard over 150 gunshots throughout the night. He told reporters that he and Captain Johnson "got lit up" by gunfire, while they were out on the streets, and they were both surprised that they did not get hit. Belmar thought the timing of the announcement, late in the afternoon, did not add to the hostilities or destruction of property. He felt the timing was good and that the police were prepared. He said, "I don't think we were underprepared." The Chief also explained how he and Captain Johnson, of the Missouri Highway Patrol, had many meetings with community leaders and protesters in an attempt to prevent any future violence. He said, "We not only were engaged, we did everything we could to prevent this."

Captain Ron Johnson said, "We talked about peaceful protest, and that did not happen tonight. We definitely have done something here that's going to impact our community for a long time. That's not how we create change. Change is created through our voice, not the destruction of our community."

Later in the evening, Governor Jay Nixon's office issued a press release to announce the mobilization of the National Guard, to protect the Ferguson police department and firehouse. The statement read, "The Guard is providing security at the Ferguson Police Department, which will allow additional law enforcement officers to protect the public." The Governor's office said they expected to call in more troops in the near future. At about 2 a.m., at least five busloads of soldiers were seen taking positions around the police command center.

By the time the national Guard arrived, more than two dozen cars were ablaze at a local car dealership., a Conoco gas station was lit on fire, and dozens of other businesses were looted and burned. The business district of Ferguson was decimated. Area hospitals reported treating two gunshot wound victims, and there were injuries to 13 other people associated with the Ferguson protest.

Once the National Guard arrived, the local police force could finally send details of officers into the areas being looted. They apprehended a man who had just looted and trashed a Phillips 66 convenience store. Along Florissant Avenue, the AutoZone, Fashions R Boutique, and a Title Max all went up in flames.

Firefighters said they could not respond right away to some fires because of the violence and gunfire in the area, but once the National Guard arrived, and they were assured of some personal security and safety, the firefighters deployed their fire trucks and dowsed the flames on Florissant.

One of the businesses that was burned during the evening was the community outreach facility, #HealStL, that St. Louis Alderman Antonio French set up to help black youths in the area. It was the unintended consequence of a fire that was purposefully set in an adjoining cell phone business, in the same building, but then spread to consume the other businesses in the vicinity. The police were also successful in capturing several suspects who were arrested for looting an O'Reilly Auto Parts store. By midnight, at least ten flights had been diverted from Lambert International Airport because of FAA flight restrictions in the area.

As a result of all of the gunfire, a young man was hit in his leg by an errant bullet. He stumbled out of his car to tell police what had happened, but when he was asked to go to the hospital to seek medical treatment, he refused, in fear of leaving his car behind, which he thought would be set on fire. He said the car, a grey Ford Mustang, was all that he had.

Ferguson Mayor James Knowles said that, before the National Guard reinforcements arrived, he had tried to contact every elected official he knew, all the way up to the Governor's officer, to try to get more troops on the ground, and prevent his town's businesses from being destroyed. He said, "They're not here. They're not responding. Right now, we're just hoping they'll respond."

Some witnesses of the night's events justified them as a result of police brutality, not only in Ferguson, but elsewhere as well. Steven Rodriguez, a resident of Ferguson, said, "This violence wasn't planned. This happened because people are sick and tired of being shot and bullied by the police." His friend, Kenneth Covington, said, "There have been so many black men killed by police, but police are never held accountable for it."

Along West Florissant Avenue, about 20 armed men stood guard to secure a perimeter around a strip-mall parking lot to prevent the businesses from being ransacked and burned. Some people claim it was the "Oath Keepers" who protected the stores.

During the evening's unrest, two police cars were set on fire. The Ferguson Market was broken into and looted, again. The Toys R Us was looted. The McDonald's had its windows smashed, again. A Little Caesar's pizzeria was looted and burned. A Public Storage was looted. The neighborhood Walgreens was set on fire, along with dozen of other businesses that were also destroyed. The rioting spread across the country, with both peaceful and violent protests raging through the night.

In the wake of the Grand Jury's decision to not indict Darren Wilson, Ferguson experienced the worst acts of rioting and civil disobedience since Michael Brown had been shot. A St. Louis County Police Sargent, Brian Schellman, reported that at least 61 people were arrested during the evening, "on charges ranging from burglary, to trespassing, to receiving stolen property." [23]

---

[23] http://bit.ly/1IeJ3XO

CHAPTER 41

WORLD RESPONSE

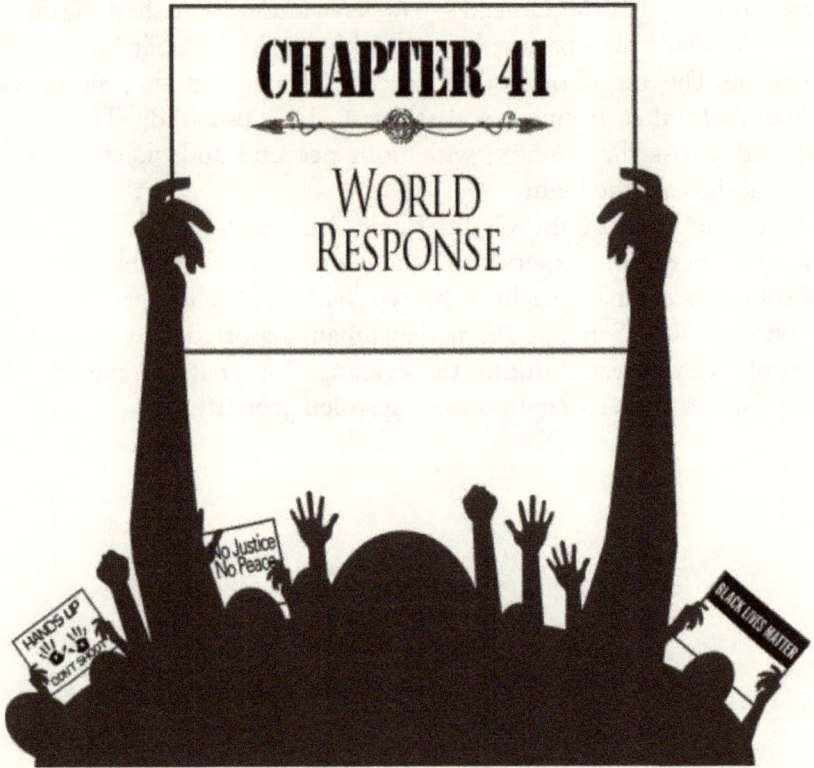

The United Nations Committee on the Elimination of Racial Discrimination (CERD) urged the American government to "use restraint," and halt further excessive use of force by police and military forces in Ferguson. The United Nations (U.N.) panel monitors compliance with a "use of force" treaty, ratified by 177 countries including the United States. The CERD panel consists of 18 experts in race relations from countries around the would, who monitor the implementation of the treaty in the hope of eliminating all forms of racial discrimination. Each member country must submit periodic reports to CERD, every two years, or whenever requested, to explain how each member country is implementing the policies of the United Nations "Convention on the Elimination of All Forms of Racial Discrimination." [24]

CERD may investigate incidents of racial discrimination in

---

[24] http://bit.ly/1k1MoiX

member countries whenever there is evidence of a violation. Once an investigation begins, the CERD panel can call upon delegates from countries that are under investigation, and require them to answer questions about their policies to prevent racial discrimination, and their adherence to the U.N. policies.

Not surprisingly, a U.N. panel was convened to investigate Ferguson. The United Nations Committee on the Elimination of Racial Discrimination questioned a delegation of United States Representatives about the harsh, military-styled tactics being employed on American citizens in Ferguson. The U.N. charged the United States with violating citizens' rights and violating the International Racial Discrimination treaty.

CERD vice-president, Noureddine Amir, admonished the United States for the harsh tactics that were used against the civilian population of Ferguson, and urged the use of restraint if tensions flare-up again, either in Ferguson or elsewhere in the country. He said, "The excessive use of force by law enforcement officials against racial and ethnic minorities is an ongoing issue of concern, and particularly in light of the shooting of Michael Brown. This is not an isolated event, and illustrates a bigger problem in the United States, such as racial bias among law enforcement officials, the lack of proper implementation of rules and regulations governing the use of force, and the inadequacy of training of law enforcement officials."

The United Nations Committee on the Elimination of Racial Discrimination urged further investigations into the US Government and their seemingly systematic policy of discriminating against minorities. The committee continued its criticism of United States policies, by suggesting the "Stand-Your-Ground" laws that have been passed in 22 states should be reviewed to "remove far-reaching immunity and ensure strict adherence to principles of necessity and proportionality when deadly force is used for self-defense." CERD's statement on Ferguson continued, "The Committee remains concerned at the practice of racial profiling of racial or ethnic minorities by law enforcement officials, including the Federal Bureau of Investigation (FBI), Transportation Security Administration (TSA), border enforcement officials, and local police."

Noureddine Amir, CERD committee vice-chairman, said in a press conference:

The excessive use of force by law enforcement officials against racial and

*ethnic minorities is an ongoing issue of concern and particularly in light
of the shooting of Michael Brown. This is not an isolated event and
illustrates a bigger problem in the United States, such as racial bias
among law enforcement officials, the lack of proper implementation of
rules and regulations governing the use of force, and the inadequacy of
training of law enforcement officials.*

The panel of experts from around the world urged the United
States to address the unfair obstacles that have been placed in front
of minorities, such as laws that have been passed to limit black
voting, though district gerrymandering, voter identification rules and
other laws that have been put in place by political parties to dissuade
minority voting and their participation in the electoral process.

The American Civil Liberties Union (ACLU) praised the findings
of the United Nations. ACLU spokesperson Jamil Dakwar stated,
"shortcomings on racial equality are playing out today on our streets,
at our borders and in the voting booth. When it comes to human
rights, the United States must practice at home what it preaches
abroad."

In response to the many accusations of racial discrimination by
the United Nations panel, United States Ambassador Keith Harper
claimed the American government has made "great strides toward
eliminating racial discrimination" but also admitted "we have much
left to do."

The main concerns pointed out in the United Nations
Committee on the Elimination of Racial Discrimination
recommendations to the United States, in the wake of the Michael
Brown shooting, include the following:

*The Committee remains concerned that members of racial and ethnic
minorities, particularly African Americans, continue to be
disproportionately arrested, incarcerated and subjected to harsher
sentences, including life imprisonment without parole and the death
penalty. It expresses concern that the overrepresentation of racial and
ethnic minorities in the criminal justice system is exacerbated by the use of
prosecutorial discretion, the application of mandatory minimum drug-
offense sentencing policies, and the implementation of repeat offender laws.
The Committee is also concerned at the negative impact of parental
incarceration on children from racial and ethnic minorities.*

The Committee reiterates its previous concern at the brutality and excessive use of force by law enforcement officials against members of racial and ethnic minorities, including against unarmed individuals.

The Committee remains concerned at the practice of racial profiling of racial or ethnic minorities by law enforcement officials, including the Federal Bureau of Investigation (FBI), Transportation Security Administration, border enforcement officials, and local police.

The Committee urges the State party to intensify efforts to effectively combat and end the practice of racial profiling by federal, state and local law enforcement officials, including by:

(a) Adopting and implementing legislation which specifically prohibits law enforcement officials from engaging in racial profiling, such as the End Racial Profiling Act;

(b) Swiftly revising policies insofar as they permit racial profiling, illegal surveillance, monitoring and intelligence gathering, including the 2003 Guidance Regarding the Use of Race by Federal Law Enforcement Agencies;

(c) Ending immigration enforcement programs and policies, which indirectly promote racial profiling, such as the Secure Communities program and the 287(g) program; and

(d) Undertaking prompt, thorough and impartial investigations into all allegations of racial profiling, surveillance, monitoring and illegal intelligence-gathering; holding those responsible accountable; and providing effective remedies, including guarantees of non-repetition.

The Committee is concerned at the obstacles faced by individuals belonging to racial and ethnic minorities and indigenous peoples to effectively exercise their right to vote, due to restrictive voter identification laws, district gerrymandering, and state-level felon disenfranchisement laws. It is also concerned at the Supreme Court decision in Shelby County v. Holder, which struck down Section 4(b) of the Voting Rights Act and made Section 5 inoperable, thus invalidating the procedural safeguards to prevent the implementation of voting regulations that may have discriminatory effect. It expresses further concern at the continued denial of the right of residents of the District of Colombia (D.C.), half of whom are African Americans, to vote for and elect representatives to the United States Senate and voting-members to the House of Representatives.

The Committee calls upon the State party to: Abolish laws and policies making homelessness a crime.

The Committee is concerned at the high number of homeless persons, who are disproportionately from racial and ethnic minorities, particularly African Americans, Hispanic/Latino Americans and Native Americans, and at the criminalization of homelessness through laws that prohibit activities such as loitering, camping, begging, and lying in public spaces.

The Committee urges the State party to intensify its efforts to prevent the excessive use of force by law enforcement officials by ensuring compliance with the 1990 Basic Principles on the Use of Force and Firearms by Law Enforcement Officials, and ensure that the new CBP directive on the use of force is applied and enforced in practice.

The Committee remains concerned that students from racial and ethnic minorities disproportionately continue to attend segregated schools with segregated or unequal facilities, and that even those who are enrolled in racially diverse schools are frequently assigned to "single-race" classes, denied equal access to advanced courses, and disciplined unfairly and disproportionately due to their race, including through referral to the criminal justice system. It also expresses concern at racial disparities in academic achievement, which contribute to unequal access to employment opportunities.

Several countries that The United States has condemned for their civil rights violations were quick to point out American hypocrisy. The Iranian Supreme Leader, Ali Khamenei, released the following statement:

Today, the world is a world of tyranny, lies and deception. The flag of defending human rights is being carried by those who are the greatest enemies of human rights! And the government of the United States is taking the lead among them! Look at what they do to the black community in their own country. This is not about the past. It is not about 50 or 100 years ago that they would claim they have already had reforms. It is about today and the major cities of the United States. Look, in a country that claims to support freedom and human rights, the problem of racial discrimination has not been solved yet. Still in that society, people are deprived of a sense of security only because they have dark skins! If necessary, the police may beat them to death over the crime of having dark skins! The same people claim that they support human rights! They turn a blind eye to the horrible crimes of the usurper Zionist regime. These bombardments, kidnaps and murders are all considered as crimes. All these-according to what they say are acts that go against human rights. The advocates of human rights do not feel at all that anti-human rights actions are occurring there. If a desperate and oppressed Palestinian shouts out and makes an aggressive move, their propaganda and political machines start to operate but all the crimes against the nations of Palestine and Lebanon are ignored by them! Today the flag of human rights is being carried by such people! Is this not a world of deception? Is this not a world of lies? Is this not a world of hypocrisy?" [25]

Egypt Response:

Egypt's Foreign Ministry called on the US to exercise restraint in its handling of the protests, mirroring language the US has used with Egypt in the past. Foreign Ministry spokesman, Badr Abdel-Aty, suggested that law-enforcement in Ferguson should adopt a policy to deal with protests that adheres to International standards, and adheres to the United States' own, unenforced, policies and laws. He hoped the investigations would reveal the truth about "Mike Brown's murder."[26]

North Korea Response:

North Korea's Foreign Ministry spokesman responded to a state-owned news agency's question about the Ferguson riots and serious racial discrimination issues in the United States. He said:

---

[25] http://on.fb.me/1lBRpHi

[26] http://bit.ly/14HH7ce

Some days ago, a black teenager was shot to death by a white policeman in Ferguson City, Missouri State. The U.S. and police ruthlessly cracked down on protesters, leveling their rifles at them and firing tear gas and smoke shells. Against this backdrop, there occurred a shuddering incident in another city in which a policeman shot another young black man to death. The U.S. is, indeed, a country wantonly violating the human rights where people are subject to discrimination and humiliation due to their races and they are seized with such horror that they do not know when they are shot to death.

The protests in Ferguson City and other parts of the U.S. are an eruption of the pent-up discontent and resistance of the people against racial discrimination and inequality deeply rooted in the American society.

The recent cases brought to light the human rights performance in the U.S. and underscored the urgent need to force the U.S. to sit in the dock of a human rights court.

The U.S. issued every year a report taking issue with "human rights performances" of other countries as if it were an "international human rights judge" but this time suffered disgrace and became a laughing stock of the world owing to what happened in it.

The U.S. had better honestly accept the unanimous accusations of the broad international community and mind its own business, instead of interfering in the internal affairs of other countries. It should not seek solutions to its problem in suppressing demonstrators but bring to light the real picture of the American society, a graveyard of human rights, and have a correct understanding of what the genuine human rights are like and how they should be guaranteed. The U.S. should know that it is bound to get itself into a big trouble unless it behaves with discretion, not knowing where it stands. [27]

Russia Response:

Russian Foreign Ministry's Human Rights Commissioner, Konstantin Dolgov, stated:

---

[27] http://bit.ly/1DxaxYJ

The United States should take care of its own internal problems instead of intervening in other countries' internal affairs on the pretext of protecting democracy." He also stated, *"The tragic events in Ferguson that followed shortly after a police gunned down an unarmed 18-year-year-old Afro-American Michael Brown are clear evidence of the high degree of tensions in US society, which remains split along racial lines."*

China Response:

China's state-owned news agency, Xinhua, released the following statement about the civil unrest in Ferguson:

BEIJING, Aug. 18 (Xinhua) -- In his landmark speech, "I have a dream," civil rights leader Martin Luther King voiced his strong aspiration for equal rights of the black people in U.S. society. Fifty years later, such a dream has been partially realized. The African Americans living in the United States today are enjoying elevated political and social status. Notably, the country is having its first African American president in history. However, despite the progress, racial divide still remains a deeply-rooted chronic disease that keeps tearing U.S. society apart, just as manifested by the latest racial riot in Missouri. Stunned and enraged by the shooting death of an unarmed black teenager by a white police officer, a large number of residents in the suburban St. Louis town in Ferguson took to the streets and staged a tense standoff with police in riot gear.

In history, racial tensions cut deep in U.S. society. Even now, the scar is obviously far from being fully healed. Some might argue that racial differences and conflicts are unavoidable in a "melting pot" like the United States, where people from virtually every corner of the world converge and seek common lives. However, it is undeniable that racial discrimination against African Americans or other ethnic minorities, though not as obvious as in the past, still persists in every aspect of U.S. social lives, including employment, housing, education, and particularly, justice. In the worst U.S. violence in recent times, the acquittal of four white policemen in the beating of a black motorist in 1992 sparked a six-day riot involving thousands of people across the metropolitan area of Los Angeles, leaving an astounding 51 people dead. In a highly-mixed society like the United States, such racial inequalities could only jeopardize social peace and security. It is highly advisable for the country to make extra efforts to effectively uproot racism in all fields so as to prevent tragedies from recurring.

The Ferguson incident once again demonstrates that even if in a country that has for years tried to play the role of an international human rights judge and defender, there is still much room for improvement at home. In its annual human rights report issued in February, the United States assaulted almost 200 countries across the world for their so-called poor human rights records. However, the U.S. human rights flaws extend far beyond racial issues. As revealed by famous whistleblower Edward Snowden, the U.S. government has hacked into emails and mobile phones of ordinary Americans as well as leaders of other countries, including traditional U.S. allies. What's more, Uncle Sam has witnessed numerous shooting sprees on its own land and launched incessant drone attacks on foreign soil, resulting in heavy civilian casualties.

Each country has its own national conditions that might lead to different social problems. Obviously, what the United States needs to do is to concentrate on solving its own problems rather than always pointing fingers at others. 28

Counter-Response from U.S. State Department:

The Obama administration defended the human rights record of the United States against the mounting international criticism of the police tactics used in Ferguson, Missouri. U.S. State Department spokeswoman, Marie Harf, said. "When things occur, as you've heard the president speak about, we look at them, as I said, transparently, honestly and openly, and we, of course, would suggest that other countries do the same thing. We here in the United States will put our record for confronting our problems transparently and honestly and openly up against any other countries in the world." [29]

---

[28] http://bit.ly/1sOr1Xn

[29] http://bit.ly/1FGiPzH

CHAPTER 42

CIVIL RIGHTS VIOLATIONS

The Human rights organization, Amnesty International, decried the civil rights violations in Ferguson in the press, in the courts and through social media. The group posted online, "US can't tell other countries to improve their records on policing and peaceful assembly if it won't clean up its own human rights record"[30] They have been heavily involved in overseeing the Ferguson riots and police response, from soon after Brown was killed. On August 14, 2014, a delegation of Amnesty International observers were deployed to Ferguson Missouri to work with the community, and protesters to develop de-escalation tactics that could be used during protests. Further, they were to act as field observers and to witness whether or not citizens' civil rights were being violated during the daily

---

[30] http://bit.ly/14K2j0A

demonstrations. What the delegation witnessed was shocking. They saw constitutional rights being stripped away, with flagrant disregard for democracy, the right to assemble and of free speech, by police officers who were determined to contain the riots, and the media, at all costs, even at the expense of liberty.

Amnesty International reviewed the legality of the Michael Brown shooting and the police response in its aftermath. They concluded that the confusing and conflicting state and federal laws on the use of deadly force by law enforcement officers should be re-written to conform to the United Nations principles of practice for the use of deadly force. Such laws have already been established in the United Nations Code of Conduct for Law Enforcement Officials and the United Nations Basic Principles on the Use of Force and Firearms by Law Enforcement Officials. [31]

The United Nations considers the use of deadly force appropriate by police officers only when it is "strictly unavoidable in order to protect life." The United Nations policy on the use of deadly force mandates that it is only to be used as a last resort, and requires that the amount of force must be proportionate to the threat encountered and designed to minimize damage and injury. In international law, police officers may only use deadly force against a suspect when it is necessary to avoid death or serious injury to the police or to others.

Christof Heyns, an independent expert appointed by the United Nations Human Rights Council to examine extrajudicial and arbitrary executions, has explained that: "The 'protect life' principle demands that lethal force may not be used intentionally merely to protect law and order or to serve other similar interests (for example, it may not be used only to disperse protests, to arrest a suspected criminal, or to safeguard other interests such as property). The primary aim must be to save life. In practice, this means that only the protection of life can meet the proportionality requirement where lethal force is used intentionally, and the protection of life can be the only legitimate objective for the use of such force. A fleeing thief who poses no immediate danger may not be killed, even if it means that the thief will escape." [32]

---

[31] http://bit.ly/1dtR5f7

[32] http://bit.ly/1wtRZIC

Contrary to the UN policies, Missouri state law allows police officers to use deadly force in circumstances where they are trying to apprehend a fleeing suspect, if the officer believes a felony has occurred.

Missouri state law 563.046 on the use of force in making an arrest states: [33]

1. A law enforcement officer need not retreat or desist from efforts to effect the arrest, or from efforts to prevent the escape from custody, of a person he reasonably believes to have committed an offense because of resistance or threatened resistance of the arrestee. In addition to the use of physical force authorized under other sections of this chapter, he is, subject to the provisions of subsections 2 and 3, justified in the use of such physical force as he reasonably believes is immediately necessary to effect the arrest or to prevent the escape from custody.

2. The use of any physical force in making an arrest is not justified under this section unless the arrest is lawful or the law enforcement officer reasonably believes the arrest is lawful.

3. A law enforcement officer in effecting an arrest or in preventing an escape from custody is justified in using deadly force only

(1) When such is authorized under other sections of this chapter; or

(2) When he reasonably believes that such use of deadly force is immediately necessary to effect the arrest and also reasonably believes that the person to be arrested

(a) Has committed or attempted to commit a felony; or

(b) Is attempting to escape by use of a deadly weapon; or

(c) May otherwise endanger life or inflict serious physical injury unless arrested without delay.

The Missouri statute on the use of deadly force seems to be unconstitutional. It is not in line with the United Nations policy on the use of deadly force, nor is it compliant with United Stated federal law.

In the court case of Tennessee v. Garner, the US Supreme Court ruled that under the Fourth Amendment to the US Constitution, Tennessee's laws on the use of deadly force by law enforcement were

---

[33] http://on.mo.gov/1nagNcF

unconstitutional. The members of the Supreme Court noted, "Where the suspect poses no immediate threat to the officer and no threat to others, the harm resulting from failing to apprehend him does not justify the use of deadly force to do so... A police officer may not seize an unarmed, non-dangerous suspect by shooting him dead. The Tennessee statute is unconstitutional insofar as it authorizes the use of deadly force against such fleeing suspects."

The Supreme Court confirmed that lethal force in the United States by police officers may not be used unless it is necessary to preserve life. The Tennessee v. Garner case grew out of an incident on October 3rd, 1974 at 10:45 PM when two Memphis police officers were dispatched to a "prowler" call that came from a concerned citizen who heard broken glass at her neighbor's house and told the police that someone was breaking in. One of the arriving police officers heard a door slam shut at the property being burglarized and then saw a young man running from the house. The officer pursued the boy into the backyard and cornered him at a fence in the rear of the yard. The officer could see that the boy was unarmed, but when the fleeing suspect began to climb over the fence to get away, the police officer shot him in the back of the head, killing him. Elton Hymon was 15 years old and had stolen only $10 from a purse on the property. His father claimed the killing was illegal and an infringement of the United States Constitution, and of the Forth Amendment in particular.

In Tennessee in the early 1980's, state law allowed law enforcement to shoot to kill fleeing criminal suspects. The Tennessee statute stated, "the officer may use all the necessary means to effect the arrest," which effectively entitled each officer to kill any suspect if they reasonably believed a crime had been committed and the alleged criminal was escaping arrest.

The Supreme Court ruled "The use of deadly force to prevent the escape of all felony suspects, whatever the circumstances, is constitutionally unreasonable. Where the suspect poses no immediate threat to the officer and no threat to others, the harm resulting from failing to apprehend him does not justify the use of deadly force to do so. It is no doubt unfortunate when a suspect who is in sight escapes, but the fact that the police arrive a little late or are a little slower afoot does not always justify killing the suspect. A police officer may not seize an unarmed, non-dangerous suspect by shooting him dead. The Tennessee statute is unconstitutional insofar as it authorizes the use of deadly force against such fleeing suspects. The Tennessee statute is unconstitutional insofar as it authorizes the use of deadly force against, as in this case, an apparently unarmed, non-dangerous fleeing suspect; such force may not be used unless necessary to prevent the escape and the officer has probable cause to believe that the suspect poses a significant threat of death or serious physical injury to the officer or others."

A lawsuit clarified that the Fourth Amendment does not permit the police to "use whatever force is necessary to effect the arrest of a fleeing felon," even if it is written into state law, as it is in Missouri. These outdated "common law" clauses were written into state law many years ago when Felonies where much more violent crimes that usually carried the punishment of death, which might have warranted the use of deadly force by police officers, especially at a time when these laws were passed, when the police did not carry guns and were much more exposed to harm than they are today.

Human Rights Violations in Ferguson:

Although Missouri's Governor, Attorney General, the Highway Patrol and the President of the United States have all admitted that most of the Ferguson protests associated with the Michael Brown shooting have been peaceful, the actions of a few rowdy rioters were somehow able to impact the rights of the majority of individuals who were acting lawfully, and exercising their constitutional rights of Peaceful Assembly, Freedom of Association and Freedom of Expression.

Amnesty International observers were immediately dispatched to Ferguson once word of the Michael Brown shooting and subsequent riots started to spread across the country. The main concerns of Amnesty International were in regard to a curfew, a new "no standing" rule, restricted assembly areas, intimidation of protesters, illegal dispersal of protests, the use of tear gas and rubber bullets on peaceful protesters, the use of long range acoustic devices against United States citizens, restrictions placed on the media and on civil rights observers, and the lack of accountability for law enforcement officers' overzealous actions.

In addition to filing several lawsuits and compiling a Ferguson impact report of law-enforcement abuses, the group has also made nine public recommendations to address the police brutality and civil rights violations they witnessed in Ferguson. They include:

The Curfew:

On August 16th, Governor Nixon declared a state of emergency in Missouri due to some early morning looting and vandalism. He then imposed a curfew to prevent further acts of civil disobedience and, he claimed, to protect the safety of the residents of Ferguson. The curfew prohibited people from being outside from midnight until 5:00 a.m. each morning. The police gave no timeline for the duration of the curfew, except to say, "until further notice." Although the curfew only lasted for two days, it was an immeasurable inconvenience for the people who needed to travel to, through and from Ferguson, at night.

When questioned by reporters, the police could not provide any details about how the curfew was going to be enforced or how the people who reside in, or travel through the Ferguson community would be affected by the nightly curfews. There were no provisions made public for people who had to travel to work at night, or for those who had an emergency. On the first night of the curfew there were seven people arrested for being out past midnight, according to the St. Louis County police, and 12 people were arrested on the second night of the curfew, with charges being filed against them for "failure to disperse'. There is no record of the number of people who were detained and later released, but never charged. Of the seven people arrested the first night of the curfew, three claim to have been on their own driveway. [34]

Governor Nixon removed the curfew on August 17th, after activating the National Guard to provide support to the local police forces. Calling in the National Guard sent a strong signal to activist organizations across the country--that Ferguson would be the first real race-riot in America in the 21st century, and nobody in the civil rights industry wanted to miss it. The activist population in Ferguson continued to increase and the police didn't know what to do next, so they outlawed standing. [35]

---

[34] http://politi.co/1EzXyXL

[35] http://on.ksdk.com/1Ad47LK

The No Standing Rule:

Once the Governor had called in the National Guard and called-off the nightly curfew, the police created a new rule which prevented protesters, or anyone else located within a newly defined "no-standing" zone, from standing still for more than 5 seconds. It was termed the 'No Standing Rule" and also called the "5 Second Rule." The new "No Standing Rule" allowed law enforcement officers to arrest protesters, or anyone else who was standing still for more than 5 seconds in the newly-identified zones. The law effectively outlawed standing still on public property in certain parts of the city. Anyone who stopped walking for more than five seconds could be arrested and charged with "failure to disperse." The only area where anyone could stand still for more than 5 seconds without the threat of being arrested was in a designated press area, but the press area was far away from where the protesters were demonstrating, so the media refused to use it. The police also reported that protesters were given a specific area to protest in, but the location of the promised demonstration site was difficult to find. Many people claimed it was never actually set up until the media realized they had been lied to and then began investigating where the supposed protest area was supposed to be.

Civil rights groups who became aware of the no standing rule immediately criticized it as being unconstitutional, and claimed it was being used as a tool to disrupt the "peaceful" protests. It was also viewed as a way for law enforcement to prevent people from congregating around activist leaders who were attempting to give speeches to the crowd. The Missouri State Highway Patrol stated that the new no standing rule was implemented to keep groups small and to prevent them from clustering together in one area. Highway Patrol Captain Ron Johnson said the no standing rule could prevent people who were committing violent acts or vandalism from blending in with the crowd of peaceful protesters.

Protesters were repeatedly told that they would be arrested if they stopped moving. On the first day of enforcement, 78 people were arrested for failure to disperse. [36] On August 18th, the day the police

---

[36] http://bit.ly/1wvs1vS

began to enforce the no standing rule, the American Civil Liberties Union (ACLU) filed a Temporary Restraining Order against St. Louis County and the Missouri Highway Patrol, claiming the new rule was illegal. A judge ruled against granting the restraining order due to the testimony of Missouri's Attorney General, who declared in court that the no-standing rule was not illegal because there had been provisions made for both the general public and protesters to have an alternate designated area, hereafter called the "protest zone," in which to congregate, rest, and demonstrate. Therefore, their constitutional rights were not violated since the protest zone was being made available to them. The Attorney General stated, "there is ample space there for protestors to gather even in the thousands, three to four acres of open land there."

Missouri's Deputy Director and General Counsel for the Department of Public Safety, Andrea Spillars, testified that the prohibition against standing was designed to encourage people to "disperse and go to the other area to protest."

It was uncovered later that Missouri's top law enforcement official and Public Safety Officer misrepresented the no-standing policy to the courts when they claimed that an alternate protest area had been established. In fact, no alternate demonstration site was established until after the ACLU filed a lawsuit claiming the no-standing rule was illegal, and after the Attorney General declared in court that a demonstration site had already been made available for protesters.

Several civil rights groups, including the ACLU, visited the site of the protest zone. They found that the designated area was fenced off. There was no sign that it was available for the intended purpose, and it was locked against entry. After word of this discovery was disseminated, the Attorney General's office issued an e-mail to the civil rights groups, telling them that the "real" designated protest zone was in a different location than that which had been identified in court.

The "new" protest area was supposedly located in a vacant parking lot across the street from the originally designated area. The ACLU immediately sent observers to see if there was really a protest area set-up as the Attorney General had reassured them. When ACLU observers arrived at the new protest site, they found the empty parking lot of a furniture store, with no protesters in sight, no facilities, and nothing to give anyone an indication that the site was intended and available for protests and demonstrations. When the owner of the furniture store was asked if his parking lot was the site of the protest zone, he claimed that it was private property and that he had not given anyone permission to use it.

Later in the afternoon, an ACLU observer overheard Captain Johnson of the Highway Patrol negotiating a deal for the furniture store parking lot to be used as the protest zone. When Captain Johnson was asked if this was really the location of the protest zone, he responded that is would be, and that he hoped to have the protest zone opened by 5:00 pm that evening, but he was still working out some details. This occurred about 24 hours after the Attorney Generals declaration that the justification for the legality of the no-standing rule was that an alternate protest zone had already been established. Thus, a full day after the no standing rule was put in place, the alternate protest area was finally opened, as noted in a press release by the Missouri Highway Patrol, titled, "New Ferguson Protester Assembly Zone and Media Staging Area."

The approved Protester Assembly Zone was finally established at an abandoned Ford dealership parking lot at 9026 West Florissant Avenue. far away from the site of the actual protests. The newly approved media staging area, which was previously located at a local McDonalds Restaurant and situated directly across the street from the initial protest area, was moved to the Public Storage facility several blocks away from the Protester Assembly Zone. Both locations were inconvenient and outside of the areas where the media and the protesters wanted to be. Further, they were too far removed from each other for the protesters to voice their concerns and for the Media to hear them. Many people thought that this was done by design, in order to limit the media's documentation of the riots and subsequent law enforcement actions. The Protester Assembly Zone and the Media Staging Area were rarely used by either group. Everyone wanted to be at ground zero, which was at the QuickTrip, but the Quicktrip had been taken over by the police so the protesters descended on the streets surrounding the Quicktrip.

On August 26th, the ACLU filed another lawsuit challenging the earlier denial of the restraining order, and seeking to compel the courts to rule on the constitutionality of the no standing rule. The justification was that there was no alternate protest location available to the general public, contrary to the claim, in court, by the Attorney General and the Public Safety Officer.

The ACLU complaint contended the St. Louis Police Department was violating the First Amendment of the United States Constitution by enforcing an illegal law, which was arbitrarily enforced, and which purposely prevented people from gathering around political leaders or activists who were giving speeches. The lawsuit also claimed that the rule was intended to prevent people from pausing on a sidewalk momentarily to catch their breath, in order to wear-out the strength and moral of the protesters and to cause an early end to the daily demonstrations. Police officers were free to enforce the rule on whoever they wanted, and as they felt was appropriate, but observers noticed that the rule was being applied disproportionately to black youths more than to any other segment of society.

A St. Louis judge finally granted an injunction that prevented the police from enforcing the no standing rule. The judge found that the new police policy violated the U.S. Constitution. further, he restricted law enforcement personnel from "telling citizens that they must keep moving, or from threatening them with arrest if they stand still, so long as those citizens are not committing a crime, engaging in violent acts, or participating in a crowd that contains other people doing those things."[37] U.S. District Court Judge Catherine Perry found in favor of the American Civil Liberties Union and ruled "The 5 second rule — a policy being enforced by some officers that required protesters to be moving at all times during demonstrations or be subject to arrest — was unconstitutional and violated the protesters' First Amendment rights." [38]The judge wrote in the ruling, "The practice of requiring peaceful demonstrators and others to walk, rather than stand still, violates the Constitution," [39]

Restricted Assembly Area:

Ground Zero for the Ferguson protests was at or in front of the QuickTrip convenience store, where the first Ferguson riots and

---

[37] http://bit.ly/1s5ZmkT

[38] http://wapo.st/1t1stqu

[39] http://bit.ly/1HaVP9f

looting occurred. Each day protesters congregated on the public sidewalks of West Florissant Avenue, across the street from the Quicktrip, to pray, protest and remember Mike Brown.

The QuickTrip parking lot and the surrounding public property were the initial staging grounds for the protesters and the media, until the police pushed them all out, on August 18th, eight days after the riots began. The same day, the police began enforcing the no standing rule. The ACLU contended in court that the imposition of the no standing rule and the misinformation about an approved assembly were designed to disrupt the demonstrations rather than provide safety to the community, as the police contended.

When an approved assembly area was finally set-up, it was located at a closed down car dealership parking lot, far away from where the demonstrators wanted to be and too far from the media to communicate their message. Therefore, neither the protestors nor the media used the designated holding pens that law enforcement tried to coral them into, except to take a short reprieve from the enforcement of the no standing rule.

Protesters complained that the police's designated protest area had no significance to them and it was far away from the media in an apparent attempt to limit their right of assembly. The ACLU wrote in their lawsuit that "International law allows the restriction of the right to freedom of peaceful assembly only if it is carried out for a legitimate aim, such as the protection of public safety, order, health, morals or the fundamental rights and freedoms of others. Restrictions must be proportionate and necessary to meet that aim. However, the broad imposition of a curfew for the entire city of Ferguson, and requirements for those protesters on W. Florissant Avenue to keep walking under threat of arrest, impede protesters from enjoying their right to freely assemble."

Intimidation of Protestors:

The ACLU complaint, contends that the St. Louis County Police purposefully employed military type tactics to intimidate the protestors. After St. Louis County took over the responsibility of policing Ferguson, the department began a campaign of harassment that provoked fear, resentment and further hostilities towards the police. On August 13th, the county police lined the protesters marching route with militarized police forces on either side of the street, with police outfitted in riot gear and with automatic weapons pointed at the demonstrators, further infuriating the crowd. In an apparent attempt to deescalate the tension, the Highway Patrol was called-in to take over policing of ferguson, but the calm did not last. Only one day after Captain Johnson and the state police walked side by side with the protesters, in apparent unity, the bond was broken. The following night, August 15th, the Highway Patrol and other supporting police agencies confronted protesters in full riot gear, batons, shields, attack dogs, tactical military weaponry and combat vehicles, in an all out assault on the community.

The Governor declared a state of emergency on August 18th and mobilized the National Guard to ferguson, take control of the city, and quell the apparent violence. A curfew was put in place and other extreme measures were used to disperse the crowds. The presence of the National Guard seemed to give local police the ability to go vigilante without much oversight. Name tags and identifying information were removed from police officer uniforms so there would be no accountability for their actions. Later that evening the National Guard, Highway Patrol and municipal police agencies from around Missouri assaulted the crowd of mainly peaceful protesters with rubber bullets, flash bang grenades, LRAD Long Range Acoustic Devices, aggressive dogs and the full force of the National Guards military arsenal. The people were pushed back, arrested, shot, injured and driven away from where they were protesting.

On the evening of August 19th, during another assault on the crowd by law enforcement, an officer with the St. Ann police department went lost control and began ranting at the protesters that he was going to kill them, while at the same time, pointing his AR-15 semi-automatic rifle right in their faces. A video recording captured him saying "I will ficking kill you." When the protesters asked for the officer's name he responded "go fuck yourself." He is known on-line as officer Go Fuck Yourself. Police have contended that the officer had a bottle of urine thrown on him just before his tirade, but that was no excuse for his outrageous behavior and excessive use of force. He resigned a few days after the incident, after a video of him threatening the protesters went viral.

According to the United Nations Basic Principles for the Use of Force and Firearms by Law Enforcement Officials, the police "shall not use firearms against persons except in self-defense or defense of others against the imminent threat of death or serious injury." The forceful police presence during the demonstrations escalated the mostly-peaceful protests into full-scale riots. Police forced protesters from the commercial business district into the surrounding neighborhoods, causing a wider scale conflict. The use of militarized assault vehicles and weaponry enraged the crowd and caused an escalation in the violence.

Dispersal of Protests:

The police have a primary responsibility to protect people's right to assemble, and to ensure that public order is maintained during protests and demonstrations. Officers are expected to be properly trained in legal riot-control measures, and safeguards should be put in place to make sure protesters rights are not violated, by either police or other agitators. During the Ferguson riots, the police used two Missouri state laws to justify their actions to quell the crowd. One law was used to order the dispersal of the demonstrators and the other law allowed the police to arrest protesters who did not disperse. It seems the police either misunderstood Missouri law, or failed to comply with it.

Under Missouri law, "a person commits the crime of rioting if he knowingly assembles with six or more other persons and agrees with such persons to violate any of the criminal laws of Missouri or of the United States with force or violence, and thereafter, while still so assembled, does violate any of said laws with force or violence."

Under Missouri law, "a person commits the crime of refusal to disperse if, being present at the scene of an unlawful assembly, or at the scene of a riot, he knowingly fails or refuses to obey the lawful command of a law enforcement officer to depart from the scene of such unlawful assembly or riot."

When a lawful command is given by the police to a crowd of rioters to disperse from an unlawful assembly, it must be clearly communicated to the demonstrators, and sufficient time must be allowed for the protesters to move away from the scene. In Ferguson that did not happen. On many occasions protesters were either given no warning or very little warning before they were confronted by police.

Police departments have, on occasion, used protestor actions, such as throwing water bottles at them, to justify the conclusion that a peaceful assembly has transformed into an illegal riot. This conclusion entitles the police to shut down the activity, and to arrest protestors if they do not disperse. There has been speculation that "agents" of the police have, on occasion, thrown bottles or used gun shots to justify shutting down peaceful assemblies, especially when they might embarrass the police force or city administrators. In Ferguson, the police seemed to have overreacted to a small number of protesters who threw plastic water bottles at them. Numerous witnesses contend that no water bottles were thrown prior to the police responding with, possibly, "excessive force." Regardless of how many water bottles were thrown or not thrown, the police did not act in accordance with protocol. They should have given the command to disperse and allowed time for reaction, announced their intent to advance, and then advanced on non-compliant protestors.

Contrary to protocol, the police gave either no warning, or only a short warning, before moving-in to disperse or arrest the protesters.

Use of Tear Gas and Rubber Bullets to Disperse Protests:

On August 11th and 12th, police fired rubber bullets, flash-bang stun-grenades, and tear-gas at protesters. Rubber bullets, grenades and tear gas were again used against the crowd of protesters on August 15th when they refused to disperse after a midnight curfew imposed by the Governor. Questionable police tactics continued to be used on protestors on August 16th and 17th. Several children were wounded by tear-gas and had to obtain medical assistance at a local hospital. On August 18th and 19th tear-gas and rubber-bullets were again used against the protesters, but this time it was for failing to keep walking, after the police began enforcing the unconstitutional No Standing Rule.

Use of Long Range Acoustic Devices:

On August 18th a group of protesters stood still in front of an advancing police line, in defiance of the No Standing Rule, until the police activated their Long Range Acoustic Device (LRAD), a piece of military equipment that produces ear-piercing sounds that cause unbearable pain to anyone in its attack zone. The LRAD was mounted on top of an armored tactical truck. Despite laws that require a warning before anti-riot control measures are deployed against the public, the police gave no warring before turning on the

LRAD, which made the protesters and the media sick with nausea. One St. Louis County cop was kind enough to supply an Amnesty International observer with a set of earplugs, then stated, "this noise will make you sick."

LRADs can pose serious health risks which range from temporary pain, loss of balance and eardrum rupture, to permanent hearing damage. Some cities in America have been sued for their use of the LRAD, due to the permanent damage it can cause to "targets." Civil rights leaders have questioned the amount of training law enforcement personnel have received in the use of these military weapons in riot-control situations. The devices are dangerous, not widely used, and the leaders are concerned that the training may be insufficient.

Orders to Disperse:

During the evening of August 18th a group of protesters, tired from walking, slowed down their pace and began milling around in one area without continuing to walk, in apparent violation of the no standing rule. In response, law enforcement personnel formed a police line in the middle of the street in front of the protesters. The law enforcement personnel were fully suited in riot gear, batons, helmets, bullet proof vests, shields, dogs and an arsenal of intimidating tactical equipment. The police line stood still for about a minute while police were pointing their guns at the demonstrators, and at the media personnel who were interspersed within the group. Then the police line began to move forward towards the crowd, without a warning being uttered, and forcibly removed them from the sidewalk. The crowd fled out of fear of being shot with rubber bullets or being gassed again.

August 19th produced the same law enforcement reactions that had occurred on the previous day; with dogs in the street, police pointing their guns directly at peaceful protesters, and repeated reminders over the loudspeaker telling people to keep on moving or they would risk being arrested. Then, without any warning, the police would rush into the crowd to arrest certain targeted individuals, seemingly at random. The rest of the protesters would flee in panic. Later in the evening a line of protesters formed directly in front of the police line. The protesters held each other, hand-in-hand, in solidarity, with their backs towards the police. Over the loudspeaker, the protesters were told to disperse immediately. Then the media was ordered to separate from the protesters and go to the media area. After a few minutes, it was announced on the loudspeakers that the media should stay in the designated area, and all other people should disperse from the area. Then the police moved in and began to randomly arrest people from the crowd. When asked why people were being arrested and forced to disperse, a police spokesman stated that it was a "riot situation." It seems that police decided to classify the peaceful protest as a violent riot when a plastic water bottle was thrown in their direction. This allowed the police to move-in and disperse the crowd with force.

Amnesty International observers reported that they witnessed a clear lack of consistency and transparency as to how police policies were carried out by the various law enforcement agencies working the Ferguson detail. Police continually told observers they did not know why people were being arrested. They also told observers that they could not answer their questions, and instructed them to "ask someone else." They repeatedly instructed the media to go away. Observers claimed the police stormed crowds of protesters arbitrarily, without any standard protocol. In some cases the officers moved on a crowd without any notice, sometimes with a little notice and sometimes with as much as 30 minutes before the police took actions to disperse the protestors.

The U.N. Code of Conduct for Law Enforcement Officials states "Law enforcement officials may use force only when strictly necessary and to the extent required for the performance of their duty." The U.N. Basic Principles on the Use of Force and Firearms by Law Enforcement Officials states that the police will "not use firearms against persons except in self-defense or defense of others against the imminent threat of death or serious injury." but even though the United Nations gives guidance to countries about proper civil rights tactics, each state has the ability to craft their own laws to protect police officers.

Events such as the shooting death of Michael Brown in Ferguson and the subsequent demonstrations by community members, are incidents of great public importance. They need to be reported honestly, and openly, without undue interference from law enforcement. Citizens who represent a civil society have a right to attend public assemblies, and the media have a right to report these occurrences. However, legal and human rights observers, as well as members of the media, have repeatedly been obstructed from carrying out their roles and responsibilities by law enforcement personnel in Ferguson.

From August 13 through October 2, at least 19 journalists and members of the media were arrested, and others were subjected to tear gas and to being shot with rubber bullets. Reporters for CNN, Al Jazeera America and other outlets reported being harassed, physically threatened, tear gassed and shot at. Law enforcement created a designated "protection zone" for members of the media. Those media members who left the designated area were assaulted and arrested. Several journalists who spoke with Amnesty International investigators feared that they would be arrested for doing their jobs.

On the night of September 20, Capt. Johnson of the Missouri Highway Patrol was asked a question about the arrests of media personnel, who were covering the protests in Ferguson. He responded, "It is difficult to tell who is media, and who is disguising themselves as such." Captain Johnson's claims that rioters were impersonating reporters is improbable and unbelievable.

In addition to the media being harassed and arrested, legal and civil rights observers have also been targeted, for doing nothing more than collecting evidence and witnessing if any human rights violations were occurring during the demonstrations.

Journalists Ryan Devereaux and Lukas Hermsmeier were arrested and held in jail over night for "failing to disperse" after they got pinned-down by police, and then rounded up and hauled away to the police holding tank. The police had earlier closed down the protest site, due to "public safety" concerns, after police reported that shots were fired in the area. When the two reporters tried to leave the area, they say they were blocked off by police and attacked with hot cans of tear gas. Amnesty International reported,

"As Devereaux and Hermsmeier attempted to return to the safety of their car in the midst of tear gas and metal canisters flying overhead, armed police officers drove up in armored vehicles and blocked their passage. After coming out behind a cover with their hands in the air, shouting, "Press!" and "Journalists" and "We're media!" an officer allowed them to pass. However, as Devereaux and Hermsmeier continued walking with their hands in the air, shouting "Press!" the same officer shot rubber bullets at them, hitting both journalists in the back. Out of fear, they dove behind a car. The officers approached with guns pointed and arrested them without reading them their rights or notifying them of their charge despite their continuous announcements that they were from the media. They were placed in a jail cell with other protestors, the majority of whom were African American. An officer subsequently denied Devereaux's request for his lawyer's phone number, claiming that it was "too late" to retrieve it. Despite Missouri Highway Patrol Capt. Ron Johnson's assurance that night that no journalists were arrested, and that even if they were, the police department had already taken proper action to release them immediately, Devereaux and Hermsmeier were not released until the next morning.

Accountability For Law Enforcement In Policing Protests:

On multiple occasions, police officers who were stationed at the Ferguson protests were caught not wearing name tags or any identifying information that would indicate who they were or what police department they belonged to. The Department of Justice sent a letter to the Ferguson Police Department directing them to comply with the requirement that officers wear name tags. The DOJ reminded the police department, "Officers wearing name plates while in uniform is a basic component of transparency and accountability ... Allowing officers to remain anonymous when they interact with the public contributes to mistrust and undermines accountability ... and conveys a message to community members that, through anonymity, officers may seek to act with impunity."

Recommendations by Amnesty International:

Amnesty International has put forth nine recommendations for the policing of protests in Ferguson, and all other law enforcement agencies in the United States. These recommendation are:

1. Governments and law enforcement authorities, in particular, must ensure that everyone under their jurisdiction can enjoy their human right to peaceful assembly, the right to freedom of expression, and freedom of movement.
2. All law enforcement agencies must comply at all times with international human rights obligations and with international standards on policing, in particular the U.N. Code of Conduct for

Law Enforcement Officials and the U.N. Basic Principles on the Use of Force and Firearms by Law Enforcement Officials, which must be the guiding principles underpinning all operations before, during and after demonstrations.

3. Ensure that all law enforcement agencies engaged in the policing of protests understand that their task is to facilitate, not to restrict, a peaceful public assembly. All necessary measures must be taken to prevent use of excessive force and other human rights violations by law enforcement officials in demonstrations.

4. Ensure that all law enforcement agencies engaged in the policing of protests review their policies in the policing of protests by taking an approach that leads to de-escalation. They should avoid unnecessary escalation through threatening appearance and/or behavior, excessive use of force, inappropriate equipment, and arbitrary arrests. They should seek dialogue with protest organizers, call for calm, and not make public statements which label an entire group of protesters as the enemy of the state, such as "we will fight vandals and criminals."

5. Ensure that all law enforcement agencies engaged in the policing of protests engage in communication with organizers and demonstrators before and during the operation in order to create mutual understanding and prevent violence. Where outbreaks of violence are highly probable, communication with organizers and demonstrators becomes even more important in order to reduce tension and to avoid unnecessary confrontation. Law enforcement officials and organizers should look together for ways to prevent violence or to stop it quickly as soon as it breaks out.

6. Ensure that any decision to disperse an assembly is be taken only as a last resort and carefully in line with the principles of necessity and proportionality, i.e., only when there are no other means available to protect a legitimate aim and when the level of threat of violence outweighs the right of people to assemble. Ensure that even in situations in which a small minority tries to turn a peaceful assembly into a violent one, police should ensure that those who are protesting peacefully are able to continue to do so, and not use the violent acts of a few as a pretext to restrict or impede the exercise of rights of a majority.

7. Ensure that the type of equipment used for the purpose of dispersing is carefully considered and used only when necessary, proportional and lawful. Policing and security equipment – such as

kinetic impact projectiles (e.g. rubber/plastic bullets), chemical irritants (e.g. tear gas/pepper spray) and stun grenades, often described as "less-lethal" weapons – can result in serious injury and even death. Toxic chemical irritants, such as tear gas, should not be fired directly at an individual, used in confined spaces against unarmed people, or in situations in which exits and ventilation points are restricted. Irritants should not be launched near vulnerable people, such as the elderly, pregnant women and children. The discharge of 'less lethal' projectiles (rubber or plastic bullets) should be prohibited, unless the projectiles have been rigorously and independently tested to ensure that they are sufficiently accurate not to cause unwarranted injury, and their use is strictly limited to situations of violent disorder posing a risk of harm to persons, where no less extreme measures are sufficient to achieve the objective of containing and stopping the violence. Semi-automatic weapons, i.e. weapons that can be put on multiple shot mode, have no place in such situations where each single shot must be justified. In general, firearms are not ordinary tools for public order management. Police should only be deployed with firearms where a level of violence is anticipated that life of people is in danger.

8. Officials must investigate effectively, impartially and promptly all allegations of human rights violations by police officials during public assemblies, including unlawful use of force, arbitrary arrest and detention; and bring all those found responsible, including commanding officers, to account through criminal or disciplinary proceedings as appropriate; and provide full redress to victims.

9. Review and revise the training provided to law enforcement officials, ensuring that more thorough training on the lawful use of force and firearms and the policing of protests as well as on respect for human rights is included. [40]

The United Nation's High Commissioner for Human Rights, Navi Pillay, criticized the police response in Ferguson. He stated, "I condemn the excessive use of force by the police in Ferguson and call for the right of protest to be respected. These scenes are familiar to me and privately I was thinking that there are many parts of the United States where apartheid is flourishing." [41]

---

[40] http://bit.ly/1wtRZIC

[41] http://bit.ly/1rvqfPD

CHAPTER 43

GRAND JURY TESTIMONY

The Grand Jury of Darren Wilson consisted of 12 jurors, of whom, seven were men, five were women, nine were white and three were black. Out of the almost sixty total witnesses that gave statements about their knowledge of the Michael Brown shooting, only two people are alive today that know exactly what occurred on August 9th, 2014; Darren Wilson and Dorian Johnson. Following is their testimony to the Grand Jury:

Dorian Johnson transcript:

During his Grand Jury testimony, twenty-two-year-old Dorian Johnson said he met Michael Brown while Brown was living with his Grandmother. Shortly after that he moved-out, and into the apartment of a friend who lived across the street from Johnson, on Canfield Drive. Dorian claimed that Michael "had to move out of his grandmother's apartment," and that the two had only been hanging-out together for a month or two. They initially had met when a mutual friend brought Brown to Dorian's apartment to play video games. They hardly spoke, but formed a friendly bond.

In his testimony to the Grand Jury, Johnson said his morning routine was to smoke some marijuana and hang-out, but on the morning of August 9th, he needed some Cigarillo cigar wrappers to smoke some pot. His quest for rolling papers would lead to an altercation with the police that would cause the death of Michael Brown and bring about a long-overdue conversation about race-relations in America.

Dorian ran into Michael Brown at 7 a.m. the morning of August 9th, while he was leaving his apartment to go to his neighbor's home to buy Cigarillo cigars, which he knew the neighbor sold, so he could roll his morning blunt (a joint made from a cigar wrapper). Brown was helping to put some children into his aunt's car when Dorian saw him in the parking lot and began a conversation. Dorian and Brown talked about sports, girls, fashion, and future plans. Dorian also claimed that he and Brown began talking about school, after Brown mentioned that he was about to attend college. Dorian told him about his personal struggles while going to Lincoln University, in Jefferson City, Missouri right after graduating from high school. He told Brown that he left school due to police harassment which he experienced both on and off campus. After Dorian dropped-out of college, he moved home to St. Louis and into the Canfield Drive apartments with his baby-mama, his dog and a roommate. He had been living on Canfield Drive for the past eight months and had known Michael Brown for only the last two of those months.

When Dorian told Brown that he was going to a neighbor's place to get Cigarillos to roll a joint, Brown said the he would "match" him, which, in stoner street lingo, means they would each roll a joint with their own marijuana, and then smoke them together. Since Brown did not know the neighbor who sold the Cigarillos, he suggested to Dorian that they go to the store to get them. Dorian agreed, and the two began their slow, meandering walk to the Ferguson Market. While on the way, Brown and Dorian stopped to talk to a couple of construction workers who were doing a job at their apartment complex. When asked by a prosecutor about the conversation they had, Dorian claimed that he couldn't hear what Brown and the construction workers were talking about, but he confirmed that they were discussing getting high. Other testimony indicated that Brown and one of the construction workers walked-off together and "disappeared" for about 30 minutes.

When the two got back together, Dorian said he asked Brown to go to his apartment and ask their mutual friend (whom Brown was living with), if he wanted to go to the store with them. Brown checked, but his roommate said he was too tired to go.

When the prosecutor asked Dorian if he knew that Brown was going to steal the Cigarillos, Dorian answered, "No." He said that while they were walking to the store he assumed Brown had money to purchase the Cigarillos, because Brown dressed well and wore "next generation clothes," so Dorian thought he had money.

Dorian told the Grand Jury that, once they arrived at the Ferguson Market, Brown asked the clerk for some Cigarillos. Before the clerk could retrieve them, Brown reached across the counter and grabbed an entire box. Brown handed the Cigarillos to Johnson, and then reached across the counter again to grab a handful of single Cigarillos. Dorian said the clerk, this time, attempted to slap Brown's hand, but he was too late and accidentally slapped the counter instead. His finger tips hit some of the Cigarillos and they fell on the floor. Brown bent down to pick them up and then made a move towards the front door, to leave the store.

Dorian said he put the box of cigars back on the counter, since he did not see Brown pay for them. He claimed he had been in the store many times, implying that he would not want to cause any trouble there. He said the store clerk looked directly at him while Brown was attempting to steal the cigars, and saw him put the cigars back on the counter. He told the Grand Jury, "The store clerk actually does notice me, like I said, it was a male store clerk and his daughter was there. She's looking directly at me, I'm looking at her face-to-face and she sees me actually put the box of Cigarillos back and I step back." Dorian explained that the male clerk came out from behind the desk to prevent Brown from leaving with the cigars. Dorian said he was trying to get out of the way because he didn't want any part of what was happening and he knew there were cameras in the store. When the clerk tried to grab Brown, he turned and pushed him backwards and said, "get back," according to Dorian. As they were leaving the property, the store clerk yelled at them that he was going to call the police.

Dorian said that while he was walking back to the Canfield apartments with Brown, he was trying to figure out what just happened. He said he felt like an accomplice to a crime. Dorian claims he told Brown, "I don't do stuff like that. What's going on?"

Brown reportedly told him to "be calm" and "be cool," and laughed it off, but Dorian said he was uncomfortable because he knew they had just committed a crime, and they were on camera.

Dorian said that he and Brown were walking down West Florissant, on their way home, when they saw a police car coming towards them. Dorian thought to himself that he was going to go to jail for the robbery, but he was surprised to see the Ferguson police truck pass on by and then pull into a McDonalds parking lot, next to the Ferguson Market, where, he said, the police like to sit. He said he and Brown turned onto Canfield Drive, on their way to the Canfield apartments, when they saw another Ferguson police truck pass them by. He said that when he saw two police cars pass by, he thought the Ferguson Market had called the police, but he was surprised that they just passed him by.

Dorian said he and Brown walked down the middle of the road for about 30 seconds, while two or three cars passed them, but no one honked or told them to get out of the street, so he didn't feel it was a problem for anyone.

They next saw Officer Darren Wilson's truck coming towards them on Canfield Drive. As the officer approached the two, who were walking in the middle of the road, he rolled down his window and said "get the fuck on the sidewalk." Johnson responded by saying, "We're just a minute away from our destination, I live on Canfield and we'll be off the street shortly." Johnson said, "He never stopped us and said hey, freeze, stop right there, let me get out of my car, anything like that. I've been stopped by police before, I know there is a way that they stop or pull up on people, suspects for committing a crime. So exactly what I said, didn't feel like he was stopping or telling us anything like we were committing a crime so much as chastising, like from a father to a son, like you are doing some wrong. Hey, put that down or don't touch that, it came off like that, that's how he said it."

Johnson said, "we continued to walk and have our conversation, but almost a split second later we heard the tires screech, and the officer, he pulled back in the truck very fast to the point at an angle, if we didn't hear his tires screech, the back of his cruiser would have struck one of us, if not both of us. It would have struck both of us or one of us because of the way he angles in reverse. He never drove and turned around, he reversed real fast. Why he reversed so fast on us, and the angle that he did in that manner. Now we are almost not inches away from his front door, like we was right in his face. He never got out of the car, he just pulled right back on the side of us, but it is almost at an angle. When he pulled-up, we are face-to-face. Me and Big Mike are shoulder-to-shoulder now and the officer is facing us." Johnson continued, "The officer pulled back. What did you say? Very loud, angry. And Big Mike, in an instant, Big Mike was finishing saying something, his door was thrust open, very complex, he thrust his door open real hard. He was so close to the door that it hit mostly Big Mike, but it hit me on my left side and it closed back on him, like real fast. Just the same speed, boom, boom, that fast. And at that time he never attempted to open the door again like to try to get back out, but his arm came out of the window and that's the first initial contact they had. The officer grabbed ahold of Big Mike's shirt around the neck area. When the door had closed back on him, he didn't say anything. His arm almost in an instant came out the window, his left arm, I remember it was his left arm, came out the window and touched Big Mike around his neck and his throat. I watched his hands, you know, they really tightened up, so yeah, he had a good grip on it, that's what I saw first. Now, from the beginning of the grab, it is a tug-of-war. Big Mike places his hands openly, one hand on top of the cruiser and the other hand more right up under the window, the side mirror. He's trying to pull off the officer's grip. They are talking to each other, they are yelling and cussing, and neither one of them can calm down, they both have angry faces on while they are talking. They both were very upset and they couldn't calm down."

When asked if he thought Officer Wilson purposefully slammed his car door into them after he backed up to confront the two youths, Dorian Johnson stated, "I cannot speculate what is in someone's mind or what their agenda is going to be, but the force that he used and the power behind it, I believe it was unnecessary." Dorian said, "He could of, and the way he backed up, if he would have backed up straight back, he would have been able to open his door, step out of his car perfectly. But because of the angle where he reversed and how close we were and how fast he did it, it happened real fast. Everything happened continuously right back-to-back. It was really with a lot of force and power that wasn't needed."

When the prosecutor asked Dorian if Officer Wilson could have been blocking both lanes the way he backed up in order to prevent them from continuing to walk down the street, Johnson replied, "Even still, like I said, if he would have pulled back straight, the altercation would have happened a lot different. I'm sure it would have happened a lot different if he'd been able to get out of the car and stand straight up, but because of how that little small incident reacted, it kind of turned the next level up a lot."

Dorian claimed that Brown was trying to pull away from officer Wilson when the gun was pulled. He said, "The left arm is not on the car anymore, the officer still has the right arm, but he's not inside the car. And when I look up and see the officer, the officer has his gun pointed, aimed at Big Mike. In my mind it was probably aimed at both of us, but I assumed he wasn't directly just trying to go for Big Mike. He had his gun pointed towards us. I'm still standing in the doorway and at the time, he said, I'll shoot. He was going to say it again, I'll shoot and almost, he didn't get to finish his sentence, the gun went off."

When asked if Big Mike or the officer's arms were inside or outside the vehicle, Dorian stated, "At the time, like I said, I see more of the officer's arm outside the car than Big Mike's arm inside the car." He continued, The gun definitely was inside the car when he fired the shot. How me and Big Mike were standing, we were standing straight up, so we definitely was outside the vehicle. The bullet came outside the car and struck him. He was never inside the car and got struck, he was outside the car when the first shot went off. The officer was inside the car, so the gun was inside the car, but when he shot the gun, bullet traveled outside his car and struck Big Mike in the chest."

Dorian then said that Officer Wilson let Brown loose after the first shot was fired and both Brown and Johnson began to run away. Dorian got behind a Pontiac Sunfire that was parked on the street, with passengers inside. Once he got behind the car, he saw brown run past him. He said Brown looked at him as he's running past and said, "Keep running bro." Dorian then heard officer Wilson get out of his car and saw him walking fast-paced toward Brown with his weapon drawn. Dorian, hiding behind a parked car, stated, "After walking past me, I kind of stand up more. I'm trying to ask the people in the first car, could they please just let me in the vehicle, I stay in the same complex. You can just drop me off. They said no, and they pulled off on the sidewalk."

Dorian then described the second shot. He said, "I'm watching the officer, he's walking and Big Mike gets past the third car, the final car before the second shot was fired. It was the second shot fired, pow, the officer shot. I don't know if it hit, I wasn't that close to see that it struck Big Mike, but the manner that he jerked and just stopped in his track, I sense that he was hit again."

When asked what Brown did after being shot the second time, Johnson said, "At that time Big Mike's hands were up, but not so much up in the air because he had been struck already in the region somewhere. It was like his hands is up and his hands is kind of down sort of."

The prosecutor asked if Brown's hands were ever near his waist. Dorian answered. "No, his hands never went down towards his waistline or anything."

Johnson said that when Brown was shot the second time, he turned around to face the officer, and yelled-out that he didn't have a gun, and then tried to say it again, but was shot by a volley of bullets before he could complete the sentence. Dorian explained, "I can see how many shots this officer is firing, it is sickening to my stomach, I'm almost bursting in tears right there. I threw up a little in my stomach initially. I got in my head that he's dead. When I see his body hit the ground, in my head I say he's dead. At the time, while he's on the ground, the officer is standing there, he doesn't look around like he's looking for me or anything like that, I'm still in plain sight. I never went anywhere until it clicked back to me that he may could be looking for me too. Again, at that time, that's more fear for my life. I just seen him gun down and kill someone I was just walking with, my friend Big Mike. I see that, I see with my own eyes he killed him. Now, I'm my head, I'm wondering what he is going to do with me."

Johnson said he took off running after he saw Brown dead on the street. He ran back to his apartment and tried to explain to his girlfriend what happened. He waited a few minutes, then decided to go back to the scene and see what was happening at the scene of the shooting.

The prosecutor asked Dorian for clarification, if Wilson ever asked Brown to stop or get on the ground. Dorian said, "No sir, and like I said, I was still on the scene to the point where I could, I was still right in the area and the only thing that I heard was Big Mike tell me to keep running. After that, there was no more words said to anybody, it was just shots fired."

Dorian said that after witnessing Brown's family convene around his body, and then told by police to get away, he felt he had to let them know what happened, so he went to Brown's grandmother's house and explained the whole story. The Brown family then asked Dorian to go back to the scene and give his account of what happened to a news crew which had quickly been mobilized to report the shooting. He mentioned that he was shocked that he was able to give an interview, in the middle of all of the police presence, without law enforcement knowing he had been with Brown at the time of the shooting. Johnson said, "They (the Brown family) actually wanted me to walk down, that was my first interview. I don't know if it was Fox 2 or anything like that, the first statement that I've given. And that was the reason I gave it, because the family, they asked me if I could do it for them because they wanted to get it out immediately. Their words, so it wouldn't be covered-up or misconstrued in any type of way. They wanted me to get it out there quickly." He continued, "There are a lot of police officers, detectives out there. While I'm talking to the camera, I'm talking to the camera crew right here in this area where the cameras are located at. They taped off pretty much this area. They taped off so all of that was taped off, nobody could come through here or there or anything like that, it was taped off. The Police force was strong right here and they are walking around, but I'm right here talking to the cameras. I'm talking to the uncles and they are standing right there. At no time, no police came or looked for me or even was saying they were looking for me." Dorian was surprised that even though he gave a statement to the news right away, nobody from law enforcement contacted him for a couple of days.

Dorian testified that the only words he could remember hearing from Brown during the altercation with Officer Wilson in the patrol car was Brown telling the officer, "get the fuck off me" and "let me the fuck go."

When asked if Brown took any steps towards Officer Wilson after Brown was shot, Johnson replied, "Half a step maybe, his foot was coming off the ground. He was being riddled with more shots and that caused him to tumble over." The prosecutor asked if Brown ran towards the officer. Johnson explained, "No. At no point in time when he turned around he made a rush towards the officer or anything like he was going to tackle the officer or anything like that.

He was standing straight up."

When asked about the location of Officer Wilson relative to his car when the second shot was fired, Johnson said, "I definitely know that his patrol car was in front of this driveway and in front of this building, and when he shot the second shot he was at the end of the building." When prosecutors questioned him how two shell casings could be found near the car door, Dorian replied, "I honestly do not know. He definitely only shot one time inside the car, it wasn't multiple shots. If they found, I mean, we don't have forensics. Both shells match his gun. If they did, I was lost after the first shot. That just shows how much more shock I was in because I definitely knew he shot once. I wasn't aware of a second shot at the car."

The prosecutor asked Johnson if there was anything stopping people from approaching Brown's body immediately after the shooting. Johnson said, "Nothing stopped anybody from the public coming up to the dead body and just looking at it. It was uncovered, his body was not covered. At the time, there was no police officers out there, nobody, just a squad car. And he was not there, there was no yellow tape. So people were just coming out of their doors, kids, you know, there is a lot of kids out. Just looking at the dead body, like he is right here laying in front of us, that's how people were able to walk up and look at his body, and take their phones out, take pictures of his body. There was nobody telling them to stop. At the time his family wasn't even out there. It is just a bunch of random people walking around coming out of the building, oh it is a dead body in our street. They are walking up to it like it's a prank or something like that. No, this is a real dead person, he's not covered, his pants are down by his knees, you could see the blood spilling from his top part, not out of his head, but you can tell that it is blood leading because it is all coming from his top part. I didn't even actually know he had got shot in his face and head until the autopsy report."

The prosecutor asked Dorian if there were any people who had gotten into the street between the body and the police car after the shooting. Johnson said, "Correct."

Dorian was asked point-blank if Brown had discussed getting high with the construction workers. Dorian answered that he could barely hear what they were saying, but he told the Grand Jury that he did hear them talking about getting high, then he lost sight of Brown and one of the construction workers for a while.

The prosecutor asked Johnson if there was anyone else who he knows of who saw the shooting and have not reported it to law enforcement yet. He responded, "I'm frankly surprised they have so many witnesses to the actual event. Prior to it happening, I only saw one person that was out there when the first shot went off all the way up to the last shot. I only saw one person. I wasn't aware of anybody, and I only saw her because before the initial first shot when the police stopped us, she was on her balcony and I just happen to glance up and see her and she stood there."

When asked if he had spoken to anyone else who witnessed the shooting, Johnson stated, "Since the day all of this, of everything that happened, I haven't spoken to anyone in Canfield, per se. They really, I haven't seen, I haven't been in that area. It was a hard time for me getting my things out of my apartment complex, so that's what I'm dealing with now actually because they don't want me consulting with nobody who may have heard something from somebody else that want to tell me something and stuff like that."

When asked if there was anything important he wanted to add. He said, "Yes. Regardless of everyone's opinion of me, I know a lot of speculation of my past and criminal record that I have, or anything like that. That day, I felt like even when the store thing happened, I didn't feel like someone should have lost their life. I feel like the incident at the car, with both Mike Brown and Officer Darren Wilson, could have been resolved without deadly force. We definitely wasn't posing a threat to his life. I just want, I just want to pray that everybody sees the evidence for what it really is. Deadly force was really not necessary, everything else, had he knew about the store incident, him stopping us, all of that that's protocol, I get that. Deadly force was never ever needed and I pray that people really see that we didn't have any weapons on us or anything like that. He could be in jail right now."

The prosecutor followed up by asking about the "speculations" of his criminal record. Johnson said, "Yes, because I stay watching the news and media outlets. I see they dug through years in my past to see an incident that happened in Jefferson City, but what they fail, they keep leaving out, is I was a freshman in college at the time, everybody makes, you know, crazy little moves their freshman year. I was just beginning, I was getting out, I was breaking out of my kid years, you know, just being on my own around new people, Atlanta people, Washington people, people I never see on a daily basis. I'm from St. Louis. So to hold that against me and Michael Brown on a day that has nothing to do with it, I feel like it is very wrong, especially for them not to dig two or three years prior in Darren Wilson's file and see if any complaints were made against him. Basically all I keep seeing is slander on my name."

The prosecutor said they didn't want to slander his name, but rather just wanted to get information. The prosecutor then asked him what happened in Jefferson City. Johnson said, "There was just basically me walking with a group of kids that I knew, we were going to a YMCA to play basketball. I didn't have membership there. They actually had membership there. So we are walking through some apartments, one of the guys, you know, he grabbed a package and, you know, he ripped it open. As we are walking towards the YMCA, I see a pool guy, he sees us, but he doesn't see anything in our hand or anything like that, but he sees us walking from out of the apartments going towards the gym. So I guess whoever's package it was, they made a call saying someone had stole something off their property like that. And I guess he too got it in his own mind that I just saw these guys coming out of those apartments. When they went to run the YMCA cameras to see who had just recently walked in, I did not pay to get in, even though I was supposed to. I kind of just walked right on past, go to the gym, play basketball. And when the police came and they ran the camera back and they saw like he didn't pay or this group right here, they came down, they grabbed basically the last group."

The prosecutor asked if he got charged. He responded, "I had a false report to an officer, I had a stealing charge that they were trying to see if I was the one that had stole it. I was going to court. At the time of me leaving court, I had been fed-up with being stopped by off-campus police and on-campus police because of the stereotypical way they look at people from St. Louis. And being stopped everyday, being late for classes and having to remake up work, I just said, you know what, Jefferson City school, Lincoln University was not for me at the time. So I left, and still having to come back to court in Jefferson City, I've been getting a lot done down here in St. Louis. I don't have a charge for the City or County of St. Louis, but when they run my name, they see Jefferson City. They detain me sometimes, some police officers let me go. A couple police officers they detain me."

When asked about the second charge of giving a false police

report, Johnson stated, "that was the same incident with the officer who actually had me. He put me in the car, took me down to the station. I had both my school campus ID and my state ID in possession of me. When the officer asked my name, I didn't say anything so much as just handed him my identification. I was mad at the time, again, I was freshman in college. I'm kind of angry with the police, so don't really want to say anything to them, but I know that he is going to ask me for identification. So I hand him my school ID and both my state ID at the same time. He is looking at both of them, he's looking at me. I have a very distinguishing feature about me. I have one of my eyes, I have a cataract, one of them is blue and the other one is brown. It is like that on both my picture ID, I have distinguished color on my eyes. So I'm sure he can see that, in my mind I know he can see it, I know he can tell that this is me, who I am. He actually called campus security from Lincoln University, they also came down and verified that's him, you know, we seen him walking around on campus. But because I never said nothing to the officer, he took that as disobedience. And he was like, you are not gong to tell me anything, so I'm just going to write down that you gave me a false report. Me being a freshman and not really wanting to talk to him, I just kind of shrug my shoulders not thinking too much of it until it got to court and it was like, this is serious, but the judge, he threw that one out of court. I never got charged for that or anything."

Dorian was then thanked for coming in and the hearing was concluded. [42]

Darren Wilson transcript:

Darren Wilson is 6 feet 4 inches tall and weighs 210 pounds. He carries a P229 .40 caliber Sig Sauer service weapon, which holds 13 bullets. He said he doesn't wear a Taser because his department only has a limited number of them and he elects not to carry one because they are uncomfortable to wear. When asked to tell his story, officer Wilson explained:

I see them walking down the middle of the street. And first thing that struck me was they're walking in the middle of the street. I had already

---

[42] http://bit.ly/11SRYP7

seen a couple cars trying to pass, but they couldn't have traffic normal because they we're in the middle, so one had to stop to let the car go around and then another car would come. And the next thing I noticed was the size of the individuals because either the first one was really small or the second one was really big. And the next thing I noticed was that Brown had bright yellow socks on that had green marijuana leaves as a pattern on them. They were the taller socks that go halfway up your shin. As I approached them, I stopped a couple of feet in front of Johnson as they were walking towards me, I am going towards them. And I allowed him to keep walking towards my window, which was down. As Johnson came around my driver's side mirror I said, 'Why don't you guys walk on the sidewalk.' Officer Wilson explained to the prosecutor that Dorian told him, 'we are almost to our destination,' and then he pointed in a northeasterly direction. And as he did that, he kept walking, and Brown was starting to come around the mirror, and as he came around the mirror, I said, 'well what's wrong with the sidewalk.' Wilson then said Brown replied 'fuck what you have to say.' Wilson said that that response drew his attention totally to Brown, stating, "It was very unusual and not an expected response from a single request. When I start looking at Brown, the first thing I notice is in his right hand, his hand is full of Cigarillos. And that's when it clicked for me because I now saw the Cigarillos, I looked in my mirror, I did a double-check that Johnson was wearing a black shirt, these are the two from the stealing. And they kept walking, as I said, they never once stopped, never got on the sidewalk, they stayed in the middle of the road. So I got on my radio, and Frank 21 is my call sign for that day, I said Frank 21 I'm on Canfield with two, send me another car. I then placed my car in reverse and backed up just past them and then angled my vehicle, the back of my vehicle to kind of cut them off, kind of keep them somewhat contained. As I did, I go to open the door and I say, hey, come here for a minute to Brown. As I'm opening the door he turns, faces me, looks at me and says, 'What the fuck are you going to do about it,' and shuts my door, slammed it shut. I haven't even got it open enough to get my leg out, it was only a few inches. I then looked at him and told him to go back and he was staring at me, almost like to intimidate me or to overpower me. The intense face he had was just not what I expected from any of this. I then opened my door again and used my door to push him backwards, and while I'm doing that I tell him, 'get the fuck back,' and then I used my door to push him. He then grabs my door again and shuts my door. At that time is when I saw him coming into my vehicle. His head was higher than the top of my car. And I see him ducking, his hands are up and he is coming in my vehicle. I had shielded myself in this type of manner and kind of looked away, so I don't remember seeing him close at me, but I was hit right here in the side of the face with a fist. I don't think it was a full-on swing, but not a full shot. I think my arm deflected some of it, but there was still a significant amount of contact that was made to my face. After he hit me, it stopped for a second. He kind of like, I remember getting hit and he kind of like grabbed and pulled, and then it stopped. When I looked up, if this is my car door, I'm sitting here facing that way, he's here. He turns like this and now the Cigarillos I see in his left hand. He's going like this and says, 'hey man, hold these.' I'm assuming to Johnson, but I couldn't see Johnson from my line-of-sight. And at that point I tried to hold his right arm because it was like this at my car. This is my car window. I tried to hold his right arm and use my left hand to get out to have some type of control and not be trapped in my car any more. And when I grabbed him, the only way I can describe it is I felt like a five-year-old holding onto Hulk Hogan. Hulk Hogan, that's just how big he felt, and how small I felt, just from grasping his arm. And as I'm trying to open the door is when, and I can't really get it open because he is standing only maybe 6 inches from my door, but as I was trying to pull the handle, I see his hand coming back around like this and he hit me with this part of his right hand here, just a full swing all the way back around and hit me right here. After he did that, next thing I remember is how do I get this guy away from me. What do I do to not to get beaten inside my car. I remember having my hands up and I thought to myself, you know, what do I do. I considered using my mace, however, I wasn't willing to sacrifice my left hand, which is blocking my face, to go for it. I couldn't reach around on my right to get it and if I would have gotten it out, the chances of it being effective were slim to none. His hands were in front of his face, it would have blocked the mace from hitting him in the face and if any of that got on me, I know what it does to me and I would have been out of the game. I wear contacts, if that touches any part of my eyes, then I can't see at all. Like I said, I don't carry a Taser, I considered my asp, but to get that out, since I kind of sit on it, I usually have to lean forward to the steering wheel to get it out. Again, I wasn't willing to let go of the one defense I had against being hit. The whole time, I can't tell you if he was swinging at me or grabbing me or punching me or what, but there was just stuff going on and I was looking down figuring out what to do. Also, when I was grabbing my asp, I knew if I did even get it out, I'm not going to be *able to expand it inside the car or am I going to be able to make a swing that will be effective in any manner. Next I considered a flashlight. I kept that on the passenger side of the car. I wasn't going to, again, reach over, like to grab it, and then even if I did grab it, would it even be effective? We are so close and confined. So the only other option I thought I had was my gun. I drew my gun, I turned. It is kind of hard to describe it. I turn and I go like this. He is standing here. I said, 'get back or I'm going to shoot you.' He immediately grabs my gun and says, 'you are too much of a pussy to shoot me.' The way he grabbed it, my gun was basically pointed this way, I'm in my car, he's here, it is pointed this way, but he grabs it with his right hand, not his left, he grabs with his right one and he twists it and then he digs it down into my hip. I can feel his finger and I distinctly remember envisioning a bullet going into my leg. Thought that was the next step. As I'm looking at it, I'm not paying attention to him, all I can focus on is just this gun in my leg. I was able to kind of shift slightly like this and then push it down, because he is pushing down like to keep it pinned on my leg. So when I slid, I let him use his momentum to push it down and it was kind of pointed to where the seat buckle would attach on the floorboard on the side of my car. Next thing I remember, putting my left hand on it like this, putting my elbow into the back on my seat and just pushing with all I could, forward. I was just focused on getting the gun out of me. When I did get it up to this point, he is still holding onto it and I pulled the trigger and nothing happens, it just clicked. I pull it again, it just clicked again. At this point I'm like, why isn't this working, this guy is going to kill me if he gets ahold of this gun. I pulled it a third time, it goes off. When it went off, it shot through my door panel and my window was down and glass fled out of my door panel. I think that kind of shocked him and me at the same time. When I see the glass come up, it comes, a chunk, about that big, comes across my right hand, and then I notice I have blood on the back of my hand. After seeing the blood on my hand, I looked at him and he was, this is my car door, he was here and he kind of stepped back and went like this. And then after he did that, he looked up at me and had the most intense aggressive face. The only way I can describe it, It looked like a demon, that's how angry he looked. He comes back towards me again with his hands up. At that point I just went like this. I tried to pull the trigger again, click, nothing happened. Without even looking, I just grab the top of my gun, the slide, and I racked it. Still not looking, just holding my hands up, I pulled the trigger again, it goes off. It went off twice in the car. Pull, click, click, went off, click, went off.*

So twice in the car. When I look up after that, I see him start to run and I see a cloud of dust behind him. I then get out of my car. As I'm getting out of my car I tell dispatch, 'shots fired, send me more cars.' We start running, kind of the same direction that Johnson had pointed, Across the street like a diagonal towards this, kind of like where the parking lot came in for Copper Creek Court and Canfield, right at that intersection. And there is a light pole right there, I remember him running towards the light pole. We pass two cars that were behind my police car while we were running. I think the second one was a Pontiac Grand Am, a green one. I don't know if it was a two door or four door, I just remember seeing a Pontiac green Grand Am. When I passed the second one, about that same time, he stopped running, and he is at that light pole. So when I stopped, I stopped. And then he starts to turn around, I tell him to get on the ground, get on the ground. He turns, and when he looks at me, he made like a grunting, like aggravated sound, and he starts, he turns, and he's coming back towards me. His first step is coming towards me, he kind of does like a stutter-step to start running. As he does that, his left hand goes in a fist and goes to his side, his right one goes under his shirt in his waistband, and he starts running at me. That was all done, like I said, the first step, his first stride coming back towards me. As he is coming towards me, I keep telling him to get on the ground, he doesn't. I shoot a series of shots. I don't know how many I shot, I just know I shot it. I know I missed a couple, I don't know how many, but I know I hit him at least once because I saw his body kind of jerk or flinched. I remember having tunnel vision on his right hand, that's all. I'm just focusing on that hand when I'm shooting. Well, after the last shot, my tunnel vision kind of opened up. I remember seeing the smoke from the gun and I kind of looked at him and he's still coming at me, he hadn't slowed down. At this point I started backpedaling and again, I tell him to get on the ground, get on the ground. He doesn't. I shoot another round of shots. Again, I don't recall how many it was or if I hit him every time. I know at least once because he flinched again. At this point it looked like he was almost bulking up to run through the shots, like it was making him mad that I am shooting at him. And the face that he had was looking straight through me, like I wasn't even there, I wasn't even anything in his way. Well, he keeps coming at me after that, again, during the pause I tell him to get on the ground, get on the ground, he still keeps coming at me, gets about 8 to 10 get away. At this point I'm backing up pretty rapidly, I'm backpedaling pretty good because I know if he reaches me, he'll kill me. And he had started to lean forward as he got that close, like he was just going to tackle me, just go right through me. His hands was in a fist at his side, this one is in his waistband under his shirt, and he was like this. Just coming straight at me like he was going to run right through me. I look down, I remember looking at my sites and firing, all I see is his head and that's what I shot. I don't know how many, I know at least once because it was the last one to go into him. And then, when it went into him, the demeanor on his face went blank. The aggression was gone. It was gone. I mean, I knew he stopped. The threat was stopped. When he fell, he fell on his face, and I remember his feet coming up, like he had so much momentum carrying him forward that when he fell, his feet kind of came up a little bit and then they rested. At that point, I got back on the radio and said, 'Send me a supervisor and every car you got.

The prosecutor interrupted Officer Wilson to ask, "Did you know that radio dispatch did not go out?" Wilson responded:

No, I didn't find out until later while I was actually driving back to the station that my portable radio was on Channel 3 and our main channel was channel 1. They did ask me why my radio for the car was laying on the floorboard. Asked me if I used that. I don't remember using that radio. I, for some reason, remember using this one. It could have been sitting in my lap, there is also that chance that I used that one. I don't know which one that I used. When I'm chasing him, my main goal was to keep eyes on him and just to keep him contained until I had people coming there. I knew I had already called for backup and I knew they were already in the area for the stealing that was originally reported. So I thought if I can buy 30 seconds of time, and that was my original goal when I tried to get him to come to the car. If I could buy 30 seconds of time, someone else will be here, we can make the arrest, nothing happens, we are all good. And it didn't happen that way. So when he ran, you know, just stay with him, someone is going to be here, you know, we'll get him.

The prosecutor then asked a series of questions. She asked Wilson, "Are you firing at him while he's running?"

Wilson, replied, "No."

The prosecutor asked, "And at some point you say Michael Brown does turn around?"

Wilson replied, "Yes."

When the prosecutor asked, "Any idea what happened to make him turn around or he just all of the sudden turns around?"

Wilson relied, "No, just turns around. His whole reaction to the whole thing was something I've never seen. I've never seen that much aggression so quickly from a simple request to just walk on the sidewalk."

The prosecutor asked, "You never did talk to him about the Cigarillos or the stealing at the Ferguson Market?"

Wilson stated, "No, I never had the chance to."

The prosecutor asked, "You said when he's coming back at you with his hand, right hand in his waistband and kind of charging, that's when you fired the last shots?"

Wilson replied, "Yes."

The prosecutor asked, "Did you think he was dead at that point?"

Wilson said, "Yes, I did."

The prosecutor asked, "What did you do after that, when he goes down?"

Wilson replied:

After that is when I got back on the radio and I said, 'send me a supervisor and every car you have.' Seconds later, I don't know how many seconds later, is when officer (redacted) followed by officer (redacted) arrived. And I believe they were the ones that were assigned to the stealing call originally. (Redacted) walked up to me and said 'Darren what do you need?' I don't remember what my reply was and he said, 'Did you call for an ambulance?' I said 'I haven't, will you?' I remember him calling twice, like he was about from me to you away on the radio calling. And then I look across and (redacted) was starting to tape off the area, but I noticed that all of our cars are parked this way, Brown is laying here. I told (redacted) to move his car to this side to block that side of the street off. He did that and then he resumed taping. After that, I walked to my car and I put my gun up. I start walking away from the scene. As I'm walking away, I walk back to my car and I don't know if the door was open or shut. I think it was shut. I open the door, I reach in, I turn my car off, shut the door. At the time, my sergeant pulled up and I walked over to him. I don't remember what started the conversation, he said something first, but I said I have to tell you what happened. And he goes, 'what happened.' I said, I had to kill him. He goes 'what?' I said, he grabbed my gun, I shot him and I killed him. He goes, 'go sit in the car.' I said, I cannot sit in the car. I said, 'Sarge, I can't be singled out. It is already getting hostile, I can't be singled out in the car. I will leave if you want me to leave.' He said, 'take my car and leave,' so I got in his car and I drove to the police station."

The prosecutor interrupted to ask, "In your mind, him grabbing the gun is what made the difference where you felt you had to use a weapon to stop him?"

Wilson said, "Yes. Once he was hitting me in the face, that was enough, in my mind, to authorize the use of force."

The prosecutor followed-up, "Okay. So if he would not have grabbed your gun while he was hitting you in the face, everything was the same, but he would not have grabbed the gun, you still would have used deadly force?"

Wilson answered, "My gun was already being presented as a deadly force option while he was hitting me in the face."

The prosecutor asked, "Did you guys have a volatile, well how can I put this? Did you not really get along well with folks that lived in that apartment complex, not you personally, I mean the police in general?"

Wilson responded, "It is an anti-police area for sure. There's a lot of gangs that reside or associate with that area. There's a lot of violence in that area, there's a lot of gun activity, drug activity, it is just a not very well-liked community. That community doesn't like the police."

The prosecutor asked, "You were pretty much on high alert being in that community by yourself, especially when Michael Brown said, 'Fuck what you say,' I think he said? You were on high alert at that point knowing the vicinity and the area that you're in?"

Wilson responded, "Yes, that's not an area where you can take anything really lightly. Like I said, It is a hostile environment. There are good people over there, there really are, but I mean, there is an influx of gang activity in that area."

The prosecutor asked, "All right, so you're driving yourself back to Ferguson, what are you thinking on the drive back to Ferguson?"

Wilson responds, "I think I'm just in shock of what just happened. I really didn't believe it because like I said, the whole thing started over will you just walk on the sidewalk and it developed into that in 45 seconds. And that's the only other thing I remember thinking about, is I heard the car radio going off and mine wasn't. That doesn't make sense. So I hit the scan button on mine thinking the scan button got messed up. I wasn't getting anything. And I did that and it still, this one is going off and mine's not. So then I looked at it and I was on channel 3. I was like, I don't know what was heard or what wasn't heard."

The prosecutor asked, "And that's when you realize that you probably, nobody probably ever heard your call for help?"

Wilson answered, "Right. I know they heard the initial one because before I put it in reverse I used the car radio, the car mike, which is always on Ferguson channel, it never changes, but I don't know when this was changed, if they even heard anything."

The prosecutor asked, "When you first went out on your call to Canfield Green, you said I'm going out Frank 21?"

Wilson replied, "I said, Frank 21, I'm on Canfield with two, send me another car."

The prosecutor asked, "It wasn't a stressful situation at that point?"

Wilson responded, "No, it wasn't, but I just had that gut feeling that someone else needed to be there and knowing that this guy just stole from the market because I saw the Cigarillos and had the black shirt, I felt that in order to effect the arrest, it would be better to have backup."

The prosecutor asked, "You asked for this other car before any words were exchanged?"

Wilson replied, "No, he had already told me, 'fuck what you have to say.'"

The prosecutor asked, "You didn't tell the dispatcher that you were having a confrontation or that you had these guys who might be suspects in the stealing?"

Wilson replied, "No, it was kind of said in a quicker way, just kind of hey, I want to get the information out, get a car started and once more develops, I can advise them more.

The prosecutor wanted to know what Wilson did once he returned to the police station, asking, "So you drive back to Ferguson by yourself, you are at Ferguson, what do you do?"

Wilson said:

> *I immediately go to the bathroom. On the way back I found that I had blood on the inside of my left hand and I already know I had blood on the inside of my left hand and I already know I had it on the back on my right hand. And just from everything we have always been told about blood, you don't want it on you, you don't touch it, you don't come into contact with it. And my original thought was that it was the glass and cut my wrist and cut my hand which is why this hand was bleeding. And so thinking that I was cut with someone else's blood on me, I had to wash my hands. So I go directly to the bathroom. I actually washed them, went to the bathroom and then it looked like I still had it like in my cuticles and stuff, so I washed my hands again. After I washed my*

hands, I go to our roll-call room. Once in there, Officer (redacted) was there working on the computer. I come in, (redacted) looks at me (redacted) said, you know, what happened. And I said, I just had to shoot somebody. I asked (redacted) to get me a pair of gloves. (Redacted) goes, gets me a pair of gloves, comes back, put the gloves on. I grab an evidence envelope, take my gun out of the holster, make it safe. I lock the slide back, take the magazine out, take the one round that's left in it out. I put it all in that bag, seal it with evidence tape and then sign it.

The prosecutor asked, "And you handled your own gun at that time with gloves on?"

Wilson said "Correct. To preserve any evidence on there, I knew his DNA was on that gun."

The prosecutor asked how he knew Brown's blood would be on the gun.

Wilson answered, "When I first took it out, without even looking at it, I knew that he had fingerprints on it and possibly even sweat from, it was warmer that day so, and he could have sweated on it. When I took it out, I also saw blood on it."

The prosecutor asked, "You saw blood?" "That could have come from when you shot him."

Wilson responded, "Yes."

The prosecutor then followed up by asking, "Is it procedure for you to make your gun safe in a shooting like this or should some else do that?"

Wilson said, "I don't really know."

The prosecutor asked why Wilson took off his police shirt before going to the hospital. Wilson explained:

I felt more comfortable too because I obviously can't wear my gun, and I don't want to be in uniform after all of this without it. So I took the shirt off, just my undershirt, my pants, my boots, go to the hospital.

While waiting to be treated in the waiting room, not in the waiting room, in the actual hospital room, Detective (redacted) began his interview and then stopped as needed for nurses, whoever came in. They took x-rays, prescribed me a painkiller for the face injuries. St. Louis County's evidence technician arrived, he photographed everything. Don't know who it is, but he came from whoever the department uses for drug tests, they gave me the drug tests. And after that, I think he left and then the assistant chief drove me and (redacted) back to the station. He had already made a phone call, the assistant chief did have Officer (redacted) get a change of clothes for me, so they were going to take my clothes. They had blood on my left hip area. So when I get back and change, St. Louis County took my pants, shirt, they already had my weapon, and then that was it, I went home for the day."

When asked how long Wilson has been a police officer, he responded, "five years."

Wilson stated that he started out with the Jennings police department, but the department was disbanded so he applied for St. Louis Country Police Department but was not selected, so he went to Ferguson. He also claimed to have worked for Pine Lawn for 8 hours, but he did not go into detail about that, and he was not questioned about why he left after only 8 hours on the job.

The prosecutor asked, "Any other incidents where you have been involved where you had to use force?"

Wilson responded, "I've used my asp before, I have used my flashlight before and I have used OC spray before."

In further questioning, Wilson admitted that he turned his face away from the window and then shot his gun through it, without knowing where the bullet might go, although he was in between two residential apartment complexes. He said he saw the bullet go into the ground in front of one of the apartment complexes and make a puff of dust when it hit the dirt. He said he shot in Brown's "general direction." He admitted that nobody at the police station swabbed his hand or his face for evidence.

The prosecutor asked, "Did you ever think about, I know you said your vehicle was running, did you ever just think about getting in that bad boy and drive?"

Wilson responded, "No I didn't. My thought is, I was still dealing with a threat at my car. You know, we're trained not to run away from a threat, to deal with a threat, and that is what I was doing. That never entered my mind to flee."

Wilson was asked if he ever touched Brown's throat, to which he responded, "Never touched his throat. Only part of him I touched was his forearm."

The prosecutor asked, "When Michael Brown was running from you, after the shots were fired within the car and they both just disappeared and you had Michael in focus, did you ever at any time fire with his back facing you?

Wilson responded, "No, I did not."

When the prosecutor asked about how Brown was able to take control of the officer's gun, Wilson stated, "He was controlling where it went, how it went and his finger was in the process of going on the trigger with mine. I could feel his fingertips on my trigger finger trying to get in the trigger guard."

The prosecutor asked one final question for Wilson; "When you got back to the police department, after you washed off everything, did you ever think at that time that I need to write a report while it is fresh in my mind?"

Wilson said, "No. The protocol is whenever you are involved in a significant use of force, that you contact you FOP representative and he will advise you of what to do, step-by-step, because they are the clear head in that situation. They have not been through a traumatic experience."

The prosecutor then interrupts to inject, "And I guess, to be fair about this, any time any law enforcement officer has asked to speak to you, you have willingly and voluntarily come in and been interviewed and answered all the questions, is that fair to say.

Wilson answered, "Yes."

The prosecutor asked, "for your own sake, did you like write down in a diary what happened, I mean, not a diary or I guess a grown man would call it a journal, but you know, have you ever like, did you afterwards, you know, write this out for your own, you know, therapeutic needs?"

Wilson said, "My statement has been written for my attorney."

The prosecutor then responded with, "Okay. And that's between you and your attorney."

Wilson confirms, "Correct. The department has not asked me for anything."

The prosecutor reconfirmed by asking, "So no one has asked you to write out a statement?"

Wilson said, "No, they haven't."

When the prosecutor asked, "Do you think that after having really thought about this over time and basically you've had to tell this scenario a few times, do you think that if there are additional details that you may not give initially, do you think that's because you're just now remembering them because you are putting so much thought into what happened or do you think that things that maybe you kind of imagined happening, didn't really happen?"

Wilson responded, "Yeah, just from what I have been told about the incident originally, is that you are supposed to have 72 hours before you are actually officially interviewed, record a statement and all of that. You tend to remember more through a couple sleep cycles then what you do as soon as it happened. It is a traumatic event, a lot of details kind of come as one detail. I mean, from what I understand, there hasn't been really anything significant that's changed."

The prosecutor asked, "So you think that when you were testifying today you said you kind of thought, had a thought process. As this chaotic scene is unfolding, do you recall actually in your mind processing this in the way you've described or is it all just reactionary?"

Wilson explained, "No, I remember actually, I picture a use of force triangle in my head when this first happened and I was going through the progression of what I could do as far as the use of force continuum is concerned."

The prosecutor asked if Wilson learned about the force triangle in the police academy, and Wilson affirmed that he did. Wilson said he started thinking about the force triangle while he was being hit in the face, before he pulled his gun out.

Wilson was asked, "Did you ever think while you were firing that you could have hit another innocent bystander?" He responded, "When I originally fired the first time, when he turned around and I raised my weapon, I remember looking behind him and seeing nothing. I didn't see a car, I didn't see a person, there is nothing behind him. And after the first round of shots, I had tunnel vision on his hand. After that, when I refocused, I still don't remember ever seeing anybody behind him."

The prosecutor asked if Wilson could remember anything significant that happened the day prior to the shooting and if he got a good night's sleep the night before the shooting. Wilson responded that nothing noteworthy happened the day prior to the shooting and he confirmed that he got between 6 to 8 hours of sleep. The prosecutor responded to Wilson's remarks by saying, "Felt rested, ready to go the next day--just had to ask, curious."

The St. Louis County prosecutor asked, "Dorian--Did you ever tell the police chief or any other officers that there was another person with him, did you ever try to look for Dorian?"

Wilson responded, "No, I haven't talked to the chief or anybody at the department in length about what happened. I told my Sergeant what happened at that time, that was the end of our conversations with anybody from the department."

The prosecutor asked if Wilson tried to identify Dorian Johnson for detectives during a follow-up interview, on September 10th. Wilson confirmed that he was presented with a photo line-up to pick out Dorian but he said the detectives never told him if he picked the correct person.

In the final questions, the prosecutor helped to support Wilson's affirmations that he acted in self defense. The prosecutor said, "You felt your life was in jeopardy when you were sitting in the vehicle?"

Wilson responded, "Yes."

The prosecutor stated, "You felt like when you exited the vehicle and the interaction with Michael Brown, he was advancing towards you, you felt like your life was in jeopardy?"

Wilson responded, "Yes."

The prosecutor stated, And use of deadly force was justified at that point in your opinion?

Wilson said, "Yes."

Wilson was then given an opportunity to give some closing remarks about anything else he thought was important to know. He said, "One thing you guy's haven't asked that has been asked of me in other interviews is, was he a threat, was Michael Brown a threat when he was running away. People asked why would you chase him if he was running away. I had already called for assistance. If someone arrives and sees him running, another officer, and goes around the back-half of the apartment complexes and tries to stop him, what would stop him from doing what he just did to me, to him, or worse, knowing he has already done it to one cop. And that was, he still posed a threat, not only to me, to anybody else that confronted him."

The prosecutor followed-up and asked, "Along those lines, you feel like, as a police officer, it is your obligation to follow that suspect?"

Wilson confirmed, "Yes."

The September 16th hearing then came to a close. [43]

Medical Examiner Testimony:

The St. Louis County medical examiner responded to a series of questions from the prosecutor regarding Brown's toxicology and the crime scene. Although it was his responsibility to measure distances and take photos, the Medical Examiner did neither. The prosecutor got directly into the matter of not taking the photos. It was her first question. She said, "Okay, and let's talk specifically about the case involving the shooting of Michael Brown. Did you take photographs?"

The Examiner answered, "No."

When asked why not, the Examiner claimed, "My battery in my camera died." He said he saw St. Louis Country taking pictures so he knew he could get pictures from them. When asked if he requested any pictures from St. Louis Country, the Examiner said, "I do not know." When asked if taking pictures was something he would normally want to do, the Examiner confirmed that his Pathologist sometimes asks for them.

The prosecutor asked if any measurements were taken. The Examiner explained that they can take measurements, if they need to, but he answered, "No," he did not take any measurements during the Michael Brown shooting investigation. When asked by the prosecutor why he felt he didn't need to take any distance measurements at the crime scene, he explained, "I got there, it was self-explanatory what happened. Somebody shot somebody. There was no question as to any distance or anything of that nature at the time I was there."

The prosecutor asked, "And if it turns out there was some concern about the distances, that's not something that you would be qualified to tell us about?"

[43] http://bit.ly/11S7lXb

The Examiner said, "If I took the measurements I could tell you about them."

Since the Medical Examiner got the call to go to the shooting scene at 1:30 but didn't arrive until 2:30, the prosecutor asked, "Is there any reason why it took you an hour to arrive?" The Examiner responded, "No Ma'am, just waited."

The prosecutor asked if the crowd was saying anything. The Examiner explained, "They were just, I don't know how to explain it. I guess voicing their concerns at what is going on, why this is taking so long, things of that nature. I assume the body was lying too long in the street, they didn't like the body being out there."

When the Examiner was asked if he had spoken to any bystanders, he said, yes, he spoke with Brown's grandmother. He explained, "I was walking back to the vehicle to make some phone calls and a lady came up and she asked me if I was the Medical Examiner. I told her I was. She asked me why the body was still there on the street, why it is taking so long. I explained to her, you know, it takes a thorough investigation and crowd control, just getting everybody into the scene was taking time to do that once everybody is there, we can get our information that we need and the evidence collected and then we can be out of here. Once everything starts, it doesn't take long." He continued, "She seemed to be fine with that. She was very pleasant." He told the Grand Jury that Brown was identified by a tattoo he had on his arm that read "Big Mike,"

When asked about Brown's injuries, the Examiner said, "There was one on the top of the head, several to his right eye, a bunch of blood, dried up blood. I guess road material, there was one here, there was an injury here, an injury on his side right here, two in the arm and one in here and a wound on his hand."

When asked if he saw any wounds on Brown's back, the Examiner said "No."

The prosecutor asked, "Did you happen to speak to the officer who allegedly did the shooting?

The examiner said, "No."

When asked if he noticed any rigor mortis in Browns' body, the Examiner said, "It was starting to set in. Correct."

The Examiner concluded that Brown had 9 injuries, which could be bullet holes. "One on the top of the head, one to the right forehead, one around the eye, and then one in the neck, close to the neck/chest area, one on the right side and the rest on the arm and one in the hand."

The Medical Examiner said he found two lighters, two $5 bills and small bag of what appeared to be marijuana in Brown's pockets.

When asked if Brown had any residue on his body indicating that the shots were fired at close range the Examiner said, "No."

When questioned about not having a charged battery for his camera and not including notes in his report the examiner tried to defend himself, stating, "This crime scene, can I say something? The crime scene was huge, he's here, some of his shoes are farther away from him. You have a vehicle and a hat, it may stretch out 100 yards. I'm just there for the body. Just trying to let our pathologist know he's here, there are other things there, this is what's going on with the body."

The Medical Examiner explained to the Grand Jury that he is the eyes and ears of the Pathologist. He said the Medical Examiners go out to the crime scene on behalf of the pathologists, to collect and review evidence, whereas the pathologist only works from the office. "He does not go to the crime scene." The Medical Examiner in St. Louis County admitted that he only works two days per week, on Saturday and Sunday, for 16 hours each day.

Detective Witness:

A St. Louis police detective was questioned by the Grand Jury about the crime scene, and specifically about why there were so few pictures taken. The detective said he wasn't able to take all of the pictures he wanted because of the crowd disturbances, but he did take some measurements. He stated that Browns body was 153 feet and 9 inches away from officer Wilson's police car. He said there were 10 shell casings found and he thought 12 shots were fired, since Wilson stated he had only one bullet left in his gun when he put it in the evidence envelope, out of a total of 13 bullets that were loaded. The detective said Wilson had been "fully-loaded," which meant that he had one live round in the chamber and a full clip of 12 rounds.

The detective indicated that there were blood splatters further away from Browns body, indicating that he moved back towards Officer Wilson after he was shot.

The crime scene detective wrote in his report that Officer Wilson was the "victim" and that the crime that was being investigated was an "Assault on a Law enforcement officer," indicating the mindset of the officers investigating the case, and also that of the County Prosecutor, who many in the community felt was too biased towards the police to prosecute the case fairly.

Bob McCulloch:

Bob McCulloch has been the St. Louis County Prosecutor for the past 23 years. The Ferguson incident was his biggest case ever, and he didn't seem too interested in stepping aside to let someone else take the spotlight. Tens of thousands of St. Louis residents signed petitions to have him removed from his position as lead prosecutor for the Darren Wilson case, but the Governor refused to replace him with a Special Prosecutor, and McCulloch refused to recuse himself from prosecuting the case. This hadn't been the first time McCulloch found himself in the limelight. He filed charges against Axl Rose, from the rock group Guns and Roses, in 1991 for inciting a riot during a performance in St. Louis. Rose jumped off the stage to confront a fan who had taken his picture. After Rose stormed off the stage and canceled the concert, the spectators began to riot and tear-up the amphitheater. Although McCulloch went to great lengths (and public expense) to prosecute the lead singer of Guns and Roses, a judge didn't agree, and found that Axl Rose did not directly incite the riot. Prosecutor McCulloch used the fame and name recognition he received from that case to stay in office from that time on. Bandmates of Guns and Roses will always remember McCulloch, but not fondly. In their Use Your Illusion I and II album inserts, the group inscribed, "Fuck You, St. Louis!"

CHAPTER 44

CLOSING

The Ferguson protests may be remembered as a flashpoint in American history and the catalyst of a renewed civil rights movement in the 21st century. The death of Michael Brown provoked a long-overdue conversation about excessive police force, racial intolerance and the injustices of the U.S. justice system.

America is at a breaking point. Ferguson was the first sign of upheaval. If quick action is not taken to mend the relations between the races in America, the country may descend into chaos.

"Those that fail to learn from history are doomed to repeat it," is an axiom that has been used many times in the past, by notable luminaries such as Winston Churchill, Edmund Burke, Henry Kissinger and Nelson Mandela. It's application regarding Ferguson may be as appropriate as any other time. The history of race relations in America must be understood to truly comprehend the plight of the African American in the United States. From their prospective, black Americans have experienced generations of persecution by a white power structure which seems determined to separate the races and relegate minorities to a second class existence. The implications of these perceptions are being felt today, in Ferguson, and elsewhere around the country.

Civil wars are often initiated over racial, economic or religious issues. America's own civil war was fought over a complex combination of issues including cultural differences, an industrial vs. an agrarian economy, state rights vs. federal rights, and the question of whether or not to allow the expansion of slavery into new territories. The "cause" which garnered the greatest support for the war in the North, from both a moral and a financial support viewpoint, was the issue of slavery—to maintain it, or to abolish it as a moral and ethical evil. One result of the war, of course, was the abolition of slavery and the economic ruin of the South. This outcome was, for the slaves, a mixed blessing—they were no longer in slavery, but they lived in economic chaos and were not welcomed into white society or the white work force. The economy and a white separatist attitude relegated them to the lowest ranks of American society.

One-hundred-fifty years have passed since the end of the Civil War. While some black Americans have found success and acceptance in white society and commerce, many others live little better than their predecessors did a century ago. As in all ethnic or racial populations, some individuals contribute little to their societies and should expect little in return. However, there are masses of minority individuals in our society who deserve better treatment from the majority than they have received. They are desperate for better acceptance and treatment from the majority, and seem more and more willing, and likely, to act out if they don't receive it. The backlash against perceived white injustice in Ferguson, Missouri may mark the beginning of a new round of racial strife in the United States. What must be done to avoid a round of devastating conflict between majority and minority segments of our society?

Americans have the right, and the duty, to protest injustice and repression. In Ferguson a large number of people exercised their right to assemble and to take issue with an action which they perceived to be unfair, unjust, and illegal. Were they correct in their perception? The answer to that is unclear, although the Grand Jury appointed to evaluate the case concluded that the evidence did not indicate that a case could be made against Officer Wilson to charge him with wrongdoing in the killing of Michael Brown.

So, we have behaviors on each side which were based on perceptions, but we have differing, countering perceptions from "the other side" as well. Which perceptions were correct? The conclusions as to the culpability of either white Officer Wilson or black Michael Brown in regard to this tragedy are closely linked to the race of the perceiver. Ferguson is 90% black, so that "side" was strongly represented in "witnesses" and overall numbers of participants supporting Brown. The Ferguson Police Department is nearly 100% white, so the white "side" supporting Wilson was represented by fewer direct participants, but backed by greater "power." Against the white power, black perception came to be expressed in protest and riot. Unfortunately, the local black population was augmented by out-of-town personnel, who were responsible for much of the riot and destruction.

Of those who came from out-of-town to support the Brown side was John Morgan, who drove from Greenville, Illinois each day after work during the protests to demonstrate against the injustice he perceived in Ferguson, and which he also has experienced in his own home town. He said, "This didn't just start yesterday. There's two sets of laws in this country; there's laws for them and there's laws for us. Michael Vick was sent to prison for killing a dog. This white guy can walk up, gun down a child in the street, in broad daylight, in front of witnesses, cars going up and down the street, and we have to go through this to get you to arrest this man." Morgan said, "That's justice in America. That's America without the makeup." [44]

What action should we take, as a nation, to avoid repetition of the Ferguson experience? Obviously, we haven't identified that answer, and we certainly haven't implemented it, in one-hundred-fifty years. The answer, if there is one, is multi-faceted and difficult, requiring insight and a firm commitment to action. Matching the demographic population of police departments to those of the communities they serve would be one of the easier actions, and is perhaps the only achievable one. Raising the economic stature of the poor population would be a long-range benefit, but we haven't demonstrated an aptitude for that in recorded memory.

---

[44] https://firstlook.org/theintercept/2014/09/04/rdevro-hed-tk/

After Ferguson; a new coalition of civil rights leaders should unite, and form a national alliance to collectively work towards equality and justice for people of all races and social status. Many passionate and intelligent individuals conducted peaceful protests in Ferguson. Such activists need to put politics and egos aside and work in concert to nurture changes in both perception and reality, together, though peaceful, planned and permitted demonstrations to put pressure on politicians, who are in power to make the changes necessary to mend the hostilities between the races and make reparations for any injustices in the past. If the people of a community feel that they are not being served by their political leaders, then it is their duty and moral obligation to register to vote. And vote them out of office, and to then elect representatives that represent them. Otherwise, they should not expect any change that would benefit them. The squeaky wheel gets oiled. That is a political fact. If enough people make enough noise, the politicians will hear their message, and respond accordingly, either through the passage of new civil rights laws or approval for funding for programs that benefit the underprivileged. Real change will only come when oppressed people register to vote, and then exercise their right to vote. Until then, they will be unheard and unnoticed by politicians or people of power.

Missouri's slogan is "The Show Me State." Ferguson could show the rest of the nation how quickly local political leaders in Missouri can be replaced by their constituents if voters feel they are being underrepresented. In only a few years, Ferguson residents could elect an all black Mayor, Council members, City Attorney, City Manager and a new Police Chief, if the residents became less apathetic about local politics and more involved in their own destiny. Approximately 70% of Ferguson resident are black. Minorities in the city have the majority quorum of voters. There destiny is in their own hands, but year-after-year minorities fail to exercise their right to vote, thereby perpetuating their own oppression from a white political structure they allow to remain in place.

Emmet Till:

If you ask most white adults what was the defining moment in the civil rights movement, many would say, Rosa Parks refusing to go to the back of the bus in Montgomery Alabama or the Selma march for voting rights, but most black adults will admit that the defining moment for them was when they first heard the name of Emmet Till.

Emmet Till was a 14-year-old black boy from Chicago, in 1955. His mother had a good job and tried to provide a good home for her family. Her son Emmet was known as a class clown. He had a suitcase of jokes he use to take to school to entertain the other pupils, who all seemed to like him. When he was offered an opportunity to visit his uncle and nephews in Mississippi he pleaded with his mother to let him go. Although she was nervous about it, she let him go to Mississippi to bond with his extended family and learn some life lessons. He soon found out how dangerous life could be for a black youth with a big mouth, in the South.

After a long day of picking cotton, Emmet and his cousins went to a neighborhood market to get drinks and Emmet bought some bubble gun. While leaving the store, Emmet whistled at a white female store clerk. Her husband, who owned the store, flew into a rage and recruited his brother to help him teach a young Till a lesson about southern culture.

Four days later, Emmet was kidnapped at his relatives home, in front of witnesses, then beaten, shot, and dumped into the Tallahatchie River. The killers were charged with murder, but an all-white jury refused to convict them of killing Till. An all-white Grand Jury refused to indict them on kidnapping charges even though there were witnesses who saw the two suspects drag Till from the home.

Till's 12-year-old cousin, Simeon Wright, who was sleeping in the same bed with Till when he was abducted, described him as "fun loving" with "no fear." Wright said, "He was always looking for something to do to make him laugh and make you laugh. He wanted to be a comedian." Wright said that Till thought it was fun to whistle at white women, but Wright warned him that in Mississippi, in 1955, "you didn't whistle at nothing white." Till didn't listen, and he was executed for his lack of southern etiquette.

After the acquittal of Till's killers, Belgium news reported, "Killing a black person isn't a crime in the home of the Yankees: The white killers of young Emmett Till are acquitted!" In Germany, the newspaper Freies Volk wrote: "The Life of a Negro Isn't Worth a Whistle."

The two brothers later admitted to the killing in a magazine interview, and were paid $4,000 for their story, after double jeopardy laws prevented them from being tried twice for the same offense.

The brothers described how they killed Till. They said they took him to the edge of the Tallahatchie River, shot him in the head, fastened a large metal fan used for ginning cotton to his neck with barbed wire, and then pushed his body into the river, in Sumner Mississippi. The motto of the town of Sumner was "A good place to raise a boy."

Jet Magazine and The Chicago Defender newspaper published graphic images of Till's corpse and badly beaten and unrecognizable face.

His death provoked an outpouring of support for the family, especially after Emmet's mother chose to have an open casket funeral so everyone could see how badly his body was mutilated. His mother, Marmie Till, explained her painful decision to let people see how badly her son was beaten, in a 1996 interview. She said, "People really didn't know that things this horrible could take place. And the fact that it happened to a child, that make all the difference in the world."

Jesse Jackson stated at the time, "With his body water-soaked and defaced, most people would have kept the casket covered. His mother let the body be exposed. More than 100,000 people saw his body lying in that casket here in Chicago. That must have been at that time the largest single civil rights demonstration in American history."

Many African Americans say that the Emmett Till murder was the turning point in their resolve to stand up and fight back. His death spawned a generation of activists fighting for their civil and human rights. Till became a symbol of racial intolerance. His legacy helped spark the civil rights movement in the 1950's, and set the stage for the violent confrontations between the police and black youths in the race riots of the 1960's. Many of those young protesters of the 1960's remembered the story of Till; who was killed when he was the same age as the protesters, and with whom they identified.

Marmie Till took comfort in knowing that her son helped start a civil rights movement. She said, "When people saw what had happened to my son. Men stood-up who had never stoop up before. People became vocal who had never vocalized before. Emmet's death was the opening of the civil rights movement. He was the sacrificial lamb of the movement."

One hundred days after Till's murder, Rosa Parks refused to give-up her seat on an Alabama city bus, sparking the year-long Montgomery Bus Boycott. Rosa Parks was so moved by the Till murder that she refused to go to the back of the bus, because she remembered what happened to Till. Parks said, "I thought about Emmett Till, and I couldn't go back to the back of the bus."

Nine years after Emmet Till died, The United States Congress passed the Civil Rights Act and the Voting-Rights Act, outlawing segregation and discriminatory voting practices. Till's name won't be remembered by whites, but blacks will never forget him.

Martin Luther King rose to prominence soon after Emmett Till was murdered. He used the tragedy as a rallying point to campaign for equal rights for all American citizens. King referenced Till many times during his passionate speeches about "the evil of racial injustice." In 1963 King evoked the name of Emmet Till, as he often did, when he said in a speech "the crying voice of a little Emmett Till, screaming from the rushing waters in Mississippi." King claimed that Till's murder "might be considered one of the most brutal and inhuman crimes of the twentieth century."

Emmett Till was the Michael Brown of his time. Till's death sparked a civil rights movement that made great strides, until the untimely death of Martin Luther King, which resulted in the untimely demise of the civil rights movement that Emmett Till had sparked. The Michael Brown killing is the catalyst that may help create a new civil rights movement in America. The only question that remains is who will the new leaders be, and will they choose peaceful over violent protesting. As Martin Luther King realized, the only way for a mutually cohesive coexistence between the races is through peaceful demonstrations.

Violence begets violence, especially in the United States of America. If protesting turns violent; a racial civil war could ensue, which, history has taught us, leaves no winners. Ferguson was America's breaking point. If swift action is not taken to mend the strife between the races, the warning of the 1968 Presidential Commission of Civil Disorders will ring true. **"None of us shall escape the consequences."**

ABOUT THE AUTHOR

Tim Suereth has lived in Florida for the past 25 years, mainly in an area of Miami known as South Beach. It's an outdoorsmans paradise; a perfect place to live for someone seeking some excitement.

Tim's excitement seeking began early in his life. He moved away from his St. Charles, Missouri home at the age of thirteen to train at the country's premier boys gymnastics training center, in Pennsylvania. Although he was the youngest team member to have ever been accepted to the program, his youth didn't deter him from quickly progressing to become one of the highest ranked gymnasts in the nation.

Tim eventually grew tired of the 5-hour daily workouts and moved home to Missouri at the age of fifteen to resume a normal life as a teenager, only 20 miles from Ferguson. Normalcy didn't last long. By seventeen, he enlisted in the Army and was sent to Ft. Carson, Colorado for three years of military service; eventually being recruited to the U.S. Army Boxing Team. After the Army, Tim moved to Florida to get an education and although his formal schooling came from the University of South Florida, his real education would come later, when he entered the world of business and politics.

After college, Tim worked as a Stockbroker with a major securities firm, but became disillusioned by the realities of being a money manager for a large corporation, so he left the firm to open his own small stock brokerage business based on Miami Beach. He subsequently helped a friend write a 4-volume book series on investing, and after the book was done, Tim refocused his efforts on aviation and spent the next year acquiring his Instrument, multi-engine and commercial pilots licenses. Once Tim became a commercial pilot, real-estate development caught his attention, and from then on, he has bought, sold and developed real estate in Florida, and now only fly's for fun.

For the past 14 years Tim has been involved with both state and national political and communications campaigns. He's been sued--

he's been slandered--and he's been bullied by billionaires for the truths he's revealed. Tim's undercover work for the United States Customs has garnered him praise as "the best they've ever worked with." He has told his stories as a ghostwriter in the past, but will now expose what he knows through his books and documentary films. Ferguson: America's Breaking Point is the first.

www.ingramcontent.com/pod-product-compliance
Lightning Source LLC
La Vergne TN
LVHW091212080426
835509LV00009B/960